# *Cases in Advertising*

# Cases in Advertising

President, Bismark Corporation
Adjunct Professor of Marketing,
Graduate School of Business,
Columbia University

**William M. Weilbacher**

Macmillan Publishing Co., Inc.
New York
Collier Macmillan Publishers
London

1981

Macmillan Publishing Co., Inc.
866 Third Avenue, New York, New York 10022

Collier Macmillan Canada, Ltd.

Library of Congress Cataloging in Publication Data

Weilbacher, William M
Cases in advertising.

Includes index.
1. Advertising–United States–Case studies.
I. Title.
HF5813.U6W4 659.2'0973 80-13540
ISBN 0-02-425120-8

Printing: 1 2 3 4 5 6 7 8 Year: 1 2 3 4 5 6 7 8

*This book is for GLADYS MANNING WEILBACHER*

# Preface

This is a book of cases that reflect the practice of advertising. In developing the cases that appear in this volume, particular attention has been paid to ensuring their reality. The cases reflect reality in several senses. They reflect real advertising decisions and real advertising processes. They reflect real advertising research information as it is applied—and sometimes misapplied—in advertising decisions and processes. They reflect the reality of individual personalities as they interact in the process of advertising and advertising decision making.

The emphasis on reality is based upon my conviction that the teaching of advertising can be dramatically enhanced by materials and situations that reflect the world of the advertising practitioner. In this approach the emphasis is on advertising as a useful business tool. Of course, advertising is not necessarily or even usually an easy business tool to use. Successful advertising requires hard thinking, relevant research, a practiced sense of how the advertising process works, and an intensity in and dedication to building advertising successes.

Many advertising students seem to find it particularly hard to grasp the realities and difficulties of advertising practice because of the knowledge of and prejudices about advertising that they have continuously acquired as advertising recipients, long before they ever appear as students in a formal course about advertising. These cases are consciously designed to help the student understand the world of the advertising practitioner and how the practitioner works to make advertising into a successful business tool.

Advertising is a business that depends very heavily upon the creativity of its practitioners. They must develop creative marketing ideas and programs; they must develop creative advertising copy ideas and campaigns; they must develop creative advertising media ideas and campaigns. Too often the word "creativity" is taken to be synonymous with loose thinking or an irresponsible license in the presentation of ideas about products. My own experience as a practitioner has demonstrated how erroneous this conception of advertising creativity is. Advertising creativity is most effective when it operates in a disciplined environment. It is the need for discipline, for rationality, as a backdrop for creative thinking that leads to the emphasis that is put upon information and upon research findings by so many advertisers. I have especially tried to reflect this emphasis in this book of cases: the cases are data rich. The student is continuously, therefore, confronted with data and research materials that reflect the essentials of each of the portrayed advertising situations in a disciplined, rational way. Thus the student's own creativity is directed and channeled as he develops his solution to the questions that accompany each case.

The questions themselves have been very carefully developed to accurately reflect the kinds of issues that the practitioner faces in each of the case situations. They also reflect my teaching experience, which suggests that case questions do most to stimulate students and their learning experiences when they are required to project themselves accurately into the situation portrayed in the case. The successful student will be stimulated by these case questions to think like a practitioner and to respond to the case situation exactly as a practitioner would.

The cases in this book have two intrinsic characteristics that deserve comment. First of all they are long. And they are based upon imaginary situations rather than upon the experience of real companies.

The cases are long rather than short in order to reflect the variety of advertising (and marketing) issues that almost invariably arise in any particular advertising decision situation. This variety of issues arises even though the advertising decision to be made is primarily concerned with one advertising element like creative development, or media planning, or market testing of advertising programs, or whatever. Thus, the cases are long in order to reflect the way in which advertising issues present themselves to the decision maker in real life. The reality of advertising practice is dense and ambiguous: short cases simply cannot reflect these real life characteristics.

The cases are based upon imaginary situations as a result of conscious choice. It is a great temptation to use real companies, real situations, real people, and real data. The use of such elements creates an illusion that appears to be lifelike. The alternative is to create imaginary case situations that are molded very closely on life. With the latter approach the author gains several degrees of freedom. He may reflect some of those aspects of advertising that rarely seem to find their way into advertising cases that are based upon real companies and events. I am thinking especially of the elements in advertising decision situations that reflect personality and organizational peculiarities. Advertising practitioners do not always behave either rationally or in ignorance of their own self interest and advertising decisions are often affected. The importance of the human element is not, of course, limited to advertising. For example, Daniel J. Kevles has this to say about the importance of the human element in the history of science in this country:

> Scientists know how human an enterprise science is, if only from the strong interest they feel in the award of credit for priority of discovery or from their community's practice of naming theories, effects and experiments after particular people. Science is shaped in the endlessly unpredictable way that social and family environment work upon individual temperament and imagination and the way that professional circumstances meld with the ordinary drives for money, status and power.*

The book is designed to supplement standard advertising texts. It is, of course, particularly well-suited as a supplement to *Advertising.*** But its general organization and emphasis on the reality of advertising make it compatible with the other leading advertising texts. It can be used with both undergraduate and graduate students. It is neither elementary or advanced: it simply reflects advertising practice as it exists. The more mature the student, the more of this reality will be absorbed and resolved, but the situations and issues remain the same regardless of the sophistication of the student or, one might add, of the advertising practitioner. No compromises are made with reality because such compromises do not make the life that the case reflects easier for the student—only more frustrating.

In assigning material of the kind contained in this book to my students, I always make several suggestions to them about how it should be handled.

* Daniel J. Kevles, *The Physicists,* Alfred A. Knopf, New York, 1978, p x.

** William M. Weilbacher, *Advertising,* Macmillan Publishing Co., Inc., New York, 1979.

1. I urge them to immerse themselves in the case itself—to read it through carefully and with thorough concentration. Almost all of the material in the case is relevant in one way or another to an understanding of the situation portrayed and the questions that are raised at the end of the case. An understanding of the arguments and the issues of the case is an imperative first step toward solution.
2. After they believe they *understand* the case, I propose that they try to identify the significant issues and the relevant advertising decisions related to these issues. Paper and pencil help here. I suggest that the students jot down what might have to be decided as a result of the material in the case and what the most appropriate advertising moves might be in each instance. A development of this context makes it easier to answer whatever actual questions are to be answered because the student has begun to feel—if he has done the job—all of the conflicting pressures and issues that the actual decision-maker becomes aware of in reaching an advertising decision.
3. Finally, I suggest that the student begin to develop his answers to the assigned questions. I implore him to be succinct: that is, to have thought through the implications of the case and his specific answers so that they may be stated with simple directness and clarity rather than in muddled verbosity. And I encourage the student to make explicit the assumptions that he has made in answering the questions. I tend to accept almost any reasonable formulation, as long as its underpinnings are explicit, and I tend to mark down unwarranted or unexplained leaps of fancy.

Over forty people responded to my request to reproduce the advertisements that appear in Case 5. Without exception, these representatives of their outstanding companies were enthusiastically helpful in clearing my request through the proper channels and in supplying the materials reproduced here. If there is not enough space to acknowledge their contributions individually, I am no less grateful for it.

Regis Redin served as art director in the preparation of advertising for Mid American Airlines and Sinugard. I admire the crisp specificity of her work. She is a good-natured and dedicated professional, and I am indebted to her for her contribution. Nancy Munro typed the text from my incomprehensible longhand with tenacity and good will, and I am grateful for her help. Martha M. Weilbacher consulted on matters of style and grammar, and, although some of the fires continue to burn, it appears that our marriage will survive.

W.M.W.

# Contents

# *Cases in Advertising*

# Case 1

# Advertising and the Marketing Process

## *THE AMELIA ETERNAL COMPANY DETERMINES ADVERTISING POLICY*

The Amelia Eternal Company was started in 1956 by Henry J. Litt. Litt was a graduate chemist. He had received his B.S. degree in chemistry from a smallish southwestern university in June of 1942. Within weeks of his graduation, he was inducted into the United States Army. At the conclusion of his army service, he applied for and was hired as a junior chemist in the product development department of Eudora Compleat, Inc., a medium-sized California fragrance and cosmetic manufacturer.

He stayed with Eudora Compleat, Inc. for almost ten years, gaining product development experience that was subsequently invaluable to him. In the years from 1947 to 1951 he pursued a master's degree in business administration in the evening studies program of the graduate business school of a large southern California university. He received his M.S. in business administration with a specialization in management and finance, and then, in the next four or five years took odd evening courses at the same university, some in marketing, some in applied chemistry, and some, for the pure exhilaration of it, in modern American literature.

In 1954, Litt was promoted to associate director of product development of Eudora Compleat. In this job, he served as chief operating officer for a laboratory group of fifteen chemists, technicians, and other specialists. He reported to Johnathan Springford, Ph.D., who had executive responsibility for product-development work at Eudora Compleat, was seven years older than Litt and who was, by Litt's admission, an able administrator with a real flair for cosmetic and fragrance development.

Litt was well paid by Eudora Compleat, was fully vested in a generous profit-sharing plan that served as the company's pension program, and was the recipient of a modest but satisfying range of fringe benefits which included a company car and membership in the company's executive dining room.

Litt could not say that he was bored in his work for Eudora Compleat since he in fact, was, not. He liked his peers and associates and he did not find working for Springford to be burdensome. He was in continuous interaction with the marketing people in the firm and had developed a singular rapport with them. His product-development philosophy was to develop and perfect products that the marketing people found easy to sell: that is, he believed that product-development work was pointless if it did not respond to needs that were real for consumers. As he pursued this point of view, he turned naturally to the marketing people and asked them, what products in effect, they felt were most wanted by consumers. This product-development-marketing relationship was an important element in the continuing success of Eudora Compleat and in retrospect it is not at all hard to understand why this would be so. Nevertheless, Litt's fraternization with the marketing people did not always make Springford happy.

"Look here, Henry," Springford remarked at lunch in the executive dining room one spring day in 1952, "I think you spend too much time hobnobbing with those guys over in sales, or whatever they call themselves now–marketing, is it? You put yourself in a vulnerable position when you do that, seems to me."

"What do you mean, 'vulnerable,' Johnny?" asked Litt. "Those guys are supposed to know what all those ladies that they're trying to sell to want to buy, aren't they? If that's true, and I think it is, then why shouldn't I spend time with them? The more I know what they think they can sell, the more likely we are to develop a product that consumers will like–and that *will* sell, therefore, and make the company money, and you happy. You got me stumped, Johnny: How can that make me vulnerable?"

"You don't know those sa–, uh, marketing guys, Henry," responded Springford. "They're fair weather friends. It's all right if you develop the products they ask for, and they sell through and make a success. But the marketing people won't always be right about what will sell, Henry. As a matter of fact, they're certain to be wrong at least some of the time. And when they give you wrong direction, it won't be their advice they'll blame–it will be your product. I say that part of *our* job is to develop those products that we know consumers want from *our* own experience and observation and from *our* knowledge of what our technology will permit us to do. Then give those products that *we* have confidence in to the sales department and it's their responsibility to sell them. If they don't do it, it's their fault, because we know how good those products that we developed from our own expertise and resources are to begin with. That's what I think, Henry, and I wish you wouldn't be so damned chummy with those sales guys. They really are setting you up for a fall."

"Okay, Johnny, I understand what you're saying," said Litt, "and what you're not saying, too: You're suggesting that maybe I've been a little naive with these marketing boys, aren't you?"

"I didn't say that, Henry," replied Springford, rather sharply. "I think what you've been doing is one way to approach your job, and if I was in your position, I'm not saying that I wouldn't have done the same thing. I'm not even suggesting that you cut it totally out–just tone it down."

Litt recognized at once that this was a topic that Springford felt strongly about. It was rare for Springford to talk about any subject either at length or with much seeming sense of conviction. He was man of mild manner, and Litt had never before heard him swear for any reason, business related or not. But there was one statement that Springford had made that confused Litt, and he kept the conversation going because of it:

"Okay, Johnny, fair enough. I'll keep my natural conviviality and outgoingness in check," he replied with a smile. "But you said something just now that I didn't understand at all. You said that the marketing people are 'certain to be wrong at least some of the time.' Why is that Johnny? If those guys don't know what will sell, who, for heaven's sake, does?"

"The point I was making," replied Springford, "is that the sales or marketing people, or whoever, almost never talk to the women who use our cosmetics; and, if they do talk to them, they don't talk to them in any organized way. They are in touch with their customers, but their customers are *trade* customers, not ultimate customers. The trade doesn't necessarily know what's really going on in their stores, and sometimes, when they talk as though they do, they are really just reflecting their own prejudices."

"You mean," said Litt, breaking in abruptly, "that the buyers in department stores and drug chains, and in the drug wholesalers, don't really know what their customers want?"

"Why should they?" responded Springford. "They talk to their wives and to women they meet at cocktail parties, but that isn't a valid reflection of the consuming public. And, of course, they have a kind of general knowledge of their sales, but that only reflects what's selling now and not necessarily what will sell in the future. That's what I meant when I said that our sales guys were almost certain to be wrong about the kind of products that the public wants, at least some of the time."

So ended the conversation between Litt and Springford about the reliability of the Eudora Compleat sales force as a source of new product ideas. Litt did not really agree with Springford's belief that new product ideas should come solely from new product development personnel, reflecting only their own intuitions and technical know-how.

"If the sales people can't be trusted to reflect the needs of the consumer, there must be some other way to keep in touch with those needs," reasoned Litt. But this was as far as his thought about the topic went in 1952. Litt might have investigated the potential of marketing research to identify consumer new-product needs, but the thought never occurred to him. He was, after all, primarily interested in chemistry and its new product-development implications. Having majored in management and finance in business school, he had probably never heard of marketing research; and, if he had, it was in passing, without serious study. And, of course, in 1952 marketing research was little more than an emerging art, the early manifestations of which rarely, if ever, dealt with a determination of the kinds of new products that women might wish in fragrances and cosmetics. Eudora Compleat did not have a market research department until 1967. And so, in ignorance of marketing research and with other matters of considerably greater importance on his mind, Litt simply forgot about this conversation with Springford, except to consciously curtail the amount of contact that he had with the Eudora Compleat marketing staff.

Some weeks later, arriving home after work, Litt was confronted by his wife Amelia. "Henry," she said, "we've had some real problems around here. The plumber has been here all day. The septic tank has been overflowing since this morning."

"Why is that?" asked Litt. "The bacterial action in the tank is supposed to go on forever. Those tanks are supposed to be trouble free forever–at least that's what the guy who sold us the place said."

"Well, that's right, Henry," said Amelia, "and that's what I told Luke Long, the plumber–but he just laughed. Luke said that everyone in the neighborhood has the same problem. There's something in the detergents that we all use that destroys the bacterial action in the tank, and then the trouble begins."

This innocent exchange marked the beginning of the Amelia Eternal Company. The problem of the detergent destruction of septic-tank bacterial action intrigued Henry Litt. He set up a small crude laboratory in his basement to see if he could figure out just what chemical and biological activity was involved, hoping that perhaps he might find a way to offset the detergent activity. Weeks passed, the laboratory gradually expanded and the equipment became more and more sophisticated as Litt spent more and more of his spare time trying to solve the problem.

Early in 1953, Litt developed a detergent product that tended to exhaust itself after combination with water for twenty or twenty-five minutes. Litt had identified the phosphate ingredient found in all commercial detergents as the element that attacked and destroyed active bacteria in household waste-disposal systems. He could not find a substitute for this phosphate ingredient in 1952 (although he and other detergent manufacturers did develop phosphate substitutes in later years). His solution was to render the phosphate harmless to bacterial action in waste-disposal systems *after* it performed its cleaning chores but before it had a chance to do further damage. The Litt detergent did an excellent job of washing dishes for lengths of time up to and including ninety minutes. But, meanwhile, a chemical change had taken place that rendered the phosphate ingredient harmless. Litt applied for, and ultimately received a United States patent for his process and formula. In the meantime, he made up two-gallon batches of the product for the use of his wife and the neighbors.

The product did an excellent job in the tasks of conventional light-duty liquid detergents: that is, in washing dishes and in bowl-washing of lingerie and other delicate clothing. It seemed mild to the hands and all the users reported that its cleaning properties were excellent. The women who used the Litt detergent were relatively indifferent, however, to Litt's claim that the product would not interfere with the functioning of the home-waste disposal systems.

"Henry, you've got a problem convincing me or my friends that your detergent won't hurt the septic tank," said Amelia one evening when they were discussing his new detergent. "First of all, the septic-tank protective feature is like preventive medicine. If it works, we won't know it for a long time; and, of course, we'll never be certain that it has worked because the septic tank can always go haywire anytime. But Luke Long says that you've only solved a little bit of the problem."

"Who is Luke Long, and what does he know, Amelia?" asked Litt.

"He's the plumber; you remember Luke," said Amelia. "And he knows, because he's the one who has to deal with the septic tank backups. He says the biggest volume of detergent going into the septic tanks is powdered laundry detergent, not the liquid. And because the laundry powders are stronger and more concentrated, he says, they are the things that really cause the trouble.

"But, anyway, Henry, can you make up about twenty gallons of that stuff of yours and put it in one-quart jars? Mildred Allenby, on the other side of the development, wants to pass some out among her friends."

"Hold on, Amelia," replied Litt. "That stuff of mine costs money to make. Maybe what we ought to do is sell some to Mildred, and let her resell it to her friends. Maybe she could even make a profit! But what good will it do her, or them, if the real villian is the laundry detergents?"

Litt solved the laundry-detergent problem in late 1953. By early 1954, he had made an arrangement with a contract packer of household cleaning items. Under the Power Safe brand name, he was selling about $2,000 worth of light duty and laundry detergents a week to a group of about thirty women, recruited by his wife, who in turn sold the products to their friends and neighbors. The price, suggested by Litt, yielded the saleswomen a 35 percent profit on each package of Power Safe they sold.

Litt resigned from Eudora Compleat, Inc. on September 1, 1954 and never again worked for anyone but himself in the newly incorporated Amelia Eternal Company. He was president and his wife, Amelia, was secretary-treasurer.

As Litt and his wife thought about their new enterprise and tried to determine what they should do to make it prosper and grow, they came to two basic conclusions. At first, these conclusions were not conclusions at all, but rather merely inclinations that they both seemed to share, almost intuitively.

The first of these inclinations was that they should move toward the production of their own products, as quickly as they could afford it from income and profits and/or as soon as their financial statements were sufficiently respectable to justify bank loans for the construction of their own production facilities. As Henry Litt put it, "Amelia, we have to make what we sell. By 'we' I mean our company, not contract packers or other outsiders. I don't want other people knowing our formulas, and I don't want outsiders responsible for our quality. This company will stand or fall on the quality of its products. If it falls, I want the satisfaction of knowing that it was our mistake, and not some guy who isn't part of Amelia Eternal."

Their second inclination was that there should be no middlemen in the Amelia Eternal marketing chain. "We'll sell as much of our product as we can, ourselves, direct to our customers," said Litt. "But, we already know that we won't have time to do much of that. So, we'll sell to others who sell to consumers, but only on a direct basis. No wholesalers, no company salesmen, no retail outlets, none of that. I never want to be more than one person away from the consumer, and I want that one person in the middle to have as much at stake personally as I do in the products of Amelia Eternal."

"Do we have to hire them, Henry?" asked Amelia. "I mean we haven't done that yet, and I think our representatives prefer to work for themselves. At least it seems to me that the best ones aren't the type that will ever work for anyone else, if they can help it."

"Let's keep it that way, Amelia," said Litt, "at least for as long as we can. Some others seem to be able to do it. Avon, for example. Let's not be greedy, either. Let our people make as much money as they can. The more they make, the more we make, after all, and if they end up rich, we'll end up very rich, won't we?"

Exhibit 1-1 shows the sales growth of Amelia Eternal from 1954 through 1979. As the sales data reveal, the company grew dramatically between 1954 and 1975, and sales evened out in the years following 1975. Nevertheless, even with the sales sluggishness of the late 1970s Amelia Eternal was a gigantic enterprise by any system of reckoning.

Henry and Amelia Litt's original inclinations about how the business should be run gradually hardened into firm policies. By 1975 the company produced seventy-nine different household cleaning products under the Power Safe brand name. The original Power Safe liquid and powdered detergents were still in the line, as were improved, nonphos-

**EXHIBIT 1-1**
**Specimen Data: Dollar Sales of Amelia Eternal Company, 1954-1979**

| | |
|---|---|
| 1954 | 29,000 |
| 1955 | 64,000 |
| 1956 | 122,000 |
| 1957 | 342,000 |
| 1958 | 456,000 |
| 1959 | 872,000 |
| 1960 | 2,899,000 |
| 1961 | 6,924,000 |
| 1962 | 12,784,000 |
| 1963 | 18,642,000 |
| 1964 | 28,642,000 |
| 1965 | 39,827,000 |
| 1966 | 47,832,000 |
| 1967 | 61,531,000 |
| 1968 | 72,963,000 |
| 1969 | 84,662,000 |
| 1970 | 91,249,000 |
| 1971 | 101,632,000 |
| 1972 | 109,724,000 |
| 1973 | 115,861,000 |
| 1974 | 123,842,000 |
| 1975 | 128,321,000 |
| 1976 | 129,673,000 |
| 1977 | 131,421,000 |
| 1978 | 127,320,000 |
| 1979 | 132,634,000 |

phate, extra-strength versions of both. In addition, the line included floor and rug cleaners, upholstery cleaners, pet shampoos, window-washing solutions, automobile cleansing lotions and waxes, refrigerator shiners, and on and on. There was literally no product for home cleaning that the Litts and their product-development staff could think of that had not been included in the Power Safe line. These products were manufactured in three geographically dispersed plants: one in Southern California, one in Mississippi, and one in upstate New York.

Drawing on his experience with Eudora Compleat, Litt introduced lines of facial-treatment, cosmetic, fragrance, and hair-care products to the company product roster in 1957. These lines grew strongly over the years as new brand names were introduced and as existing brand lines were expanded. By the early 1970s there were five or six cosmetic brands in the line at any one time, as well as ten to twelve fragrance brands, three treatment brands and three or four hair-care brands. Collectively, these various lines and brands constituted a total of 706 individual items, not counting shades, in 1979.

This proliferation of makeup lines and brands had many advantages. In the first place, it permitted the company to present products at a variety of price points, each competitive to those that existed in the retail marketplace. Secondly, the variety of makeup brands gave Amelia Eternal considerable flexibility in meeting both the needs of their customers and their individual sales resistances. Whatever objection a potential purchaser might have against a particular item in a particular line of merchandise, there was always another comparable item from another brand within the line that might overcome the objection.

In addition, the arrangement facilitated the introduction of new makeup products into the company's lines and the discontinuation of products whose sales potential had been exhausted. New makeup formulations could be introduced into a single brand line, for example, and, if they were successful, expanded to other brand lines. This approach tended to minimize the costs of introducing new products while providing a flexible format for assessing consumer response to all of the new product ideas that were developed in the research and development laboratories. Meanwhile, if it were necessary to discontinue an item within a brand, it was frequently possible for the sales representative to offer a comparable substitute product from another company brand.

Finally, the proliferation of lines and brands provided an ideal basis for developing promotional programs of one kind or another with the sales representative group. It was relatively easy to direct sales attention to one brand of merchandise or another by offering special extra discounts or bonus gift-merchandise point certificates for sales of one or two items from the brand during the promotional period. Such promotions tended to develop extra sales across the brand as a whole and thus provided not only sales stimulation, but also extra incentive to the sales representative groups.

The cosmetic, facial-treatment, hair-care, and fragrance products are all manufactured by Amelia Eternal in their own plants. There are three Amelia Eternal cosmetic, facial-treatment, hair-care, and fragrance production plants. They are adjacent to, but physically separate from, the plants that produce the household cleaning products. Litt had considered producing all of the Amelia Eternal products within a single plant facility, and in fact, in the early days of the company, this is exactly how it had been done. But, as sales and profits grew, Litt decided to separate the two production processes. There were production economics to be realized from combined production facilities, but they were relatively minor.

More important, however, was Litt's strong feeling that the two types of products simply did not belong together in the same production plant. As he explained his feeling to Amelia: "It's just not right to be making fine fragrances right next to dog shampoos, and, even though it doesn't make any difference, really, I still don't like it one bit. Eventually, we want to encourage our sales representatives to visit our factories. The factories must appear to have the same characteristics that we say our products have. If we say that our products have the highest possible quality and are made of pure non-synthetic ingredients, it seems to me that this will be a lot more believable if we separate the household products from the makeup products—don't you agree, Amelia?"

Amelia agreed, and that was that. The Amelia Eternal household products were produced in sparkling new factories that were distinct from, yet adjacent to, the sparkling new factories that turned out the four product categories that the Litt's referred to, collectively, as makeup products.

All of Amelia Eternal makeup products were designed to be effective, yet without side effects either for the environment or for the user herself. This principle had been established at the very beginning when the liquid and laundry detergents had been designed to protect the bacterial action of home waste-disposal systems.

But the principle was generalized to all of the subsequent product-development work. As Litt put it in his introductory speech to new research and development employees: "We design products here to have two distinct characteristics. They must do what they are designed to do, but, beyond that, our products must be completely benign. This means that our products don't do anything they aren't supposed to do. They musn't upset the bacterial action in septic tanks; they musn't give pet dogs skin sores; they musn't cause allergic reactions to those who use them; they musn't discolor fabrics or cause fabrics to wear out prematurely.

"If there is ever a doubt in your mind about a product, then that product should not enter the Amelia Eternal line. And, I charge you with the responsibility of devising a broad range of tests to assure yourselves and Amelia and me that every product that is introduced by Amelia Eternal has these characteristics."

Thus, it happened that Amelia Eternal household products were biodegradable and Amelia Eternal makeup products were hypoallergenic before those words found their way into the American vocabulary. Litt did not set out to make products with these specific characteristics; rather, he set out to produce products that would do exactly what they were supposed to for the consumer, without, at the same time being in any way objectionable. This made his products biodegradable and hypoallergenic, but it made them considerably more. Amelia Eternal products were simply and totally acceptable to consumers, and Litt insisted that any consumer objection or complaint about any of his products that was revealed to the sales representatives be brought to his personal attention, at once.

Over the years this policy became a powerful factor in the success of Amelia Eternal. The reputation of the company's products grew by word of mouth, and this policy was continually presented as a strong selling point by the Amelia Eternal representatives. As the decade of the seventies unfolded, it was true that no Amelia Eternal product, household or makeup, had ever contained an ingredient subsequently found or suspected to be carcinogenic.

The growth of the sales representative organization paralleled Amelia Eternal dollar-sales growth. As Exhibit 1-2 reveals, the size of the Amelia Eternal sales-representative force stood at 34 on December 31, 1954, and at 63,099 on the same date in 1979.

The Litt policy of direct selling to consumers through sales representatives had been refined and articulated over the years. In the beginning, of course, the sales-representative staff had been a small group of Amelia's friends and neighbors, hand picked by her. For a year or two this system worked satisfactorily, as the business gradually grew in the geographic area around the housing development in which the Litt's lived. Shortly, however, requests began to arrive for Amelia Eternal products from friends and relatives of the California sales representatives. These friends and relatives were widely dispersed geographically, and it was no longer feasible for Amelia Litt to screen them, nor to train them. The way to increased sales was clearly through an expansion of the Amelia Eternal sales-representative staff. But it was equally clear that some sort of plan would have to be developed so that this expansion could take place in an orderly way and to insure that the sales-representative force would develop a dedication and integrity that would match the qualities of Amelia Eternal products themselves. Amelia and Henry discussed the problem in mid-1955.

"I think that what we should do, Henry," said Amelia, "is to let anyone sell our products who wants to. Put them on a cash-with-order basis, and just 'let it rip.'"

"We can't be that free and easy about it, Amelia," replied Henry. "We have to have some assurance that the people who are representing us are going to put the company in a good light, that they are honest, and that they will work hard. Beyond that, we've got to

**EXHIBIT 1-2**
**Specimen Data: Growth of Amelia Eternal Sales Organization, 1954-1979**
**(Representatives As of 12/31 of Each Year)**

| Year | Sales Representatives | Sales Organizers | Amelia Belles |
|---|---|---|---|
| 1954 | 34 | | |
| 1955 | 59 | | |
| 1956 | 102 | | |
| 1957 | 241 | 2 | |
| 1958 | 321 | 8 | |
| 1959 | 612 | 14 | |
| 1960 | 1,858 | 22 | |
| 1961 | 4,002 | 26 | |
| 1962 | 6,082 | 34 | |
| 1963 | 8,906 | 43 | |
| 1964 | 13,626 | 69 | |
| 1965 | 18,947 | 72 | |
| 1966 | 22,755 | 103 | 2 |
| 1967 | 29,273 | 112 | 3 |
| 1968 | 34,711 | 147 | 3 |
| 1969 | 40,258 | 170 | 4 |
| 1970 | 43,411 | 206 | 6 |
| 1971 | 48,350 | 210 | 9 |
| 1972 | 52,199 | 225 | 12 |
| 1973 | 55,119 | 240 | 13 |
| 1974 | 58,916 | 276 | 15 |
| 1975 | 61,047 | 285 | 17 |
| 1976 | 61,690 | 302 | 20 |
| 1977 | 62,521 | 321 | 24 |
| 1978 | 60,570 | 365 | 29 |
| 1979 | 63,099 | 379 | 34 |

find some way to give them information about the company and its products and try to teach them how they can be most effective salespersons for Amelia Eternal."

"Okay," Amelia said in reply, "why don't we ask applicants to write a letter telling why they want to become an Amelia Eternal sales representative, and why they have chosen to do this rather than to do some other sort of work. If we get such a letter, we'll know the person is literate and we'll know that she has enough interest in us to take the trouble to write a letter. Then we'll send her a set of our product specification sheets and order forms. She can study the specification forms and use them as a basis for selling our products. If we find people who are really successful, we can meet with them periodically and build up their morale and sales skills. You know, that's what I do with the girls around here who sell for us—we meet every week or two to talk about our products and how to sell them. That way we keep in pretty close touch, and yet they're still their own boss."

In this exchange were the seeds of the development of the Amelia Eternal direct sales organization. To this day, no one can become an Amelia Eternal sales representative unless she writes Amelia Litt a letter telling why she wants to work for Amelia Eternal.

This simple process serves as an effective screen for new sales representatives. Many women write the letter and qualify as a sales representative who do not really like the work when they try it and drop out. But many women write the letter, receive the specification sheets, try direct selling, and are immediately successful at it. In 1957 fourteen of the Amelia Eternal representatives sold $10,000 or more of Amelia Eternal merchandise. They were designated "Amelia Eternal Super-Sellers" and were invited to come to Los Angeles to meet with the Litts, discuss the Amelia Eternal products and the new makeup line, and exchange experiences based on successful sales tactics and strategies.

During these 1957 meetings, two of the "super-sellers" approached Amelia Litt and suggested that they be authorized to recruit sales representatives in their home towns. As Madeline Tobias, sales representative in Oshkosh, Wisconsin, put it: "I don't know how many sales representatives you have in Oshkosh. I may be the only one. But, I'll tell you, there's business for us that is going begging in Oshkosh. I simply don't have the time to sell all the business that is there. What I want to do is find some other girls, train them, supervise them, and let them loose. They would order merchandise through me, and I'd collect from them and pass it on to you. Of course, if I were to do this, I'd like a little percentage on top of what I usually make, for the extra effort. Maybe we could take it out of their commissions—what would they know if we set their commissions so they made 30 percent instead of 35, like I make, and I took in the 5 percent for my trouble?"

The Litts jumped on this idea. It solved two problems that they had been agonizing over since the company began—that is, how could they maintain some kind of control over sales representatives who were geographically distant from the home office; and how could they recruit new sales representative prospects in areas where their representation was sparse without physically traveling to markets all over the country.

Before the Los Angeles meetings broke up, the Litts had created the title "sales organizer." They appointed Madeline Tobias sales organizer for Oshkosh, Wisconsin, and Gladys Emery sales organizer for Nutley, New Jersey. At the same time, they developed a set of rules that were to be followed by the sales organizers as they recruited new sales representatives:

1. Each candidate must write a letter to Amelia Litt telling why she wants to be an Amelia Eternal sales representative and why she has chosen this kind of work in preference to others. This letter is to be forwarded to headquarters when the new representative is signed on.
2. There will be no exclusive Amelia Eternal sales territories. Any sales representative may sell anywhere in the United States, or abroad, for that matter.
3. Amelia Eternal sales representatives will be encouraged to maintain suggested retail prices.
4. Sales organizers will sell the "Starting Your Own Business with Amelia Eternal" sales-training kit to each sales representative for $3.00 and use the materials in that kit as a basis for training the sales representative. [This kit had recently been developed for use with women who wrote in and expressed a desire to sell Amelia Eternal products. It replaced the specification sheets and order forms that had been previously sent to such applicants when they signed on. The $3.00-charge did not yield profit for Amelia Eternal but did recover the cost of producing the kit. Also, this charge served as an additional measure of the desire of potential sales representatives to join Amelia Eternal. The kit was, it turned out, ideally suited for use by the new sales organizers in their recruiting efforts.]

5. Each sales organizer will be required to hold a biweekly meeting with her sales representatives to discuss the product line, the new products to be introduced, selling techniques, field problems, etc.

The sales-organizer program was an immediate success. Each of the original two sales organizers recruited eight additional sales representatives, and the dollar-sales yield from Oshkosh and Nutley increased by over three-hundred percent. It was clear to the Litts that the sales-organizer program held the key for the long-term expansion of Amelia Eternal sales. The trick was to find qualified candidates. They were convinced that the only way to identify a potential sales organizer was on the basis of her performance as a sales representative. Thus the annual sales-representative national meetings served as the primary opportunity to recruit new sales organizers on the basis of their demonstrated sales success in the previous year, on the basis of their stated desire to become a sales organizer, and on the basis of the Litt's personal assessment of them as potential key field representatives of the Amelia Eternal Company.

In 1966, it became apparent that another level of local supervision could properly be added above the sales organizers. In the largest markets where several sales organizers were working independently of one another, there was a continuing need for coordination of activities, an occasional need for adjudication of territorial jurisdictional disputes, and an intense need for a forum in which to thrash out common selling problems. Thus, the next level of sales supervision was created. The new "super"-supervisors were called "Amelia Belles." They were selected from the ranks of the sales organizers. The most successful sales organizer in a particular market was typically chosen by the Litts as the Amelia Belle for that market, and installed in an appropriate ceremony at the annual sales representative meetings. Amelia Belles continued their own sales-representative work and also continued as sales organizers. Each Amelia Belle received a 2 percent bonus from headquarters on the total sales achieved by all sales organizers who reported directly to her.

By the late 1970s, there were a total of 379 Amelia Eternal sales organizers and 34 Amelia Belles. The average sales organizer earned $34,769 in 1979, and the highest-earning sales organizer received $82,349 in that year. The average Amelia Belle earned $96,432 in 1979, and the most successful earned $327,426. The average sales representative earned $673 in 1979; but, in assessing this figure, it must be remembered that every sales organizer and every Amelia Belle also still worked, at least some of the time, as a sales representative.

In addition to cash income from commissions (and, in the case of the Amelia Belles, cash bonuses), all of the sales representatives accumulated bonus points that were redeemable for merchandise-bonus awards. These merchandise-bonus points were awarded for performance under various promotional programs that were in force almost continually throughout the year. A sales representative earned merchandise-bonus points for a variety of accomplishments during the promotional period: They might be awarded for sales of a new product; for sales of specific items in the line; for joint sales of three or more items from within the line; or for whatever sales results were specified under the terms of the particular promotion. The more successful sales representatives earned television sets under the merchandise-bonus program, and some of the sales organizers as well as all of the Amelia Belles owned a car that had been earned in this way.

The basic company communication with the sales representatives was a four-color magazine called the *Amelia Eternal Success.* The *Success,* as it was known to the sales representatives, was published twelve times each year. Its editorial style was brisk, punchy, and self-confident. The *Success* was designed to convey five kinds of information to the sales representatives:

1. It was the basic source of information about Amelia Eternal promotions. The lines and items to be promoted were identified; the length of the promotion, the savings that it offered to consumers, and the bonus-merchandise points that it yielded to the sales representatives were all specified.
2. It provided a continuous flow of information about individual Amelia Eternal products. In addition, a good deal of information about Amelia Eternal laboratory-testing programs designed to insure product quality and integrity was also presented in the *Success.*
3. Tips about how to improve representative sales-success were also featured in the magazine. Frequently this material was written by sales representatives who had developed new and particularly successful selling procedures or techniques. Descriptions of such selling successes written by the sales representative responsible for them seemed to impart a practical orientation to such material, and it seemed to be especially well accepted by the sales-representative group.
4. The *Success* announced and described new products. It also announced product deletions and explained how long deleted products might be available to those customers who had used them in the past.
5. Finally, the *Success* provided a medium through which the Litts could announce new company policies as they were introduced and explain the workings of the company policies already in force.

Successful sales representatives participated in an elaborate and magnificently executed series of sales meetings. Each Amelia Eternal sales region held two sales meetings a year at a resort somewhere within the sales region. All sales representatives whose six-month sales exceeded $3,000 were invited to these biannual meetings free of charge, and they were welcome to bring their spouses for a slight charge, somewhat below the actual out-of-pocket cost to Amelia Eternal.

The annual sales meeting attracted all sales representatives who had sold at least $10,000 worth of Amelia Eternal products in the preceding year. These annual sales meetings were held in glamorous cities like New Orleans or San Francisco, in offshore United States locations like Puerto Rico or Hawaii, or occasionally in foreign capitals like Paris or Rio de Janerio. Once again, the sales representatives qualifying to attend the annual sales meetings attended on an all-expense-paid basis, and spouses were welcome to attend, too, for a modest, standard surcharge.

The regional sales meetings lasted for three days, and the annual sales meetings lasted for six days. All of these meetings were carefully planned to include a heavy dose of information about Amelia Eternal, its products, and how to sell them; an equally heavy round of recreational programs; and, a small but emotionally potent inspirational message.

The Litts themselves were depended upon to provide the inspirational portion of these programs. They both attended every sales meeting until the mid-seventies and as many as they were physically able to, after that. They were a superb personification of every sales representative's dream. Millionaires several times over, the Litts were known to have risen from humble beginnings to overwhelming success with a business conception that was simple and honest, and with an ever-renewing dedication to quality products—

products that genuinely served a consumer who could not be harmed through their use.

Henry became, as the years passed, a remarkable platform performer in these sales meetings. He carefully blended sentimental reminiscenses of his life with Amelia and his experiences with the company with observations about the honorable and rewarding experience that representing Amelia Eternal had become for everyone of the successful sales representatives. From this theme, he gradually began to express his pride in his audience, mentioning the names of those who had delivered especially outstanding or unusual performances in the immediately preceding sales period. By the end of the recitation of individual performance, he moved, frequently in tears, to his peroration; here he expressed the hope that he would see all of his friends at the next meeting and that he would see others who worked so well for the sales organizers and who were about to qualify for the sales meetings.

His closing line remained invariant from year to year. "I want everyone of you to carry one thought home with you: If you're not here next time, you will have let me down, personally. You owe it to me, to Old Henry Litt, to see your face and shake your hand at ____," and he would give the place of the next meeting in the sequence. The standard response was a chant, often repeated as many as twenty or thirty times: "We'll see you there, Henry."

As the chanting went on, Henry at first stood for a few moments, tears streaming down his face, humbly looking down into the audience, seeking eye contact with as many individuals in the crowd as he was able. Shortly, however, he seemed to snap back into the reality of the moment, and, as the chanting continued, moved quickly off the stage, to return almost immediately with the radiant Amelia. The chanting then was overwhelmed by a standing ovation for beloved "Miss" Amelia.

If Henry was remarkable as a platform performer, "Miss" Amelia was practically beyond description. Her appearances were always short, never amounting to more than seven or eight minutes. After she had been led onto the stage by Henry, she looked directly at him, smiled, and dismissed him. She then remained in the center of the stage, alone, diminuitive and radiant, waiting until every last vestige of applause died away. Often this took three minutes or more, yet she would wait patiently for it to occur, refusing to speak until the silence was absolute.

When she did speak it was with such a low voice that those in the rear of the auditorium found it necessary to lean forward, straining, to catch her voice. But she always spoke loudly enough so that she was, in fact, heard by everyone present. Her presentation had remained the same, word by word, from the late 1950s. It was a short, succinct statement of what Amelia Eternal offered to its customers.

Amelia began quietly, slowly, radiantly: "I want to tell you all, once again, what our company, is, and what it does . . .

"Amelia Eternal is . . .

"A continuing relationship between sales representatives and customers . . .

"It is a special relationship. There is no hard sell. Every product is guaranteed to be effective yet not harmful . . .

"We offer every makeup item a woman needs to maintain her sense of serenity and beauty . . .

"We offer every household product a woman needs to make her home what she wishes it to be . . .

"And we offer you, our sales representatives, a way to self-confidence and solid accomplishment . . .

"The heart of our business is in the warmth of the relationship you build with your customers. You have the products to do it. You have the skills to do it . . .

"But most of all, you special people here in this room have the humanity to do it. I salute you."

At this point the curtain fell and the sales meeting came to its official end. The applause often continued for eight or ten minutes, but the Litts themselves never responded to it. Instead, they removed themselves as quickly as they could from the convention site, believing that the impressions made by their presentation should be final, without any further exposure to the sales representatives until Henry and Amelia appeared, once again, at the next sales meeting.

The mixture of product quality, interactive sales organization, strong compensation arrangements, and the periodic sales meetings climaxed by the Litt appearances produced a superb sales and profit performance for Amelia Eternal throughout the decade of the sixties and into the seventies. But in the period 1975 through 1979, sales leveled off and profits began to decline as costs, especially selling costs, continued to drift upward.

Exhibit 1-3 suggests what was happening. As the exhibit shows, sales increased more than threefold between 1965 and 1975. Profits virtually tripled in the same period, although they did not increase as rapidly as sales; and, in that same ten-year period, before-tax profit as a percentage of sales declined from 28.5 percent in 1965 to 23.4 percent in 1975.

Between 1975 and 1979, dollar sales remained virtually the same, although unit sales dropped off quite sharply as price increases were imposed across the Amelia Eternal line with increasing frequency. The total number of packages sold by Amelia Eternal declined by 18.7 percent between 1975 and 1979.

Meanwhile, sales costs were rising. Commissions increased from 34.7 percent of sales in 1965 to 41.6 percent of sales. "Commissions" as computed by the Amelia Eternal accounting department included commissions earned by sales representatives, company bonus payments to Amelia Belles, and the cost of merchandise-bonus-point programs. There were two fundamental reasons why the proportion of sales accounted for by commissions had risen steadily over the fourteen-year period. In the first place, Amelia Belle cash bonuses became a factor in the Amelia Eternal compensation system after this level of sales supervision was introduced in 1966. Although not all Amelia Eternal sales were subject to an Amelia Belle Bonus, it was true that, by 1979, roughly two-thirds of sales did pass through an Amelia Belle sales organization, and thus qualified for the payment of the 2 percent direct, Amelia Belle bonus. Thus, between 1965 and 1979, roughly 1.3 of the total increase of 6.9 percent in sales commissions was attributable to the Amelia Belle bonus program.

The balance of the increase in sales commissions—that is, 5.6 percent of total sales in 1979, was attributable to increases in the cost of the bonus-merchandise program. Most of the impact of the Amelia Belles program upon sales commissions had been felt by 1975. Thus, the Amelia Eternal accounting department believed that most of the 3.9 percent increase in sales commissions as a proportion of sales occuring between 1975 and 1979 came from the bonus-merchandise program.

This meant, as all of those involved were quick to agree, that sales promotional activities had been stepped up significantly, as sales stabilized. An analysis of the sales promotions offered in the *Success* in 1975 and 1979 confirmed this trend. There had been a total of 42 promotions in the 1975 calendar year, and the average sales representa-

**EXHIBIT 1-3**
**Amelia External Company Sales and Costs of Sales, Selected Years**

| | 1955 | | 1970 | | 1975 | | 1979 | |
|---|---|---|---|---|---|---|---|---|
| | $ | 100% | $ | 100% | $ | 100% | $ | 100% |
| Sales at Consumer Prices | $39,827,000 | 100.0 | $91,249,000 | 100.0 | $128,321,000 | 100.0 | $132,634,000 | 100.0 |
| Selling Costs | | | | | | | | |
| Sales Commission | 13,820,000 | 34.7 | 33,671,000 | 36.9 | 48,377,000 | 37.7 | 55,176,000 | 41.6 |
| Sales Meetings | 1,438,000 | 3.6 | 3,376,000 | 3.7 | 5,389,000 | 4.2 | 6,632,000 | 5.0 |
| Sales Communications | 239,000 | 0.6 | 821,000 | 0.9 | 1,668,000 | 1.3 | 1,857,000 | 1.4 |
| Cost of Goods Sold, (including factory overhead) | 8,642,000 | 21.7 | 20,440,000 | 22.4 | 30,284,000 | 23.6 | 32,761,000 | 24.7 |
| Administrative Expense | 4,337,000 | 10.9 | 9,673,000 | 10.6 | 12,576,000 | 9.8 | 11,405,000 | 8.6 |
| Total Cost of Sales | 28,476,000 | 71.5 | 67,981,000 | 74.5 | 98,294,000 | 76.6 | 107,831,000 | 81.3 |
| Profit Before Taxes | 11,351,000 | 28.5 | 23,268,000 | 25.5 | 30,027,000 | 23.4 | 24,803,000 | 18.7 |

tive earned approximately 1,206 merchandise-bonus points with a gross merchandise value of approximately $342. (The net merchandise value—that is, the discounted price actually paid for the merchandise by Amelia Eternal—was $179.). In 1979 there were a total of 106 promotions offered in *Success.* This did not mean that the company's promotional activity had increased by two-and-one-half times because individual promotions were not equal in their cost to the company. In fact, it appeared that the average promotion in 1979 was *more* costly to the company than its counterpart in 1975. Thus, the gross merchandise value of the bonus points earned by the average sales representative in 1979 was $892 (net value $459).

In addition, as Exhibit 1-3 reveals, the cost of the sales meetings had also escalated between 1965 and 1975. Most of this cost escalation could be attributed to inflation, but there had been some tendency to increase the quality of the meetings and the relative attractiveness of the meeting places in the 1970s, and especially after 1975.

Sales communications cost refers to the cost of maintaining written contact with the sales representative group. It includes all communication costs with sales representatives except those attributable to sales meetings. More than 90 percent of this overall cost in each year is accounted for by the editorial preparation and printing of the *Success* Magazine. Increases in this cost category have also been primarily due to inflation. However, a comparison of the content and graphics of the *Success* in 1979 with those of 1975 would suggest that some significant attempt had been made to make the magazine more interesting and more readable during the late 1970s, and this effort involved some extra direct cost.

Cost of goods had also shown slight proportional increases during the fourteen-year period, and administrative or home-office expenses had decreased proportionately.

The overall effect of increased costs, especially selling costs, is seen in the proportionate decline in profits over the years, but especially between 1975 and 1979. A percentage decline of 4.7 is recorded in these years, and this amounts to a dollar-profit decline of $5,224,000, as sales remained relatively stable. If sales had increased between 1975 and 1979 at the rate of the period 1970 to 1975, the decline in profit percentage would not have been reflected in an absolute decline of profit dollars. It is the plateau of company sales that is affecting the company's profitability in 1979, as costs rise inexorably, reflecting both inflation and valiant attempts to remedy the sales slump.

Over the years, the Litts had built a solid home-office organization to run the company for them, as their attention and energy was increasingly absorbed by the sales meeting programs and other direct contact with the sales representatives. As the momentum of the company slowed during the 1970s, Henry Litt delegated more and more responsibility to his staff. Finally, in October of 1978, Litt relinquished the title of chief executive officer to Morgan G. Harris, age 52. Harris had been with Amelia Eternal since 1964.

Harris was a trained accountant and had been originally recruited into the company to oversee the transition that accompanied the computerization of sales, inventory, and financial records that occurred in the late 1960s. Harris executed this assignment brilliantly and in the process had gained the friendship and the respect of the Litts. In 1969 he was appointed chief financial officer of the company; in 1973, executive vice-president; and in 1975 president and chief operating officer. When Harris became chief executive officer in 1978, he also assumed the title of chairman, as Henry Litt moved up to founder-chairman.

"Morgan, I want you to run the company," explained Henry Litt. "Amelia and I will be here to help you, and we'll go to as many of the sales meetings as we're able. But, it's your show now, Morgan, and it's your responsibility. We both know that things are slowing down. I don't know why this is–maybe we've run out of customers. Or maybe the old ways don't work with this new generation of sales representatives. I don't know. But somebody has got to find out what's going on and how to fix it. I'd do it myself, but I want to enjoy life a little before my health goes. Amelia's not as well as she looks, either, and I think we owe it to her to let her have a little fun before it's too late."

Morgan Harris did not have anything to say in immediate response to this. He was not much of a talker, and he remained quiet for a few moments, thinking about what Henry Litt had said. Finally, he replied: "Okay, Henry, I'm not sure what's wrong around here. It looks to me that whatever we've done hasn't fixed the problem. I think we've got to start thinking about our marketing programs. Maybe we need some fresh marketing approaches–and some new marketing brains."

"Okay, Morgan, whatever you say," replied Henry Litt. "I'd take some time studying and thinking about it before you start bringing in any of these marketing hotshots, though. You know those guys promise the world and sometimes they don't deliver all that much, either. Amelia thinks our current marketing programs are pretty sound, and I'm inclined to agree with her. But it's your job, Morgan, and we'll keep ourselves out of your way."

Morgan Harris was certain that Henry Litt was completely sincere when he said that he and Amelia would keep themselves out of his way as he set about to improve the fortunes of the Amelia Eternal Company. But he also knew that it would be impossible for the Litts to ignore either the company or any substantial changes that he, Morgan Harris, made in the way that it was run. Amelia Eternal was, after all, identified with the Litts, and no one except the Litts had run it since they started it in 1954. "I may fix this company," Harris thought to himself, "get sales going up again, and improve profits; but to do it, I've got to find a way to make whatever I do acceptable to the Litts."

Harris decided that he could not use traditional management processes in the company to accomplish his purposes. In the first place, the bulk of the decisions, over the years, had been made by the Litts themselves, usually Henry, without consultation with anyone else in the company, except perhaps Amelia. Now Henry had given up the chief executive title, and Harris knew that he should not depend upon Henry Litt for decisions. But Harris recognized that it was likely that Henry Litt would gradually move back into this decision-making role if something were not done to fill the vacuum that had been created by his promotion to founder-chairman.

Alternatively, Harris could make the needed decisions himself. But when he had made decisions in the past, he had always done so in consultation with Henry Litt. Harris suspected that Henry would expect to be consulted under the new organization structure, regardless of what he had said to the contrary, and that if he were not consulted, he would become annoyed and insist that all decisions be reviewed by him. "I really can't keep him, or Amelia, for that matter, out of it," thought Harris. "They still own 73 percent of this company, and founder-chairman or not, Henry will have to be convinced that what we do is in the best interests of the Litts and of the company, and in that order."

Finally, Harris decided that the only way to resolve the problem of imposing control was to seek help from outside specialists. He decided to hire the management-consulting firm of Keltner, Boudreau, and Gordon to assess the overall situation of Amelia Eternal and to make specific recommendations concerning what reforms should be undertaken to improve the sales and profits of the company.

When Harris broached this plan to Henry Litt, he was pleasantly surprised by the reaction. "I think that's a darned good idea, Morgan," said Henry. "I've known Eddie Collins down at their Los Angeles office for years, and he's a smart man, and he's had a lot of experience with a lot of companies, and I bet they can say some really sound things to us. Go ahead, that's the right way to tackle it!"

Keltner, Boudreau, and Gordon assigned a team led by Edward Collins, executive vice-president in charge of its Los Angeles office. Collins was assisted by five others who specialized, respectively, in marketing, accounting, information processing, organization control, and management structure. This group studied Amelia Eternal for three months. No interim reports were issued, and no one at Amelia Eternal had any idea what conclusions the KB&G team was reaching while it methodically reviewed the company, its internal workings, and its external relations.

Finally, in March 1979, Eddie Collins wrote the following letter to Morgan Harris:

---

# Keltner, Boudreau, and Gordon

- Management Consulting -

March 9, 1979

Dear Morgan:
We have now completed our investigation and review work for the Amelia Eternal Company. Our final and detailed report and its recommendations will be in your hands next week. In the meantime, I believe that it may be appropriate for me to summarize briefly this report for your private consideration, and I do so in this letter.

1. Our major findings concern the direct-selling operations of Amelia Eternal.
   a. The average age of the Amelia Eternal representative is 49 years. If we eliminate those representatives that have been with the company for less than two years, the average age of the representatives is 54 years.
   b. Overall, the representatives have worked with Amelia Eternal for a total of 9.3 years on average. If we eliminate those who have been with the company for two years or less, this average tenure with the company jumps to 12.1 years.
   c. Two years seems to be the crucial length of time for representative service. If a representative stays for two years, she is likely to stay for a considerably longer length of time. When a representative is recruited, the odds are about 3 to 1 against her staying for two years or more. That is, three out of four of your new recruits drop out before they have stayed in the representative force for two years.
   d. Representatives are largely recruited by those women who are already in the sales-representative force. Even those women who apply to the company for an appointment as representative are immediately referred to a local sales organizer if there is one. The heavy drop-out rate for newly appointed representatives suggests that the recruitment process is not as successful as it should be.

e. Your sales-representative coverage is very spotty. We estimate, for example, that Amelia Eternal has no sales-representative coverage at all in 83 of the 217 television coverage areas that constitute the continental United States. Our analysis also indicates that your representative coverage is very sparse in many of the television-coverage areas in which you do have some representation.

f. Sales representatives seem to specialize in the products that they sell. Some representatives seem to sell mostly household products, whereas other representatives seem to sell mostly makeup products. Among those who concentrate in cosmetics, it is not unusual for sales to come from only one or two of the Amelia Eternal brands. It is hard to know whether these representatives that have been de facto specialists are really capable of broadening their sales efforts to other lines and brands. It may be that your sales representatives are inherently limited in respect to the breadth of products that they can sell effectively. You should know a lot more about this than you do. If, for example, the 60-odd percent of all representatives who primarily sell only makeup or household products could be encouraged to extend their sales presentations to include the second line of products, we believe that company sales could grow at least 22 percent within a year.

g. Our analysis indicates that many sales representatives set a particular earnings goal for themselves and are content, once having reached that goal, to suspend their active selling. These goals are usually stated in terms of the monthly commissions that the sales representatives have decided that they want or need to make. The result of this informal goal setting is that your representatives don't work as hard as they might. In some cases the representatives simply fill orders from customers that they have serviced for years and make no attempt to seek out and sell new customers.

A great deal of this informal goal setting is traceable to the nature of your sales representative force: over 75 percent of the representatives view their work as part time. They think of it as an activity to produce supplemental income rather than as the prime or only source of family income. This attitude is probably inherent in a direct-sales activity of the Amelia Eternal type depending, as it does, on neighborhood women with spare time on their hands as a source for the bulk of the sales representatives. This informal goal setting rather severely inhibits company sales progress, however, and raises questions about the desirability of experimenting with alternative compensation arrangements to stimulate extra selling activity on the part of the incumbent representatives. It also suggests the possibility of attempting to recruit more full-time Amelia Eternal sales representatives.

2. We have studied the sales-meeting program in great detail. We recognize its fundamental strengths, and we recognize it as one of the bulwarks of the Amelia Eternal direct-sales system. Yet we believe that the sales meetings have several shortcomings.

   a. The sales meetings are one of the two major ways in which your company communicates with the outside world. As a communication channel, the sales meeting has many strengths, not the least of which is the opportunity for productive interaction with the sales-representative force. But, the sales meeting is a limited communication device. In the first place, it can only convey direct information to the sales organization. The assumption is, of course, that the sales organization becomes an effective intermediary between the company and its ultimate customers. Thus, one hopes that the sales organization transmits all or most of the information that it receives at the sales meetings on to the ultimate customers and that the sales meeting is a primary stimulant to sales and, ultimately, to company earnings.

We have, of course, seen evidence that the sales meeting, as such, often does not have this desired stimulative effect upon sales. The fact that many sales representatives specialize in either makeup products or household products suggests that the hopeful assumptions about sales-meeting effects are ill founded. And, the practice of informal quota setting by the sales representatives also suggests that the sales meetings do not have as great an effect on sales effort as one might wish or hope.

b. A second problem with the Amelia Eternal sales meeting is that they are quite limited, by design, in terms of their coverage of the sales representatives. Only those representatives who reach specific goals are qualified to attend the sales meetings. We estimate that only about 35 percent of Amelia Eternal sales representatives have ever attended a sales meeting. And those sales representatives who do attend tend to be the old-timers who have carved out successful franchises and are more or less set in their ways. It is, we would expect, exactly this group who is least likely to be positively affected by the sales meeting in terms of carrying its effects back into the field selling activities. It is hard to be certain about this, of course. In theory, the sales organizers should be carrying the messages of the sales meetings back to their representative networks, and they should be doing it with a good bit of zeal and passion. We simply question whether it really works out this way in practice.

c. Finally, we believe that the Amelia Eternal sales-meeting format has become relatively flat and tired. In those meetings that we attended, we felt that the standard format was followed a bit too slavishly, and that the content of the meeting day to day was a little too predictable and dull. Surely, as you have recognized, the device of moving the meetings from location to location does a great deal to introduce a sense of anticipation and novelty into the program. But too little else is done to "jazz" the meetings up and make them distinctive, different, and really interesting. For example, does every meeting have to devote a full half day to sales-success stories? These have a certain sameness about them, and not every sales representative or sales organizer, for that matter, has a really scintillating platform presence. For example, must every meeting have as its climactic moment the appearance of Henry and Amelia Litt? This may have been a truly stimulating event in years gone by, but the Litts are not as dynamic as we suspect they once were; and a good deal of their dynamism seems now to be dissipated in a sentimentality that is not only ineffective, but sometimes even embarrassing. The old-timers like it, perhaps, because they have come to expect it. Those newer sales representatives who have managed to qualify for meeting attendance find the Litt appearances of limited usefulness, at best.

3. The *Success* is an important communication tool. It is all the more important because it is the only company communication received by those sales representatives who do not qualify for the sales meetings. We are

frankly impressed by the *Success*. The sales representatives respond favorably to it, and its content is fresh, stimulative, and responsible. We would not change the *Success* in any significant way. We would only raise the question as to whether it might be supplemented with other direct company communication (personal letters for example) to those newer sales representatives whose sales records seem promising, but who do not yet qualify for company sales-meeting participation.

4. A major problem for Amelia Eternal will be to develop some substitute for the Litts. These two brilliant, successful, and engaging people epitomize the company to all who work for it. It is difficult to imagine the company in the absence of the Litts, for they seem to be almost interchangeable with it in the minds of the sales representatives and the home office and manufacturing employees. Their role and status in company affairs is difficult to overemphasize.

   It is imperative that you, as their successor manager and as their designated surrogate leader, recognize the burden that has been put upon you and that you make definitive plans as to just how you will accept and discharge the responsibilities of this role. You must consciously design a personality for yourself that will have substance that is meaningful to the sales representatives. This substance must have meaning in its own right, and it must have meaning as a substitute for the Litts.

   Morgan, whether you like it or not, the Litts will not be active in this company forever. Your appointment as chairman and chief executive officer suggests that they have already decided to phase out of day-to-day participation in company affiars and is so interpreted by the sales representatives. If you do not wish to become the public figure that replaces them in your company, or if you do not believe you are capable of it, it is imperative that you decide who will become this figure. If you decide to undertake this role, you must devote every one of your waking minutes to the formulation of the personality that you will project to your sales representatives and to the world.

5. We have reviewed the company's promotional programs in considerable detail and we are, frankly, disappointed in them. The merchandise-bonus-point system is sound in concept, but it does not seem to motivate the sales representatives to extra effort. The sales representatives seem to accumulate merchandise-bonus points as they go along; and when they have enough to cash them in for something that appeals to them from the catalog, they do so, and thus begin accumulating points again. We believe that the bonus-point program must be restructured to provide genuine motivation to the sales representatives to increase their sales productivity, and to do this by seeking out new customers for Amelia Eternal, as well as by selling Amelia Eternal merchandise that the representatives have a tendency to ignore. Our feelings about this merchandise-bonus-point program are especially important because it is this program that has absorbed the bulk of the increases in sales costs that have been incurred in the past four or five years. You have been depending upon this program to turn the company's sales and profits around and it simply hasn't worked.

6. Finally, it is inconceivable to us that a company that had, last year, $127 million in sales to consumers makes no attempt to communicate with consumers through advertising. We are unanimous in our belief that you should begin to build a base of consumer awareness and understanding through advertising. The benefits of such an approach are so obvious that

I won't burden you with them in this letter. But I do believe that this is the first subject that we should discuss as we begin to talk about ways in which you can begin to revitalize this exciting company.

In addition to the initiation of an advertising program, let me list in summary fashion some objectives which we believe you must develop programs to accomplish:

A. First, you must find ways to recruit new representatives. The present system is almost no system at all. You do little to seek out representatives and you have no program to identify those candidates with outstanding potential nor those who are more than likely to fail. You can no longer depend upon referrals from your existing sales representatives. The current system will, incidentally, get worse as the incumbent sales representatives get older, and it could be argued that they have already reached an average age at which their sales representative referrals will be increasingly of mediocre quality.

B. Your compensation and promotional programs must be revised so that they motivate the sales representatives to extra effort. This is a complex subject, and one that will require ingenuity and field testing. But there must be better ways, and we must find them!

C. We believe that your product lines are too long and too redundant. You offer for sale almost anything that the research and development people perfect that meets company standards of quality and integrity. Your inventory load is horrendous, and you do entirely too much small-batch manufacturing. Your manufacturing and warehousing costs can be very significantly reduced, if you will reduce the number of items in your line by, let us say, for example, 50 percent. Yet if you were to eliminate items in the company lines that constitute the lowest selling 50 percent, the net impact on sales would be less than 10 percent. This won't be easy. But it will permit vast savings in overhead. There is another reason to do it. It will permit you to focus company sales and promotional efforts behind that handful of Amelia Eternal products that contribute the bulk of company sales and that have won genuine and widespread consumer acceptance. The company has been emphasizing breadth and depth of product lines, and in the process, ignoring the very items that have, almost inadvertently, become the heart of your business. This is a great opportunity for Amelia Eternal, and it is one that we must seize immediately!

D. Amelia Eternal is not now a national company. It must become one, mustn't it? If you can generate $127 million in sales from your present lopsided and disproportionate sales-representative coverage, it seems evident that an immediate way in which to increase sales is to increase geographic coverage. We have already talked about improving the quality of Amelia Eternal representatives. Now we are talking about the pressing need to increase the quantity of high-potential sales representatives and to do it in those geographic areas that now lie dormant.

E. Finally, we must find ways to make the sales meetings more effective. Their content simply must be modernized. And, we believe that you must find ways to broaden their coverage to include promising younger sales representatives that do not now qualify for attendance. Perhaps the bonus-point promotional programs can be used to qualify previous non-sales-meeting attendees for attendance. Perhaps some other system must be worked out. But somehow you must find ways to expand the coverage of the meetings and you must work on the content so that it really does motivate the attendees to sell more.

I hope that all of this will strike you as constructive, Morgan. This has been a critical letter. But rarely in our experience have we seen a company with greater potential for progress. As we work together to develop programs to exploit this potential, I am certain that you will find sales and profits responding immediately and very positively.

---

Morgan Harris read the Collins letter twice on the day that he received it. He said nothing about it to his associates, nor, heaven forbid, to the Litts. He did not look at it again for six days. Then he read it again, twice, and called Eddie Collins on the phone.

"Eddie, I've read your letter," said Harris, "several times, in fact. And I've thought about it a good deal, and now I want to talk to you about it. No one else over here has seen it, and I don't want them to see it, until you and I have talked and I'm satisfied on several points."

"Okay, Morgan," replied Collins. "Can I come over right now?"

And so Collins and Harris met on the afternoon and into the evening of March 16, 1979. In total they talked for seven hours and forty-five minutes. At the end of their conversation, Morgan Harris had been convinced that he must do a number of things that had been recommended by Collins in the March 9 letter. But, he was not totally convinced that Amelia Eternal should initiate a program of consumer advertising. A good deal of their long conversation centered on this question.

"Eddie," said Harris, "you know perfectly well that the Litts have never approved of consumer advertising and that at least part of our reason for not advertising is that they don't believe in it. I've heard Henry say time and again that advertising isn't honest, that it would not reflect the kind of products that he makes and believes in, and that this company can depend upon the sales representatives to reach the public. He believes that the sales meeting is a genuine and optimum alternative to consumer advertising."

"But, damn it, Morgan, you know better than that. Read what I said in my letter," exploded Collins.

"Okay, Okay, Eddie," replied Harris. "Cool off. I know what you've said in your letter. But you really didn't tell me what advertising would accomplish for us. Rather you told me all about the problems with our representatives and the sales meetings, and so on. I'm not saying that I disagree with you about this advertising issue, Eddie. I'm just pointing out that you didn't make a positive case for advertising; you made a negative one. And when we talk to Henry Litt about this—and believe me, before this company does any advertising at all he'll have to be convinced—you'd better be prepared to make the case *for* advertising, not just the case *against* our sales meetings, representatives, and sales promotions."

"Okay, Morgan, I get the point," said Collins. "And I think you're absolutely right. But you said that it wasn't just Henry's objections that had been responsible for Amelia Eternal not advertising in the past. What else is there? I can't imagine that there can be more than that."

"You surprise me, Eddie," responded Harris. "There are just rock-bottom business reasons. How much will a consumer-advertising program cost us?"

"I really don't know. Advertising agencies are the ones who know the answer to those questions. And the good ones won't try to answer until they have some sort of idea of the objectives that you are trying to accomplish."

"Come on, Eddie, you can't duck it," snapped Harris. "If you are going to come in here and tear our business apart, and put it back together and decide that—what word did you use that made us look like baboons—ah, it's 'inconceivable' that Amelia Eternal hasn't advertised: Eddie if you're going to come on like that, you *have* to know at least something about what you're talking about. If you're going to get tough with us on generalities, you can't go soft on specifics. I mean it, Eddie. I won't put up with it from you *or* all those MBAs you've got working for you down there."

"Okay, Morgan," smiled Eddie. "It's your turn to cool off. It could cost you $10 million a year to do the job. It might cost as much as $15 million. That's what some of my advertising pals told me by way of an educated guess. It's probably about right. One thing is for sure—it will cost some really big bucks."

"Eddie, do you know what our before-tax profits in this company were last year?" asked Harris. They were roughly $26,600,000. We're pretty sure that they'll drop below $25 million this year, and maybe below $24 million. You come in here and start talking about an advertising program that will shoot half our profits before taxes. You won't guarantee that it will work, and neither will any of those ad guys either.

"Now, my guess is that everything else you propose—*everything*—won't cost more than $3 million, maybe $4 million at the outside. I think you're dead right on these other things—we should have moved in some of these areas years ago. But then, you want me to put $15 million on top of $4 million and tell Mr. Litt that he'll have pre-tax profits of not more than $4 million.

"Wow, Eddie, you're an optimist! And you must be a better salesman than I am, because I know that I'd have trouble working that one past Henry, and especially little old Amelia. She can be a bearcat when it comes to profits."

"Well, Morgan," said Collins, "we're not going to resolve this one today. I'll think about it some more and you think about it some more, too. I'll just say one thing to you: Most of the companies in this country that are successful in selling to consumers spend more on advertising than they make in profits. That's the way they do it. You've been getting a free ride for too long, Morgan. You are going to have to face up to the realities, I'm afraid. Look, do I want to say all this to you? Of course not. My life would be simpler and my fees just as large if I just forgot about this advertising business. But I won't because, in good conscience, I simply can't do it."

"Okay, Eddie," said Harris, almost wistfully. "But tell me what it will do for me. And tell me why I've got to spend $10 or $15 million to reach my customers even though Henry and I are already spending, uh, uh, roughly six-and-one-half million on sales meetings that are already reaching the customer through the representatives."

"You may have to do both, Morgan. You may have to do both, whether you want to or not."

On that note, Collins excused himself and went home.

## *QUESTIONS FOR CASE 1*

1. What could consumer advertising be expected to accomplish for the Amelia Eternal company? List five specific effects that a consumer-advertising program could be expected to accomplish.

2. What would be the marketing implications of an Amelia Eternal Company decision to advertise?

3. Would consumer advertising accomplish the same objectives as the Amelia Eternal sales meetings? If you answer is "yes," describe the joint effects which these two marketing programs could be expected to accomplish. If your answer is "no," describe the differences in the effects of the two programs and describe the degree to which they complement each other.

4. Can Amelia Eternal afford the cost of a consumer-advertising program? Is it possible to justify a consumer-advertising expenditure in terms of the specific effects to be accomplished that you have given in answer to Question 1? Discuss your asnwer.

5. Is it possible that Amelia Eternal consumer-advertising expenditures might increase the sales generated by the bonus-point-merchandise promotional programs? How might these two programs interact? What restrictions would such advertising-promotional program interactions place on the content of the consumer-advertising program?

6. Write a recommendation to Morgan Harris concerning a consumer-advertising program for Amelia Eternal. Be sure you tell Mr. Harris what advertising will do for his company and how he can justify its cost.

# Case 2

# Determining Advertising Appropriations

*STAR COLA COMPANY INTRODUCES STAR-D COLA*

The Star Cola Company was founded in 1928. Its headquarters, offices, and main manufacturing facility are located in Louisville, Kentucky. Like its major competitors, Star manufactures soft-drink essences or syrups and sells them to a network of local bottlers throughout the United States. The bottlers, in turn, convert the essences into STAR soft drinks and bottle and can them in containers of standard design provided by Star Cola Company. In addition to providing the soft-drink essences, packages, and a variety of management services to the bottlers, Star also sponsors national advertising and promotional activities in behalf of the company soft drinks.

The basic product in the Star Cola Company line is STAR COLA. In addition, over the years, Star has introduced several other soft-drink products including a line of generic soft drinks–orange, cream, root beer, ginger ale, club soda, and so forth (1951)–under the brand name of ELF; a lemon-lime drink called FRESH (1962); and a diet-cola drink under the DIET-LIGHT COLA brand name (1972).

The sales results for these several brands are shown in Exhibit 2-1. As the exhibit reveals, Star Cola Company has shown a vigorous growth since 1955. The new products have made an important contribution to this growth because STAR COLA itself has shown only a steady but hardly spectacular growth in these years. DIET-LIGHT COLA has spurred company sales strongly since its introduction in 1972, and especially since 1977.

But, noteworthy as the sales growth of DIET-LIGHT COLA has been, it has not kept

**EXHIBIT 2-1**
**Specimen Data: Star Cola Company Sales to Bottlers by Brand for Selected Years, 1955-1979 (000 omitted)**

| Year | Total | STAR COLA | ELF Line | FRESH | DIET-LIGHT |
|---|---|---|---|---|---|
| 1955 | $28,720 | $26,796 | $1,924 | - | - |
| 1960 | 34,831 | 32,879 | 2,042 | - | - |
| 1965 | 36,945 | 29,379 | 3,724 | $3,842 | - |
| 1970 | 41,822 | 33,319 | 3,892 | 4,611 | - |
| 1971 | 43,204 | 35,356 | 3,642 | 4,206 | - |
| 1972 | 45,321 | 36,345 | 3,782 | 4,132 | $ 1,062 |
| 1973 | 49,272 | 37,587 | 3,911 | 3,982 | 3,792 |
| 1974 | 54,832 | 41,446 | 3,281 | 4,206 | 5,899 |
| 1975 | 56,911 | 40,728 | 3,392 | 5,371 | 7,420 |
| 1976 | 59,306 | 41,838 | 3,962 | 4,873 | 8,633 |
| 1977 | 62,918 | 45,109 | 4,014 | 4,764 | 9,031 |
| 1978 | 71,432 | 49,631 | 3,862 | 5,213 | 12,726 |
| 1979 | 84,693 | 50,873 | 3,982 | 5,006 | 24,832 |

*Source:* Star Cola Company Annual Report.

up with industry growth in the diet soft-drink category. As Exhibit 2-2 shows, DIET-LIGHT COLA accounts for 13.5 percent of total industry diet soft-drink sales in 1979, and this percentage has actually fallen since 1974, in spite of the four-fold growth in DIET-LIGHT sales in that period.

As the senior executives of Star Cola Company reviewed the events in the cola market during 1979 and the first months of 1980, it became clear to them that, in spite of the Star Cola Company's impressive sales achievements, the soft-drink market was quickly getting away from them. The explosive growth in the diet soft-drink segment of the market found Star Cola Company with too few diet soft drinks in their product line.

**EXHIBIT 2-2**
**Specimen Data: Diet Soft-Drink Sales to Bottlers and DIET-LIGHT Market Share, 1972-1979 (000 omitted)**

| Year | Diet Soft-Drink Sales | DIET-LIGHT Cola Sales | DIET-LIGHT Cola Market Share |
|---|---|---|---|
| 1972 | $ 13,974 | $ 1,062 | 7.6% |
| 1973 | 28,625 | 3,792 | 13.2% |
| 1974 | 34,845 | 5,899 | 16.9% |
| 1975 | 47,261 | 7,420 | 15.7% |
| 1976 | 58,730 | 8,633 | 14.7% |
| 1977 | 62,715 | 9,031 | 14.4% |
| 1978 | 83,176 | 12,726 | 15.3% |
| 1979 | 183,941 | 24,832 | 13.5% |

*Source:* Star Cola Market Research Department.

It would be easy enough for Star Cola to introduce diet versions of the ELF line and of FRESH. This would strengthen the company position with its bottlers and would provide more depth in company offerings in the diet soft-drink market. But the really difficult question facing Star Cola management was whether or not DIET-LIGHT COLA should be the sole company entry in the crucial cola segment of the diet soft-drink market.

Key officials of the company were deeply divided on this issue. When DIET-LIGHT had been introduced in 1972 it was thought of as little more than a novelty. The basic flavor appeal of STAR cola and its major competitors Coca-Cola and Pepsi-Cola came from the synergistic action of the cola flavoring with sugar. There was, in the view of company officials, no way in which a cola drink could be made to taste like a cola drink in the absence of sugar, and especially when dependence was placed upon saccharine to achieve sweetness in the formulation of diet-cola drinks. Star Cola introduced DIET-LIGHT in 1972 to fill out the company line. It was as good a non-sugar-cola drink as STAR could make, and there seemed to be some demand for it; but no one of responsibility in the company could believe that consumers would ever buy either DIET-LIGHT or the competitor's diet-cola drinks in any significant volume. Thus the management of the Star Cola Company was dumfounded when the diet soft-drink market grew so vigorously during the late 1970s and when sales of DIET-LIGHT had grown to half the volume of those of STAR COLA.

By 1979 a major breakthrough in the formulation of diet colas had been made by the research and development group at Star Cola. They had found an additional ingredient—a synthetic chocolate flavor—that, when added to DIET-LIGHT syrup in minute quantities, produced a cola flavor that was virtually indistinguishable from STAR COLA itself.

Some Star Cola officials, including Robert Harmon, president, and Albert Falcone, treasurer, believed that DIET-LIGHT should be reformulated using the synthetic chocolate flavor and reintroduced in the marketplace as a "new, improved DIET-LIGHT"; but Marketing Director John A. Watercomb disagreed. The three men met with Star Cola Chairman Malcolm A. Middlestadt to discuss this issue in early July of 1980.

Robert Harmon opened the meeting. "I still can't quite understand, John, why you believe that we shouldn't reformulate DIET-LIGHT. It seems to me that that is the logical and easy thing to do. Just make the product better, and let consumers know about it. Isn't that the right way to go?"

John Watercomb responded to Harmon: "I think that there really are two reasons why we shouldn't reformulate DIET-LIGHT, Bob," said Watercomb. "But you put the cart before the horse, as far as I'm concerned. It's not so much what I'm against as what I'm for. I believe, very strongly, that we should introduce a diet cola under the STAR brand. It's because of this that I wouldn't use our new product to reformulate DIET-LIGHT. I've got a better way to use that really super new diet-cola drink.

"Why am I so anxious to put out a diet cola under the STAR name? First of all, because the new product tastes like STAR COLA. If it tastes like STAR COLA, it should have the STAR name. We know that STAR COLA appeals to consumers. Our blind taste tests prove that most consumers can't distinguish STAR from COKE, and those that can usually perfer STAR. The STAR name gives a broad base of acceptance and allegiance when we introduce a diet cola that really tastes good and really tastes like STAR COLA.

"But there's even more to it than that. DIET-LIGHT seems to have found a place for itself. We can't sneeze at more than $25 million in sales. DIET-LIGHT doesn't taste like the new product. I don't even think it tastes very good, but we seem to have found a lot of customers who like it. If we reformulate DIET-LIGHT, we have a good chance of losing a lot of business that we now have. And I don't think that there's any chance at all of building as much new business with the new product under the DIET-LIGHT name as under the STAR name, simply because we have changed the product. The market opportunity exists because the new product does taste like STAR COLA, not because it *doesn't* taste like DIET-LIGHT. You agree with all this, don't you, Malcolm?"

"Well, John, maybe I do," said Middlestadt. "Let me put it this way, I think what you're talking about makes real marketing sense. I think that new product is a real winner. And the way the diet drinks are growing, I believe that we must do everything in our power to stay up with them. If we don't, we're going to stay just a nice little cola company in Louisville, a fading Number Four in an industry that the big boys will have really taken over. So, from the marketing standpoint, you've convinced me that we ought to bring out the new product under the STAR name, alright. The thing I don't know about is where the money to do this is going to come from. You haven't said anything about it, but I imagine it will cost us a lot more to launch a new brand, than it will to reintroduce an improved DIET-LIGHT. Isn't that right?"

"Yes, that's right, Mal," said Watercomb. "We would want to continue to support DIET-LIGHT with an advertising appropriation that is consistent with its sales growth. It is, after all, growing so fast that it would be criminal not to continue to give it at least a normal level of advertising support. If we were to reformulate DIET-LIGHT and reintroduce it as a product with an important new flavor, I believe that the major change in advertising would be in the copy. As I've just said, I think we'd lose sales if we reformulate DIET-LIGHT, but the sales loss wouldn't be so great as to seriously impact the DIET-LIGHT advertising appropriation. What we would really lose would be sales momentum.

"But then, if we were to introduce a new diet form of STAR COLA—we're thinking of calling it STAR-D, incidentally—we would have to find some money to support introductory advertising. To really make an impact in the marketplace we'd recommend investment spending on advertising in the first year."

"What kind of dollars are you talking about, John?" asked Treasurer Albert Falcone.

"Well, Al." responded Watercomb, "we'd be going for a 10 percent share of the market in the first year. We think the diet drinks are going to reach about $300 million in 1980. Using that as a base, we're talking—rough figures—about $30 million in sales and about 50 percent over our normal advertising percentages. So, we usually spend about 20 percent of sales on advertising; and to get STAR-D started we recommend an introductory advertising appropriation somewhere around 30 percent. Let's say—still rough figures—$9 million in the first year."

"Nine *million* dollars?" gasped Falcone. "Where on earth are we going to get that kind of money? John, you know as well as I do that we are only going to net a little more than $10 million in this fiscal year. The thought of spending $9 million *extra* dollars on advertising next year is simply preposterous!"

"Well, Al, it's a lot of money, alright," responded Watercomb, "but we're not talking about advertising just to spend the money. We're talking about what we have to do to keep this company in the soft-drink market. I really think that we're discussing survival here this morning, Al."

"But, for pete's sake," snapped Falcone, "where is the money going to come from? We'll have to borrow it, if the banks would lend it to us for advertising, which I doubt, and then we're talking interest rates of more than 20 percent. I wouldn't do *that* if we needed a new plant, but at least if we were going to put up a new plant I'd have something tangible and I'd know that sooner or later I'd get the money back. When you talk about 'investing' in advertising, what do you mean? A plant is an *investment*—it's tangible, and it will produce income, returns, for years to come. You have no idea whether this scheme of yours, that will cost $9 million, will work or not. That's not an investment—that's an adventure. It might work, and then again it might not; but there is no *predictable* known return from it. I just don't think that we can operate this company on that basis. It's not prudent—it's just foolishness you're talking about, John."

At this point, President Robert Harmon jumped in. "Al is right, Mal. You must know that. What will our stockholders think if we borrow as much money as we make in a year, or more, and spend it all on advertising?"

"Okay boys, calm down, all of you," said Malcolm Middlestadt. "My problem is that I suspect that everyone's right on this. We can't afford *not* to introduce a diet cola under the STAR brand name, and we can't afford to do it either. John, I don't think that I'm entirely clear about how you decide how much to spend on advertising on either our existing products or our new products. Would you write a memorandum about how you do this that explains exactly *what* you do, and then we'll meet again and try to figure out what we should do without putting the company into bankruptcy.

About a week later, John Watercomb released the following memorandum:

---

# THE STAR COLA COMPANY

Office Memorandum

July 10, 1980

| | | | |
|---|---|---|---|
| To: | Malcolm A. Middlestadt | cc: | R. L. Harmon |
| From: | John A. Watercomb | | A. M. Falcone |
| Subject: | Star Advertising Appropriation Policy | | |

You asked me to describe just how we determine the size of advertising appropriations for Star brands.

The first step in determining an appropriation is to make an estimate of the sales that the company will generate during the period for which we are calculating the advertising appropriation. Usually, we establish advertising appropriations a year at a time, and usually we make the sales estimate for the subsequent calender year in early October. You review the sales forecasts and marketing plans for a given year in the last weeks of October of the preceding year. The marketing plans include, of course, the recommended advertising appropriation for the following year.

Once we have a sales estimate, we simply multiply it by 20 percent to develop the recommended advertising appropriation. Of course, the question that this process begs is just why we use 20 percent. Why not 18 or 25, or whatever? It was the custom of the company to use 20 percent when I joined Star in 1971. There were, as far as I could tell, three reasons why this percentage had been adopted.

First, it appears that 20 percent is about what our competitors spend to support their brands with advertising. There are competitive advertising studies in the files that have been produced by the advertising agency and date back to the early 1950s, and that's what these studies show. So the first reason that we use a 20 percent advertising appropriation is because that's what our competitors feel that they can afford to do. Incidentally, the competitive advertising-expenditure analyses are updated every year, and the 20 percent figure still seems to be holding up for the industry.

Secondly, we seem to be able to live, as a company, with the 20 percent appropriation level. There aren't any memoranda or analyses in the file that document this. The point remains, nevertheless, that we have continued to be a growing, prosperous company over the years that we have spent about 20 percent of our total sales revenues on advertising. This is really a very, very important consideration. I'm sure that the treasurer's department would prefer that we spend less on advertising and, for that matter, cut all of our other expenses, too. Then we'd all make a lot more money, if sales held up after we'd finished making the cuts. But the plain fact of the matter is that neither the treasurer's department nor anyone else in the company has ever been able to prove, or come anywhere near to proving, that a cut in advertising would work in the long run, or even in the short run, for that matter.

Finally, the company did make some effort to investigate this whole matter of how much to spend for advertising, in the early 1960s. I am attaching the summary results of these market tests to this memorandum for your perusal (Exhibits 2-3, 2-4, 2-5). They were judged inconclusive by the

**EXHIBIT 2-3**
**Specimen Data: Test of Advertising Appropriation Level for STAR COLA, 1961, 1962, 1963**
**Test Condition I: Increase Advertising Weight By 50 Percent (Knoxville, Tennessee; Omaha, Nebraska; Atlanta, Georgia)**

| | Sales | Advertising |
|---|---|---|
| Pre-test Year (1961) | | |
| (Normal Advertising Weight) | | |
| 1st Quarter | $132,839 | $22,631 |
| 2nd Quarter | 158,910 | 28,411 |
| 3rd Quarter | 197,249 | 50,689 |
| 4th Quarter | 166,041 | 35,073 |
| Test Year (1962) | | |
| (Advertising Weight Increased 50 Percent) | | |
| 1st Quarter | $126,076 | $33,947 |
| 2nd Quarter | 141,321 | 42,617 |
| 3rd Quarter | 174,832 | 76,034 |
| 4th Quarter | 149,711 | 52,610 |
| Post-test Year (1963) | | |
| (Normal Advertising Weight) | | |
| 1st Quarter | $130,811 | $21,542 |
| 2nd Quarter | 152,348 | 27,044 |
| 3rd Quarter | 189,612 | 48,251 |
| 4th Quarter | 141,229 | 33,386 |

**EXHIBIT 2-4**
**Specimen Data: Test of Advertising Appropriation Level for STAR COLA, 1961, 1962, 1963**
**Test Condition II: Decrease Advertising Weight by 50 Percent (Chattanooga, Tennessee; Columbus, Ohio; Oklahoma City, Oklahoma).**

| | Sales | Advertising |
|---|---|---|
| Pre-test Year (1961) | | |
| (Normal Advertising Weight) | | |
| 1st Quarter | $119,842 | $20,724 |
| 2nd Quarter | 127,683 | 24,813 |
| 3rd Quarter | 177,244 | 36,122 |
| 4th Quarter | 115,231 | 30,887 |
| Test Year (1962) | | |
| (Advertising Weight Decreased 50 Percent) | | |
| 1st Quarter | 130,642 | $10,362 |
| 2nd Quarter | 144,789 | 12,407 |
| 3rd Quarter | 179,842 | 18,036 |
| 4th Quarter | 178,927 | 15,444 |
| Post-test Year (1963) | | |
| (Normal Advertising Weight) | | |
| 1st Quarter | $143,250 | $20,956 |
| 2nd Quarter | 136,872 | 25,091 |
| 3rd Quarter | 164,231 | 36,516 |
| 4th Quarter | 124,647 | 31,233 |

marketing people employed by the company in 1964. I am hardly a researcher but I have looked over the detail of the tests and they seem to me to have been soundly conceived and executed. At least there is nothing about these tests that immediately leaps out to my eye as improper. But the results are more than inconclusive; they just seem crazy. As you can see, sales declined in the markets in which advertising was increased, and sales increased in markets in which advertising was decreased! Whoever heard of such a thing?

Of course, those tests were conducted at a time when many of our bottlers were manipulating consumer prices, especially during slack seasons. And this price manipulation wasn't limited to our bottlers; everyone in the industry was doing it. Unfortunately, no one kept any market-by-market pricing histories during this period. Or if they were kept, they haven't survived. So it's impossible to develop any insight into price-advertising interactions that were taking place during the tests.

In addition, of course, is the probability that the bottlers, unbeknownst to our people, increased their own advertising expenditures or more probably their promotional expenditures, in the markets when we withdrew advertising—and that they decreased advertising and promotional expenditures in the markets when we increased our advertising expenditures.

Anyway, in retrospect, the whole testing program seems to me to have been a can of worms, not because of the *way* the tests were run, but because it is so difficult to control test-market pricing and bottler advertising and promotional activities. Maybe the tests *were* conclusive. It seems to me that

**EXHIBIT 2-5**
**Specimen Data: Test of Advertising Appropriation Level for STAR COLA, 1961, 1962, 1963**
**Test Condition III: No Change in Advertising Weight (Nashville, Tennessee; Cincinnati, Ohio; San Antonio, Texas)**

| | Sales | Advertising |
|---|---|---|
| Pre-test Year (1961) | | |
| (Normal Advertising Weight) | | |
| 1st Quarter | $136,820 | $24,213 |
| 2nd Quarter | 169,931 | 30,817 |
| 3rd Quarter | 204,297 | 47,643 |
| 4th Quarter | 190,952 | 40,665 |
| Test Year (1962) | | |
| (Normal Advertising Weight) | | |
| 1st Quarter | $149,327 | $24,697 |
| 2nd Quarter | 170,422 | 31,433 |
| 3rd Quarter | 209,312 | 48,596 |
| 4th Quarter | 186,939 | 41,478 |
| Post-test Year (1963) | | |
| (Normal Advertising Weight) | | |
| 1st Quarter | $159,293 | $25,085 |
| 2nd Quarter | 174,832 | 31,926 |
| 3rd Quarter | 219,612 | 49,358 |
| 4th Quarter | 178,263 | 42,129 |

I've heard that Anheuser-Busch ran tests something like this at about the same time and got about the same results. But, even if this is true, it doesn't help us in trying to analyze what happened in Star tests that were completed more than fifteen years ago.

At this point in time it seems best to me to forget about the market tests; that is, I think we might just as well act as if they had never occurred. Rather, I would defend our current level of advertising appropriation simply on the grounds that it is consonant with the spending level of our competitors and on the grounds that, under this appropriation policy, Star has been a prosperous, growing company for at least thirty years.

That leaves us with the question of advertising appropriation determination for a totally new brand. This is the case that we face with STAR-D. I am going to make the assumption that we all are agreed that it is imperative that we introduce our new diet-cola formulation as a STAR brand, rather than taking the much more limited, and, I would judge, ultimately self-defeating course of using the new formulation for the DIET-LIGHT brand.

The basic objective in introducing a new brand is to make a very strong impression with consumers. We want them to become aware of our new brand, and we want them to perceive that our level of advertising is sufficiently high to suggest how confident we are that they will like our new product. In essence, we want the advertising to imply that we are willing to warrant consumer satisfaction by spending a very significant advertising sum to inform consumers that this new product exists.

We do this by spending at a rate significantly in excess of the rate at which we would spend to sustain one of our existing brands. In this case, a higher level of advertising is required to inform consumers and to carry the burden of implied warranty besides. Our experience with the introduction of the ELF line and the FRESH brand is that an advertising appropriation 50 percent higher than the normal, or 20 percent, level—that is, an advertising appropriation of 30 percent of anticipated sales—is adequate. This is, incidentally, the same level of expenditure that our competitors seem to use when they introduce a new soft-drink product.

---

A few days later, Middlestadt received a second memorandum, this one from Star President, Robert Harmon:

---

# THE STAR COLA COMPANY

Office Memorandum

July 14, 1980

| | | | |
|---|---|---|---|
| To: | Malcolm A. Middlestadt | cc: | J. A. Watercomb |
| From: | Robert L. Harmon | | A. M. Falcone |
| Subject: | Star Advertising Appropriations Policy | | |

I have now read John Watercomb's excellent memorandum on this subject and I would like to make one or two comments upon it:

1. I believe that we must, as a company, have firmer bases for determining advertising appropriations policy than merely that it parallels what our competitors are doing and that it has not done any harm. This is the way that companies ran their affairs in the 1940s, but not today. We must know more, and do better.
2. I also believe that it must be possible to set specific goals for our advertising programs, if not in sales terms, then at least in terms of what advertising is supposed to do in accomplishing consumer knowledge of, awareness of, and attitudes toward our company brands. I gather that our competitors do this as a routine matter, and I believe that it is high time that we did it, too.
3. Finally, I am *very* intrigued by the whole question of the market tests of advertising that we ran back in the sixties. I think that John is absolutely right when he says that no good purpose would now be served by trying to make a contemporary analysis of events that are fifteen years in the past. But shouldn't we make some effort to start a new program of market testing to develop our own knowledge of advertising effects—so that in establishing our own policies we are not simply dependent on what our competitors *seem* to be doing?

---

Malcolm A. Middlestadt studied these two memoranda at considerable length. On the one hand, his instinct was to support his marketing director because he was the corporate official directly responsible for the determination of marketing policies and especially for the determination of company policy in respect to advertising appropriations. On the other hand, the company president seemed to be challenging the marketing director's judgment on professional grounds, rather than on the more general ground of whether or not Star Cola Company could afford to do what Watercomb was recommending. It was one thing for a company president to react to a marketing director's recommendations by saying that they were acceptable but that the company could not afford them. It was a totally different matter for a company president to say that a marketing director's recommendations were unsound and ignore the broader question of whether they were affordable or not.

Middlestadt did not really feel himself prepared to deal with this situation. A financial expert by training, he could easily respond to the proposal that it was fiscally unsound to borrow $9 million to support the introduction of a new brand through advertising, if that was in fact what his senior personnel were recommending. But arguments about what the appropriate level of advertising for his company's brands should be were simply beyond Middlestadt.

It seemed to Middlestadt that both his president, Robert Harmon, and his marketing director, John Watercomb, were ducking the basic issue. Watercomb seemed to be saying that the company would not survive unless it introduced a new diet-cola brand, STAR-D. Watercomb also appeared to be saying that it was necessary to introduce that brand with an advertising expenditure consistent with historic practice in the industry and that any expenditure at a lower rate would be doomed to fail.

Harmon, on the other hand, was ignoring the issue of the necessity of introducing a new brand in order to assure that the company's future position in the soft-drink market would be maintained. Instead, his position was that Watercomb was using an incorrect basis to determine the level of company advertising appropriations, and that there had to be a better, more modern way in which to make this determination. Middlestadt noted that Harmon did not, or perhaps could not, say just what that better way to determine advertising appropriations for Star Company brands might be.

Finally, after giving the whole matter considerable thought, and with considerable frustration over his own felt inadequacy to make a final decision in a situation of considerable urgancy and ambiguity, Middlestadt reached a decision. He would not depend upon himself to decide what the Star Company should do, nor would he depend upon himself to adjudicate between the divergent viewpoints of his two associates. Instead, he decided to seek outside counsel from a management-consulting firm to help him resolve the issues that confronted the Star Cola Company.

Middlestadt turned the problem over to the management-consulting firm of Iver L. Snead and Associates. This firm had been formed in Louisville in 1946 by Iver Snead, Sr. He had retired from the business in 1976, turning it over to his son, Iver L. Snead, Jr., who was then thirty-eight years old. Middlestadt had played golf with the senior Snead for years and through this activity had casually come to know a good deal about Snead and the Snead firm. He knew that it was the leading management-consulting firm in Louisville; that it had done work for most of the leading companies in Kentucky, as well as in surrounding states; and that most of its clients were well-enough satisfied with its work to return, often time and again, to the Snead firm with new assignments. It was hard to find anyone in corporate managerial circles in Louisville or its environs who had a bad word to say about Iver Snead, his son, or their firm.

Middlestadt informed his colleagues of his decision to bring in the Snead firm and their collective reaction was one of almost enthusiastic relief. Harmon and Falcone welcomed the introduction of a third, outside, party into the dispute which had developed within the company about advertising appropriation policy. While neither Harmon nor Falcone would admit it, either to each other or to anyone else, they both quietly assumed that Snead Associates would support their view that the Star advertising appropriation policy was in need of drastic revision, and that this revision would be accomplished by the Snead people with consequent lowering of Star advertising expenditures.

John Watercomb also welcomed the appointment of the Snead firm, but for drastically different reasons. In the first place, Watercomb was relieved. He had found himself, in recent weeks, supporting a company advertising appropriation policy that he sensed was inherently unsound. He suspected that there must be a better way to determine how much to spend on advertising than the way in which Star had been doing it, yet he had no idea what that better way might be. In addition, he knew that if there were to be a better way to settle upon the size of advertising appropriations, he should have introduced it to the company–if not when he was hired in 1975, then shortly thereafter. The fact that he had not seen fit to recommend a change in the appropriation policy made him, de facto, an endorser of it. And if this were not enough, his support and explanation of it in recent weeks had unequivocally linked his career with it. The fact that he knew or sensed that the appropriation policy was outmoded and yet had done nothing to change it, put Watercomb on the spot, and he knew it. Thus, he hoped that the general upheaval that the Snead firm would inevitably cause in the Star Company would lead to a new advertising appropriation policy without causing him either embarrassment or difficulty in his work.

Middlestadt, Harmon, and Watercomb met with Iver L. Snead, Jr., and two of his associates in late July of 1980. Meetings between the Snead people and various members of the Star management group continued, off and on, throughout the late summer and early fall of 1980. Finally, on October 16, 1980, the Snead Firm delivered a detailed report, presenting their conclusions about the way in which they believed that the Star Company should appropriate its advertising dollars, and the recommended action that Snead Associates believed that the Star Company should take to implement a new advertising appropriation policy. This lengthy report was accompanied by a letter from Iver L. Snead, Jr., to Malcolm A Middlestadt, summarizing the major findings and recommendations contained in the formal Snead report. The letter is reproduced on this and the following pages.

---

# IVER L. SNEAD ASSOCIATES

Client Communication

October 16, 1980

To: Malcolm A. Middlestadt
From: Iver L. Snead, Jr.

Dear Mal:

The purpose of this letter is to provide you with a rather informal summary of the findings from our study of Star Company advertising appropriation policy as well as our recommendations.

I. Our first major finding is that the advertising appropriation policy followed by your company, based as it is on competitive practices, is old-fashioned. It is old-fashioned in the sense that Star Company has been following this procedure for at least thirty years; and it is old-fashioned in the sense that many other methods for determining what an advertising appropriation should be have been developed by other companies in recent years.

But the real question is not whether your method is old-fashioned but whether or not it is outmoded. Our experience indicates that many other consumer-goods companies follow methods of advertising appropriation that are not fundamentally different from the method followed by your company. There is a good deal of rhetoric about this in the business press; and if one does not read and listen carefully, one can easily gain the impression that very complicated approaches to the problem are in widespread use in American industry.

This is not necessarily the case. Many firms do exactly what you do. Other companies set advertising appropriations that differ somewhat from those of their competitors, but rarely does this reflect any particularly unique knowledge on the part of these firms in respect to how to use advertising. When one probes into these situations, one usually discovers that they reflect some pattern of events that traces far back into the history of the firm, yielding some de facto competitive strength or weaknesses.

An example of a historically determined disparity between advertising expenditures and the industry average may be traced, for example, to a particular strength in product engineering or, for another example, to particular economics in production or direct-selling expense. Under such circumstances, the firms in question may have had more money available for either profit or advertising and may have made the historical decision to spend it on advertising at a higher rate than the industry norm in order to build a more solid base of consumer acceptance for the years ahead. Other firms, in the same circumstances, may let, for example, their superior products fend for themselves in the market place. In this case, the firms substitute design superiority for advertising and depend upon the design superiority to attract customers that, in its absence, would have come to the company through consumer response to relatively heavier advertising pressure. When a firm is at a competitive product design or quality disadvantage, it may have to spend more on advertising to keep pace with the other firms in the industry that have developed an inherent basis of competitive superiority.

II. Our second major finding is that some firms have consciously set out to abandon sole dependence upon the competitive environment in the determination of their level of advertising expenditure. We have found three distinctly different positions among these firms.

A. Some firms set goals in so-called communications terms. They seem to believe that it is impossible to establish any kind of a direct relationship between advertising and sales. That is, they believe that advertising expenditures create or contribute to an environment within which sales are made, but that it is impossible to determine what level of advertising expenditures will cause a particular level of sales. Rather, these firms say, if advertising is to create the ideal sales-causing environment, it will establish a particular level of brand- or product-awareness among the consuming public; it will create certain levels of brand or product knowledge among that public; and it will create favorable consumer attitudes toward the advertised brands or products. Even if these companies do not know how much to spend on advertising to create a particular sales result, the argument goes, they do know that levels of brand- and product-awareness and knowledge and favorable attitudes will vary depending on how much is spent for advertising. Sales cannot occur in the absence of consumer awareness, knowledge, and favorable attitudes. Therefore, these firms plan their advertising appropriations to achieve as much consumer brand- and product-awareness, knowledge, and favorable attitude as they can because they believe that the higher the level of brand- and product-awareness, knowledge, and favorable attitude that are achieved, the higher sales will be.

The firms that espouse this point of view then measure consumer brand- or product-awareness, knowledge, and attitudes and relate changes in these measurements with changes in advertising inputs. That is, these firms try to relate changes in advertising copy or advertising media plans or advertising appropriations to changes in consumer brand-awareness, knowledge, and/or attitudes. The more sophisticated firms in this category do a good deal of market testing in which advertising inputs are systematically varied; and the effects of these variations on consumer brand awareness, knowledge, and attitude are continuously measured.

We are frankly skeptical of this approach to advertising appropriation determination. The specific reasons for this skepticism are detailed in the attached report. In brief, they are:

1. The only reason that we can think of for any company to advertise is to make sales. If the effect of advertising upon sales can not be demonstrated, then we say that the company should not advertise.
2. We believe that consumer brand-awareness and knowledge as well as favorable brand-attitudes are usually necessary before sales are made. But we do not believe that the achievement of such communication goals are sufficient to achieve sales. That is, we believe that it is perfectly possible for a consumer to be aware of a brand, know a good deal about its distinguishing attributes, and hold favorable attitudes toward the brand and its attributes, and yet consistently buy some other product-brand that he or she happens to prefer. In fact, in many, if not most, product categories, we believe that there are no "bad" brands as such, and that most brands are well known and favorably regarded by most consumers; and yet the market is more or less divided among these acceptable brands. Soft drinks are probably an excellent example of just such a competitive situation.
3. Probably the most dangerous aspect about dependence upon communication measurements for the determination of advertising appropriations is that this method tends to become institutionalized within the firm. Employees over a period of time, come, to depend upon communications goals and measurements exclusively and lose, in the process, all sight of the philosophy that underlies this dependence. Because there is very good reason to believe that the accomplishment of communications is a necessary but not a sufficient condition to

cause sales, companies that follow this procedure face the very real danger of making very bad advertising appropriation decisions without even realizing it. At least the firms that closely follow competitive practices in setting advertising appropriations rarely get very far out of line with industry practice and will tend to be successful if they have competitive products and advertising copy.

Thus, we conclude that the Star Company advertising appropriation policy should not be tied to the relative achievement of company communications goals, for the reasons given above. We see no harm, incidentally, in initiating a program of communications-effect measurements for the Star brand if you wish to do so. We have attached (Exhibit 2-6) a dummy data sheet that indicates the kinds of data such a continuing measurement program would produce. These data are purely hypothetical, but at least they should give you some "feel" for the kinds of numbers that would be available if such a program were to be undertaken.

Some of our clients have had such a research program in place for years and they seem to find it of considerable help in assessing the effects of advertising copy in producing increases in consumer awareness, knowledge, and favorable attitudes about their brands, even if, as we believe, the data generated are of little help in deciding how much money to appropriate for advertising.

B. Another group of firms have gotten into the habit of periodically market testing the level of advertising expenditures they make for their individual brands. Usually, such tests are made when there seems to be some strong marketing reason to change the level of advertising pressure behind a particular brand, either upward or downward.

The objective of these tests is always the same: to measure changes in sales and profits that are associated with changes in the level of advertising appropriation.

1. When the test is of a higher level of advertising spending, the issue is whether that increased pressure will generate a higher long-term level of company sales that will generage higher levels of brand profits than would have been achieved in the absence of the greater advertising expenditures. Normally, the advertising is increased for a period of time—a year or two—and the increase is financed out of brand profits during this period. If the new, higher level of sales is achieved, it at least will recapture the profits that have been allocated to increased advertising. This recapture of invested profits due to a higher level of sales is called a "payout." Most test plans of these types anticipate that a payout will be achieved in a year or two, although sometimes payout periods are longer. If the new higher level of sales is achieved, it will generate a higher level of advertising expenditure than was spent for the brand prior to the test; and this higher level will help to sustain the higher level of sales in the post-test period. Once payout has been achieved, the brand will throw off more profits, too, as a result of the higher level of sales. So the net effect of the successful test is to raise the brand's sales and profits to a higher level without *extra* cost to the company. If, of course, the test does

**EXHIBIT 2-6**
**Specimen Data: Illustrative Communication Measure Results for STAR COLA as Prepared by Snead Associates**

| | 1/1/80 | 7/1/80 | 1/1/81 |
|---|---|---|---|
| Aware of Star Cola | 56% | 60% | 60% |
| Unaided* | 26 | 28 | 24 |
| Aided with Brand Name** | 30 | 32 | 36 |
| What Other Product Is STAR COLA Most Like?† | | | |
| Correct | 62% | 63% | 62% |
| Incorrect | 38 | 37 | 38 |
| How Would You Rate STAR COLA?‡ | | | |
| For Taste | | | |
| Excellent | 42% | 40% | 36% |
| Very Good | 27 | 24 | 23 |
| OK | 20 | 26 | 22 |
| Not as Good | 9 | 4 | 8 |
| Poor | 2 | 6 | 11 |
| For Refreshment | | | |
| Excellent | 40% | 41% | 37% |
| Very Good | 26 | 23 | 19 |
| OK | 22 | 24 | 23 |
| Not as Good | 10 | 5 | 9 |
| Poor | 2 | 7 | 12 |
| As a Thirst-Quencher | | | |
| Excellent | 62% | 64% | 62% |
| Very Good | 27 | 23 | 25 |
| OK | 3 | 2 | 4 |
| Not as Good | 4 | 6 | 3 |
| Poor | 4 | 5 | 6 |
| Availability in Vending Machines | | | |
| Excellent | 28% | 30% | 36% |
| Very Good | 22 | 24 | 27 |
| OK | 18 | 21 | 26 |
| Not as Good | 10 | 12 | 6 |
| Poor | 22 | 13 | 5 |
| Availability in Restaurants and Cafes | | | |
| Excellent | 42% | 44% | 42% |
| Very Good | 38 | 39 | 41 |
| OK | 12 | 14 | 10 |
| Not as Good | 7 | 1 | 7 |
| Poor | 1 | 2 | 1 |
| For Friendliness | | | |
| Excellent | 37% | 36% | 29% |
| Very Good | 22 | 20 | 17 |
| OK | 16 | 18 | 22 |
| Not as Good | 16 | 18 | 24 |
| Poor | 9 | 8 | 8 |

**EXHIBIT 2-6 (Continued)**

| | 1/1/80 | 7/1/80 | 1/1/81 |
|---|---|---|---|
| For Good Times | | | |
| Excellent | 51% | 54% | 58% |
| Very Good | 22 | 24 | 30 |
| OK | 10 | 12 | 6 |
| Not as Good | 15 | 9 | 5 |
| Poor | 2 | 1 | 1 |
| As an All-Round Cola Drink | | | |
| Excellent | 28% | 27% | 29% |
| Very Good | 32 | 34 | 36 |
| OK | 22 | 21 | 13 |
| Not as Good | 12 | 14 | 12 |
| Poor | 6 | 14 | 10 |
| What Advertising Slogan Does STAR COLA Now Use? | | | |
| Correct | 25% | 32% | 47% |
| Incorrect | 12 | 8 | 4 |
| Cannot Recall Slogan | 63 | 60 | 49 |

* The question asked: What brands of soft drinks can you think of?
** The question asked: Have you ever heard of STAR COLA?
† This question is asked to determine specific consumer knowledge of what kind of product STAR COLA is. (Correct answers include: COKE, PEPSI, ROYAL CROWN, and other true Cola products.)
‡ The responses to the scale questions are based on respondents who are aware of STAR COLA *and* know specifically what kind of a product it is.

not "pay out," it is considered a failure; and a loss is incurred equal to the profits that were invested in advertising that were not recouped through extra sales–that is, the loss is equivalent to the shortfall in payout. Exhibit 2-7 gives a hypothetical example of how a brand like Star might test an extra advertising expenditure of $5,500,000 and presents two hypothetical outcomes of such a test.

If the market test pays out and is thus judged a success, it will be expanded nationally and will, presumably, generate the same results that have already been experienced in the smaller test area. If the original market test is bungled, there is, of course, always the possibility that the national expansion will not reflect the test results. In addition, if market or competitive conditions change after the market test is completed, there is also the probability that national results will not follow the same patterns as those obtained in the market test. The possibility that national experience may not follow test market results exactly, or at all, suggest that there is a risk in expanding a market test to the national level; and this is certainly very true. The risks inherent in the implementation of such market-test results on a national level may be minimized in

**EXHIBIT 2-7**

**Illustrative Results from a Market Test of an Increased Advertising Appropriation for STAR COLA as Prepared by Snead Associates**

**Current (1980) STAR COLA National Advertising Appropriation: . . . . . . . $10,684,000**

**Proposed (1981) National Advertising Budget:* . . . . . . . . . . . . . . . . . . . $16,026,000**

**Test-Market Sales and Advertising Appropriations:**

| | Atlanta | Cleveland | San Diego |
|---|---|---|---|
| 1979 Advertising Appropriation | $120,200 | $ 179,400 | $ 82,000 |
| 1980 Advertising Appropriation | 128,200 | 191,200 | 87,600 |
| 1981 Advertising Appropriation (Test of Extra Weight) | 192,312 | 286,900 | 131,400 |
| | Hypothetical Outcome A | | |
| 1979 Sales | $543,800 | $ 947,600 | $429,600 |
| 1980 Sales | 558,100 | 996,400 | 447,400 |
| 1981 Sales | 724,800 | 1,527,300 | 728,624 |
| 1979 Advertising/Sales Ratio | .22 | .19 | .19 |
| 1980 Advertising/Sales Ratio | .23 | .19 | .20 |
| 1981 Advertising/Sales Ratio | .27 | .19 | .18 |
| | Hypothetical Outcome B | | |
| 1979 Sales | $543,800 | $ 947,600 | $429,600 |
| 1980 Sales | 588,100 | 996,400 | 447,400 |
| 1981 Sales | 602,243 | 897,600 | 477,800 |
| 1979 Advertising/Sales Ratio | .22 | .19 | .19 |
| 1980 Advertising/Sales Ratio | .23 | .19 | .20 |
| 1981 Advertising/Sales Ratio | .32 | .32 | .28 |

* Advertising budget increase is based on 1980 sales and assumes zero natural or unstimulated sales growth in 1981. The tax consequences of an increase in advertising expense on after-tax profits are ignored.

two ways:

a. First, it is very important that such market tests be very carefully and meticulously planned and administered. It is important that such tests be implemented in at least three separate markets and, if great relevance is to be placed on the test results, it is important that a payout be achieved in each of the individual test markets.

b. Second, it is important that the marketer be alert to changes in market conditions—like new competitive brands or marketing activities—that may be expected to invalidate the test results. If it is reasonable to assume that the test results have been invalidated, then it would be foolhardy to expand the test program to the national level.

2. When a level of advertising that is below current levels is tested, the assumption is that there will be no consequent effect upon sales and that, therefore, brand profits will increase. We know of several situations in which such tests have seemed to indicate that sales will remain steady when advertising is reduced,

and we know of one instance in which sales actually appeared to increase when advertising was decreased. Market tests of lower advertising appropriations levels should certainly be made, and we would consider them to be appropriate for consideration by Star. However, we believe that these tests may lead to inappropriate conclusions unless great care is taken. Specifically:

a. It is very important that all marketing variables, other than the level of advertising spending, be closely controlled while such tests are underway. If for example, prices are not controlled during a test of decreases in advertising weight, an apparent sales increase may be due to lower prices, rather than to less advertising.
b. It is very important to monitor sales results in the test markets long after the lowered advertising appropriation has been implemented. Sales decay may set in some time after advertising pressure is decreased. If this is the case, the continuous monitoring of the test markets will show the delayed effects and may provide an early warning of delayed national sales declines.
c. Finally, after the test of lower advertising pressure is expanded nationally, it is very important to monitor changes in the competitive environment. A decrease in advertising spending may lead to higher brand profits under one set of competitive circumstances but not under others. For example, if a competitor subsequently increases his own advertising appropriation very significantly, the effect on the brand that has cut its advertising pressure may be especially severe, particularly if that brand does not immediately increase its advertising expenditures to meet the new competitive threat.

3. The introduction of a new product frequently provides an especially appropriate opportunity for market testing of alternative advertising appropriations, and it is common practice for those firms that continually test appropriation policy to introduce new products into test markets under two or more advertising appropriation levels.

C. Finally, a few firms have consciously set out to determine the relationships that exist for their brands between advertising and sales. They attempt to determine the basic nature of these relationships over a fairly broad range of advertising expenditures and sales responses. The object of such work is to determine what the ideal advertising appropriation for a brand will be at any given time. This kind of work differs from the kind of testing program previously described in that these previously described programs usually try to determine what will happen in a *specific situation* if the level of advertising is changed by a specific amount. There is, therefore, no attempt in this former kind of testing to develop any *general* understanding of the fundamental relationships between sales and advertising.

Apparently, the STAR Cola testing program that was initiated in the 1960s set out to determine the basic relation between STAR COLA sales and advertising expenditures in behalf of the brand. We have nothing to add to Mr. Watercomb's observations about these tests. The observed sales results from these tests certainly are perplexing: It seems quite possible to us that they reflect uncontrolled market factors rather than a sales response to changes in advertising pressures.

One general point should be made about such testing programs. Because they seek fundamental knowledge about advertising-sales relationships rather than the effect of a particular change in advertising in a specific situation, they tend to involve a wide range of individual tests requiring significant amounts of time and money to successfully conclude and interpret.

III. There are a few general observations to be made about the situation that now confronts the Star Company:

A. First of all, it seems to us that in your deliberations about whether or not to introduce STAR-D you have missed a fundamental point. In our conversations and in the various company communications that we have received, it has been assumed that STAR-D is an either/or kind of proposition. *Either* the company introduces STAR-D nationally with an advertising appropriation of $9 million *or* the company does not. It appears to us that it is well within the capabilities of your company to manufacture STAR-D in relatively small quantities, for market-test programs. No new equipment would be required; stock containers can be used; the formula has been developed and involves the use of readily available materials and ingredients. We assume that your bottler relations are such that there will be no trouble in finding as many bottlers as a test program requires to participate in a marketplace determination of the viability of STAR-D. If the bottlers are apprehensive that they may lose money by participating in such a test, you can always, as a last resort, offer to indemnify them against such loss.

   So, as we perceive the Star Company decision, it is whether or not you wish to *test* the viability of STAR-D in the marketplace through a series of carefully planned and executed market tests, including tests of alternative levels of advertising pressure. Your decision does not, and most decidedly should should not, depend upon whether or not to take STAR-D national immediately and spend $9 million in advertising this national introduction.

B. The introduction of STAR-D will *not* involve an outright, nonrecoverable, expenditure of $9 million. STAR-D will, of course, achieve consumer sales. For every sale that is made, some contribution to advertising expense will be made. If, for example, STAR-D were to achieve $30 million in sales during its first year, there would be no nonrecovered advertising expense, since the level of sales would throw off, at a 30 percent advertising-to-sales ratio, exactly $9 million. The 30 percent advertising-to-sales ratio does not, of course, yield much in profits, but would it not be worthwhile for your company to forego profits during the introductory year if, in the process, you were to build a $30,000,000 business for STAR-D? We would certainly think so. You may argue that it is unlikely that STAR-D will build first-year sales of anything like $30 million. Our point is that, whatever the sales of STAR-D, they will make some contribution to the advertising investment: The $9 million is not a net cost of building the franchise. For example, suppose that STAR-D sales are $20 million in the first year. Sales at this level will pay out-of-pocket and overhead costs of manufacturing this volume of STAR-D and they will throw off 30 percent, or $6 million, in advertising. The remaining $3 million would, presumably, be recaptured from second-year profits on the $20 million sales base built in the introductory year.

Sooner or later, barring a total market failure for STAR-D, the $9 million advertising investment will be recouped and a base for profitable future operations developed. The risk that STAR-D may in fact become a total market failure, which is, in our judgment, slight in any event, can be assessed with considerable accuracy in the market test program.

C. One other aspect of market tests of STAR-D and of the STAR-D advertising appropriation should be mentioned. Market testing focuses executive attention on the economics of brand performance. The company and its long-term profitability is protected in the process of *planning* for market tests, because Star Company's management can always insist that no market-test plan that is fiscally irresponsible can be implemented for a Star Company brand, even in the test market. Thus, market expenditures tend to be rational, almost as a by-product of the market-testing program itself.

Taking all of the preceeding into consideration, we make the following recommendations to the Star Company:

1. STAR-D should be considered as a new brand for the Star Company: the diet companion to STAR COLA.
2. The evaluation of the viability of STAR-D as a new Star Company brand should be accomplished through the type of market-testing program described above.
3. Alternative advertising appropriations should be incorporated into the market-test evaluations of STAR-D's viability in the market.

---

Malcolm A. Middlestadt received the complete Snead Associates report and the covering memorandum reproduced above on October 17, 1980. He immediately distributed copies to Messrs. Harmon, Falcone, and Watercomb and asked that they evaluate the report and its recommendations, in writing, no later than October 24, 1980. Here are the memoranda received by Middlestadt in response to this request:

---

# THE STAR COLA COMPANY

Office Memorandum

October 23, 1980

To: Malcolm A. Middlestadt
From: John A. Watercomb
Subject: Snead Associates Report

I have now read the Snead Associates report dated October 16, 1980. I am in complete agreement with its contents and recommendations.

---

# THE STAR COLA COMPANY

Office Memorandum

October 24, 1980

To: Malcolm A. Middlestadt
From: Albert M. Falcone
Subject: Snead Recommendations

I've read the Snead report, and I have plenty of trouble following their reasoning and recommendations.

In what follows, I'm going to be candid, which is what I assume you're looking for.

I think the Snead report is a lot of hot air. They make the numbers move with mirrors. We spend $9 million but it doesn't cost us anything, they say. I say $9 million is $9 million and no amount of blue-sky theorizing about future sales that we haven't made, and may not—probably won't—make, can make that go away.

I'm not going to criticize the Snead people for their ignorance of tax accounting because that's my problem. I'll just say that you can't wish away the tax-effects of advertising expense in a footnote. In fairness though, I'll have to admit that the tax treatment of advertising expenditures as an expense will tend to produce profits where Snead implies only a break-even if what they call "payout" is achieved—which I don't believe it will be.

But they haven't thought about the most important two aspects of their scheme:

1. What effect will the introduction of STAR-D have on the sales of STAR COLA?
2. What effect will the introduction of STAR-D have on the sales of DIET-LIGHT COLA?

I think it is naive to assume that our bottlers' sales force can force $30 million in new sales out of the distributors' network we now have without losing an immense amount of sales from our current products (which the new brand will *have* to displace on retailers shelves) and in the consumption of consumers. Our retailers have just so much sales space to give us, and our consumers can drink just so much cola.

# THE STAR COLA COMPANY

Office Memorandum

October 25, 1980

To: Malcolm A. Middlestadt
From: Robert L. Harmon
Subject: What to do about the Snead Report

I think Al Falcone has put his finger on a potentially serious shortcoming of the Snead Associates report. As you know, I don't think we can afford to spend $9 million on the introduction of STAR-D. I have believed this ever since the issue came up and nothing in the Snead Associates report, including their visionary plan to pull STAR-D up by its own bootstraps, has changed my mind.

If we must introduce STAR-D, and I am beginning to accept the proposition that we must, I have the following suggestion to make: Instead of establishing a separate advertising appropriation for STAR-D, why don't we use the existing STAR COLA advertising program to introduce STAR-D? What I have in mind is to shorten every STAR COLA television commercial from thirty seconds to about twenty-five, show a picture of the STAR-D can, and have an announcer say: "STAR COLA is now available as a diet cola, too—try new STAR-D today!"

This way we get the advertising exposure that we achieve from STAR COLA's ten-million-plus advertising budget, it doesn't cost us a dime extra—let alone $9 million—*and* I'll bet my reputation that it won't hurt STAR COLA all that much either.

## *QUESTIONS FOR CASE 2*

1. Should Malcolm A Middlestadt accept all three of the Snead Associates recommendations? Why or why not? In answering this question be sure to consider the viewpoints expressed in the memoranda written by John Watercomb (October 23); Albert Falcone, (October 24); and Robert Harmon (October 25). Have Snead Associates recommended a new general advertising appropriation policy for Star Company? What is it?

2. Evaluate in detail Robert Harmon's proposal that the announcement of STAR-D's availability should be tagged onto regular commercials for STAR COLA. Is this the ideal way to build a STAR-D business? What implications does this recommendation have for the long-term growth of the Star Cola Company?

3. Albert Falcone makes a distinction (page 30) between investment in plant and equipment and investment in advertising. Is this distinction valid? Analyze Falcone's remarks on this topic and tell whether or not you agree with him, and why.

4. In what ways did the Star Company market tests that were conducted in 1961, 1962, and 1963 differ from those conducted by Anheuser-Busch during the same period of

time? Do you agree with Watercomb's assessment of the test results? Is it possible that the Anheuser-Busch test results were conclusive while those of Star Company are inconclusive? Why might this be so? Could both sets of test results be incorrect? Why might this be so? If the results of both sets of tests are correct, what is the implication of the results for STAR COLA?

5. Watercomb states (page 33) that a goal of the STAR-D advertising program would be to imply to consumers "that we are willing to warrant consumer satisfaction by spending a very significant advertising sum to inform consumers that this new product exists." Is this a legitimate advertising goal? What kind of information about the STAR-D product would be communicated by advertising designed to fulfill this goal?

6. Is there any reason (or reasons) why one firm in an industry is likely to spend distinctly more or less on advertising one of its brands than competing firms spend in advertising for directly competitive brands? Why or why not?

7. Analyze the reasons why Snead Associates reject communications goals as a basis for establishing advertising appropriation policy. Do you agree with the Snead Associates position, or not? Why? Be sure to consider the data in Exhibit 2-6 in answering this question.

8. Interpret the data presented in Exhibit 2-7. Would it be desirable to monitor sales results in these hypothetical test markets through 1982? Why or why not?

9. On page 45, the following statement is made: "Sooner or later, barring a total market failure for STAR-D, the $9 million advertising investment will be recouped and a base for profitable future operations developed." What does this statement mean? What does it imply about the success of STAR-D?

10. What alternative advertising appropriations should be incorporated into the market-test evaluations of STAR-D's viability in the market? What kinds of considerations are involved in making decisions about what alternative levels of advertising spending to test?

# Case 3

# Setting Advertising Goals

## *ATLAS HOME-APPLIANCE COMPANY APPRAISES ITS ADVERTISING ACTIVITIES*

The Atlas Home-Appliance Company manufactures and sells a full line of electric kitchen appliances. This standard "white goods" line includes refrigerators, ranges, dishwashers, clothes washers, clothes dryers, trash compactors, and microwave ovens. The Company was founded in 1923 and was acquired in 1958 by Universal Electronics, Ltd., as that latter firm took the first steps toward becoming one of the largest industrial conglomerates in the United States. Atlas continued, after its acquisition by UEL, to operate with almost total autonomy. Financial controls were imposed upon Atlas by UEL, and Atlas five- and ten-year plans and new-product development protocols were developed according to UEL guidelines. But beyond this, UEL was content to let Atlas and the Atlas management run its own business, as long as it remained profitable and as long as its sales base and the profits that it generated continued to increase.

Atlas did continue to increase its sales and profits throughout the decade of the sixties and into the early years of the seventies. Beginning in 1972, however, Atlas sales and profits ceased to grow; and by 1975 a distinct decline had begun. The Atlas sales and profit data for 1960 through 1976 are shown in Exhibit 3-1.

In its history as a conglomerate, UEL had encountered falling sales and profits in more than a few of its subsidiaries and had, as a result, developed a fairly detailed response to such situations. The basic UEL approach was to bring UEL employee-specialists into the sluggish company, with the mandate to evaluate its operations fully. UEL had created a team of employee-troubleshooters with experience in finance, production,

**EXHIBIT 3-1**
**Specimen Data: Sales and Profits in Atlas Home-Appliance Co., Division of Universal Electronics, Ltd., 1960–1976 (000's omitted)**

| Year | Sales | Profits | Profits in Percent of Sales |
|---|---|---|---|
| 1960 | $ 623,000 | $ 63,000 | 10.1% |
| 1961 | 729,000 | 69,000 | 9.5 |
| 1962 | 964,000 | 87,000 | 9.0 |
| 1963 | 1,021,000 | 94,000 | 9.2 |
| 1964 | 1,329,000 | 121,000 | 9.1 |
| 1965 | 1,344,000 | 135,000 | 10.0 |
| 1966 | 1,438,000 | 149,000 | 10.4 |
| 1967 | 1,527,000 | 161,000 | 10.5 |
| 1968 | 1,572,000 | 168,000 | 10.7 |
| 1969 | 1,594,000 | 174,000 | 10.9 |
| 1970 | 1,632,000 | 179,000 | 11.0 |
| 1971 | 1,658,000 | 181,000 | 10.9 |
| 1972 | 1,661,000 | 168,000 | 10.1 |
| 1973 | 1,649,000 | 142,000 | 8.6 |
| 1974 | 1,623,000 | 147,000 | 9.1 |
| 1975 | 1,572,000 | 126,000 | 8.0 |
| 1976 | 1,432,000 | 97,000 | 6.8 |

*Source:* Atlas Home-Appliance Financial Records

materials procurement, physical distribution, and marketing; and it was this team that was first directed to review the operations of Atlas Home-Appliance in early 1977. If this team should discern problems that it could not handle with its own relatively limited personnel resources, or if a particular kind of expertise were required, an outside management-consulting firm would then be employed to work in tandem with the UEL troubleshooters in developing solutions for the ailing subsidiary.

This process had been brilliantly successful in resuscitating several UEL subsidiaries during the 1960s and early seventies, and UEL management believed that its perfection was a crucial element in the total success of their eighty-billion-dollar (1977) company. Even though the managers of UEL liked the results that their troubleshooters produced for the corporation, the process was hardly popular with the subsidiaries that underwent what had become known throughout the corporation as the "treatment." The net effect of the "treatment" was disrupting; and established, indigenous managers simply do not like to have their work disrupted. But it was hard to object to the success that the program had achieved in every instance in which it had been employed. And, many Atlas employees decided, it was undoubtedly better to undergo disruption at the hands of fellow UEL employees than to turn one's fate over to "outside" management consultants.

The UEL team investigated every aspect of the Atlas Appliance Company business during the early months of 1977. As the results of their observations and analyses came together, it became clear that the heart of the Atlas problem lay in the marketing area. Atlas production technology and physical plant were totally up to date and appeared to be more modern than most of the leading competitors. Atlas accounting procedures were impeccable and its financial policies were totally acceptable since they had been substantially under the control of UEL since the early 1960s. Although there appeared to be some shortcomings in Atlas materials procurement, they were not major, were easily correctable, and could not have conceivably been responsible for the sales and profit history that concerned UEL. Finally, Atlas was very experienced in the methods of physical distribution and the company had, over the years, pioneered many warehousing and transportation innovations that had since become standard throughout the industry. It was a company boast that any Atlas dealer could have an Atlas product within thirty-six hours after the order was received by the Atlas Distribution Expediting Division.

But all was not well in the marketing area. Reproduced below is a memorandum written by Rodney A. Claridge, the chief UEL marketing troubleshooter, to Stanley L. Simpkin, president and chief executive officer of the Atlas Home-Appliance Company. This memorandum details the marketing shortcomings of Atlas.

---

# UEL Internal Consulting Group "Can Do"

June 1, 1977

To: Stanley L. Simpkin, President
Atlas Home-Appliance Company
From: Rodney A. Claridge, Senior Marketing Consultant Officer
Subject: Marketing Activities at Atlas

A major conclusion of our investigation is that Atlas marketing strategy and tactics are very significantly behind those of the rest of your industry. Your marketing programs are outmoded and unimaginative. They must be thoroughly overhauled. Your total marketing budget is woefully inadequate by contemporary standards. You should be spending at least 50 percent more than you are on marketing, and perhaps twice as much. You need new people, more aggressive programs, and a new attitude about marketing.

The following paragraphs will briefly outline the reforms that are required, as we see them. I simply state the requirements without documenting them in this memorandum. Rest assured that this documentation exists, and in detail, for every one of these recommendations.

1. Atlas retail distribution must be substantially upgraded. Atlas has fallen behind in seeking new outlets for the retail distribution of its products. The problem of retail distribution has two aspects: First, the company has not kept track of basic population shifts and has made no significant effort to align its retail-distribution capabilities with the ebb and flow of household population. As a result, the company is woefully underrepresented in shopping centers and malls. In addition, the company has remained too dependent upon the specialist appliance retailer. Over 75 percent of Atlas franchised dealers are independent appliance retailers. There has been little change in this percentage in the past twenty years. As a result, Atlas is not properly represented among mass merchandisers, nor in department stores, and its products

are virtually nonexistent in the order centers of the so-called catalog retailers.

We conclude, therefore, that a massive effort must be made, and as promptly as possible, to upgrade and revitalize the retail selling facilities of the company. We understand, incidentally, that such an effort cannot be made without upsetting and disrupting existing trade relations. However, the company has no alternative but to add a significant number of new retail outlets. If long-term Atlas dealers are antagonized in the process, so be it. These dealers will shortly discover that they have no viable alternative to staying with Atlas.

2. There are some basic shortcomings in the Atlas product line. These tend to be marketing shortcomings rather than product-design failures as such. Atlas products are, generally, as absolutely reliable as they are absolutely uninspired. They have been designed to perform their basic functions, to perform them as well as or better than competitive products, and to perform them with great dependability over an extended period of time. But there are woefully few differentiating or salable features built into Atlas products. They are stodgy, rather than spectacular; dull, rather than promotable. Too much attention has been given over the years to the engineering soundness of the Atlas line, and too little to the features and characteristics that have consumer appeal.

   We conclude, therefore, that Atlas should make a genuine effort to find out what features are important to consumers when these consumers set out to buy white-goods items. Once Atlas knows the things that consumers look for in appliances, every product in the line should be reviewed in the light of that knowledge. Product designs should then be developed to make Atlas appliances more attractive to consumers. Ideally, in this process of product-line review, it will be possible to maintain the basic design integrity that now characterizes Atlas products. But it must be anticipated that situations will arise in which potential consumer appeal and design integrity will be in conflict. When this kind of situation arises, we strongly urge that the final design decision be made on the basis of ultimate consumer appeal. Hidden virtues rarely sell products, no matter how important they may seem from the standpoint of the engineering department.

3. Too little attention has been paid to sales-training programs for retail salesmen. We know that appliance manufacturers tend to despair of ever achieving adequate sales support at the retail level. Retail salesmen are, it is true, hard to train and inspire; and it is also true that once a salesman is trained, he almost inevitably quits and finds some other, better-paying job. Nonetheless, these facts do not, in our judgment, justify the virtual abandonment of retail sales-training programs by Atlas. It is absolutely certain that if the retail salesman is given no factory help in becoming a better salesman, he will, in fact, never become a better salesman. To reason that too few salesmen actively avail themselves of factory programs or take full advantage of them misses the point that if there are no programs, nothing at all can be accomplished.

   We conclude, therefore, that Atlas must make a major effort to create new sales-training materials that can be used by the retail salesman. These materials should include: training manuals that are brightly written and filled with accessible and cogent information about the

Atlas product line; incentive programs that reward the retail salesmen for learning about Atlas; filmstrip product presentations that, once mastered by the salesman, can be used in explaining product features to potential customers; whatever innovative materials Atlas and its suppliers can develop that will help every Atlas retail salesman to know as much about Atlas products as he can.

The development of a sparkling new package of Atlas sales-training programs is especially important as the company expands and modernizes its retail distribution system. Such retail-training programs will be vital in ensuring that new Atlas retailers and their sales personnel receive all the help they need in introducing the Atlas line in their stores and to their customers.

4. Atlas has been remiss, too, in ignoring, to a major degree, the opportunities that are inherent in vigorous trade-promotion activities. Most of the aggressive home-appliance producers have a well-thought-out annual calendar of trade-promotion activities and events. These activities and events help the trade both to stimulate consumer demand during periods in which sales are at seasonal low points and to add momentum to retail sales during periods of traditionally higher product movement. Trade promotions should also be geared to specific classes of trade. For example, programs that are effective with independent appliance retailers are usually totally inappropriate for mass merchandisers, and vice versa.

   The aggressive manufacturers thus are likely to have two or three distinct promotional calendars, one for independent appliance retailers, one for department stores, and one for mass merchandisers. Each of these separate calendars features an annual sequence of events geared specifically to the demonstrated needs of each class of trade. Field promotion managers must be recruited and trained as the factory employees who work with the major accounts in implementing these promotional events. And, these managers must have the authority to revise and modify the individual promotion programs to meet the requirements of key accounts.

   All of this is a far cry from current Atlas trade-promotion practice, which neither recognizes the peculiar promotional needs of individual classes of trade nor makes available a regular sequence of promotion activities and events to any retailer who wishes to avail himself of it. (We should add that the Atlas cooperative-advertising program is well conceived and administered. It certainly meets all the Federal Trade Commission standards and tests for such programs. It is tragically underutilized because of the lack of a well-organized factory trade-promotion program. If there were superior factory trade-promotion programs, there would be, we believe, a very significantly higher utilization of cooperative-advertising funds. The trade would tend automatically to advertise promotional events, utilizing cooperative-advertising monies in this effort. Without adequate promotional programs it is inevitable that cooperative advertising funds will largely remain unspent.)

5. Finally, there is the whole matter of factory-sponsored advertising. Close analysis indicates that Atlas spends advertising monies at about one third the rate of the leading competitive manufacturers. For example, Federated Appliance Corporation had a factory advertising

> budget of about $12 million for its white-goods line in 1976. Our best estimates place the Federated Appliance white-goods sales in 1976 at approximately $1.6 billion, or about the same as Atlas sales. Yet the Atlas factory advertising appropriation in 1976 was $3,800,000. Atlas expends no money on television while every one of its leading competitors spends three quarters or more of their total advertising appropriation in this medium. Atlas advertising copy is severely handicapped by a lack of product features, as we have noted above, that readily lend themselves to exploitation in advertising. In summary, we believe that Atlas advertising has been humdrum, ineffectual, and totally lacking in aggressiveness.

What Atlas is, in summary, is a company that has made its mark as a manufacturer rather than as a marketer. Atlas has a superb product line which now must be marketed much more aggressively than it has been in the past. Our experience is, incidentally, that it is much easier to turn this kind of situation around than it is to overcome fundamental product-design or manufacturing problems. In our judgment, recent sales and profit problems reflect more aggressive marketing competition from other leading firms and especially Federated Appliance in the years since 1972. Federated has demonstrated the sales effectiveness of aggressive marketing during this period. Federated has strengthened its distribution, improved the consumer appeal of its products, organized its sales-training efforts, developed a comprehensive trade-promotion policy, and increased its advertising appropriations. Atlas has fallen behind competitively, but it should be relatively easy to catch up if, and we emphasize *if,* Atlas is willing to make a determined marketing effort in the years ahead.

We would recommend that a three-phase program be initiated by Atlas management. In the first phase, attention would be focused on expanding and strengthening distribution; improving sales-training programs; organizing promotion activities; and on the development of product innovations with genuine consumer appeal. We would expect that this phase would take at least two years to complete, so that by the middle of 1979 Atlas would be well on its way to much stronger retail representation. Essential to the achievement of stronger retail representation is the development of lively competitive sales-training and trade-promotion programs. Both these activities, if properly conceived and carried out, will help make it easier to achieve broader and stronger retail representation.

Meanwhile, as a second phase of this effort, the more attractive products should be available by mid-1979, too, and their availability will help to solidify gains in retail distribution as well as to make the sales-training programs more meaningful and to provide promotional program opportunities. Coincidentally, as the third phase, a very much stronger advertising program should be launched in the fall of 1979 in support of the broader retail distribution and in conjunction with the availability of Atlas products with enhanced consumer appeal. This new advertising program will be stronger in two senses. First, Atlas should invest significantly more money in advertising than ever before, bringing the level of the advertising appropriation at least to competitive parity. In addition, the content of Atlas advertising messages will have considerably greater competitive bite because Atlas products will, by this time, be inherently much more advertisable than ever before and because, hopefully, you will have found an advertising agency with a higher level of advertising skill to execute these more competitive messages.

Thus, by late 1979, we believe that it will be possible to begin to reap the benefits of the newly aggressive marketing program developed and implemented during the preceding two years.

We will be happy to meet with you and your colleagues at your convenience to discuss the steps that should now be taken to implement these recommendations.

---

Stanley Simpkin had been president and chief executive officer of Atlas Home-Appliance Company since 1973. Now 57 years old, Simpkin had joined Atlas as an apprentice product-development engineer directly after his graduation from college with a bachelor of mechanical engineering degree in 1947. Simpkin was, thus, an old-line Atlas employee and he had resented the UEL takeover of the company in 1958 when he was chief product-development engineer. Now, reading the Claridge memorandum, Simpkin resented its imperious tone and, more fundamentally, resented bitterly the fact that Atlas Home-Appliance, under his leadership, had come to a sales and profit point that required that outsiders be brought in to tell him how to run the business.

"But," thought Simpkin, "it could be worse. They could have fired me. It would have been easy enough to rationalize. I never have known much about marketing, and heaven knows it would be easy for them to replace me with a younger, more marketing-oriented man."

When it dawned on Simpkin that it was within his grasp to survive this time of trouble, he immediately set about to do everything within his power to make sure that this possible new lease on life became both actual and permanent. Within a two-month period after receiving the Claridge memorandum, Simpkin completely reorganized the Atlas Home-Appliance Company marketing department. He recruited, with Claridge's help, Justin A. Applebaum, from the Apex Television Division of UEL to be the Atlas director of marketing. Together, Applebaum, Claridge, and he then created three totally new positions within the marketing department: a director of trade relations, responsible for expanding retail distribution, creating retail sales-training programs, and developing retail sales-promotion programs; a director of marketing research; and a director of advertising. Long-term Atlas employee Roger L. Schneidken was appointed director of trade relations on August 1, 1977, and long-term Atlas employee Albert L. Toledano was appointed director of advertising on the same date. On September 6, 1977, Justine L. Swartzell, previously in the marketing research department of Federated Appliance Corporation, was appointed director of marketing research for Atlas Home-Appliance Company (see Exhibit 3-2).

Simpkin himself took responsibility for the redesign of the Atlas product line in order to give it heightened product appeal.

By the spring of 1979, Atlas had made very significant progress in implementing the program outlined in the Claridge memorandum of two years before. A total of 378 new Atlas dealerships had been instituted during that period for a net gain of 283, as 95 old-line Atlas dealers terminated their relationships with the company. Sales-training programs had been developed and accepted by the retailers; and spot field-checks indicated to Simpkin that the level of salesmanship in Atlas retail outlets had become, if still far from perfect, very significantly better as a result. Trade-promotion calendars for individual trade classes were now an established fact, and the trade utilization of Atlas cooperative-advertising funds had increased 35 percent in 1978 over 1977 and appeared

**EXHIBIT 3–2**
**The Atlas Home-Appliance Company Marketing Organization, January 1, 1978**

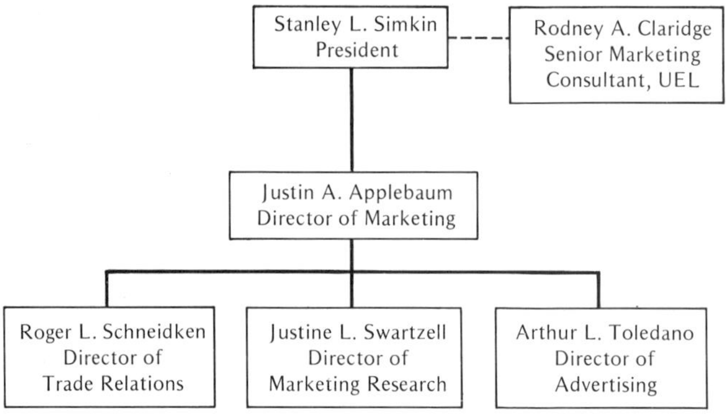


to be running about 52 percent higher in early 1979 than during the comparable period in 1977.

And, product improvements had been realized in the Atlas line of home appliances. Now, for example, an ice-cube maker was standard in all Atlas refrigerators, and the interior of all Atlas refrigerators were now significantly articulated into individual storage areas for different kinds of food such as meat, vegetables, butter, eggs, soft drinks, and the like. The top of the line electric range, for further example, now had a self-cleaning oven as a standard feature, and all the Atlas ranges featured newly developed Sensi-Speed top burners which heated quickly and changed heat levels with equal speed. Similar product innovations had been widespread throughout the Atlas line, each solidly based on the needs of consumers as identified by Justine Swartzell's marketing research projects.

This left the Atlas advertising program for the 1979–80 model year to be determined. Simpkin was completely at sea as far as advertising was concerned. He had no idea what it could be expected to accomplish nor what various levels of accomplishment might cost. He met, from time to time, with Al Toledano, his new director of advertising and sought to sort out, in more or less casual conversations with him, the relevant issues that affected advertising decisions. In these meetings, Simpkin did his best to pump Toledano for ideas and thoughts without revealing to him how totally inept he felt in the advertising area. But after months of this sparring with Toledano, Simpkin now felt considerable pressure to move forward with the advertising plans for 1979–80.

"Al," Simpkin said, as he and Toledano were eating lunch in the Atlas executive dining room one day in late March of 1979, "I really don't know at which end of this advertising problem to start; but believe me, we have got to come to grips with the advertising program for next year. We don't have a lot of time left—now that we're getting all these new retailers, and these new products are beginning to come off the line. You've got to tell me where to start, so we get to specific solutions and get to them right away."

"I don't know what you mean by that, Stanley," responded Toledano. Toledano had been a highly competent advertising manager for Atlas Home-Appliance. Given an advertising budget and some sort of basic direction as to the advertising messages to be delivered, he could oversee the development of the advertisements and their subsequent placement in a list of media vehicles. Past Atlas advertising basically had been limited to magazine insertions that showed colored pictures of particular Atlas appliances and described their features and specifications in a straightforward, factual manner. Toledano knew that this rather perfunctory advertising era was past when he was promoted from advertising manager to advertising director. He realized that he was now expected to assume some sort of a policy role within the company. He also sensed that Atlas advertising was expected to do more for Atlas than it had in the past and that more money was to be spent to accomplish this. But Toledano was totally confused as to what changes might be required in the advertising program, and he had no idea at all about what goals might be accomplished as a result of this new advertising activity. Throughout the winter of 1978 and 1979 in his meetings with Stanley Simpkin, Toledano had done his best to conceal his confusion and ignorance; and since Simpkin was even less well-prepared to make decisions in this area than was Toledano, he, Toledano, had been able so far to get by with generalities and circumlocutions. Now, suddenly, as Simpkin asked about "which end of the advertising program to start at," Toledano sensed that he was going to have to be a lot more specific with Simpkin, and pretty quickly.

"What I mean," said Simpkin, "is that I can't figure out whether we should decide how much to spend for advertising first, or whether we should decide what we want our advertising to accomplish *before* we make up our minds about how much to spend."

"Well, Stanley," replied Toledano, "as far as I can see, the only justification for advertising is that it sells products. We can start there. We know what fraction of sales we've spent over the years on advertising. If we want to increase its effect on sales, then we increase the fraction of estimated sales we spend on advertising."

"You mean," asked Simpkin, "that if we double our advertising budget that our sales will double?"

"Oh, no, Stanley," said Toledano smiling, "nothing like that. I wish it were that easy. But of course it isn't. We can safely say that if advertising is doubled, sales will be higher than they otherwise might have been—if everything else is equal. Then there's the matter of the strength of advertising copy. I mean if we could only get better copy out of that agency of ours, we could get more sales without increasing our expenditures at all."

"But let me be clear about this, Al." said Simpkin. "You really don't have any idea about the sales we'll get if we increase advertising dollars. Have I got that right?"

"Yes, that's right, Stanley," said Toledano. "Nothing precise, although we'll get more sales for sure; and the better the copy, the more the sales."

"Well, actually, Al," said Simpkin, beginning to show some irritation, his voice raising just a notch or two, "when you think about it, there's no reason at all why advertising should actually cause specific sales in our business and a lot of reasons why it shouldn't."

"Oh, I wouldn't go that far, Stanley," said Toledano, rather uncertainly, now quite sure that he had no idea where this conversation was leading, but not liking the drift of it one bit.

"Well, I would, Al," said Simpkin. "We've spent the last year and a half doing all kinds of things to help our sales. We all decided, and you agreed, as I recall, that we wouldn't change our advertising approach or increase the appropriations until we got all these other things done. If it were as simple as spending more dough on advertising, we wouldn't have been waiting around for a year and a half; and we wouldn't have spent all this money on recruiting new retailers, writing sales-training programs, increasing our trade-promotion expenditures, and redesigning every product in our line.

"Start thinking, Al. When you do, you'll realize that we only spend about one quarter of one percent of our sales on advertising. I'll be the first to admit that $3,800,000 is a lot of dough to spend on anything, even advertising, but it's peanuts in our business. Even over there at Federated, they only spend three quarters of one percent—three times as much as we do—still peanuts for them. If advertising was really effective in causing sales, wouldn't we already be spending more, a lot more, Al? I think we would. What all this means to me is that advertising has a role to play in the white-goods business, but it's not a *decisive* role. It's not like soap or cigarettes or whatever, if it is decisive there—who knows? But in *our* business it doesn't carry the load. It helps other things, so I don't think we can simply sit around here and say it helps make sales, and let it go at that. I think we have to know *how* it helps make sales. What are your thoughts, Al?"

"I think you're right, Stanley, dead right," said Albert Toledano, with a considerable amount of conviction.

"Okay, what are you going to do about it?" asked Simpkin.

"I think we ought to have a meeting, and pose this problem—and kind of kick it around, get a lot of different inputs from people around the company, and then sort it all out, and then we'll be able to make up our minds," said Toledano breathlessly. He ended with an almost wistful smile on his face and looked expectantly at Simpkin.

"Okay, Al," said Simpkin, still irritated both with Toledano and with his own indecisiveness, "you can hold a meeting if you want. But not one of those meetings where a topic is announced and then everyone comes in and lets off a lot of hot air and opinions. First, Al, you have to write a memorandum about Atlas advertising and what it does for us, and what it should be expected to do for us. Do that, and then we can have a meeting about it if you want, but be sure you have an agenda for the meeting too, that's keyed to your memorandum so that the people you include know what they are going to have to talk about, and have a chance to prepare their thoughts."

By then, lunch was over. Toledano said he would prepare the memorandum within two or three days and set up the meeting within a week; and Simpkin agreed with the timing. With that, the two men went their separate ways, neither really satisfied with what he had said—Simpkin feeling discontented about the competence of his director of advertising, and Toledano beginning for the first time to experience a fearfulness that he might not be able to do his job.

Here is the memorandum prepared by Toledano at Simpkin's request and circulated some eight days following their luncheon discussion:

---

# ATLAS HOME-APPLIANCE COMPANY

Memorandum

April 3, 1979

| | | | |
|---|---|---|---|
| To: | Stanley Simpkin | cc: | Rodney A. Claridge |
| From: | Albert Toledano | | Justin Applebaum |
| Subject: | Advertising Objectives for Atlas | | Justine Swartzell |

You have asked me to describe the objectives that we should set for accomplishment by the Atlas Home-Appliance Company factory-advertising program in 1979-80.

This is a new topic for Atlas. Until our recent conversations, it had never been raised in this company. I've delayed writing this memorandum for a few days while I've canvassed other advertisers and their experience in this area. I've also had lengthy conversations with representatives of the Association of National Advertisers (ANA), an organization that has devoted an immense amount of time, money, and talent to determining just how the effects of advertising can be determined. So, in what follows, you'll see a lot of new ideas (that really come from a lot of different sources), as I believe they apply to Atlas.

We have, in the past, as we have discussed, assumed that Atlas factory sponsored advertising causes sales. Certainly, this has never been very well spelled out. We have held the conviction that if advertising expenditures were increased, sales would go up, and that if advertising expenditures were decreased, sales would go down. But we never addressed the question of why sales would react to changes in advertising, nor have we addressed the question of the relation of advertising to other marketing activities that also affect sales results.

I would like to suggest that advertising must be expected to accomplish two quite different, but not unrelated, goals for Atlas.

In the first place, advertising must have some effect upon sales, if it is to be worthwhile. Why should we spend money on advertising if it is not causing or affecting sales? That would just be foolishness. Therefore, we should make some effort to find out the effect of increased or decreased advertising expenditures on sales. There must be some relation between the two, even if it isn't exact or very strong. If we are content only to *assume* that advertising has some positive effect upon sales, then we still have to find out what the nature of that effect is. Otherwise, we may be wasting millions of Atlas dollars that might just as well go into profits.

So our first objective for Atlas advertising is that it must help to cause sales; and we must find some way of demonstrating this to be true.

But it can also be argued that advertising must communicate certain kinds of information to consumers, in order to cause sales. Thus, advertising does something to consumers that makes them more *likely* to buy the advertised brand. This creation of consumer predisposition to purchase a brand is how advertising causes sales, the argument runs. If advertising causes consumer awareness of Atlas appliances, transmits specific information about Atlas appliances, or increases consumer intention to purchase Atlas appliances, it can be said that advertising has done its job and that this will ultimately be reflected in sales results.

Some proponents of this point of view believe that it is unnecessary to determine the exact relation of advertising to sales because this is difficult to do with all the other marketing factors that cause sales. They say that it is enough to set *communications* goals for advertising. If the right communications goals are set and achieved, they say, that is sufficient—advertising cannot be expected to consummate the final sale.

I've talked to a lot of knowledgeable people about this in the last week or so and I've concluded that we must set both sales and communications goals for Atlas advertising. It is absolutely true that advertising must first communicate information about products before it can be expected to facilitate sales. We should set communications goals, therefore; but we cannot, in my view, abdicate our responsibility to the profitability of the corporation. We must also try to determine just what the ultimate effect of our advertising is on sales, after the communications goals have been established and accomplished.

Could the five of us meet on Tuesday, April 10, in the main conference room to discuss an agenda which includes this proposal and a discussion of just what advertising communications goals might be most appropriate for Atlas?

---

Stanley Simpkin was well pleased with the content of this memorandum. "He hasn't really come to grips with the question of what specific things advertising must communicate to cause sales," Simpkin thought to himself. "But he has suggested that to be effective our advertising must communicate, and that sure seems sound to me. And he hasn't given up hope that we'll be able to figure out just what a particular level of advertising can be expected to contribute in extra sales dollars. At least he's thinking, and I doubt that he ever really thought about all this before the last week or two."

So Simpkin was content to let the matter ride until the meeting proposed by Toledano for April 10. Others were not so content, however. Three days later, the two following memoranda also reached Stanley Simpkin.

---

# ATLAS HOME-APPLIANCE COMPANY

-Memorandum-

April 6, 1979

| | | | |
|---|---|---|---|
| To: | Stanley Simpkin | cc: | Rodney A. Claridge |
| From: | Justin Applebaum | | Albert Toledano |
| Subject: | Advertising Objectives for Atlas | | Justine Swartzell |

I have just finished reading A. Toledano's April 3 memo on this same subject. I'm sorry that I've not had the time in recent weeks to join the discussions that you have been having with Al about advertising objectives for Atlas. I am glad that I've been asked to participate in the meeting next Monday because I've had some very specific experience with these matters at Apex Television Division.

Let me summarize what we learned there about how advertising works:

1. It's very difficult to determine, in any precise, mathematical way, exactly what a given advertising expenditure will contribute in terms of sales results. When you think about it, it's obvious why this is so. We spent a lot of time and an *immense* amount of money at Apex trying to develop a mathematical model of this process; and in the end, although we accumulated a lot of thick reports, it was a fiasco. We really didn't know one thing more after the time and money was spent than we did before. I don't say that it can't be done or that we shouldn't try to do it; but it will be time-consuming, expensive, and, in the end, we may simply fail.
2. We didn't have much better luck when we tried to establish communications goals for Apex. It is possible to set awareness and knowledge and attitude goals for the trade and the consumer, especially when you have products with relatively attractive and new features. The trouble with all this is that it's very hard to sift out people who are really in

the market for one of your appliance items and measure the degree with which you have successfully communicated with them. And it's very difficult to determine what you must communicate to these potential purchasers, in a competitive environment, to bring them over to you.

This is especially true when you use television. I mean television is *very* good at communicating ideas and information to vast numbers of people. Almost everyone who sees your television commercials gets the message, at least after they have been exposed repeatedly to a television campaign. But the key group—those people who are in the market to buy—are almost impossible to identify. Our evidence indicated that they are also affected by competitive messages and information from friends; and that your advertising may not be absorbed by them, or they may discount it and form totally different attitudes as a result of exposure to it, than just the casual viewers do. Thus, even though they know what you are saying, it may not motivate them to buy your product.

It doesn't always happen this way, of course. And often population effects of advertising are a valid reflection of the effects upon those people who are genuinely ready to buy. But we learned to be a little skeptical of the measurements we could make of advertising goals in communications terms. Too often we accomplished our communications goals and nothing happened to sales.

3. As we worked at trying to find some valid way to measure the effect of our advertising programs, we became more and more convinced that we should try to isolate some sort of advertising impact on consumers that was more directly related to ultimate sales results than just what the advertising happened to communicate to consumers. We were almost forced to find some other effect, because as I've said, too often we found that our advertising communicated very well but created no discernible sales results at all.

But what kinds of advertising effects might then lie between simple communication of advertising content and the ultimate effect of sales? We thought about this for a good long time before it dawned on us that successful advertising might be expected to cause some sort of consumer behavior, even if that behavior did not culminate in the actual purchase of one of our products. Specifically, we realized that successful advertising should create a greater desire on the part of consumers to go to a store and look at our products than would unsuccessful advertising for the same product. To put it another way, a great advertising campaign would cause many more prospective purchasers of a product to come into one of our dealer outlets to look at our brand than would a less effective advertising campaign.

We reasoned that a superior way to measure advertising effect, therefore, was to make a measurement of store traffic during a period when a particular new advertising campaign was introduced. During 1976 and 1977 we ran several advertising experiments in a group of test markets. In each of these experiments we ran a particular television advertising campaign for a specific product at very high expenditure levels for a period of two weeks; we measured traffic into our dealers' stores for the two weeks *before* the advertising heavy up period, for the two weeks of the heavy advertising, and for an extra week after the heavy-up, besides.

It was immediately apparent that there was a lot of traffic in the stores after we started the heavy television advertising. We had trouble, however, in making absolutely sure that this extra traffic was really caused by our advertising. At first we believed that we could measure the effects of the advertising by stationing an interviewer in our dealers' stores and having him count the number of people who showed interest in the product that had been advertised. Thus, we believed that an interviewer could *observe* and count the number of consumers that came into some sort of contact with the product that was advertised. This sounds simple enough, but in practice it turned out to be very difficult. Sometimes the interviewers attended to the wrong product. Sometimes they misunderstood what we meant by "coming into actual contact with a product"—that the consumer must actually touch the advertised television receiver—and simply counted people who looked at the set, or walked past it. Sometimes the interviewers left early or arrived long after the stores were open for business. And none of the interviewers stayed on their stations consistently throughout the day. (There were all kinds of incidents to take them away from their stations: coffee breaks, visits to rest rooms, phone calls, errands, and so forth.)

In summary, after many attempts and much frustration, we concluded that it was impossible to make accurate measurements of store traffic created by specific advertisements through the use of in-store observers. We concluded that some other, more mechanical means of measurement was necessary.

In the end, we arranged to install a mechanical counter on the tune-in button of the advertised television receivers displayed in our dealers showrooms in the experimental test markets. This device, developed by the product-engineering department of Apex TV, counted one for every time a television receiver was turned on, and this count accumulated as each receiver was turned on over a period of days and weeks. Installation of the counter was very simple—even a nonmechanical market-research supervisor could do it. Once the counter was installed, it only required that it be "read" at the end of the two-week control period preceding the initiation of advertising and read once again at the end of the three-week period following initiation of the advertising campaign.

The counter had two shortcomings as a measure of advertising effect. First, it only measured set turn-ons. It was argued that advertising could create store traffic that did not, once in the store, actually turn on the advertised television receiver. However, it seemed to us that anyone who was seriously interested in purchasing a television set would be very likely to take a look at the picture provided by a demonstration model. Thus, we believed that a mechanical count of the number of times an advertised product was turned on in a retail outlet was a very valid indication of possible purchase prospects created by the advertising.

The second problem with the television-receiver counter was that, at least in the beginning, too many of the sets with counters installed were sold off the retail floors by our dealers. People would come into the store, turn on a demonstration receiver, like the picture that they saw, and then insist that they purchase that very receiver. Of course, when this happened, our advertising-effects measurement was ruined. We solved this problem by printing up a batch of stickers that said: "Demonstration television—not for sale." These stickers were placed on all floor models within which the counters had been installed; and this stopped the selling of these sets out from under the research program.

All in all, the experiments based on the measurement of advertising effects by mechanical counters was a total success. Through it we learned a great deal about the kinds of advertising content that could cause increases in store traffic of prospective buyers; and we also learned the intensity-level of television advertising that produced traffic with greatest efficiency. It would seem to me that we should undertake just such a program of advertising experimentation for Atlas. Certainly, it will be easy enough to engineer counters to measure the number of times refrigerator, range oven, or dishwasher doors are opened in the dealer's showrooms. I would certainly recommend this approach in preference to spending a lot of time and effort trying to measure the direct effect of advertising on sales or to making expensive and ambiguous measurements of the degree to which advertising programs achieve communications goals.

---

# ATLAS HOME-APPLIANCE COMPANY

-Memorandum-

April 9, 1979

To: Albert Toledano
From: Justine Swartzell
Subject: Advertising Objectives for Atlas

cc: Stanley L. Simpkin
Rodney A. Claridge
Justin Applebaum

In anticipation of your meeting tomorrow on this subject, I thought you might like some input from the research standpoint. I have read both your memorandum on advertising objectives for Atlas and the memorandum that Justin Applebaum circulated last Friday. I am not in total agreement with either one of them. Justin is right when he says that it will be very tough to relate specific advertising expenditures to specific sales results. There are a lot of marketing factors involved in causing sales, and advertising is only one of these. In addition, we spend relatively little on advertising and it is likely to get lost in the shuffle of other marketing events.

There is also, in my mind, the very real question of just when and how a specific advertising expenditure has a specific effect on sales. I tend to think of advertising in our product category as a kind of relentless force that continually keeps our products in the consciousness of the consumers, providing them with information that will increase the probability of their considering our products when they *do* get around to purchasing. We have to remember that relatively small numbers of households actually buy the products we sell in any given year. Our factory advertising should be conceived of as a program of continuing preparation for these consumers. Its purpose is not to create immediate sales but to increase the probability that a consumer will come to an Atlas dealer when he or she ultimately gets around to making a purchase.

Our product-promotion programs and our cooperative-advertising expenditures should be geared to converting immediate-purchase intentions into sales. Price features and promotional events make sales happen. Factory advertising must precede these specific sales-generating activities: Factory advertising makes our brands acceptable to consumers in a general sense. It guarantees that they will look at our appliances when they get ready to purchase because factory advertising has more or less "forced" them to consider Atlas appliances as one of two or three acceptable brands. If the consumer doesn't accept our brand in the first place, no amount of specific promotion or cooperative advertising price features can force him to buy Atlas.

Because of the role I believe factory advertising plays in the marketing of our products, I am very much in favor of establishing communications goals for it. We should find it relatively easy to agree that consumer awareness of Atlas is important for every one of the appliances that we make. It should also be relatively easy to identify the specific aspects of our products that will predispose consumers toward Atlas when they do find themselves in the appliance marketplace.

I think that measuring the traffic that particular advertisements apparently create is much better adapted to the assessment of cooperative-advertising programs than to factory-advertising campaigns. The use of counters to measure door openings, or whatever, is certainly ingenious enough; but factory advertising should not have the specific responsibility of bringing consumers into physical contact with our appliances at any particular time.

---

Late in the afternoon of Monday April 9, 1979, Stanley Simpkin called Albert Toledano into his office.

"Al," said Simpkin, "I think you ought to cancel that advertising goals meeting that you've got set up for tomorrow."

"Why do you think that, Stanley?" asked Toledano.

"Because, if I read these memoranda that I've been getting all week correctly, the people around here are in disagreement on the basics about advertising. Until we can figure out—you and I should do this, not the whole gang—what our advertising is supposed to accomplish, we really have no right to call a meeting to decide about advertising goals. It's not, as far as I can see, a question of *how* we should measure but *what* we should measure that will be meaningful in terms of advertising goals for Atlas."

## *QUESTIONS FOR CASE 3*

1. What is a "factory-advertising" program? What is a "cooperative-advertising" program? How are factory-advertising programs financed? How are cooperative-advertising programs financed? What is the purpose of factory-advertising programs for home appliances? What is the purpose of cooperative-advertising programs for home appliances?
2. Is it difficult to prove that advertising causes sales in the home-appliance industry? Does the home-appliance industry differ in the sales effectiveness of its advertising from the soft-drink industry (see Case 2)? How and why?
3. In what sense do sales cause advertising in the home-appliance industry?
4. How would you define the goals of the Atlas Home-Appliance Company factory-advertising program? Do you believe that Atlas should adopt sales goals, behavioral goals, communications goals, or some, or all of these, for its factory-advertising program?
   a. If you believe that Atlas should set sales goals for its factory advertising, tell how the company executives should go about setting specific sales goals.

b. If you believe that Atlas should set communications goals for its factory advertising, list at least four communications goals that the company might adopt.
c. If you believe that Atlas should set behavioral goals for its factory advertising, tell the kinds of behavior that should be used as a basis for such goals.

5. How would you define the goals of the Atlas Home-Appliance Company cooperative-advertising program? Do you believe that Atlas should adopt sales goals, communications goals, or behavioral goals, or some, or all of these, for its cooperative-advertising program?
   a. If you believe that Atlas should set sales goals for its cooperative-advertising, tell how the company executives should go about setting specific sales goals.
   b. If you believe that Atlas should set communications goals for it cooperative-advertising, list at least four communications goals that the company should adopt.
   c. If you believe that Atlas should set behavior goals for its cooperative advertising, tell the kinds of behavior that should be used as a basis for such goals.

6. Stanley Simpkin seems somewhat apprehensive about holding a meeting to discuss advertising goals for Atlas, at least until some sort of basic groundwork has been laid. Albert Toledano, on the other hand, apparently believes that a meeting will be helpful in setting advertising goals for Atlas whether groundwork for such a meeting has been laid or not. What would be the purpose of such a meeting from Simpkin's standpoint; from Toledano's standpoint? Would the meeting envisaged by Simpkin be likely to be more productive than the one envisaged by Toledano, or vice versa? Why do you believe this to be so?

7. Why is it necessary for a company to have explicit advertising goals? Under what circumstances might a company not need such explicit goals?

8. What is the relation of advertising goals to advertising appropriations? Is this relation likely to be different if advertising goals are stated in sales terms rather than in communications terms? If you believe the nature of advertising goals is related to advertising appropriation determination, tell why. If you don't think the nature of advertising goals bears a relation to the determination of advertising appropriations, tell why.

# Case 4

# Determining Advertising Creative Strategy

## *THE AMELIA ETERNAL COMPANY DETERMINES ITS ADVERTISING APPROACH*

After considerable discussion, Henry Litt and Morgan Harris agreed that Amelia Eternal would undertake a program of consumer advertising and that it would commence in 1980. (Reread Case 1 thoroughly for a description of the Amelia Eternal Company and the events that preceded this decision.)

Litt had finally, and reluctantly, accepted Harris's belief that an advertising program could help the sales of Amelia Eternal products by creating consumer awareness of this company, and by facilitating the process of attracting qualified, younger sales representatives to the company.

In addition, Litt and Harris agreed to appropriate \$12 million for this program in 1980. They did not know how these funds would be spent at the time the appropriation was determined, but they accepted Eddie Collins's estimate that consumer advertising for Amelia Eternal would require between \$10 million and \$15 million to be effective. Both Litt and Harris agreed that the \$12 million appropriation was a planning figure rather than a final commitment. But Harris believed that it was important that Henry Litt agree to a particular figure before the company immersed itself in the development of advertising plans since it would represent an agreement by Litt to the principle that consumer advertising should be used for the Amelia Eternal Company and that the advertising expenditure should be at a significant level.

During the month of April 1979, Harris and several of his associates heard formal presentations from five advertising agencies soliciting the Amelia Eternal account. The five agencies had been selected on the basis of a detailed report from Keltner, Boudreau, and Gordon in which leading advertising agencies were described, and in which a recommendation was made to limit the search for an advertising agency to those five considered best qualified by KB&G. The agencies were given an outline of the points that Amelia Eternal wished covered in each presentation. These included: a brief history of the advertising agency; a listing of its accounts; representative creative work from the five current agency accounts considered by the agency to be most similar to Amelia Eternal from the standpoint of the advertising problem that had been solved by the agency; a statement of the agency's creative philosophy; a statement of the procedures that had been established by the agency to insure that its creative philosophy was reflected in its advertising work; a list of the advertising accounts that the agency had lost or resigned in the past three years; a brief statement telling why each account was lost or resigned; and a statement describing how the agency preferred to be compensated if it were awarded the Amelia Eternal account.

All of the competing agencies were based in New York City. Keltner, Boudreau, and Gordon had strongly recommended that only New York agencies be included in the search. It was their belief that the quality of creative work produced by New York agencies was, on the average, somewhat better than that produced by West Coast advertising agencies. In addition, KB&G believed that the typical New York agency had much more creative depth than its counterparts on the West Coast. This was true, KB&G believed, because the larger New York advertising agencies were very much larger than those on the Coast and thus had many more copywriters, artists, and production personnel working for them. In addition, New York was the city in which most of the major advertising agencies were located, and thus New York tended to attract the best and most diversified talent in the business.

None of the advertising agencies were asked to make speculative creative presentations to the Amelia Eternal group because Harris believed that such presentations would merely confuse the issue. None of the agencies could be presumed to have a grasp of the characteristics of the Amelia Eternal business nor of the problems that Harris, Henry Litt, and Keltner, Boudreau, and Gordon perceived this business to have. The advertising solutions to these problems would depend upon the development of agreed-upon advertising strategies. Harris and Litt did not know exactly what those strategies would be and expected to work with their new advertising agency in developing and perfecting them.

Harris and Litt set aside one week to hear the advertising agency presentations. Each agency was given from 9:30 to 11:30 A.M. on a specific day to make its presentation. On the following Saturday morning Henry Litt, Morgan Harris, and three others who had been in the audience for the agency presentation (Edgar Fontaine, director of sales promotion; Angela Haswell, director of field operations, and Stanton Thornton, newly appointed director of advertising) met to decide which agency they would choose.

Morgan Harris opened the meeting with the following statement: "Okay, gentlemen, and Angie, we all know why we're here; and I suppose we all have a golf game this afternoon, so we want to get this over with some dispatch. Stanton is the one who will have to work with these birds, and with his background in the advertising agency business and all, I think we should hear what he thinks we ought to do." (Thornton had been recruited from a large New York advertising agency where he had been in account-management work for seventeen years.)

Thornton stated that his preference was for the firm of Aesop and Acton, a middle-sized agency that specialized in packaged-goods advertising and an agency that had made a bright, sound, and interesting presentation to the Amelia Eternal officials on the preceding Thursday morning. Thornton explained the reasons for his choice in a quiet, rational way. His major point was that Aesop and Acton had shown the most detailed and sophisticated procedure for approaching and solving advertising problems.

"These people really know how to take an advertising problem apart. They get to the heart of the matter fast, and they know exactly how to generate the research knowledge that they need to do it. But once they've identified the problem that advertising must solve and laid out the proper strategies to do it, they let their creative people have their head. Their creative work appears flashy, but it's better than just flashy–it's smart. It's right on strategy, everytime. It executes the strategy in a contemporary and brilliant way. These people are real pros. And, although the other agencies are good, a couple very good, Aesop and Acton is the best of the bunch at making advertisements that succeed."

Thornton went on in this vein for something over a half an hour, before relinquishing the floor to Harris, concluding: "But, I've talked too long–what do you others think–am I all wet?"

All of the others had rated Aesop and Acton either first or a close second, except Henry Litt. "I liked Gregory, Bartwood, and Burynge best; and I'm frankly surprised that all the rest of you rated them fourth or fifth. I thought these Aesop and Acton folks were a little too slick–too used to manipulating consumers with all their talk about research, devising alternative strategies, executing strategies, and so forth. Gregory was a lot more old shoe and comfortable. I thought they came off as more honest and less dedicated to exploiting the consumer, come what may."

"But, Mr. Litt," broke in Thornton, "what do you look for in a salesperson? Someone who appears forthright and not very aggressive, or a lady who plots her sales presentation every step of the way and refuses to take 'no' for an answer?"

"Okay, young man, you win," said Henry. "That is, if all the rest of you agree about Aesop and Acton. What about you, Morgan? You've been your usual quiet self, and I haven't really heard where you stand on this."

"I think it takes a pro to know a pro, Henry." replied Morgan Harris. "Especially in the advertising agency business. The only one in this room that knows an advertising agency from a bale of hay is Stanton, and I agree with him. Since he obviously feels strongly about it, I especially agree with him."

Aesop and Acton was thereupon appointed advertising agency for the Amelia Eternal Company. They were notified on the following Monday; and the next day three account people (an account management supervisor, and account supervisor, and an account executive), plus the agency's director of research, a creative director, and creative group head, arrived from New York at the Amelia Eternal offices to begin a series of meetings that ultimately led to the development of advertising creative strategy for the Amelia Eternal Company.

Morgan Harris and Henry Litt both agreed that consumer advertising for Amelia Eternal should accomplish three fundamental pruposes. First, they believed it should familiarize American women with Amelia Eternal, its method of selling, and the philosophies upon which its products were based. Second, they believed that it should bring specific Amelia Eternal products to the attention of American women. Finally, they believed that consumer advertising should make it easier for the company to recruit superior representatives throughout the United States, rather than only in those geographic areas in which Amelia Eternal had heretofore been successful.

It was agreed, in the first Amelia Eternal-Aesop and Acton meeting that before advertising strategies could be developed to accomplish those specific goals, it would be desirable to know something about current awareness and knowledge of Amelia Eternal among American women.

August Roenfeld, account management supervisor of Aesop and Acton, explained the need as follows: "I think we could develop creative strategies right now that would serve Amelia Eternal well, but I'm certain we can develop *better* strategies if we have some idea of current consumer awareness and knowledge of Amelia Eternal. We'll know what we have to build on in the minds of the consumer, and we'll know what prejudices and misinformation we have to overcome."

The major decision made in the first agency-client meeting was, therefore, to design appropriate consumer research. This responsibility was assigned to the Aesop and Acton research department. About two weeks later, the agency returned to Amelia Eternal offices, presented a plan for the recommended research, received approval to implement this research plan and returned to New York to initiate the approved work.

The approved research project involved a projected national sample of 3,500 respondents. These respondents were to be contacted on the basis of a stratified probability sample designed to be fully projectable to the United States adult female population, fifteen years of age and older. Each respondent would be asked a series of questions designed to develop three distinct types of information: awareness of Amelia Eternal Company and knowledge about it; awareness of Amelia Eternal products and experience with them; and attitudes toward Amelia Eternal Company and its products. The plan was to repeat the study on an annual basis, so that progress in accomplishing the stated Amelia Eternal advertising goals might be assessed, and so that changing consumer awareness, knowledge, and attitudes could be factored into Amelia Eternal advertising planning in the years ahead. The cost of this 1979 study was $87,249.

The results of the first of these annual research audits of consumer awareness, knowledge, and attitudes toward Amelia Eternal Company became available in June of 1979. (The highlights of the study findings are presented in Exhibits 4-1 through 4-9.)

Miss Charlton Putney, director of research for Aesop and Acton, presented the research findings in chart form to Amelia Eternal executives, including Henry and Amelia Litt and Morgan Harris, on June 11, 1979. In her introductory remarks Charlton Putney emphasized that the research findings suggested significant potential and opportunity for Amelia Eternal both in terms of untapped sales, and in terms of the room which existed to improve consumer knowledge of and attitudes toward the company.

As she went through her charts, there was a good deal of sharp and almost defensive questioning about the study, especially from Amelia Litt. She could not imagine that so few women knew about Amelia Eternal, nor could she imagine that so many consumers had unfavorable attitudes about the company, its products, and sales representatives. Miss Putney continually fended off Amelia Litt's remarks by reminding her that the company had been extremely successful in spite of the lack of general knowledge about it and the sometimes unfavorable attitudes toward it. In addition, she stressed the opportunities for the company that were implicit in the research findings.

**EXHIBIT 4–1**
**Specimen Data: Awareness of Amelia Eternal Company, 1979**

| American Women Fifteen Years and Over | Base: 3349<br>100<br>% |
|---|---|
| Unaided Awareness: | |
| What door-to-door sales companies have you ever heard of? | |
| Avon | 54 |
| Encyclopedia Britannica | 26 |
| Shaklee | 25 |
| Electrolux | 24 |
| Amway | 14 |
| Amelia Eternal | 11 |
| Other companies mentioned | 37 |
| Don't know any direct or door-to-door sales companies | 31 |
| (Average companies mentioned by those respondents who could identify a direct or door-to-door sales company) | 2.8 |
| Aided Awareness: | |
| Please tell me which of the companies on this list you are familiar with: | |
| Avon | 92 |
| Encyclopedia Britannica | 84 |
| Amelia Eternal | 19 |
| World Book Encyclopedia | 51 |
| Amway | 27 |
| Fuller Brush | 90 |
| Electrolux | 72 |
| Shaklee | 21 |

Direct Questioning about Amelia Eternal:

Have you ever heard of the Amelia Eternal Company?

| *Yes* | *No* |
|---|---|
| 24% | 76% |

*Source:* Audit of Consumer Awareness, Knowledge, and Attitudes: The Amelia Eternal Company, 1979.

Finally, Miss Putney summarized all of the research findings in the following seven points:

1. Consumer awareness of the Amelia Eternal Company is low both absolutely and when compared to other direct-sales companies. At best, only one in four women fifteen years of age or over has ever heard of Amelia Eternal.
2. Awareness of the Amelia Eternal Company is highest among older women, women

**EXHIBIT 4-2**

**Specimen Data: Awareness of Amelia Eternal Company by Age, Income, Education, and Geographic Region, 1979**

| | | Age | | | | | Household Income | | | |
|---|---|---|---|---|---|---|---|---|---|---|
| | Total | 15–24 | 25–34 | 35–49 | 50–64 | 65/over | Under $7,500 | 7,500 14,999 | 15,000 19,999 | 20,000 & over |
| American Women 15 years and over—Base: | 3349 | 703 | 636 | 737 | 791 | 482 | 996 | 1,012 | 502 | 839 |
| | 100 | 100 | 100 | 100 | 100 | 100 | 100 | 100 | 100 | 100 |
| | % | % | % | % | % | % | % | % | % | % |
| *Unaided Awareness* | | | | | | | | | | |
| Ever heard of Amelia Eternal | 11 | 4 | 9 | 12 | 16 | 14 | 12 | 10 | 14 | 9 |
| *Aided Awareness* | | | | | | | | | | |
| Familiar with Amelia Eternal | 19 | 10 | 12 | 18 | 24 | 35 | 20 | 21 | 18 | 16 |
| *Direct Questioning* | | | | | | | | | | |
| Know of Amelia Eternal | 24 | 12 | 15 | 21 | 26 | 55 | 26 | 25 | 24 | 21 |

| | | Education | | | Geographic Region | | | |
|---|---|---|---|---|---|---|---|---|
| | | Any College | Graduated High School | Did Not Graduate High School | North East | South | West Central | West |
| American Women 15 years and over—Base: | 3349 | 837 | 1,407 | 1,105 | 636 | 737 | 1,038 | 938 |
| | 100 | 100 | 100 | 100 | 100 | 100 | 100 | 100 |
| | % | % | % | % | % | % | % | % |
| *Unaided Awareness* | | | | | | | | |
| Ever heard of Amelia Eternal | 11 | 4 | 12 | 15 | 7 | 6 | 12 | 16 |
| *Aided Awareness* | | | | | | | | |
| Familiar with Amelia Eternal | 19 | 10 | 21 | 23 | 12 | 9 | 21 | 29 |
| *Direct Questioning* | | | | | | | | |
| Know of Amelia Eternal | 24 | 11 | 27 | 30 | 18 | 10 | 22 | 41 |

*Source:* Audit of Consumer Awareness, Knowledge, and Attitudes: The Amelia Eternal Company, 1979.

**EXHIBIT 4-3**
**Specimen Data: Consumers' Ability to Name One or More Amelia Eternal Household Product, 1979**

| | |
|---|---|
| American Women Fifteen Years and Over | Base: 3349 |
| | 100 |
| | % |
| Have heard of the Amelia Eternal Company | 24 |
| Amelia Eternal Household Products Named: | |
| Super Power Safe Laundry Detergent | 8 |
| Super Power Safe Dishwashing Detergent | 6 |
| Power Safe Auto Gloss | 3 |
| All others | 11 |
| Average Number of Household Products Named by Each Respondent | 1.17 |

*Source:* Audit of Consumer Awareness, Knowledge, and Attitudes: The Amelia Eternal Company, 1979.

**EXHIBIT 4-4**
**Specimen Data: Consumers' Ability to Name One or More Amelia Eternal Makeup Products, 1979**

| | |
|---|---|
| American Women Fifteen Years and Over | Base: 3349 |
| | 100 |
| | % |
| Have heard of the Amelia Eternal Company | 24 |
| Amelia Eternal Makeup Products Named: | |
| Eternal Moisturizer | 6 |
| Sheen Soft Shampoo | 5 |
| Sheen Soft Neutralizer | 5 |
| Elegant Eve Night Cream | 4 |
| Eternal Lipstick | 4 |
| Misty Mascara | 4 |
| All Others | 17 |
| Average Number of Makeup Products Named by Each Respondent: | 1.88 |

*Source:* Audit of Consumer Awareness, Knowledge, and Attitudes: The Amelia Eternal Company, 1979.

**EXHIBIT 4–5**
**Specimen Data: Consumer Experience with Amelia Eternal Sales Representatives, 1979**

| American Women Fifteen Years and Over | Base: 3349 |
|---|---|
| | 100 |
| | % |
| Have heard of the Amelia Eternal Company | 24 |
| Recall having been called upon by Amelia Eternal representative | 16 |
| Recall purchasing an Amelia Eternal household product | 7 |
| Recall purchasing an Amelia Eternal makeup product | 13 |
| Have been called upon by an Amelia Eternal sales representative in past four weeks | 10 |

*Source:* Audit of Consumer Awareness, Knowledge, and Attitudes: The Amelia Eternal Company, 1979.

who did not graduate from high school, and women who live in the West. Awareness of Amelia Eternal is marginally lower among upper-income women than among lower-income women.

3. Individual Amelia Eternal products are not widely known among women fifteen years of age and older. Thus, women who are aware of the company can spontaneously name only 1.17 Amelia Eternal household products, on average. The comparable statistic for Amelia Eternal makeup products—with the much longer makeup product lines—is only 1.88.
4. Coverage by Amelia Eternal sales representatives has been light, relative to market potential. More than eight out of ten women fifteen years of age or over never recall having been called on by an Amelia Eternal sales representative. And nine out of ten women fifteen years of age and over have not been called upon by Amelia Eternal in the past four weeks.
5. Market coverage by Amelia Eternal sales representatives is weakest among younger women, upper-income women, and better-educated women in the northeast, south, and west central geographic areas. These data suggest, but do not prove, that the sales representatives tend to be older women with lower incomes who did not graduate from high school and who live in the East; and that these women tend to concentrate their sales calls among population segments most like themselves.
6. Amelia Eternal sales representatives are rated (by women upon whom they have recently called) as friendly and enthusiastic about Amelia Eternal products. But the sales representatives are also characterized as being relatively uninformed about Amelia Eternal products and as not having a particularly well-groomed appearance.
7. Consumers rate the Amelia Eternal Company highest because it offers an opportunity to get to know and like a friendly sales representative; because the sales

**EXHIBIT 4-6**
**Specimen Data: Consumer Experience with Amelia Eternal Sales Representatives, 1979**

| | | Age | | | | | Household Income | | | |
|---|---|---|---|---|---|---|---|---|---|---|
| | Total | 15-24 | 25-34 | 35-49 | 50-64 | 65/over | $7,500 | 7,500 14,999 | 15,000 19,999 | 20,000 & over |
| American Women 15 years and over—Base: | 3349 | 703 | 636 | 737 | 791 | 482 | 996 | 1,012 | 502 | 839 |
| | 100 | 100 | 100 | 100 | 100 | 100 | 100 | 100 | 100 | 100 |
| | % | % | % | % | % | % | % | % | % | % |
| Have heard of Amelia Eternal Co. | 24 | 12 | 15 | 21 | 26 | 55 | 26 | 25 | 24 | 21 |
| Recall having been called upon by Amelia Eternal representative | 16 | 8 | 9 | 17 | 20 | 29 | 18 | 16 | 17 | 13 |
| Recall purchasing household product | 7 | 2 | 6 | 8 | 10 | 9 | 9 | 8 | 6 | 4 |
| Recall purchasing makeup product | 13 | 8 | 9 | 12 | 19 | 17 | 14 | 14 | 13 | 11 |
| Have been called upon by Amelia Eternal sales representative in past four weeks | 10 | 2 | 4 | 7 | 14 | 28 | 13 | 11 | 10 | 5 |

| | | Education | | | Geographic Region | | | |
|---|---|---|---|---|---|---|---|---|
| | | Any College | Graduated High School | Did Not Graduate High School | North East | South | West Central | West |
| American Women 15 years and over—Base: | 3349 | 837 | 1,407 | 1,105 | 636 | 737 | 1,038 | 938 |
| | 100 | 100 | 100 | 100 | 100 | 100 | 100 | 100 |
| | % | % | % | % | % | % | % | % |
| Have heard of Amelia Eternal Co. | 24 | 11 | 27 | 30 | 18 | 10 | 22 | 41 |
| Recall having been called upon by Amelia Eternal representative | 16 | 6 | 17 | 22 | 2 | 1 | 15 | 38 |
| Recall purchasing household product | 7 | 2 | 5 | 13 | 2 | 2 | 6 | 15 |
| Recall purchasing makeup product | 13 | 5 | 11 | 22 | 4 | 1 | 9 | 33 |
| Have been called upon by Amelia Eternal sales representative in past four weeks | 10 | 2 | 8 | 19 | 1 | 2 | 4 | 29 |

*Source:* Audit of Consumer Awareness, Knowledge, and Attitudes: The Amelia Eternal Company, 1979.

**EXHIBIT 4-7**
**Specimen Data: Consumer Attitudes toward Amelia Eternal Sales Representatives, 1979**

| American Women Fifteen Years and Over | Base: 3349 |
|---|---|
| | 100 |
| | % |
| Have heard of the Amelia Eternal Company | 24 |
| Have been called upon by an Amelia Eternal sales representative in the past four weeks | 10 |
| How would you rate the Amelia Eternal sales representative on friendliness? | |
| Very friendly | 72 |
| A little friendly | 18 |
| Not too friendly | 6 |
| Quite unpleasant | 4 |
| How would you rate the Amelia Eternal sales representative on personal appearance? | |
| Very well groomed | 26 |
| Quite well groomed | 32 |
| Not too well groomed | 30 |
| Downright sloppy | 12 |
| How would you rate the Amelia Eternal Sales representative's enthusiasm for her products? | |
| Very enthusiastic about products | 91 |
| Somewhat enthusiastic about products | 7 |
| Not too enthusiastic about products | 2 |
| Unenthusiastic about products | – |
| How would you rate the Amelia Eternal sales representative's knowledge about her products? | |
| Very knowledgeable about products | 20 |
| Somewhat knowledgeable about products | 41 |
| Not too knowledgeable about products | 19 |
| Didn't know anything about products | 20 |

*Source:* Audit of Consumer Awareness, Knowledge, and Attitudes: The Amelia Eternal Company, 1979.

representatives themselves are pleasant; because these representatives offer pleasant continuing service; and because the company provides a broad line of makeup products. On the negative side, Amelia Eternal product quality and fashion products are not highly regarded; nor are Amelia Eternal home calls considered a real alternative to shopping in stores. Finally, the Amelia Eternal guarantee of satisfaction is not well regarded by consumers.

**EXHIBIT 4-8**

**Specimen Data: Consumer Attitudes* toward the Amelia Eternal Company, 1979**

| | |
|---|---|
| American Women Fifteen Years of Age and Over | Base: 3349 |
| | 100 |
| | % |
| Have heard of the Amelia Eternal Company | 24 |
| Attitude-scale ratings*: | |
| 1. Amelia Eternal offers a broad line of household products | 4.2 |
| 2. Amelia Eternal offers a broad line of makeup products | 5.1 |
| 3. Amelia Eternal offers fashionable, up-to-date makeup products | 3.2 |
| 4. Amelia Eternal representatives provide service that is pleasant and free from hard sell | 6.7 |
| 5. Amelia Eternal representatives provide individual attention and continuing personal service | 5.1 |
| 6. Amelia Eternal representatives offer a real alternative to shopping in stores. | 2.2 |
| 7. Amelia Eternal offers an opportunity to get to know and like a friendly representative | 8.6 |
| 8. Amelia Eternal guarantees complete satisfaction from every product you buy. | 4.1 |
| 9. Amelia Eternal products are totally effective, yet are completely harmless to their users | 1.3 |

* Each respondent who had heard of the Amelia Eternal Company rated it on each attitude scale and gave the company a numeric rating varying from 1 (low) to 10 (high). The higher the consumer rating, the better Amelia Eternal scored.

*Source:* Audit of Consumer Awareness, Knowledge, and Attitudes: The Amelia Eternal Conpany, 1979.

> Demographically, attitude ratings follow levels of awareness and experience—high among older, lower-income women who have not graduated from high school and who live in the West.

There was a long, heated discussion after the research results and conclusions had been presented. Amelia Litt was still startled by what she considered to be the negative thrust of the findings.

"Miss Putney," asked Amelia, "how can you be so certain about these results? If I understand your approach, the bulk of your findings came from about a thousand women. Can we really trust just a thousand women to reflect what's going on in a business with sales of $130 million a year?"

"It's not a thousand, Miss Amelia" broke in Management Supervisor August Roenfeld. "The study was based on more than 3,300 women, and that's a good-sized sampling for this kind of work, isn't it Charlton?"

"Well yes, Augie, 3,300 respondents is very adequate for this kind of work," responded Charlton Putney, "but Miss Amelia is right in that almost all of our data are based on the 24 percent of the women who had ever heard of Amelia Eternal. And that works out, Augie, to 804 respondents. All that I can tell you, Miss Amelia, is that surveys

**EXHIBIT 4–9**

**Specimen Data: Consumer Attitudes toward the Amelia Eternal Company: Selected Demographic Groups, 1979**

| | Age | | | Education | | Geographic Region | |
|---|---|---|---|---|---|---|---|
| Attitude-Scale Ratings of Women Fifteen Years and Over Who Have Heard of Amelia Eternal Company: | All Women | 15–24 | 65/over | Any College | Did Not Graduate High School | North East | West |
| 1. Amelia Eternal offers a broad line of household products | 4.2 | 4.0 | 4.7 | 3.0 | 4.8 | 3.2 | 4.9 |
| 2. Amelia Eternal offers a broad line of makeup products | 5.1 | 4.6 | 5.6 | 4.1 | 5.9 | 4.3 | 6.0 |
| 3. Amelia Eternal offers fashionable, up-to-date makeup products | 3.2 | 1.2 | 6.2 | 1.1 | 6.3 | 1.3 | 5.9 |
| 4. Amelia Eternal representatives provide service that is pleasant and free from hard sell | 6.7 | 3.2 | 9.1 | 2.8 | 9.2 | 3.4 | 9.4 |
| 5. Amelia Eternal representatives provide individual attention and continuing personal service | 5.1 | 2.6 | 7.8 | 2.4 | 8.1 | 2.7 | 7.9 |
| 6. Amelia Eternal representatives offer a real alternative to shopping in stores | 2.2 | 1.1 | 3.1 | 1.1 | 3.2 | 1.2 | 3.5 |
| 7. Amelia Eternal offers an opportunity to get to know and like a friendly representative | 8.6 | 6.9 | 9.7 | 6.2 | 9.6 | 7.1 | 9.5 |
| 8. Amelia Eternal guarantees complete satisfaction from every product you buy | 4.1 | 2.4 | 6.2 | 2.1 | 6.4 | 2.6 | 6.6 |
| 9. Amelia Eternal products are totally effective, yet are completely harmless to their users | 2.3 | 1.1 | 3.4 | 1.1 | 3.5 | 1.3 | 3.7 |

*Source:* Audit of Consumer Awareness, Knowledge, and Attitudes: The Amelia Eternal Company, 1979.

of this type are being conducted all the time and in behalf of all of the leading companies. With samples of the size we used here, the results are very, very dependable. In fact, without getting into the mathematics, it is very unlikely that any of the statistics that you've seen today is in error by more than 7 or 8 percent."

"I'm not so concerned about the study, Amelia," said Henry Litt, "as I am about what I can do about it. You people are down here to advise us about how to advertise. I can't see how advertising is going to help me solve the sales-representative problem; and you've convinced me that a major source of our trouble is that the sales representatives are too old and, worse yet, too darned much like each other. But the other thing that really worries me is that we have so many problems, how can advertising solve them all? I have the impression based on what you said in your first presentation, August, that you would want to find a single advertising idea with great potential to positively affect our customers and possible customers out there. I get done looking at this research, and I'm faced with ten or twelve things that we can say about this company; and I'll be darned if I can figure out what one to pick."

"Mr. Henry," responded August Roenfeld, "I agree that it won't be easy to pick the right strategy for Amelia Eternal. And we're really not prepared today to talk about it, because we just got the research data last Thursday ourselves. We'll be back here in ten days with the strategic issues all thought through, as we see them. Then we'll have a real shirtsleeves session and work it out with you jointly. But before we plunge in together, we owe you our own analysis and some firm recommendations: Maybe, too, we'll have to do some more research to sort out alternative strategies. We'll see about that before we come back to you; but we'll be back within ten days, alright?"

"Yeah, that's okay, that ten days, with me," said Morgan Harris, "and we'll all look forward to hearing what you have to say. It's a tough problem. I'll tell you what I think about all this research we saw today. We spent a lot of dough to do this to help us decide what advertising strategies to use. You've got a lot of data here that tell me that Amelia Eternal has a lot of problems, lot of problems; and yes, Miss Putney, I'll give you your point—we have a lot of very real opportunities, too.

"But all these data don't tell us one thing about what strategy we should choose. August you say you may want to do more research. I guess that's okay with us. But if we do anymore and spend anymore money on it, I hope it will do more than describe the disease this company's got, next time around.

"I for one—and I'm not being critical, mind you—am getting sick of hearing what's wrong with us. I want to hear how we're going to start to make some fixes. So we'll see you in ten days, and we'll be mighty interested in what you have to say."

"Right, Morgan," said Roenfeld, "we'll be back on the twenty-first, and we'll have some answers for you. And please don't jump to too many conclusions about the research until you see what we have to say then.

"Well," Roenfeld thought to himself, "the honeymoon's over, and now we begin to play hardball."

The representatives from Aesop and Acton returned to the Amelia Eternal offices on June 21. The presentation on that day was made by the senior Aesop and Acton account representative, August Roenfeld. He also played the major agency role in the discussions that the presentation was designed to, and inevitably did, stimulate.

The first prop that was introduced by Roenfeld is shown in Exhibit 4-10. It lists the goals for Amelia Eternal advertising that had been developed in previous discussions with

**EXHIBIT 4-10**
**Amelia Eternal Advertising Goals and Implied Advertising Strategies**

| Advertising Goals | Implied Advertising Strategy |
|---|---|
| 1. Familiarize consumers with Amelia Eternal | |
| a. Amelia Eternal is a direct-sales company offering makeup and household products | A. Describe Amelia Eternal as direct-sales company of household and cosmetic products. |
| | B. Describe Amelia Eternal as a relation between consumers and representatives. |
| | C. Use product sampling to facilitate representative welcome to consumer homes. |
| b. Amelia Eternal is committed to consumer satisfaction and service. | D. Describe product quality and guarantee of satisfaction. |
| | E. Describe products as effective yet harmless and guarantee of satisfaction. |
| | B. Describe Amelia Eternal as a relation between consumers and representatives. |
| 2. Bring specific Amelia Eternal products to the attention of consumers. | F. Describe Amelia Eternal product lines in performance terms. |
| | G. Describe specific individual Amelia Eternal brand items in performance terms. |
| | C. Use product promotion to facilitate representative welcome in consumer homes. |
| 3. Recruit superior sales representatives. | H. Idealize the sales representative and her job. |
| | B. Describe Amelia Eternal as a relation between consumers and representatives. |
| | I. Create separate recruitment advertising to identify prospective sales representatives. |

Morgan Harris and Henry Litt. It then lists advertising strategies implied by each of the goals.

As Roenfeld introduced this chart, he made the following comments: "The first thing that we do is to establish what we want our advertising to accomplish. Now, in our discussions, three goals have emerged: You have emphasized that advertising should describe the company, familiarize the consumer with the company's products, and help you recruit high-potential representatives.

"Of course, implicit in all of these goals is the fundamental objective of increasing sales. We understand that. But in stating these nonsales advertising goals, we are really talking in a kind of verbal shorthand: We are saying that sales will increase if more consumers know about Amelia Eternal; and we are saying that sales will increase if more consumers know how good Amelia Eternal products are; and we are saying that sales will increase if Amelia Eternal has more and better sales representatives.

"The next problem is to begin to develop some notions about what advertising can convey to consumers to achieve the goals that we have set. It may not be possible, incidentally, to create advertising that will increase consumer knowledge about Amelia Eternal *and* about its products *and* help you recruit better representatives.

"We have to be very clear in our thinking about this. It's easy to load a lot of ideas into advertising and end up confusing the consumer. Another important issue is whether our advertising merely has to make consumers and potential sales representatives aware of Amelia Eternal and its products, or whether it must correct misapprehensions about them. The research that we showed ten days ago is especially helpful in this connection.

Finally, depending upon what consumers already know, as revealed by the research, we have to develop some points of view about the sequence in which information is directed toward them. If, for example, no one has ever heard of Amelia Eternal we might be well advised to describe what the company is before going into too much advertising about its products.

"With all of this as kind of background, we can begin to think about the best advertising strategy for Amelia Eternal with all of these considerations–goals, consumer knowledge, and the best way to sequence information–firmly in mind.

"As you remember from our original presentation, we think of advertising strategy as a simple statement of the idea that we would like to convey to consumers in our advertising. It is the strongest idea that we can develop about our product or service. It is the single idea that most clearly and compellingly differentiates our product or service both as an entity in its own right and relative to its competition. Sometimes there are only one or two things that we can conceivably say about a particular product or service that will present it in a favorable light. Sometimes there are a lot of things that might be said.

"Whatever the case in the particular situation, we must analyze the available strategies and see which one seems to hold the greatest potential. As this chart shows, there are a lot of ways that we might proceed for Amelia Eternal, and I want to discuss them in considerable detail. Your problem is complicated because Amelia Eternal is three things at once: a unique distribution system; a unique customer relationship; and two quite different kinds of products, with different lines of products, with different names and all. Usually, we can take distribution and customer relations more or less for granted, but in this case they form a unique part of what your company is.

"Before I get into the strategies, are there any questions?"

There were no questions. It was quite obvious from the expressions on the faces of the Amelia Eternal people that what they had heard so far was not quite what they had expected. Some of those in the room, notably Amelia Litt, Edgar Fontaine, and Angela Haswell had somewhat disturbed looks, as if they did not fully understand what had just been said. Roenfeld thought quickly about retracing some of his steps and reexplaining what he had been saying; but his quick appraisal of the audience indicated that Morgan Harris, Henry Litt, and Stanton Thornton had a good understanding and he decided to plunge ahead rather than risk letting their minds wander.

He referred to his exhibit chart and pointed out that the first goal, the familiarization of consumers with Amelia Eternal, could be broken down into two parts: letting consumers know that Amelia Eternal is a direct-sales company and/or telling them that Amelia Eternal had specific policies that guarantee consumer satisfaction and service.

"There are three ways, at least, to convey to consumers that Amelia Eternal is a direct-sales company," continued Roenfeld. "We can simply describe the company: that is, tell the consumers that we have representatives that call on them in their homes and that sell household and makeup products. The research certainly indicates a need to do this. This is the simplest and most direct statement we can make about the company. Properly executed, such advertising will create knowledge about, and favorable attitudes toward, Amelia Eternal. It should help your sales representatives gain access to households they have not previously called upon. Incidentally, the research finding about representative grooming is a worry in any advertising that presents the representatives. We don't want to suggest beautifully groomed representatives unless the representatives are at least somewhat attractive. We believe some immediate thought should be given to spiffing up the way the women turn themselves out, advertising or no.

"But we can take this description of the company one step further. We can give consumers a reason for wanting to welcome the Amelia Eternal representative. Under strategy *A*, we simply inform them about who we are. Under strategy *B*, we try to motivate them to welcome the sales representative. In this approach, we would try to idealize the relationship between the sales representatives and the consumer. The representative would be presented as a potential confidant, a helper in attaining personal beauty and ease of household maintenance. This should work well for the representatives, but only if you're certain that the average representative can deliver the kind of relationship that we portray. This is certainly what Miss Amelia talks about in the annual sales meetings. But we're concerned with the research findings about representative grooming and that the representatives don't know or present their product lines with as much authority as they might.

Only 20 percent of the sales representatives were characterized in the research as very knowledgeable about their products. The research indicates that the representatives are perceived as friendly and pleasant and helpful. But the only reason for adopting an advertising strategy that projects the relationship between the consumer and the sales representative is to provide a basis for selling the products of your company. We don't want to suggest all this warmth and friendliness if it just generates coffee klatches—we want it to lead directly to sales. And the only way it can is if the sales representatives are knowledgeable enough about their products to exploit the consumer receptivity such an advertising strategy should create.

"We could even carry this approach one step further. Advertising could be created to pave the way for promotional items to be delivered by the sales representatives into consumer homes. For example, you might create a twenty-five-cent trial size of Super Power Safe Detergent that would be sold by the sales representatives. Or you might offer an Eternal fragrance sample for $1.00, or whatever. These sample sizes should always be of products of wide appeal and proven sales-generating power. Such a promotion would have only one basic objective, and that is to broaden sales-force coverage of consumers. As such, it is totally different in effect from the limited promotions you run through the *Success.* In each instance, the consumer would be motivated to welcome the sales representative because of the attractive bargain that the sales representative offers.

This strategy (*C*) would not be the basis of a continuing advertising campaign, of course. More likely, you would only want to develop such a promotion once or twice a year in order to give the sales representatives a nudge in calling on consumers who they have never called upon before or on consumers they call upon only infrequently. Thus, this is a strategy that might be invoked jointly with another, longer-term strategy. Once again, as with any strategy that is designed to help the representative to gain access to new customers, the more attractive the sales representatives appear in terms of grooming and the more knowledgeable they are about Amelia Eternal products, the better.

"There is an alternative way in which to familiarize consumers with the company. Instead of describing the company or what it does, under this alternative we would convey what the company stands for. Amelia Eternal is committed to customer satisfaction and service. Attaining consumer understanding of the company in these terms might be achieved by an advertising strategy (*D*) that stresses the basic *quality* of Amelia Eternal products and the guarantee of complete satisfaction that backs them up. Alternatively, an advertising strategy (*E*) might be adopted that stresses the inherent *nature* of Amelia Eternal products—the fact that they are totally effective yet are also guaranteed to be totally harmless.

"Frankly, we are not especially interested in either of these strategies. We present them because they reflect two ways in which Amelia Eternal is unique. But it is difficult to develop executions of this kind of strategy without getting into advertising that is either of the brag-and-boast variety or that seems to be technical and heavy handed. In addition, although your products are of especially high quality and are particularly effective, yet totally benign, consumers do not like the suggestion that the products they are already using are not of high quality, effective, and benign. Thus, advertising that is based on such strategies often has credibility problems.

"Strategy *B* may also, as indicated on the chart, be executed to stress consumer satisfaction and service, rather than simply to idealize the customer–sales-representative relationship. But we think the customer-representative relationship is strongest when it primarily reflects warmth, friendship, and help, rather than abstract qualities like satisfaction and service. In any event, it would probably be impossible to execute strategy *B* without suggesting a degree of satisfaction and service; we simply believe that overemphasis on these qualities would not make the strongest advertising for Amelia Eternal.

"The second objective that we have talked about might be called the build-the-product approach or build-the-brand. The notion here is that if, through advertising, we can make the consumer want Amelia Eternal products enough, the work of the sales representatives will be greatly facilitated. The more the consumer wants a particular brand or product, so the argument goes, the easier it will be to gain access to the homes of potential new customers, and the easier it will be to coax more sales from current Amelia Eternal customers.

"We would think of this as a kind of typical packaged-goods approach to consumer marketing. Its strength is that it focuses on what your company has to sell: that is, it makes your brands and products the heroes and overcomes the current dependence upon the sales representatives to do all the selling. This approach can be implemented through either of two advertising strategies. First, we can develop advertising that describes your several lines of products and describes the performance standards they meet. This approach (Strategy *F*) would emphasize the breadth of the Amelia Eternal product assortments as well as the general qualities of those specific assortments that sets them apart from the competition.

"A second strategy (*G*) for product selling would be to select and promote three, four, or five individual products that are now among your leading items or that represent, in your judgment, products of outstanding sales potential. This is traditional brand advertising. In its favor is the fact that it can support individual products of proven or assumed sales potential on their specific merits. It can be argued that this kind of advertising leaves the rest of your lines unsupported; but this is not a change from the current situation and there are, after all, still the sales representatives whose responsibility it is to push all of the products in the line.

"The major shortcoming of the brand-product approach is that it ignores your unique distribution system and the potential relationship between customers and sales representatives that it represents. Your brands and products, whatever their competitive merit and strength, are not presented in the same competitive arena as are other brands and products. This characteristic reflects both the fundamental shortcoming of Amelia Eternal marketing and its overwhelming strength. We wonder whether it is really possible to ignore or downplay this unique characteristic in your advertising.

"The second problem with the brand-product approach is that your merchandise lines are so very long. We believe that you are well advised to consider the Keltner, Boudreau, and Gordon recommendation that your lines be shortened. But even if you were to drop half of the products that you now offer, your product lines would still be very long and complicated. If the lines are advertised as entities, the advertising executions must stick to generalities and are likely, we fear, to be inherently bland. If you adopt the brand-advertising approach, you are likely, we suspect, to shortchange the lines and cause consumer disinterest in the bulk of the individual products that you offer.

"Regardless of our reservations about product-based advertising strategies, we are reluctant, as you will shortly see, to recommend against them once and for all.

"Strategy *C*—the product sampling strategy—is also well adapted to a product-based advertising strategy. It would probably work especially well under the brand-advertising variant, but it could also enhance the impact of a line-advertising approach. It would still have the basic purpose of making representative access easier but would, under product-advertising strategies, provide a product-sampling based extension of the product based strategic approach on a periodic basis—say once or twice a year.

"We want to come back to this topic of brand-product advertising and its relation to your unique sales-representative system of distribution. But, before we do this, I would like to spend just a minute or two talking about the final objective that you wish to set for Amelia Eternal advertising—that is, how it can facilitate the recruiting of superior sales representatives.

"As you can see from the chart, we believe there are three advertising strategies that might be employed to help the recruiting of superior representatives. In the first place, strategy *H* would create advertising that idealizes the sales representative and her job. Such advertising would be not unlike that executed under strategy *B*, except that it would emphasize the sales representative for herself rather than the relationship that she develops with her customers. It might also be used as a basis of advertising similar to that created under strategy *A*, simply describing the Amelia Eternal system, or under strategy *D*, describing Amelia Eternal products in terms of the satisfaction they bring. In fact, any advertising created under strategies that emphasize the representative's relation to the consumer is likely to idealize the sales representatives, at least to some extent. Strategy *H* would simply lead to advertising in which the primary emphasis was on the sales representative.

"One important thing to keep in mind about the advertising objective of recruiting superior sales representatives is that its geographic emphasis will probably differ from advertising created with the other two objectives in mind. That is to say that if we advertise to increase consumer awareness of Amelia Eternal's distribution system (strategy *A*) or its products (strategy *D*), we would be inclined to spend the bulk of the advertising dollars in geographic areas where the sales-representative system is strong and where customer coverage is not weak. This would mean geographic emphasis in the western area certainly, probably in parts of West Central, and possibly in a few markets in the Northeast and the South. But, if the objective of the advertising is to help recruit superior sales representatives (*H*), we would want broader geographic coverage, wouldn't we? We would be advertising in markets where customer coverage is not particularly strong and where there is good sales-expansion potential if superior sales representatives are recruited and trained.

"If all of this is right, it suggests that strategy *H* might not be the best strategy to boost Amelia Eternal sales in those geographic areas where the company is now underrepresented. Better perhaps to look upon the recruitment of sales representatives as a separate problem and to adopt strategy *I*. If we were to create advertising whose sole purpose was to identify new sales representatives, it could be carried on independently of other Amelia Eternal programs. And such advertising could be coordinated with local recruiting and training activities, while you develop specific programs to broaden and strengthen your sales-represenitive cadre. So, as you will shortly see, we will recommend that Amelia Eternal treat its third advertising objective as a separate problem, with a separate advertising strategy and, consequently, a separate advertising campaign.

"Now, before we have a general discussion about all this, I would like to briefly outline the agency's conclusions and recommendations. As I do this, I'll be referring to the second chart (reproduced here as Exhibit 4-11).

"We view the Amelia Eternal marketing problem to be twofold. First, there is the problem of generating more sales in those areas in which current sales-representative

**EXHIBIT 4-11**
**Advertising Strategy Recommendations for Amelia Eternal Company**

| Market Condition | Recommended Strategy or Strategy Sequence |
|---|---|
| 1. Established markets | B. Amelia Eternal relationship<br>or<br>G. Brand Development<br>Market test to determine whether B or G generates greater sales response.<br>↓<br>C. Occasional advertised promotions |
| 2. Underdeveloped markets | I. Recruitment advertising<br>↓<br>A. Amelia Eternal System Introduction<br>↓<br>B. Or G strategy based on market tests in established markets<br>↓<br>C. Occasional advertised promotions. |

coverage is strong. This is not, in our opinion, a regional problem, but a market-by-market problem. There are strong Amelia Eternal markets in the Northeast, the South and the West Central. We believe that either strategy *B* or strategy *G* is best adapted to improving sales in such relatively developed markets. We don't know which of these strategies is likely to be more sales productive; and we believe that each should be developed into advertising and that this advertising should be market tested.

"As you strengthen your sales-representative force in markets that are not now sufficiently well covered, you should utilize advertising that is based on strategy *I*. At some point, as these markets are developed, you will want to let consumers know what Amelia Eternal is and does and thus help your newly recruited and strengthened sales-representative force gain a sales base. Under this set of market conditions, we would imagine that advertising created under strategy *A* would be ideal and that it would continue until the market becomes sufficiently mature to sustain advertising under either strategy *B* or *G*.

"Finally, there would, occasionally, be an opportunity to stimulate the entire Amelia Eternal process in the mature Amelia Eternal markets, with an advertised product promotion, following advertising strategy *C*."

At the end of his formal presentation, August Roenfeld sat down and said nothing at all. He smiled a little, almost tentatively, obviously expecting that someone in the Amelia Eternal Company group would immediately pick up the ball and respond to the long and carefully thought-out explication of advertising strategy that he had made.

No one said anything.

Three minutes passed as the various Amelia Eternal employees assumed various aspects. At first most of them looked either thoughtful or just confused. Then they began to look at each other, as if to stimulate someone else to start talking. Everyone looked at Henry Litt for a bit, but it soon became obvious that he had no intention of saying anything, refusing eye contact with anyone in the room. He stared resolutely away from everyone, first at the oak conference table top and then at the ceiling.

Morgan Harris looked at Stanton Thornton, expectantly; and Stanton Thornton, ignoring Morgan Harris's glance, looked at Amelia Litt, expectantly. Amelia Litt simply looked confused.

Finally, August Roenfeld, with obvious effort said, softly and rather slowly, "Well, we've given you a real lot to chew over here this morning. Maybe you'd all like to think about it and then sit down with us for a discussion in a day or two."

"But, Mr. Roenfeld, we can't do everything that you're suggesting," said Amelia Litt. "It's too complicated and how will we know we're right? You want us to advertise in five totally different ways. I just think we ought to tell Mrs. Consumer that she can always depend upon the quality of the products that our girls sell, that they're nice and friendly, and that they come door to door; and that our products never hurt anyone or damage their possessions; and that we're a wonderful company to work for. Don't you agree, Henry?"

Amelia's outburst seemed to jar Henry Litt out of what had become almost a trance. He looked up and down the table quickly and then said, "I'll be darned if I know what we should do. What do you think, Morgan?"

"I don't know what to think, Henry. I want to think about this, and then I want to sit down with the agency again and talk it through with them. I'll say this, though, Augie, you've learned a lot about our business, and you've given our problems a lot of thought, and I think you've done a good job, and we'll be back to you one way or another, and pretty quickly."

On this note, the meeting disbanded and the representatives of the advertising agency returned to New York.

As events transpired, there was no second meeting between the agency and Amelia Litt representatives to discuss the Roenfeld strategy presentation. As Morgan Harris thought about the agency presentation, he concluded that it was time for Stanton Thornton to start acting like an advertising manager rather than an interested bystander. He invited Thornton to join him in his office a few days later.

"What do you conclude about the agency presentation, Stanton?" Harris asked.

"I think they're all wet about the relationship between the sales representatives and the customer, Morgan," responded Thornton. "I think we should be advertising the product lines and not trying to build brands. I would use advertising that describes the company in underdeveloped markets, while we bring the sales-representatives structure up to snuff. And then I'd depend upon product-line advertising."

"What did you think of what Miss Amelia said?" inquired Harris. "In the meeting, I mean."

"I thought she missed the point, Morgan," said Thornton. "I mean, the trick is to decide what you're going to say in advertising and then say it. And she just listed all the different things that we might say in the advertising, didn't she? I don't think she likes the whole process or even really understands it. I don't want to be critical, you understand, but gosh, it must have discouraged the agency that her comments were the only substantial ones that anyone from Amelia Eternal made after that meeting."

Harris got a little red in the face after these remarks. "As far as I know, *you* were in the room, Stanton. And you are the advertising manager of this company—at least that's what we hired you for. Anyway, I think the agency did a very good job the other day. I think they made two points that we have to resolve. The first point is that this company faces different marketing situations in different markets and that advertising must be developed to respond to those different marketing situations. The second point is that we have to decide whether our sales representatives are strong enough or can be made strong enough to carry this company. If they are, then they become the benefit that we sell the customer. If they aren't, then our products are the benefit we sell the customers.

"I can't think of any way to find out which of those approaches are stronger except maybe test marketing, as they suggested. If I were you, I'd get ahold of one of our sales-meeting videotapes and see how Amelia describes what this company is, *before* you decide that we should ignore the relationship of the sales representative to the consumer in the advertising.

"Anyway, you know now where I stand. I want you to think it all through; and then I want you to write a letter to the agency giving them direction and indicating what agenda we should follow the next time we get together. No more Roman circus meetings, Stanton. Let's decide on a company viewpoint and figure out how we can get this thing moving forward.

"And, uh, Stanton, let me see that letter you write to the agency, before you send it, okay? And don't worry about the Litts. I'll handle them. They just want us to do something about this, but they're not going to tell us what to do. That's our job, and don't you forget it either, Stanton."

## *QUESTIONS FOR CASE 4*

1. Write the letter that Stanton Thornton has been asked to send to Aesop and Acton in response to August Roenfeld's advertising strategy presentation. Be sure to cover the following points in your answer:
   a. Do the marketing situations facing the Amelia Eternal Company differ from market to market? What is the implication for advertising strategy?
   b. Are the sales representatives important to Amelia Eternal? In what ways? What implications does the sales-representative system have for Amelia Eternal advertising strategy?
   c. Discuss the differences between the product-line-advertising strategy (*F*) and the brand-advertising strategy (*G*) and indicate which seems best for Amelia Eternal.
   d. Discuss means of choosing between a product-line strategy (*F*) and a brand-advertising strategy (*G*), other than executive judgment.
   e. Address the question of a market test of a product- (*F*) or brand- (*G*) advertising strategy versus a market test of the sales-representative–customer-relationship advertising strategy (*B*). Are there other ways of choosing between these strategies than test marketing? What are they?
   f. Under what conditions should the advertising strategy that calls for a description of the Amelia Eternal Company (*A*) be used? Is this strategy really a viable alternative for the company? Why?
   g. Under what conditions should the advertising strategy that calls for advertised product promotions (*C*) be used by the Amelia Eternal Company? Must this strategy be limited to one or two uses a year? Why or why not?
   h. Under what conditions should the advertising strategy that calls for a separate recruitment campaign (*I*) be used by the Amelia Eternal Company? The agency does not recommend this strategy for mature markets. Do you agree or disagree?
   i. Do you agree with the agency proposal or not? Why? If you disagree, what do you propose for Amelia Eternal?

2. Roenfeld presented an agency position on advertising strategy for Amelia Eternal without giving a preview to the Amelia Eternal employees who were to attend the meeting. Is this wise? What advantage might have been gained if Roenfeld had given Stanton Thornton a preview of his presentation? What are the potential disadvantages of such a preview presentation?

3. What items should appear on the agenda of the next meeting between Amelia Eternal and Aesop and Acton? Who should attend this meeting?

4. August Roenfeld proposed a total of nine advertising strategies to accomplish three Amelia Eternal advertising goals. Are these the only strategies that might have been put forward to accomplish these goals? If your answer is "yes", explain why you believe this to be so. If your answer is "no", give one or two alternative strategies for each of the advertising goals.

5. The Aesop and Acton recommendations suggest that various advertising strategies be followed in sequence. Would it not be possible to implement, simultaneously, an advertising strategy to accomplish each of Amelia Eternal's goals? That is, why shouldn't Amelia Eternal try to accomplish each of its advertising goals at the same time?

6. Aesop and Acton states that the purpose of an advertising strategy is to identify the single differentiating thought that is to be communicated in advertising. Yet Aesop

and Acton recommends that Amelia Eternal use five advertising strategies at one time or another. Has the agency contradicted itself? Discuss.

7. Should Amelia Eternal be a national advertiser? Under what circumstances? Why?

8. Was the marketing research presented in the Exhibits of help in formulating and evaluating advertising strategies? Explain your answer.

# Case 5

# The Analysis of Advertisements*

Advertisements fall into fairly clear categories that reflect the specific techniques used in their creation. Advertisements can therefore be classified according to these creative techniques. If such a classification does not tell a great deal about how individual advertisements came into being, it does provide an objective basis for looking at advertisements and a convenient way of thinking about them. In addition, such a classification clarifies the kinds of advertising elements that have been chosen by the individual advertising creator to present a particular advertising message and to deal with a particular problem.

Two general categories of advertising techniques can be identified as *advertising appeals* and *advertising executions.* An *advertising appeal* is the device by which specific consumer response is solicited in the advertisement. An *advertising execution* is the way in which the specific appeal is transformed into advertising.

The appeal can be said to form the underlying content of the advertisement, and the execution the way in which that content is presented. Advertising appeals and executions are usually independent of each other; that is, a particular appeal can be executed in a variety of ways and a particular means of execution can be applied to a variety of advertising appeals. Advertising appeals tend to adapt themselves to all media, whereas some kinds of executional devices are more adaptable to some media than to others.

* The text of this case is excerpted from: William M. Weilbacher, *Advertising* (New York: Macmillan, 1979), pp. 215-255.

## *ADVERTISING APPEALS*

An advertising appeal is the device by which specific consumer response is solicited in the advertisement. The following list identifies thirteen major kinds of advertising appeals in three groupings:

1. Product- or service-related appeals.
   A. Product/service features appeals.
   B. Product/service competitive advantage appeals.
   C. Favorable product/service price appeals.
   D. News about product/service appeals.
   E. Product/service popularity appeals.
   F. Generic appeals.
2. Consumer-related appeals.
   A. Consumer service appeals.
   B. Consumer saving through use appeals.
   C. Consumer self-enhancement appeals.
   D. Fear appeals.
   E. Subsidized product trial appeals.
3. Nonconsumer or nonproduct/service-related appeals.
   A. Corporate citizenship appeals.
   B. Investor appeals.

### *Product or Service-related Appeals*

A product- or service-related appeal focuses on the product or service and its characteristics; some aspect or feature of the product or service is described in some way. The benefit to the consumer is secondary or implied, rather than overt. The appeal is specific to a particular product or service, not to the category as a whole. There are six kinds of appeals that relate directly to the specific product or service.

***Product/Service Feature.*** Advertisements that use a product- or service-feature appeal describe the product or service and its dominant feature(s) or characteristic(s). Various assertions are made about its capabilities. Straight product/service-feature advertising makes no comparisons with competitors, does not feature price, tells no news about the product/service, and does not cite the popularity of the product/service as a reason for its excellence. Product/service-appeal advertisements say that the consumer should consider purchase of the product or service because its specific feature or features make it a good product or service.

***Product/Service Competitive Advantage.*** In this type of advertising appeal, an explicit reference is made to competitive products or services, often by name; and the product/service advantage depends upon performance that is superior to competition on some particular criterion or criteria.

***Favorable Product/Service Price.*** This type of advertising appeal makes a direct offer of products/services at a particular price, or at a reduced price. A great deal of retail advertising falls into this category; it includes all retail advertising in which some sort of price offer is dominant in the advertisement. The distinguishing characteristic of price-appeal advertising is that it constitutes the most important appeal in the advertisement.

Many advertisements give price information but make it subsidiary to some other advertising appeal such as product features, for example. Such subsidiary price emphasis does not, of course, serve as a basis for a price-appeal classification.

*News about Product/Service.* The key aspect of the product/service news-appeal category is that news about the product dominates the advertising. Frequently the news is that the product/service is totally new. Or the news may be that an established product/service has been modified or improved in some way. Whatever the product or service characteristics or qualities may be, its advertisements are classified in the news-about-product-appeal category if the word *new* or *product news* is dominant.

*Product/Service Popularity.* A product/service-popularity appeal asserts that the product or service is widely used, that it is a popular brand, or that it is number one in its category. Whatever the exact form of the appeal, its thrust is that the reader or viewer of the advertisement should use the product because of its widespread acceptability or popularity.

*Generic.* A final classification of product/service-appeal advertising is the generic appeal. In such advertising, a product or service category is promoted for its own sake; but individual makes or brands of the product are not singled out. Such advertising may be sponsored by a dominant producer in the field, or it may be sponsored by an industry association representing all or many of the individual producers.

## *Consumer-related Appeals*

Consumer-related appeals describe the product/service in terms of overt consumer benefits. The primary emphasis is on what the product/service will do *for the consumer* rather than merely on what the product/service is or does. In many advertisements the difference between product/service-related and consumer-related appeals is subtle. In the product/service-related appeal, the product or service is described in its own terms and the main thrust of the advertisement centers on the product/service rather than upon consumer use or satisfaction. If the product/service stands alone in the advertisement, the advertisement is likely to depend upon a product-related appeal. If the product/service is subordinated to the effect that it has with or upon consumers, the advertisement is likely to depend upon a consumer-related appeal.

*Consumer Service.* Advertisements that offer a consumer service instruct the consumer how the product or service may be used to advantage. Consumer service appeals either tell the consumer what to do with the product/service or explain the various ways in which the product/service may be used for satisfaction.

Ingredient products often use consumer-service appeals in advertising. Many food products, for example, are used solely or primarily as ingredients in the preparation of food recipes. Advertising for such products often provides new recipes of presumed interest to the homemaker that include, incidentally, the use of the particular ingredient product sponsoring the advertisement.

*Consumer Savings through Use.* Consumer-savings-through-use appeals offer the consumer an opportunity to save money or reduce expense through the use of the product/service. Product/service price is not emphasized in advertisements that fall into this category. How expensive or inexpensive the product/service may be is not at issue in such advertisements. The point is that regardless of what the product/service costs, its use will result in the reduction of some other, often continuing, consumer expense.

***Self-Enhancement.*** Advertisements in this category suggest that the use of a particular product/service will enhance or improve some inherent quality of the user—make him or her in some way more attractive, or more involving, or more beautiful. Advertisements for cosmetics, clothing, and products that may be conspicuously consumed frequently use such self-enhancement appeals. Advertisements of this classification suggest that the products deliver value not because of their utilitarian features or benefits, but rather because of their ability to add a personal dimension to the user that he or she had not previously had.

***Fear.*** Fear appeals are used in advertising to portray a threatening situation that can be resolved through product/service use. The advertising shows some sort of fear-provoking circumstances, such as the possibility of physical danger or economic loss, and then suggests that the advertised product or service will remove the basis of fear, if the product is purchased and used.

***Subsidized Product Trial.*** When this appeal is used, the advertiser offers a free sample, a price reduction, or some other purchase incentive to encourage consumer use or trial. The purpose of this advertising is to facilitate consumer use of the sponsoring product or service, and the appeal is based directly on the premise that extra sales will ultimately be generated because of such product trial.

### *Nonconsumer or Nonproduct Service-related Appeals*

All of the advertising appeals reviewed up to this point have presented some aspect of the product or service per se, or some product or service effect upon or relative to the consumer. We now turn to appeals that are based either upon the good works of corporations or nonprofit organizations, or upon some sort of generalized corporate or organizational activity for which public support is desired.

***Corporate Citizenship.*** Advertisements based upon corporate-citizenship appeals seek to portray a company or corporation in some sort of favorable light or to present its side of a controversial issue.

Corporate-citizenship advertising always has a distinct purpose, no matter how benign it may appear on the surface. The company sponsoring the advertising wants to present a description of its responsible good works to the public so as to foster favorable public attitudes and/or actions in support of the company.

***Investor Solicitation.*** A second type of corporate advertising appeals to the investment community. The purpose of such advertising is to suggest to the potential investor that the company is well managed, profitable, and/or makes a wide range of well-known products. Such advertising proceeds on the assumption that well-known companies and corporations with good reputations are likely to be at least as attractive to investors as those companies that they have never heard of and know nothing about.

## *ADVERTISING EXECUTIONS*

Advertising appeals are the devices used to solicit consumer response. As you have seen, these appeals cover a broad spectrum; most of those in common use fit into the thirteen categories described. But to identify the appeal that is used in an advertisement is not to describe an advertisement. An advertising appeal may be transformed or executed in a variety of ways. That is to say there are a variety of advertising executions that the creator of advertisements may use as he prepares an advertisement.

We identify twelve kinds of advertising executions in the following pages.

1. Factual: Straightforward Statement.
2. Factual: Provocative or Intriguing Statement.
3. Product Comparison.
4. Demonstration.
5. Still Life.
6. Metaphor: Imputed Qualities.
7. Dramatization.
8. Spokesperson.
9. Testimonial.
10. Borrowed Interest.
11. Humor.
12. Hyperbole.

### *Factual: Straightforward Statement*

Almost all advertising presents facts about the product, corporation, or service that is being advertised. Thus, it might be said that a factual classification is no classification at all, but rather a description of all advertising. But some advertisements depend upon a more or less straightforward presentation of the product facts without much embellishment or dependence upon other executional devices.

### *Factual: Provocative or Intriguing Statement*

In some cases the straightforward factual statement is embellished with a provocative or intriguing assertion about the product or service. Sometimes, it is difficult to distinguish between the straightforward statement and the provocative statement.

### *Product Comparison*

In the product comparison technique, two or more products are compared; and the sponsoring brand is found to be superior on one or more counts. In some instances, the product comparison is made against generic competition; that is, brand names are not mentioned. But often names are named.

### *Demonstration*

In demonstration advertising, the product characteristics and/or competitive strengths take center stage. The product may be demonstrated in actual use or it may be shown in some sort of staged demonstration, designed to highlight or emphasize a particular competitive strength.

### *Still Life*

In still-life advertising, the center of attention is on a stark representation of the product or some visual reminder or representation of the product. In these advertisements, the product or its representation stands alone, usually with very short supporting copy. The advertisement seems to be either a visual poster in behalf of the product or, in the case of television, a simple camera exercise in the photographing of the product from a variety of vantage points.

### *Metaphor*

An advertising metaphor suggests the effect or experience of product use through an association of the product with a person or an atmosphere that is neither directly nor literally related to the product. Sometimes it is hard to distinguish the metaphor technique from the still-life technique. The key is in what the central picture or image represents. If it is a literal representation of the product or service, it is an example of still-life. If the picture seeks to associate the product or service with a person or concept that does not literally represent or denote the product, it is an example of metaphor.

### *Dramatization*

In the dramatization technique, some sort of drama is created around the product or service. Inevitably, the product or service stars in the drama. The use of dramatization, of course, is especially well suited to television; and a good share of all the messages on television involve dramatization.

Dramatization customarily takes one of two forms: straight drama or problem-solution drama. In straight drama the product or service is shown in a real-life setting, at work, doing whatever it is intended to do. The problem that the product/service solves is more or less implicit and is usually not an inherent part of the dramatic presentation. In problem-solution drama, a particular problem is presented and the advertised product is then introduced as a solution to that problem. The overt theme of the advertisement is how the product-hero solves a particular problem.

### *Spokesperson*

In the spokesperson technique, a person speaks in behalf of the product. The person may be an unknown or a celebrity. Often the spokesperson technique is combined with some other technique such as factual product comparison or product demonstration. In such situations, one must judge whether the dominant effect of the commercial depends upon the spokesperson's presentation and personality or whether the dominant effect derives from another technique.

Usually, when a celebrity spokesperson is used, the dominant technique is the use of the spokesperson. But it is not necessary for the spokesperson in a commercial to be a celebrity for the commercial to epitomize the spokesperson technique. Unknown people may also serve as spokespersons.

### *Testimonial*

The testimonial technique is similar to the spokesperson technique in that a person, or persons, speaks in behalf of the product. In the latter technique, the spokesperson merely presents the product in the advertising, making descriptive and assertive statements about it. The testimonial technique also presents someone who describes the product, but the person's assertions about it are based on his or her own experience. The person explicitly testifies in behalf of the product.

### *Borrowed Interest*

In the borrowed-interest technique, the focal point of the advertisement has high inherent interest but has no direct relation to the advertised product. Classic uses of borrowed interest are to show young children, voluptuous ladies, or appealing puppies to entice viewer attention to the advertisement. But borrowed interest is not limited to such obvious attention attracters.

### *Humor*

Humor is used in advertising to attract attention and to direct attention to the product in a pointed and involving way. Of all the executional techniques used in advertising, probably none is more controversial than humor. This controversy springs from two main factors. First, one man's humor is not necessarily another's. Humor in advertising may not amuse many of the people exposed to it, hilarious as it may seem to the creator. Second, and probably more serious, is that humor may overwhelm the selling message, drawing attention and interest to itself and away from the product advertised.

Exhibits 5-1 through 5-23 present a series of advertisements based upon a variety of advertising appeals and advertising executions. They have been chosen both to reflect this variety and to show superior contemporary advertising practice.

## *QUESTIONS FOR CASE 5*

1. Analyze the advertisements presented in Exhibits 5-1 through 5-23. Tell what advertising appeal is used in each advertisement.
2. Analyze the advertisements presented in Exhibits 5-1 through 5-23. Tell what advertising execution is used in each advertisement.
3. What advertising strategy underlies each of the advertisements presented in Exhibits 5-1 through 5-23? That is, state the key thought about the advertised product or service that each advertisement attempts to present to its intended audience. What audience action is implied by this key thought about the advertised product or service?
4. Choose five advertisements from these exhibits that you think would be most commercially effective. Tell why you believe each advertisement you choose would be commercially effective.

## EXHIBIT 5-1

## Aqua Fresh Tooth Paste Advertisement, reproduced with the permission of Beecham Products

MOTHER: As long as I'm paying your dental bills you're using a fluoride toothpaste.

DAUGHTER: But mother, I need this gel for fresh breath.

STORE CLERK: Ladies! Try new double protection Aqua-fresh.

ANNCR: (VO) Aqua-fresh gives you all the cavity fighting fluoride of the leading paste...

...and all the breath freshener of the leading gel ...

(SFX: ZAAP) ...concentrated in one toothpaste.

STORE CLERK: So...?
MOTHER: Well, if it has all my fluoride...
DAUGHTER: And all my breath freshener...

MOTHER & DAUGHTER: We'll take the Aqua-fresh.

ANNCR: (VO) New double protection Aqua-fresh. Fights cavities and freshens breath.

EXHIBIT 5-2

Armstrong Solarian Tile Advertisement, reproduced with the permission of Armstrong Cork Co.

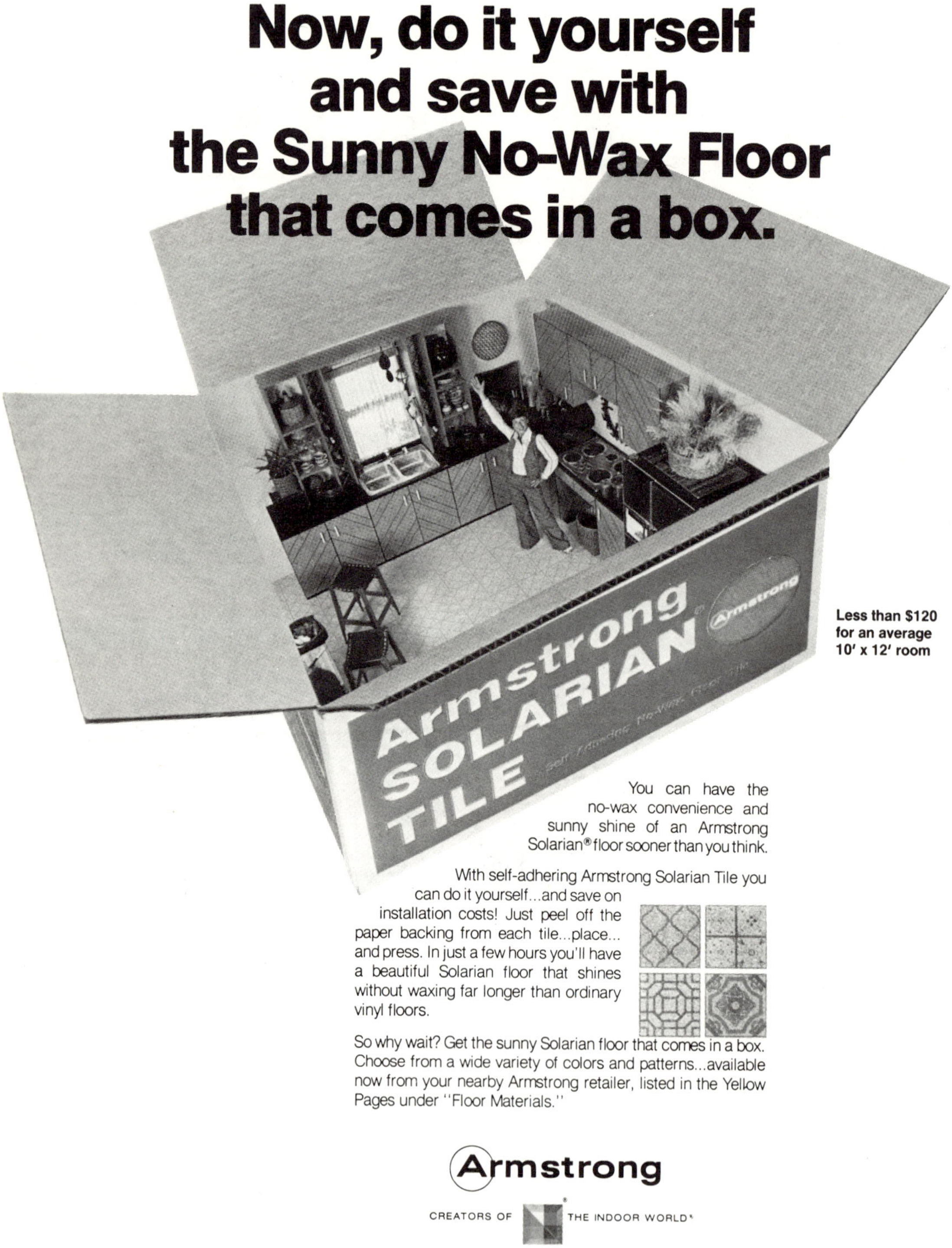

**EXHIBIT 5–3**

**BMW Automobile Advertisement, reproduced with the permission of BMW of North America, Inc.**

The extraordinary road-holding ability of the BMW 320i is graphically illustrated, above, travelling at a high speed through turn #6 at the Sears Point International race course. Note: as the BMW goes into the turn, the unique angling of the MacPherson front struts reduces the lean of the inside front wheel, while the outside front wheel remains vertical; inside and outside rear wheels remain vertical due to semi-trailing arm design in the rear.

Like all honeymoons, the first few months of new car ownership are generally a period of adjustment.

A time when man accommodates himself to the idiosyncracies of his machine—those little quirks of engineering that make the act of driving something to be endured rather than something to be enjoyed.

Perhaps because of our long involvement in motor racing—where such an antagonistic relationship would be intolerable—we at the Bavarian Motor Works in Munich, Germany, take a wholly different approach to building automobiles.

An approach that begins with the seemingly unusual engineering concept that, above all, a car must function as one with its driver.

YOU DRIVE A BMW.
IT DOES NOT DRIVE YOU.

When you drive the BMW 320i for the first time, you will experience a curious sensation of being part of the car itself—an exhilarating feeling of control.

When you press the accelerator, the two-liter, K-Jetronic, fuel-injected engine responds without lag.

Its four-speed transmission (automatic is available) slips precisely into each gear.

The suspension—independent on all four wheels—is quick and clean through the corners.

Its rack and pinion steering is sharp and accurate.

Careful study has been made of the critical relationship between seat location, visual position, steering wheel angle, pedals and controls.

Instruments are clearly visible and illuminated at night by an optically beneficial orange light; controls are readily accessible.

Pedal direction and pedal pressure have been carefully balanced to reduce fatigue and facilitate effortless gear changing.

All told, the only major adjustment you will have to make as the new owner of a BMW 320i is that you will have no adjustments to make at all.

If the thought of owning such a car intrigues you, call us anytime, toll-free, at 800-243-6000 (Conn. 1-800-882-6500) and we'll arrange a thorough test drive for you at your convenience.

**THE ULTIMATE DRIVING MACHINE.**

Bavarian Motor Works, Munich, Germany.

**EXHIBIT 5-4**
**British Airways Advertisement, reproduced with the permission of British Airways**

# "Our Dollar Stretcher™ Holidays will stretch your money all over Britain."

Being Britain's own airline, we know better than anyone where all the right places—and the best values—are in Britain. (You needn't take our word for it. Just our tours, including 2-week versions of these plums if you like.) Here, a small sample, courtesy of Robert Morley.

**OUR FLY/DRIVE HOLIDAY,**
**7 DAYS $175.** An Avis car for two, unlimited mileage (petrol on you) and 7 days to see Britain—from the lush green valleys of Wales to the lochs and highlands of Scotland.

**OUR FAMOUS LONDON SHOW TOUR,**
**8 NIGHTS $195.** The *original.* And still an unbeatable value. Theatre-area hotel, private bath, Continental breakfast, 3 hit shows, Lucullan banquet evening, and much more.

**OUR LONDON/PARIS SHOW TOUR,**
**7 NIGHTS $245.** 4 nights in London, 3 in Paris. Fine hotels with private bath and Continental breakfast, 2 theatre tickets in each city—including the Folies Bergère in Paris—and a cruise down the Seine.

**OUR DOLLAR STRETCHER FARES.**
**NEW YORK TO LONDON FROM $309 ROUNDTRIP.**
Combine our Dollar Stretcher Fares—available from all 9 gateway cities—with a Dollar Stretcher Holiday, and you'll find no one gives you better value for your money. With my space running out, and possibly my air, I suggest you send for our tell-all brochures. Or call your Travel Agent or British Airways (check your telephone directory for our local toll-free number).

Tour prices are per person, based on double occupancy, and lower before April 1. Book our Dollar Stretcher Fare 21 days in advance, stay 7 to 60 days. Airfare subject to change.

## EXHIBIT 5-5

**Calgon Hold Advertisement, reproduced with the permission of Beecham Products**

(SFX: PHONE)
1st WOMAN: 4 more hours. (COUGHS) I'll never make it.

2nd WOMAN: Excuse me Honey, I'll have to put you on hold.

You too. Here...take Hold!

1st WOMAN: (COUGHS) ...got cough drops.

2nd WOMAN: Hold is better than leading cough drops.

(VO) Read the label.
1st WOMAN: (VO) ...has dextromethorphan.

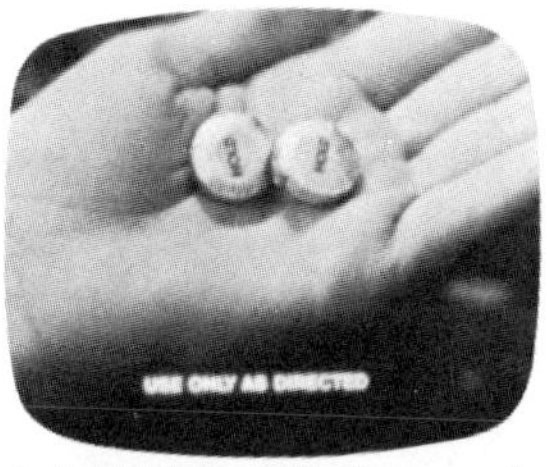


2nd WOMAN: (VO) Real cough medicine.
1st WOMAN: (VO) Two Hold work up to 4 hours!

(SFX: PHONE)

Hey! Hardly coughed and my shift is over.

2nd WOMAN: Why get hung up ... over a cough.
1st WOMAN: Yeah.

ANNCR: (VO) New Hold 4 hour cough suppressant.

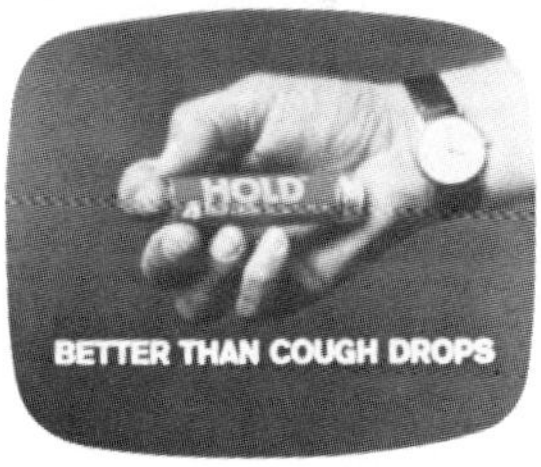


Better than cough drops.

## EXHIBIT 5-6

**Dime Savings Bank Advertisement, reproduced with the permission of Dime Savings Bank of New York**

1. CHORUS SINGS: The road to riches starts at the Dime.

2. ANNCR: The road to riches starts at the Dime,

3. where daily compounding of your regular deposits can spell out a brighter tomorrow for you.

4. Get started now towards your goal of future financial security

5. with a savings account, saving certificate,

6. or tax deferred retirement plan at the Dime.

7. The Dime Savings Bank of New York.

8. CHORUS SINGS: The road to riches

9. starts at the Dime.

## EXHIBIT 5-7

## Hellman's Real Mayonnaise Advertisement, reproduced with the permission of Best Foods, CPC International, Inc.

You can see the word mayonnaise on a lot of different jars...

but when you see the word "real"...

and the word "Hellmann's", you know that in the jar, there's a great-tasting mayonnaise...

because Hellmann's is always FRESH. Fresh when you spoon it...

Fresh when you spread it...

Fresh when you serve it.

No wonder Hellmann's is the best-selling mayonnaise in the whole country.

No wonder it wears – this blue ribbon!

Hellmann's! The great-tasting mayonnaise. Because it's always FRESH.

## EXHIBIT 5-8
**Hertz Rent-A-Car Advertisement, reproduced with the permission of The Hertz Corporation**

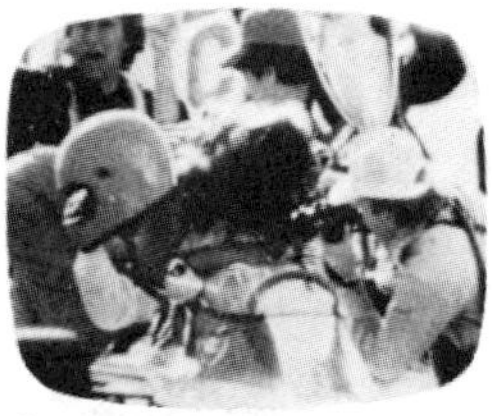

1. (MUSIC THROUGHOUT) SONG: Everybody...

2. Loves the winner.

3. Only the winner

4. can really make things happen.

5. O.J. SIMPSON: (OC) In rent-a-cars, Hertz is the winner. Number <u>One.</u> With more cars.

6. More locations.

7. (VO) More people to help you.

8. (OC) And more services to speed you on your way.

9. (VO) No wonder the presidents of over 90% of America's top 500 companies...

10. (OC) carry Hertz cards.

11. SONG: Everybody

12. loves the winner... Everybody...

## EXHIBIT 5-9
## Lipton Flavored Teas Advertisement, reproduced with the permission of Thomas J. Lipton, Incorporated

WOMAN: Want a little spice in your life?

Well I got it with Lipton's new Flavored Teas.

With Orange & Spice...

I feel I'm in a tropical paradise.

Lipton's Mint Flavor...

really refreshes me.

Lemon & Spice...

cheers me up.

Lipton Cinnamon...

makes me feel slightly devilish.

And Lipton Black Rum Flavor...

whisks me down to the islands.

Try 'em hot

or iced.

And spice up your life, with Lipton's new Flavored Teas.

EXHIBIT 5-10

Master Lock Advertisement, reproduced with the permission of Master Lock Co.

1. At a rifle range outside Los Angeles...

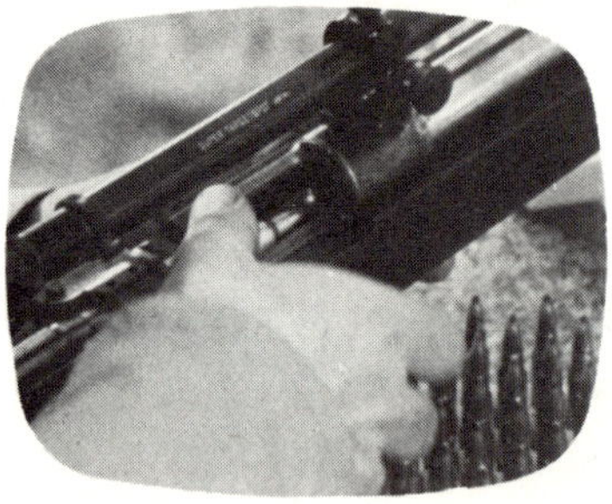

2. a high-powered 30 caliber rifle...

3. was fired at a distance of 40 yards...

4. to try and open this Master padlock.

5. The Master Lock Model No. 15 sustained considerable damage...

6. but did not open.

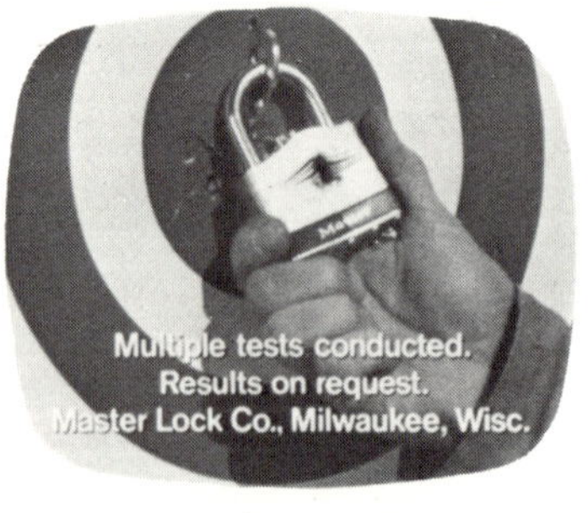


7. Repeat: did not open.

8. Whatever your protection needs, there's a Master Lock ready to do the job.

**EXHIBIT 5-11**
**Mazola Margarine Advertisement, reproduced with the permission of Best Foods, CPC International, Inc.**

(SFX: BIRDS)

TENAYA: Dolls made of corn husks.

We made them for the children,

after a good harvest of maize...

what you call corn.

Today Mazola Margarine knows all about the goodness of corn.

That's why Mazola Margarine...is made from corn oil goodness.

Mazola Margarine has no cholesterol... naturally.

And Mazola always tastes naturally fresh and delicious.

(SILENT)

Remember Mazola Margarine.

It gets goodness from maize.

**EXHIBIT 5-12**

**McDonald's Advertisement, reproduced with the permission of McDonald's Corporation**

**EXHIBIT 5-13**

**Mrs. Paul's Supreme Light Batter Fish Fillets Advertisement, reproduced with the permission of Mrs. Paul's Kitchens, Inc.**

**EXHIBIT 5-14**
**Neutrogena Body Oil Advertisement, reproduced with the permission of Neutrogena Corporation**

## EXHIBIT 5-15

### Pharmaceutical Manufacturers Association Advertisement, reproduced with the permission of the Pharmaceutical Manufacturers Association

(Operating room; door bursts open)

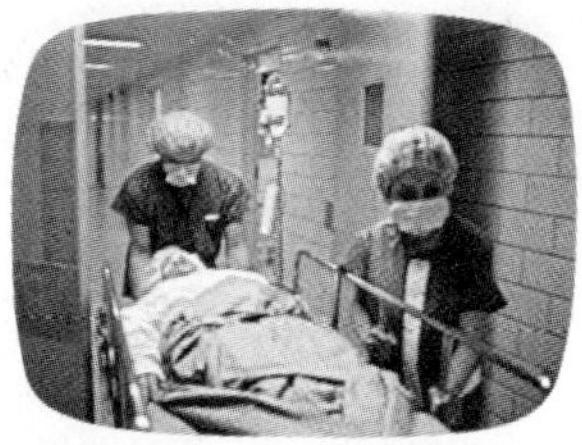

Gallstone surgery...average hospital stay... ten days. Cost to Americans last year...one billion dollars. (Cash register ring)

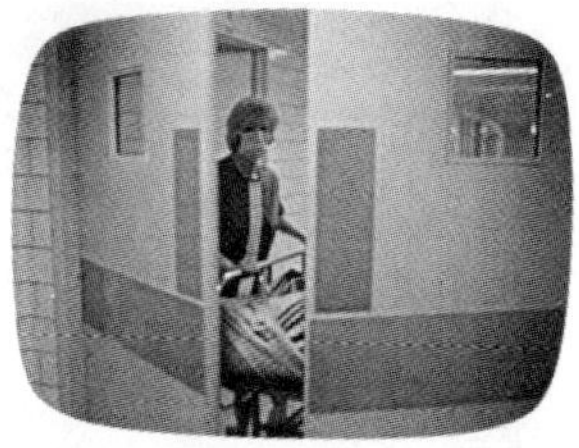

(Door bursts open)

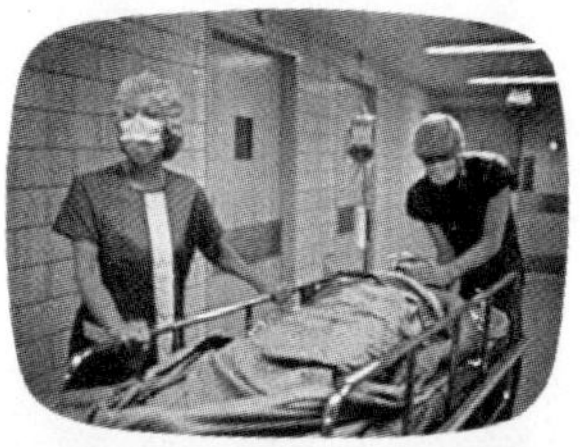

Ulcer surgery...average stay...fourteen days. Cost to Americans last year...over seven hundred and fifty million dollars. (Cash register ring)

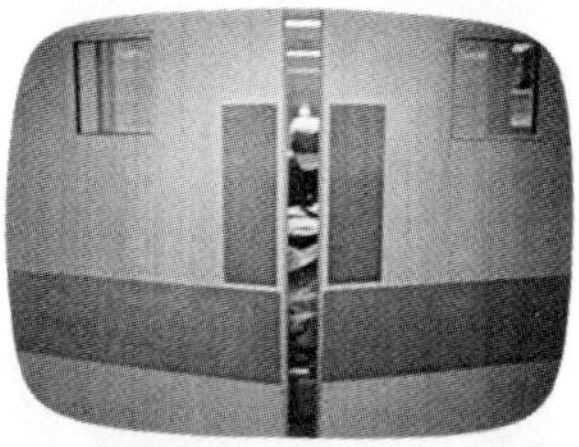

(Door bursts open)

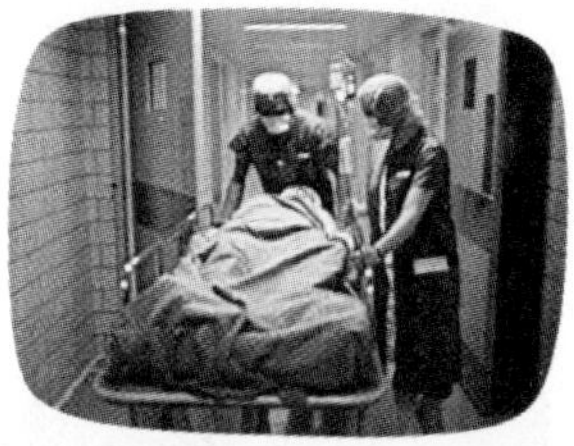

Coronary artery by-pass...an estimated seventy thousand operations last year. Cost...some seven hundred million dollars. (Cash register ring)

Suppose there were drugs to eliminate...or at least reduce the need for these operations. Think of the money we'd all save.

(Heartbeat sound) Think of the time away from work and family we'd save.

Well, some of those drugs do exist. Some are ready now. Others are being tested.

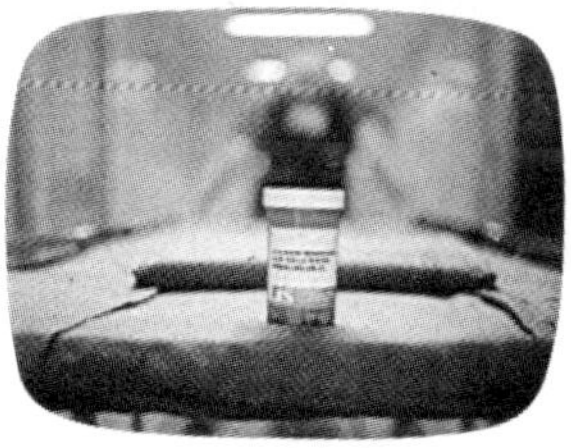

Pharmaceutical research is vital...

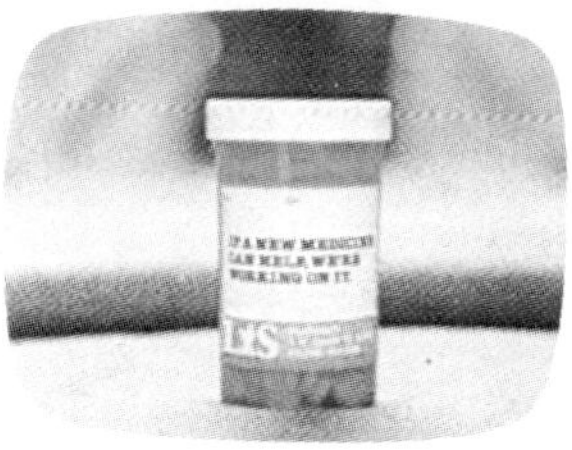

because one of the best ways to keep costs down is to keep the money-saving medicines coming.

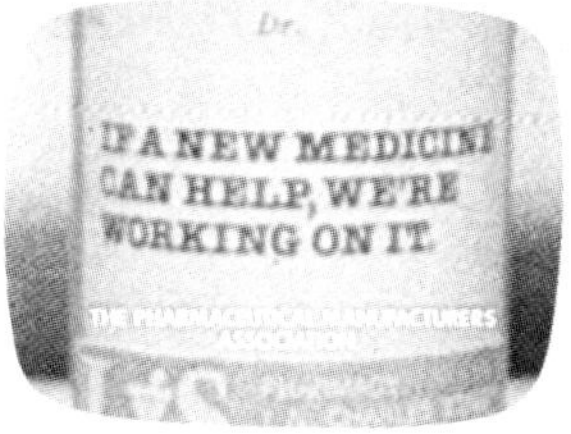


A message from the Pharmaceutical Manufacturers Association. If a new medicine can help, we're working on it.

## EXHIBIT 5-16
## Polaroid OneStep Camera Advertisement, reproduced with the permission of Polaroid Corporation

Jim: Polaroid's OneStep is the world's simplest camera; even a woman can use it.

Mariette: How'd that go again?

Jim: I thought that would get her attention.

Mariette: I could have 1000 women here in half an hour.

Jim: You never focus, you just point it and press the button.

Mariette: All marching with big signs.

Jim: The sharp clear color develops in minutes. You're beautiful when you're angry.

Mariette: You had a nice career there for a while.

Jim: Get the OneStep; this may be my final appeal.

EXHIBIT 5-17

Sandoz Pharmaceuticals Advertisement, reproduced with the permission of Sandoz, Inc.

# YOU SAID IT—WE DID IT

From your suggestions have come many SANDOZ service innovations.

| YOUR SUGGESTION | | OUR SERVICE |
|---|---|---|
| • Give us simpler dating of products for easier inventory control. | 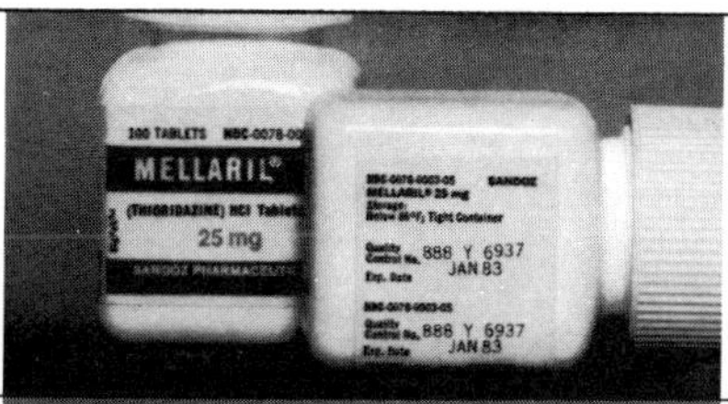  | • Semi-annual dating (January or July) for our products with a shelf life of over two years. |
| • Make returns as easy and as economical as possible. | 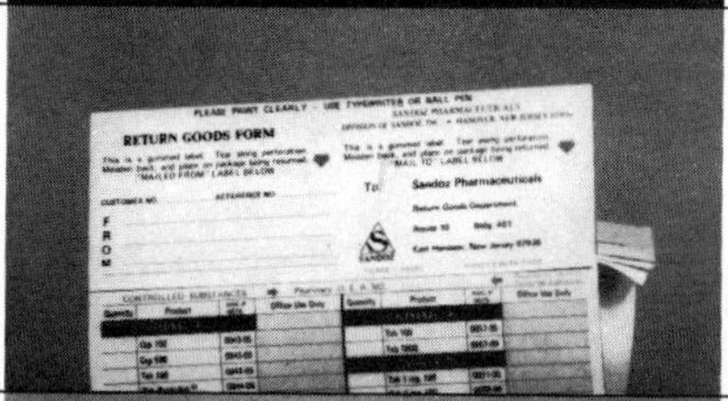  | • Revised return-goods policy with computerized system to speed up service. |
| • Make label-reading easier. | 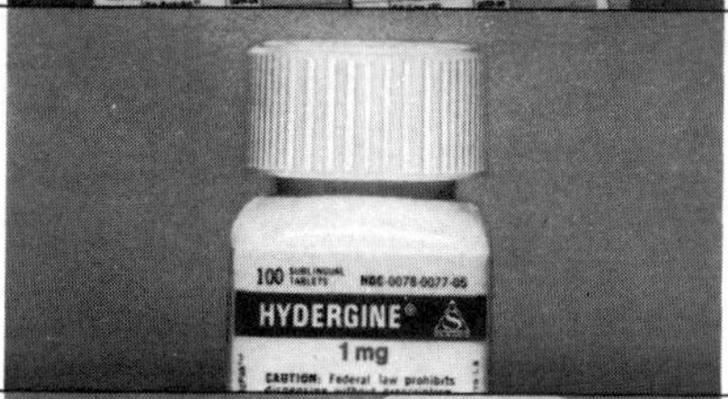  | • Greater label clarity with "up-front" identification of strength and product form. |
| • Help keep children from getting into medications. | 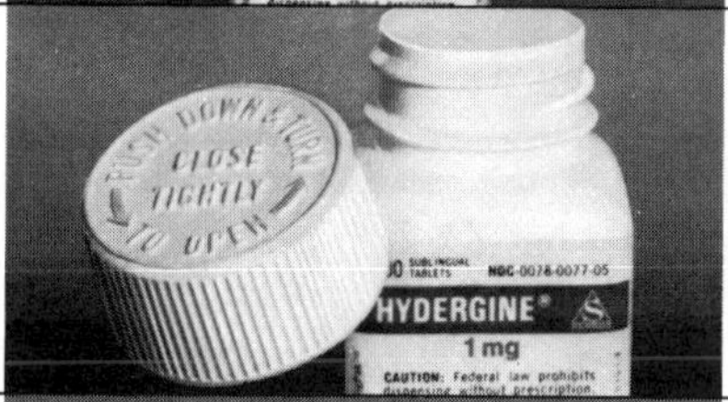  | • Child-resistant closures on bottles of 100 for all products. |
| • Provide realistic liability coverage. | 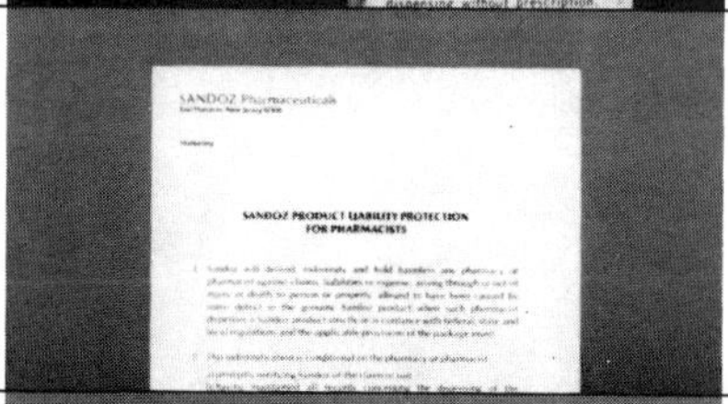  | • Comprehensive pharmacy liability policy. |
| • Give us visual aids in medical matters. |   | • A film library at the disposal of the pharmacist. |



SDZ 7-891

SANDOZ

SANDOZ PHARMACEUTICALS,
EAST HANOVER, NEW JERSEY 07936

WE SERVE YOU BETTER...BECAUSE WE LISTEN.

## EXHIBIT 5-18
**Santa Fe Industries Advertisement, reproduced with the permission of Santa Fe Industries, Inc.**

*The "Old Prospector" reports from Wall Street*

**PROSPECTOR:** Howdy!
**CABBIE:** I seen everything. What are you doin' on Wall Street?

**PROSPECTOR:** Gettin' the mornin' fix on gold. Maybe catch the security analysts' luncheon next Tuesday.
**CABBIE:** Better get your pants pressed. Listen if you're looking for Sutter's Mill, you make a left at the Brooklyn Bridge and you go west about 3.000 miles.

**PROSPECTOR:** Already been there.
**CABBIE:** Where ya from?
**PROSPECTOR:** Santa Fe Territory.

**CABBIE:** Nothin' doin', huh?

**PROSPECTOR:** (AGHAST) Nothin' doin'! Why it's big and boomin'! Santa Fe is into coal . . . oil . . . uranium . . . lumber. They got truck lines and pipelines . . . real estate and construction . . . and a main line to California and Texas.

**CABBIE:** Santa Fe? No kiddin'!

**PROSPECTOR:** Sales over 2 billion dollars.

**CABBIE:** Hey—What's their net income per common share?
**PROSPECTOR:** You thinking primary or fully diluted, Mister?
**CABBIE:** Fully diluted.

**PROSPECTOR:** Well, let's see now . . . Santa Fe Industries . . . net income per share . . . fully diluted . . . comes to . . .

EXHIBIT 5-19
Seagram's V. O. Advertisement, reproduced with the permission of Seagram Distillers Company

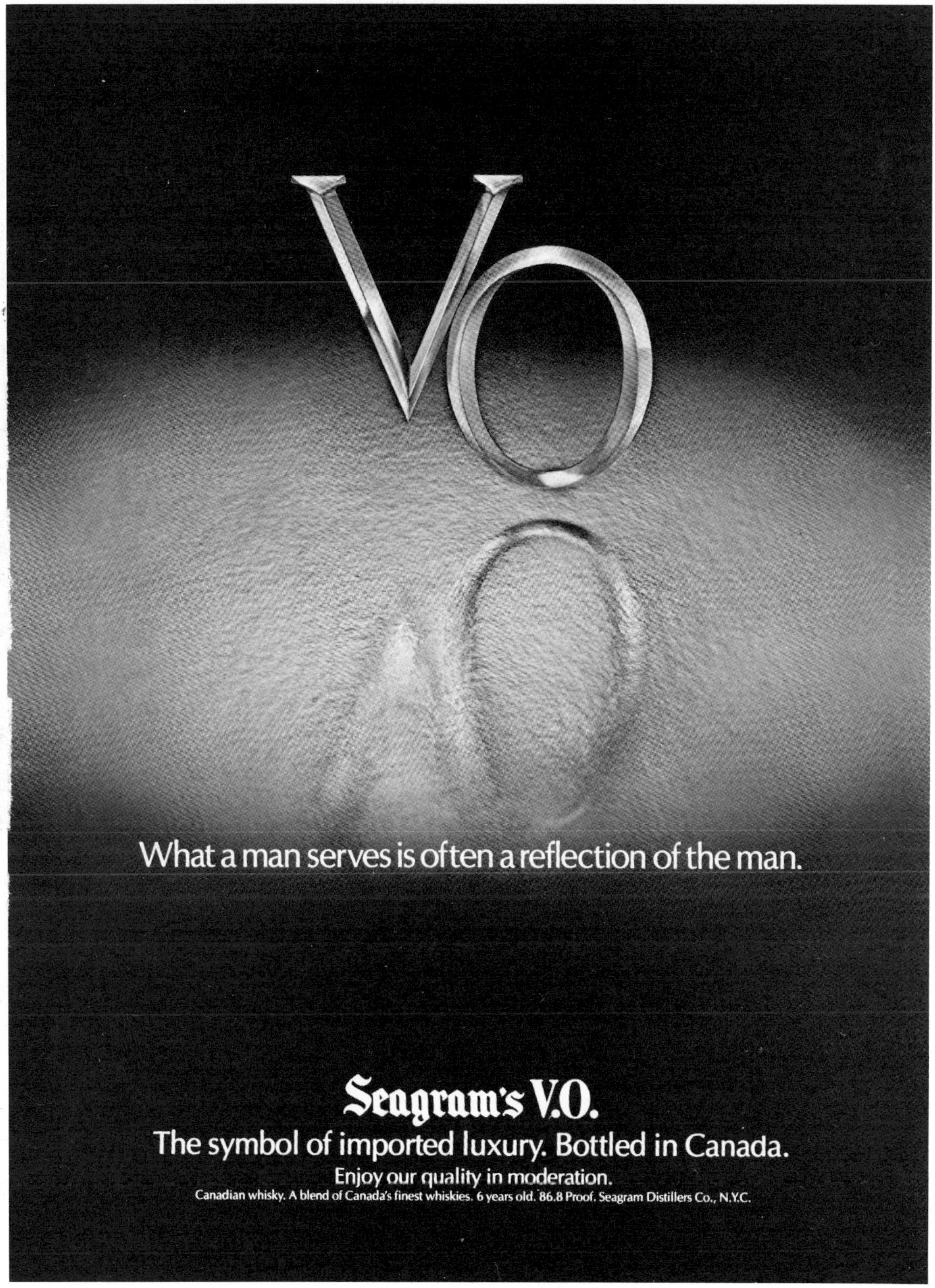

## EXHIBIT 5-20
## Sony Audio Tape Advertisement, reproduced with the permission of Sony Corporation of America

(MUSIC THROUGHOUT)

ANNCR: (VO) Sound has color.

That's why Sony is introducing

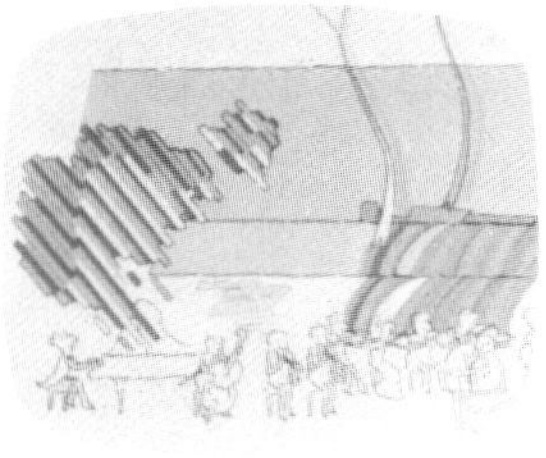

audio tape with Full Color Sound.

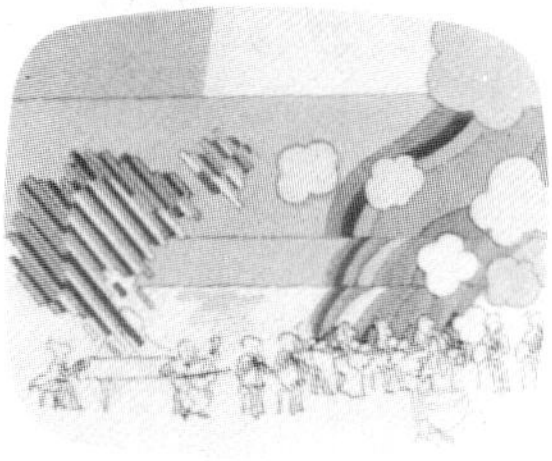

It can actually record more sound

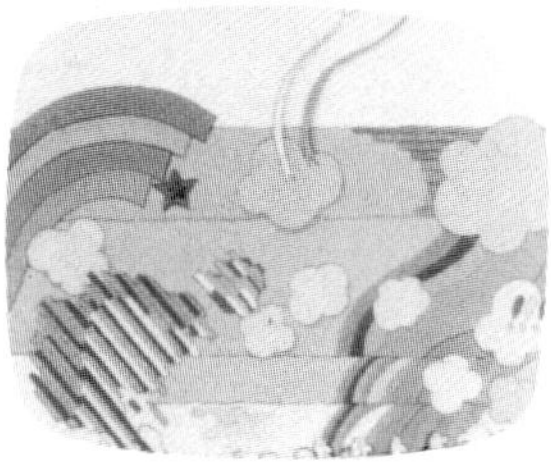

than you can hear...to reproduce

every shade of color that's in the sound itself.

(MUSIC ENDS)

Sound has color.

SFX: CLICK
(MUSIC UP)

Listen to it all on Sony tape,

with Full Color Sound.

## EXHIBIT 5-21

**Volkswagen Rabbit Advertisement, reproduced with the permission of Volkswagen of America, Inc.**

1. (MUSIC UNDER AND THROUGHOUT) INT: (VO) Sir, isn't that a Volkswagen Rabbit?

2. MAN: Sure is.
INT: (VO) But the roads aren't even plowed.

3. MAN: You're telling me?

4. (MUSIC)

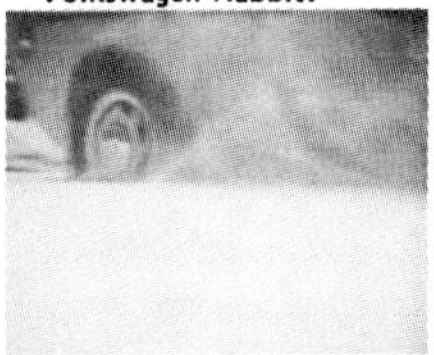

5. INT: (VO) That Rabbit sure goes through snow.

6. And you're not even using snow tires.

7. MAN: That's right. Got front wheel drive.

8. INT: (VO) So you're the man who drives the snowplow.

9. How long have you been doing that?

10. MAN: How long have there been Volkswagens?

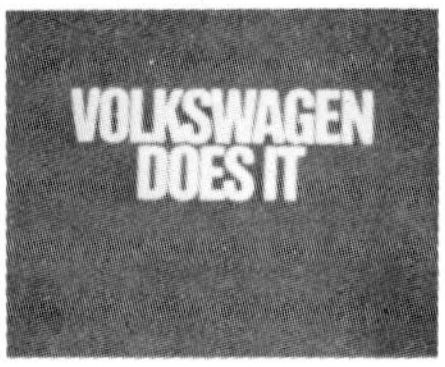


11. SINGERS: (VO) Volkswagen does it

12. (SILENT PAUSE) again!

## EXHIBIT 5-22
### Westinghouse Advertisement, reproduced with the permission of Westinghouse Electric Corporation

ANNCR: (VO) Products, once made in America,

now are coming into America from all over the world.

We've lost markets at home and overseas to nations

whose ability to produce more efficiently

has grown faster than our own. . .

Today Westinghouse has technology to help reverse that trend.

With manufacturing control systems and energy-efficient machinery

to help American industry win back our competitive edge.

Technology from Westinghouse. A powerful part of your life.

**EXHIBIT 5–23**

**White-Westinghouse Refrigerator Advertisement, reproduced with the permission of White-Westinghouse Appliance Company**

# Case 6

# Determining Advertising Media Strategy

## *MID AMERICAN AIRLINES ALLOCATES ADVERTISING FUNDS*

Mid American Airlines is the eighth largest airline in the United States. It was founded in 1922 by L. M., "Lorry," Freiquist, who was then twenty-four years old. Freiquist had been bitten by the aviation bug as a boy in the period after the Wright Brothers' first faltering flight. It was an exciting time for young Freiquist. He followed the progress of aviation with fascination, as the Wright Brothers themselves and other innovators made longer and longer flights in the constant drive toward improving airplanes. This small group made the dream of flying a reality in the years before World War I and captured the imagination of America, especially its youth and, in particular, Lorry Freiquist.

Freiquist enlisted in the Army Air Corps late in 1917, shortly after his nineteenth birthday. The air corps was not a branch of the service that was easy to enter. It was relatively small, and there were thousands of young men in the United States who had grown up in awe of flyers and flight and wanted—just as Freiquist did—nothing more than to sacrifice themselves for their country as a flyer. Freiquist was more persistent than most. He was bright and in superb physical condition; and he had the added advantage of a newspaper-editor father in Kansas City, Missouri, who was well-connected politically and well-connected in the air corps. So, Freiquist ended up in the air corps in 1918 with enough time to learn how to fly before the Armistice in November but not enough to actually get to France or engage in air combat.

Freiquist was a superb aviator. His army flight instruction transformed his adolescent love of flying into an addiction that shaped the entire course of his life. He stayed in the

Army Air Corps as long as he was able and was finally discharged in the summer of 1920, a seasoned pilot with 463 hours of flight to his credit. Other men had flown more hours but, between combat losses and training accidents of one kind or another, few of them had lived to tell the tale.

Returning to civilian life, Freiquist had only one interest—to find some commercial basis upon which he could continue to fly. Meanwhile, he worked off and on as an automobile mechanic and sometime-automobile-race driver on the dirt tracks of the Kansas City area. He saved as much money as he could—and tried to figure out how he could buy himself a surplus army Jenny so he could use it to make a living. Late in 1921 he met O. B. Dukes, aged twenty-one, who was as interested in flying as Freiquist but who had never flown and wanted to learn. Dukes had inherited about $20,000 from a recently deceased grandmother; and he was willing to invest this in a new flying company with Freiquist, if Freiquist would teach him to fly.

Their company was called the Dukes-Freiquist Aviation Company. A surplus army Jenny was immediately acquired. In the first year of the company's existence, Freiquist flew the Jenny in Kansas city and surrounding towns, making some money in sightseeing rides and some more from prize money and fees for stunt flying in the local air shows. By 1923 Dukes, also, had developed into a first-rate flyer, and the company acquired a second Jenny. The men branched out into synchronized flying exhibitions and simulated dog fights in air shows throughout the Midwest and Southwest.

In 1925 the Dukes-Freiquist Aviation Company solicited contracts for airmail flights between Kansas City and Houston and Kansas City and Dallas. Much of this mail flying was still done by the Army Air Corps, but Freiquist's air corps connections, as well as the undiminished influence of his father, paved the way to a contract award to D-FAC. It was at this time that the name of the company was changed, with some optimism, to Mid American Airlines.

Throughout the next several years, Mid American Airlines continued to add airmail contracts for routes connecting Texas and Kansas City. The equipment in the Mid American fleet was gradually upgraded and increased. By the early 1930s the company owned five aircraft, including a new, twin-engined Lockheed Electra that was used to carry a few passengers, as well as the mail, between Kansas City and Houston. In 1935 the company acquired a DC-1 from the new Douglas Aircraft Company for passenger service. By 1941 Mid American Airlines had a fleet of eight DC-3 aircraft and was firmly established as a passenger airline in the Southwest.

The company continued to operate throughout World War II; and in the post-war period acquired more routes, larger aircraft, and a solidified position as the leading passenger air carrier in the Southwest. In 1952, Mid American merged with a regional carrier in the Northeast called Northern Star Airlines. This airline had much the same kind of history as Mid-American, except that it had developed in Boston, and its route system connected Boston with cities in New York, Connecticut, Michigan, Ohio, and Pennsylvania. Northern Star had been founded by H. H., "Pop," Hutchenrider shortly after World War I. Hutchenrider had, by 1952, reached his seventieth year. He came to the reluctant conclusion that he would have to sell his airline, for three reasons.

First of all, he could no longer compete effectively with the developing East-West trunk carriers like American, United, and Trans-World. These other lines could offer service equal to that provided by Northern Star. But more important, these trunk lines went beyond Cleveland and Detroit and Buffalo: That is, their systems took passengers to Chicago, to the mid west and to the West Coast beyond. Because of their more extensive route structures, they tended to siphon off the cream of the long-haul business originating in eastern cities serviced by Northern Star. Hutchenrider knew that he would have to sell out to some airline that could offer the traveler a more extensive set of destinations from coast to coast.

In addition, Hutchenrider was seventy years old and failing. He had been a legend in the airline industry. It was said that he ran Northern Star out of his hat. He hired good people who were operationally oriented: fine pilots, superb mechanics, good ground-agent personnel. They ran his airline for him and he did everything else himself. There was no one to succeed him, because there was no one else who was either mentally or physically capable of doing the job that he did routinely. Nor had he ever taken the trouble to train a secretary, let alone a successor. At seventy, Hutchenrider knew that he was still capable of a day's work that would humble many men who were half his age; but he also knew that he had lost a step or two and that if he didn't sell soon, his airline would surely begin to collapse.

Finally, he was losing credibility with the investment community exactly when the airline industry was emerging from the hand-to-mouth, operationally oriented existence of the immediate post-war period. Air travel was on the verge of becoming a mammoth industry. Its capital needs were sizeable in 1952 and would soon become immense. There were not many bankers who could be counted upon to finance the expansion of a regional airline run by a seventy-year-old one-man-band, no matter what his past accomplishments and no matter what his personal vision of the future.

And so, in 1952, Hutchenrider approached Lorry Freiquist. Hutchenrider recognized that the Mid American route system would nicely complement his own, if it were possible to obtain permission from the Civil Aeronautics Board to fly routes that would connect the two systems. In addition, Hutchenrider believed that Lorry Freiquist was one of the few airline executives in the world that could understand Northern Star and take it over without destroying the airline.

CAB approved the Northern Star-Mid American merger in 1952 and in 1953 granted Mid American a series of routes that effectively melded the two airlines into a single system. At the time of the merger Freiquist was fifty-two and Dukes fifty. Both were in their prime, ready to take the Mid American system to whatever success it could sustain. Both men are still active in the airline management in 1980, although they have long since passed operational control on to others like President (and former MAA pilot) John Stuart and Executive Vice-President for Sales and Marketing, Thomas Eldridge. The long tenure of Freiquist and Dukes has left its mark on Mid American. It still reflects the interest and preoccupation of its founders in flying and flight operations as such. There is no formal marketing department in the airline. Marketing is equated with sales, and marketing decisions tend to be made by men and women who have moved up through the airline's sales organization.

MAA is divided into three geographic operating divisions. These divisions are based on flight operational needs and have no marketing rationale at all. In spite of its eighty-two-year-old chairman, its quaint organization, and a management almost totally unsophisticated in modern marketing concepts and methods, it is one of the best-run and most profitable airlines in America.

Exhibit 6-1 shows the Mid American system as it exists in 1980. The basic configuration is similar to the system that emerged after the Mid American–Northern Star merger in 1952. Some markets have been added in the intervening years, including Las Vegas, Phoenix, Tucson, and Denver. Other markets have been dropped. The relative importance

**EXHIBIT 6-1**
**The Mid American Route System, 1980**

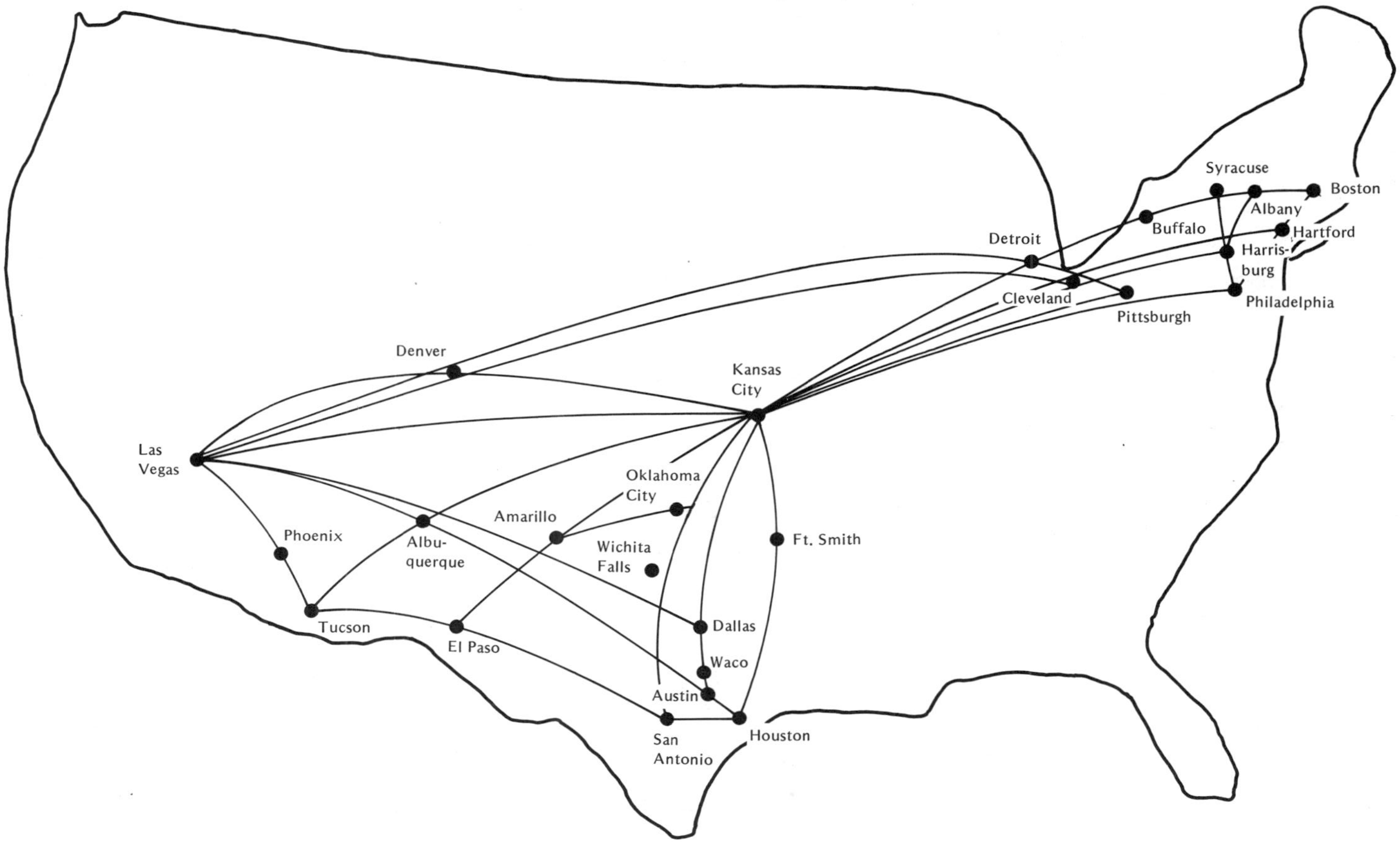

**EXHIBIT 6-2**
**Mid American Airlines Cities**

| Western Division | Eastern Division | Kansas City Division |
|---|---|---|
| Houston (headquarters) | Detroit (headquarters) | Kansas City (headquarters) |
| Las Vegas | Cleveland | |
| Phoenix | Pittsburgh | |
| Tucson | Buffalo/Niagara Falls | |
| El Paso | Syracuse | |
| Albuquerque | Harrisburg | |
| Denver | Albany/Schenectady/Troy | |
| Amarillo | Hartford/Springfield/Westfield | |
| Wichita Falls | Philadelphia | |
| Dallas/Ft. Worth | Boston | |
| Austin | | |
| Waco | | |
| Oklahoma City | | |
| Fort Smith | | |
| San Antonio | | |

of other markets and routes changed as the years passed and as other airlines grew competitively stronger or weaker in Mid American markets and over Mid American routes.

In 1980 Mid American serves a total of twenty-six markets. These markets are grouped into the three operating divisions that Exhibit 6-2 shows. Kansas City is the hub of the Mid American system. Most Mid American passengers connect in Kansas City whether they are flying to the northeast from the southwest, or vice versa. Mid American does operate a significant and increasing number of nonstop flights connecting cities like Boston and Detroit with Houston or Dallas or Las Vegas. But Kansas City is still the operational heart of the Mid American system, the site of the Mid American maintenance base, and a marketing center of importance to the whole airline. Mid American corporate headquarters is in Kansas City, as well as the staff for the Kansas City division.

In addition, there is a Western division (headquartered in Houston) that encompasses the original Mid American Airlines system, and an Eastern division (headquartered in Detroit) that is composed of the old Northern Star Airlines system. Each of these divisions is responsible for its own operations and for its own sales and marketing activities. The divisional operating and sales-marketing managers report to corporate directors of operations and sales-marketing. The relationships are shown in the Mid American Airlines organization chart in Exhibit 6-3.

Exhibit 6-4 ranks the twenty-six MAA markets in order of total airline emplanements. An emplanement is defined as one passenger boarding one commercially scheduled airline flight once. It reflects total air traffic but does not reflect the composition or quality of that traffic. An MAA "emplanement" in Houston may represent a passenger bound for Boston or for Dallas. Because of the distance and fare differential involved, the Boston passenger is considerably more important to MAA than the Dallas passenger.

The exhibit also shows Mid American emplanements in each of the markets that it serves and its share of total emplanements. Houston, for example, generated 109,854

**EXHIBIT 6–3**
**Mid American Airlines Organization Chart, January 1, 1980**

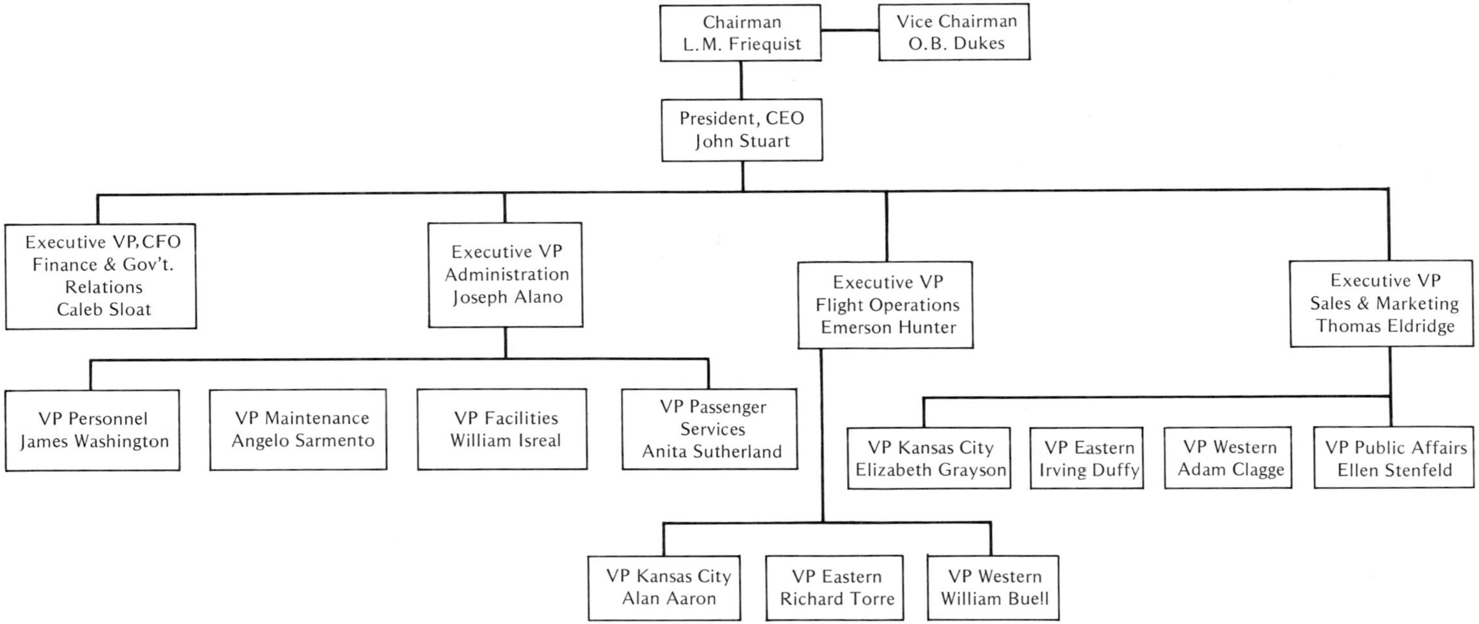

**EXHIBIT 6-4**
**Mid American Airlines Share of Total Monthly Commercial Airline Emplanements, 1980**

| Market | Total Monthly Emplanements | Mid American Airline Emplanements | MAA Share |
|---|---|---|---|
| Dallas/Ft. Worth | 802,749 | 87,543 | 10.9% |
| Denver | 738,692 | 69,448 | 9.4 |
| Boston | 621,832 | 34,926 | 5.6 |
| Detroit | 495,631 | 42,961 | 8.7 |
| Pittsburgh | 484,342 | 57,592 | 11.9 |
| Houston | 477,411 | 109,854 | 23.0 |
| Philadelphia | 418,433 | 32,135 | 7.7 |
| Las Vegas | 408,317 | 73,412 | 18.0 |
| Cleveland | 391,206 | 41,694 | 10.7 |
| Phoenix | 301,679 | 39,836 | 13.2 |
| Kansas City | 279,842 | 94,623 | 33.8 |
| Buffalo/Niagara Falls | 209,311 | 18,411 | 8.8 |
| Hartford/Springfield/Westfield | 176,482 | 11,831 | 6.7 |
| Albuquerque | 107,395 | 39,246 | 36.5 |
| Oklahoma City | 101,531 | 27,951 | 27.5 |
| San Antonio | 99,426 | 18,591 | 18.7 |
| Albany/Schenectady/Troy | 89,431 | 9,412 | 10.5 |
| Syracuse | 77,219 | 12,321 | 16.0 |
| Austin | 76,531 | 26,512 | 34.6 |
| Tucson | 42,351 | 13,824 | 32.7 |
| El Paso | 41,896 | 19,721 | 47.1 |
| Harrisburg | 34,876 | 6,543 | 18.8 |
| Fort Smith | 16,413 | 8,922 | 54.4 |
| Amarillo | 12,619 | 7,654 | 60.7 |
| Waco | 10,742 | 8,125 | 75.6 |
| Wichita Falls | 8,394 | 6,921 | 82.5 |

emplanements for MAA in the average month in 1980. This accounts for 23 percent of all monthly emplanements in the market.

Kansas City is a relatively less important market than Houston in terms of total emplanements. It generates 94,623 emplanements each month for MAA, and this total is about one third of all Kansas City passengers. Thus, one out of three passengers who board a commercial flight in Kansas City flies on Mid American Airlines.

Mid American tends to dominate emplanements in smaller Texas cities like Amarillo, Waco, and Wichita Falls, as well as in Fort Smith, Arkansas. The airline serves over half of those who emplane in these markets, but because the markets are so small, they have relatively slight significance to the overall operations of MAA.

The relative importance to MAA of each of its markets is revealed in Exhibit 6-5 which shows passenger revenue in each market for 1980. Kansas City is the top generator in the MAA system, and it delivered $166,674,000 to MAA in 1980. Six cities generated $40,000,000 or more in MAA revenue in 1980. These were Kansas City, Houston, Las Vegas, Denver, Boston, and Pittsburgh. Together, these six markets accounted for $525,150,000 in 1980, or 65 percent of total MAA revenues.

**EXHIBIT 6-5**
**Mid American Airlines: Passenger Revenue by Market, 1980**

| Market | Revenue (000 omitted) |
|---|---|
| Dallas/Ft. Worth | $ 39,345 |
| Denver | 47,142 |
| Boston | 46,957 |
| Detroit | 32,281 |
| Pittsburgh | 41,367 |
| Houston | 119,208 |
| Philadelphia | 28,505 |
| Las Vegas | 103,802 |
| Cleveland | 29,204 |
| Phoenix | 20,676 |
| Kansas City | 166,674 |
| Buffalo/Niagara Falls | 17,543 |
| Hartford/Springfield/Westfield | 13,214 |
| Albuquerque | 21,868 |
| Oklahoma City | 18,183 |
| San Antonio | 6,421 |
| Albany/Schenectady/Troy | 8,721 |
| Syracuse | 4,567 |
| Austin | 4,926 |
| Tucson | 3,854 |
| El Paso | 4,756 |
| Harrisburg | 5,093 |
| Fort Smith | 4,426 |
| Amarillo | 5,031 |
| Waco | 4,925 |
| Wichita Falls | 3,801 |
| | $802,490 |

The Civil Aeronautics Board has authorized Mid American Airlines to operate a total of 343 routes involving pairs of the twenty-six markets that constitute its system. It is possible to travel on Mid American Airlines from any city in its system to any other city. Some city pairings, however, generate a considerable amount of revenue and others generate little or no revenue at all. This is because in the case of some city pairings other airlines offer better service (nonstop as contrasted with two- or three-stop MAA service, for example, or service at more convenient times or with greater frequency). For example, it is possible to travel from Philadelphia to Denver on MAA, but almost no one does. United Airlines offers three nonstop flights a day from Philadelphia to Denver, while MAA offers two-stop service twice a day, one flight departing at 7:15 A.M., and the second flight departing at 4:15 P.M. MAA has never developed the Philadelphia-Denver route because it does not have nonstop authority to do so, and because United has aggressively developed this franchise. However, in other city pairings—Detroit to Las Vegas is a good example—MAA has the dominant position.

Every airline flies a relatively small number or routes that generate a disproportionate amount of revenue, and Mid American is no exception. These heavy revenue routes tend to be relatively longer ones connecting cities in which the airline has developed a relatively strong competitive position. In the case of Mid American, 21 city pairs generated $415,772,000 in 1980, or 51.8 percent of the airline's total revenue. These 21 city pairs are listed in Exhibit 6-6. As the exhibit reveals, 20 of the 21 top revenue-producing city pairs for MAA involve either Kansas City, Las Vegas, or Houston.

Each city pair represents two separate routes. That is, the city pair Las Vegas-Kansas City is represented by Las Vegas to Kansas City flights and by Kansas City to Las Vegas flights. Thus the 21 city pairs that generate the most revenue for MAA represent a total of 42 distinct routes. The emplanements originating in one city in a pair are never exactly equal to the emplanements originating in the other. For example, emplanements in Las Vegas for Kansas City in a given year are not exactly equal to the emplanements in Kansas City for Las Vegas. Traffic between the cities in a pair is normally about equal, but each route in the city pair must be analyzed separately if one is to know exactly how much traffic (and revenue) each city in the pair generates.

The 42 routes that are represented by the 21 top revenue-generating MAA city pairs are shown in Exhibit 6-7. This exhibit also shows the share of market emplanements accounted for by each route, the annual number of passengers boarded on Mid American on each route, and the revenue that is generated by these passenger emplanements.

Las Vegas-Kansas City accounted for 151,896 MAA passengers in 1980 and developed $19,746,000 in revenue for the airline. Kansas City-Las Vegas generated fewer passengers (141,036) and, accordingly, contributed less revenue ($18,335,000). The fares on which such revenue figures are based are an average of first class, tourist, and other

**EXHIBIT 6-6**
**Top Twenty-one City Pair Revenue Producers for Mid American Airlines, 1979**

Las Vegas – Kansas City
Las Vegas – Boston
Las Vegas – Cleveland
Las Vegas – Detroit
Las Vegas – Houston
Las Vegas – Oklahoma City
Houston – Denver
Houston – Pittsburgh
Houston – Boston
Houston – Buffalo
Houston – Kansas City
Houston – Albuquerque
Kansas City – Boston
Kansas City – Philadelphia
Kansas City – Detroit
Kansas City – Pittsburgh
Kansas City – Cleveland
Kansas City – Dallas
Kansas City – Albuquerque
Kansas City – Denver
Dallas – Pittsburgh

**EXHIBIT 6-7**
**Mid American Airlines:**
**Routes Accounting for a Majority (51.81 Percent) of Gross Revenue, 1980**

| Route | Share of Market Emplanements | Mid American Airline Passengers | Mid American Airline Revenue $(000) |
|---|---|---|---|
| Las Vegas to | | | |
| Kansas City | 3.1 | 151,896 | $ 19,746 |
| Boston | 1.5 | 73,500 | 16,979 |
| Cleveland | 1.0 | 48,996 | 8,917 |
| Detroit | 1.3 | 63,696 | 11,465 |
| Houston | 2.2 | 107,796 | 14,876 |
| Oklahoma City | 1.0 | 48,996 | 5,733 |
| Houston to | | | |
| Las Vegas | 2.2 | 126,036 | 17,393 |
| Denver | 2.7 | 154,680 | 16,551 |
| Pittsburgh | 1.4 | 80,208 | 10,267 |
| Boston | 0.9 | 51,564 | 8,405 |
| Buffalo | 0.8 | 45,828 | 6,553 |
| Kansas City | 2.6 | 148,956 | 13,108 |
| Albuquerque | 1.0 | 57,288 | 5,729 |
| Kansas City to | | | |
| Houston | 3.9 | 130,968 | 11,525 |
| Las Vegas | 4.2 | 141,036 | 18,335 |
| Boston | 1.8 | 60,444 | 8,402 |
| Philadelphia | 1.6 | 53,742 | 6,503 |
| Detroit | 1.4 | 47,016 | 4,090 |
| Pittsburgh | 1.9 | 63,804 | 6,317 |
| Cleveland | 1.6 | 53,742 | 4,944 |
| Dallas | 3.7 | 124,248 | 8,946 |
| Albuquerque | 2.9 | 97,380 | 9,251 |
| Denver | 3.2 | 107,460 | 8,597 |
| Albuquerque to | | | |
| Kansas City | 7.6 | 97,944 | 9,305 |
| Houston | 4.9 | 63,148 | 6,315 |
| Oklahoma City to | | | |
| Las Vegas | 4.1 | 49,953 | 5,845 |
| Dallas to | | | |
| Kansas City | 1.3 | 125,232 | 9,017 |
| Pittsburgh | 1.0 | 96,324 | 11,944 |
| Boston to | | | |
| Las Vegas | 0.9 | 67,152 | 15,512 |
| Houston | 0.8 | 59,700 | 9,731 |
| Kansas City | 0.8 | 59,700 | 8,298 |
| Cleveland to | | | |
| Las Vegas | 1.1 | 51,636 | 9,398 |
| Kansas City | 1.0 | 46,944 | 4,319 |
| Detroit to | | | |
| Las Vegas | 1.1 | 65,424 | 11,776 |
| Kansas City | 0.8 | 47,580 | 4,139 |

**EXHIBIT 6-7 (Continued)**

| Route | Share of Market Emplanements | Mid American Airline Passengers | Mid American Airline Revenue $(000) |
|---|---|---|---|
| Denver to | | | |
| Houston | 1.9 | 168,420 | 18,021 |
| Kansas City | 1.2 | 106,368 | 8,509 |
| Pittsburgh to | | | |
| Houston | 1.3 | 75,552 | 9,671 |
| Dallas | 1.8 | 104,616 | 12,972 |
| Kansas City | 1.2 | 69,744 | 6,905 |
| Buffalo to | | | |
| Houston | 1.5 | 37,680 | 5,388 |
| Philadelphia to | | | |
| Kansas City | 1.0 | 50,208 | 6,075 |
| Total Revenue, Forty-two Routes | | | $415,772 |
| Total Revenue, System | | | 802,490 |

fares actually charged to ticketed passengers flying the route involved. The average fare on a route may be computed by dividing gross revenues by gross emplanements; this average is weighted by actual fares charged in proportion to the frequency with which they were charged.

The highest average fare among the top 21 revenue-producing city pairs on the MAA system in 1980 was $231.00 from Las Vegas to Boston. Because the distribution of fare classes was virtually the same on flights in either direction in this city pair, the average fare generated was virtually the same from Boston to Las Vegas and from Las Vegas to Boston.

Market-research studies are available which show the demographic characteristics of airline passengers. Exhibit 6-8 summarizes data from one such study which was syndicated by a major marketing-research firm in 1979 and purchased by many of the leading airlines, including MAA. This exhibit shows data for all airline passengers, as well as for adult male passengers and adult female passengers. It includes individuals who have taken one or more airline trips during the year 1979.

The single dominant finding in this research is that a relatively small minority of U.S. adults travel by air. In 1979, only 15.6 percent of all adults traveled on a commercial airplane one or more times. And airline travel is equally distributed among males and females. The typical airline traveler tends to be relatively older; a professional or manager in the upper-income groups; college educated; and resident in A and B counties in metropolitan areas. The distribution of demographic traits is remarkably similar between males and females.

It is a commonplace that a relatively small group of air travelers are heavy users of air transportation. Exhibit 6-9 suggests the demographic characteristics of this heavy-traveler group. It is based on U.S. adults that made five or more air trips in 1979. This table reveals that males are much more likely to be frequent air travelers than are females. This is especially true of males between thirty-five and fifty-four years of age who are also

**EXHIBIT 6-8**
**Demographic Characteristics of U.S. Domestic Air Travelers, 1979**

| | % All Adults | % Male Adults | % Female Adults |
|---|---|---|---|
| Adults Who Have Taken One or More Air Trips in Past Year: | 15.6 | 15.8 | 15.5 |
| Age: | | | |
| 18–24 | 14.6 | 14.8 | 14.4 |
| 25–34 | 15.7 | 15.9 | 15.5 |
| 35–44 | 16.7 | 17.5 | 15.9 |
| 45–54 | 18.5 | 18.3 | 18.7 |
| 55–64 | 15.9 | 15.8 | 16.0 |
| Occupation: | | | |
| Professional, Managerial | 28.6 | 32.2 | 24.1 |
| Clerical, Sales | 13.6 | 17.1 | 10.1 |
| Other Employed | 10.8 | 9.1 | 12.5 |
| Household Income: | | | |
| $20,000 and over | 25.9 | 27.8 | 23.9 |
| 15,000–$19,999 | 15.3 | 14.2 | 16.4 |
| 10,000– 14,999 | 12.7 | 9.4 | 15.9 |
| 5,000– 9,999 | 9.6 | 8.1 | 10.9 |
| Less than $5,000. | 7.6 | 7.1 | 8.1 |
| Education: | | | |
| Attended/Graduated College | 27.5 | 27.7 | 27.4 |
| Graduated High School | 13.5 | 12.1 | 14.9 |
| Did Not Graduate High School | 7.6 | 7.8 | 7.4 |
| Marital Status: | | | |
| Married | 15.8 | 16.1 | 15.4 |
| Single | 17.6 | 15.9 | 19.2 |
| Widowed, Separated, Divorced | 13.4 | 13.5 | 13.4 |
| Locality Type: | | | |
| Metropolitan Central City | 16.6 | 16.1 | 17.1 |
| Metropolitan Suburban | 17.5 | 18.4 | 16.5 |
| Non-metropolitan | 11.3 | 11.1 | 11.6 |
| County Size: | | | |
| A | 17.9 | 18.6 | 17.3 |
| B | 16.5 | 17.2 | 15.7 |
| C | 13.6 | 13.0 | 14.3 |
| D | 10.3 | 9.2 | 11.5 |

*Source:* Syndicated Market Research Study.

professionals and managers in upper-income groups, college educated, and residents of B counties in metropolitan suburban areas.

But the actual disproportion in male flying and female flying in this heavy traveler group is even more extreme than that suggested by comparing Exhibits 6-8 and 6-9. This is because there is a small group of males who take many more than five air trips in a year. The effect of this small group is shown in Exhibit 6-10.

**EXHIBIT 6-9**
**Demographic Characteristics of Heavy Domestic U.S. Air Travelers, 1979**

| | % All Adults | % Male Adults | % Female Adults |
|---|---|---|---|
| Adults Who Have Taken Five or More Air Trips in Past Year: | 3.6 | 4.8 | 2.4 |
| Age: | | | |
| 18–24 | 3.4 | 4.0 | 2.7 |
| 25–34 | 3.9 | 5.2 | 2.6 |
| 35–44 | 4.3 | 5.9 | 2.6 |
| 45–54 | 4.6 | 6.6 | 2.5 |
| 55–64 | 3.4 | 4.5 | 2.3 |
| Occupation: | | | |
| Professional, Managerial | 8.4 | 12.9 | 3.8 |
| Clerical, Sales | 3.0 | 4.4 | 1.6 |
| Other Employed | 2.0 | 2.0 | 1.9 |
| Household Income: | | | |
| $20,000 and over | 6.8 | 9.4 | 4.1 |
| 15,000–$19,999 | 3.7 | 4.4 | 3.0 |
| 10,000– 14,999 | 2.3 | 2.6 | 2.0 |
| 5,000– 9,999 | 1.6 | 1.5 | 1.6 |
| Less than $5,000. | 1.2 | 1.3 | 1.1 |
| Education: | | | |
| Attended/Graduated College | 7.4 | 9.9 | 4.8 |
| Graduated High School | 2.6 | 3.3 | 1.9 |
| Did Not Graduate High School | 1.3 | 1.3 | 1.3 |
| Marital Status: | | | |
| Married | 3.6 | 4.8 | 2.4 |
| Single | 4.3 | 5.0 | 3.5 |
| Widowed, Separated, Divorced | 3.0 | 4.2 | 1.8 |
| Locality Type: | | | |
| Metropolitan Central City | 3.5 | 4.4 | 2.7 |
| Metropolitan Suburban | 4.4 | 6.2 | 2.5 |
| Non-metropolitan | 2.5 | 3.0 | 2.0 |
| County Size: | | | |
| A | 4.1 | 5.4 | 2.7 |
| B | 4.2 | 6.0 | 2.4 |
| C | 3.2 | 3.8 | 2.5 |
| D | 2.0 | 2.2 | 1.7 |

*Source:* Syndicated Market Research Study.

As the exhibit shows, about 8 percent of all air trips taken by males in 1979 were taken by those who flew only once during the year. The comparable proportion of total trips taken by females was 21.2 per cent. But 73.9 percent of all of the trips taken by male adults in 1979 were taken by men who flew five or more times. The comparable proportion of total trips taken by females who flew five or more times in 1979 is 36.5 percent.

**EXHIBIT 6-10**
**Domestic Air Trips Distributed by Frequency of Flying, 1979**

| Number of Domestic Trips in 1979 | % All Adults | % Male Adults | % Female Adults |
|---|---|---|---|
| 1 Trip | 12.5 | 8.2 | 21.2 |
| 2 Trips | 13.5 | 8.2 | 23.8 |
| 3–4 Trips* | 12.6 | 9.7 | 18.5 |
| 5 Trips or More† | 61.4 | 73.9 | 36.5 |

*The average male adult in this category took 3.5 domestic air trips in 1979; the average female adult took 3.1 domestic air trips in 1979; the average adult in this category took 3.3 domestic air trips in 1979.

† The average male adult in this category took 11.2 domestic air trips in 1979; the average female took 5.1 domestic air trips in 1979; the average adult in this category took 9.0 domestic air trips in 1979.

*Source:* Special Analysis of Syndicated Market Research Study.

Thus, the average male who flew five times or more in 1979 took many more trips in total than did the female who flew five or more times. As the note reveals, the average-trip-per-person data support this interpretation: The average male who flew five times or more in 1979 actually flew 11.2 times as contrasted to the average female flyer in this category who took only 5.1 air trips in 1979.

All of this means that a very small group of men account for a very high proportion of the total airline emplanements. This small group is hard to identify for study; and because of this and the projected expense of such a study, no reliable measurement of this premier group's demographic characteristics is available to Mid American Airlines. Thomas Eldridge, executive vice-president of Mid American Airlines, believes that this group consists primarily of senior business executives and government officials. Thus he believes that a high proportion of these frequent air travelers fall in the higher-income, college-educated, professional and managerial groups. This belief is based on Eldridge's observations over the years of MAA travelers, and the few heavy airline travelers that he has come to know.

Mid American Airlines has historically allocated about 1.8 percent of its gross revenues to advertising. No one at the airline is prepared to defend this advertising expenditure level: It appears to be adequate for advertising tasks that MAA undertakes in the course of each marketing year and seems to be in line with the advertising-to-sales ratios of most of the major airlines. Thomas Eldridge prepares an advertising appropriations recommendation each year that is based on the 1.8 percent rule, and it is more or less routinely included in the upcoming annual MAA fiscal projections and budgets. Thus, as plans for 1981 were being prepared in the early fall of 1980, Eldridge estimated that the MAA advertising allocation for 1981 should be set at $15,660,000, or 1.8 percent of estimated MAA 1981 revenues of $870,000,000.

In general, these advertising expenditures are used to accomplish two quite distinct tasks. First, Mid American Airlines sponsors an advertising campaign designed to create a favorable image of the experience a traveler may expect on MAA. The campaign is based on the advertising line "Mid American goes all the way for you." This line is executed to convey the many ways in which Mid American "goes all the way" in serving its passengers. Thus, Mid American goes all the way in meals it serves; in the sophistication of its reservation system; in the training of its cabin attendants; in the breadth of its route coverage of the northeast and southwest; in the convenience of its scheduled departures; and so forth.

Second, a separate Mid American advertising campaign is designed to convey specific information in individual Mid American markets about destinations served, frequency of service, and fare structures and discounts. One of the requirements of the advertising idea upon which the umbrella-image campaign is based is that it must be compatible with this second, local destination-scheduling-fare advertising program.

"Mid American goes all the way for you" has been judged to be especially compatible with the local advertising activities. It is translated into headlines such as:

"Mid American goes all the way for you to Las Vegas."
"Mid American goes all the way for you in low discount fares."
"Mid American goes all the way for you to Houston, six times a day."

A pool of image television commercials has been developed for use in 1981. They are similar to those used in 1979 and 1980, except that they are based on "freshened" executions and include the new Mid American flight attendants' uniforms and the new Mid American corporate logo.

A variety of fairly standard newspaper formats in 300, 700, and 1,000 lines are available for local destination-scheduling-fare advertising use; and new newspaper formats and copy are developed as needed by the Mid American advertising agency. In addition, sixty-second radio-commercial formats have been developed for local destination-scheduling-fare use based on the "Mid American goes all the way for you" theme.

In recent years Mid American has allocated about 30 percent of its advertising appropriations to the television-image campaign and about 70 percent to the local destination-scheduling-fare activities. This allocation does not, however, reflect the relative levels of sales-marketing-department activity devoted to the two individual advertising programs.

The image campaign is more or less set. Once or twice a year the advertising agency proposes new television commercials for production; and because these commercials in recent years have merely continued the agreed-upon and apparently successful advertising theme, the approval and production of this work is relatively routine. This is not to say that the image-advertising campaign is not taken seriously, nor that it does not command the attention of top airline and agency management. But the making of four or five television commercials a year is, to a degree, cut and dried, and important or not, they can be produced in a relatively easy-going and untroubled manner.

If the work on the image advertising is calm and relaxed, in contrast, the day-to-day work on local advertising is simply chaotic. Standard Formats in newspapers and for radio tend to routinize at least some of the work, but each advertisement in a market is run for a specific reason and must be thought out in terms of that specific reason. No local destination-scheduling-fare advertisement is, therefore, completely routine: Each one is a special case. Often the Mid American advertising department and its advertising agency prepare and release 50 or 60 newspaper and/or radio advertisements per week. And when new fare or discount structures must be announced or when new competitive expressions of "Mid American goes all the way for you" must be adapted to local market conditions, these 50 or 60 advertisements must be created practically from scratch, rather than adapted from existing formats.

The corporate and divisional sales-marketing staffs and the relation between them reflect the continuing needs of this local destination-scheduling-fare advertising program. The basic creative direction for all Mid American Airlines advertising rests with the corporate sales-marketing department. This department, in conjunction with the Kansas City office of Bennington, Bartley, and Avignon advertising agency is responsible for the preparation of the image-advertising campaign, as well as for the standard formats used in the local destination-scheduling-fare advertisements. The general strategy to be followed in the local destination-scheduling-fare advertisements is also determined by the corporate sales-marketing department. Thus, general decisions about whether to feature destinations, schedules, fares, or combinations of these and/or other elements in the local advertisements are made by the corporate staff. However, the specific content of advertisements that will run in individual markets is determined by the divisional sales-marketing offices. These offices also participate in the determination of the general local content strategy that is set in corporate headquarters; and the divisional offices have relatively great flexibility in deviating from this content strategy, as local competitive conditions require. Bennington, Bartley, and Avignon maintains branch offices in Houston and in Detroit, where, local advertising is executed and placed under the supervision of the Mid American divisional offices in these cities.

Media budgets for individual markets are developed in the divisional offices and are subject to approval by the corporate sales-marketing department. In general, individual-market budgets are a standard percentage of the gross Mid American revenues in each market. The standard percentage is computed by multiplying the company advertising-to-sales ratio (1.8 percent) by the fraction of the total advertising appropriation allocated to local destination-scheduling-fare advertising. As we have seen, seventy percent of total appropriated funds were allocated to local advertising programs in 1980. Thus, the advertising budget for Denver in 1980 would be computed, on the formula basis, as follows:

MAA Revenues in Denver (from Exhibit 6-5) × Advertising/Sales Ratio × Local Allocation = Denver Budget
$47,142,000 × 1.8 × 0.7 = $593,989.00

Local budgets may be set above or below the formula if unusual competitive conditions prevail. Divisional offices often recommend such deviations but implement them only after corporate approval has been received. For example, Las Vegas has never received a formula-based advertising appropriation. It is assumed that most of the traffic into and out of Las Vegas is connected with the resorts and casinos and that most of it will eventually return home more or less the same way that it arrived. The dollars that are not spent in Las Vegas are allocated to other Western-division cities.

A major advertising issue for Mid American Airlines is the determination of the proportion of total advertising funds to be committed to the overall image campaign and the proportion to be committed to the local advertising programs. In addition, there is considerable continuing controversy within the company about which local media should be used in local advertising programs. Both of these questions receive sharp debate in the annual planning meetings of divisional and corporate sales-marketing personnel held in September each year.

Thomas Eldridge reserves the right to make final decisions in respect to the allocation of advertising funds and to approve divisional media selection criteria. But he is not autocratic about this. He believes that it is his job to consider the divisional points of view and compromise them with his own sense of corporate needs and goals in as democratic a fashion as possible. Thus, he asks each divisional sales-marketing vice-president to prepare a memorandum in August of each year detailing his or her views on important media matters that should be discussed before the upcoming annual advertising planning meetings for the next year. Inevitably, the question of how much advertising money should be allocated to local purposes surfaces in these annual "media memos," as do views concerning the ideal local media for MAA use, both generally and in specific markets.

The sales-marketing executives in the divisions are talented and good-natured and over the years have developed a rather warm feeling about the annual "media debates" that always develop in Mid American advertising planning sessions. They seem convinced that the process Eldridge has settled upon is a fair one, that their views receive a fair hearing, and that the final compromises are reasonable and, in general, quite good for the company.

Here are the annual media memoranda written by divisional sales-marketing vice-presidents in August of 1980.

---

# MAA SYSTEM

Internal Communication

August 21, 1980

To: Thomas Eldridge
From: Elizabeth Grayson, Kansas City Division

You asked for my comments about media matters in your memo of August 7.

1. I continue to believe that we have, historically, allocated too much money to the local advertising programs. I believe this for the following reasons:
   a. The real purpose of our advertising is to convince travelers and prospective travelers that the MAA experience is superlative, that our product is better than our competitors'. We seem to get about one third of the Kansas City emplanements every year. This has not changed much in the last five years. I believe that we can get a larger share of the pie only by increasing our market share on high-volume, long-haul routes where we are in competition with other airlines. Where else will the business come from?
   b. But what competitive effect can our local advertising program accomplish? Our fares are exactly the same as everyone else's, so it is not to our advantage to advertise them. We are so dominant in this market that everyone knows that we fly to the Southwest and Northeast. Telling our customers that we fly to Las Vegas or Boston, therefore, accomplishes no real purpose: they already know this. And advertising our schedules is just plain foolish. If we have a good competitive schedule to a market, we'll get the business. If our departures or routings are competitively inferior, why should we advertise it? Why, for example, should we tell customers that we fly one stop to Philadelphia when United advertises three daily nonstops?

   c. Let's just blanket our market with television that tells people we go "all the way for them," instead of dribbling money away in newspaper advertisements that simply accomplish no good competitive purpose.
2. If we must continue with the local programs, then at least let's use more radio. Newspaper is simply too expensive. We can reach roughly three times as many people with a dollar spent in radio rather than in newspapers. You will object, I know, that we can't convey as much information on the radio as we can in newspapers, that it's difficult to talk rates and schedules on the radio. But this is just the information that is so pointless. Can't we, at least, have a radio version of the television advertising for use in the local advertising program rather than just the local formats?
3. Finally, I believe that a good case can be made for outdoor. We've never used this medium; yet according to a study made by the agency every one of the other top ten airlines uses it, and some spend a great deal of money on it. "Going all the way for you" could, I would think, be executed with considerable distinction in outdoor. And, if we must tell the world where our planes go, destinations could easily be featured in an outdoor campaign. I know that effective use of outdoor posters requires the development of franchise positions and that this can take a good deal of time; but what a wonderful asset we would be developing!

I'll have an agency analysis of outdoor for Kansas City ready for the September planning meetings so that we can get a specific idea of what MAA would achieve from such a program and what it would cost.

---

# MAA SYSTEM

## Internal Communication

August 23, 1980

To: Thomas Eldridge
From: Irving Duffy, Eastern Division

I'm responding to your annual media memo request.

Up here in Detroit we are now, as we always have been, strictly in favor of local advertising. There are some mighty strong reasons for this, and I'll detail them below, but the one overriding factor is that Mid American is a small airline in Eastern Division markets. If you'll refer to MAA emplanement shares, it's clear that we are not a major factor in any of the Eastern division markets. In Boston only 5.6 percent of those who board commercial flights fly with MAA. Mostly, we are at 10 or 11 percent of emplanements in these markets, or below. The exceptions are Syracuse (16.0 percent) and Harrisburg (18.8 percent), and of what intrinsic importance are these to the overall system?

We have some really fine routes out of the Eastern division to Houston, Las Vegas, and Kansas City; but we must remember that, on the whole, in our markets, we're small potatoes.

Which brings me to local advertising. MAA really doesn't have much consumer awareness in Eastern division markets. Our customers tend to use Mid American because they have to use us. More often than not, we are the only convenient way to get from one place to another. Sure, we have some competition; but in general, the routes we get our passengers on, we are the best, if not the only, alternative, if you're going to travel by air. I'll admit that this doesn't totally reflect the nonstop routes to the Southwest where we often do have competition. But even in those cases, our advertising objective is to let people know that we exist, and why we exist. Telling them that MAA goes all the way for them is okay, if you've got all the money in the world, and if consumer awareness is high.

I say this every year, and I'll say it again now, we aren't like Kansas City or even Las Vegas or Houston. We have to give our customers hard information about where we fly, how often, and for how much. If I had my way, we'd spend all of our local money in newspapers and most of our money locally.

I say "most of our money locally" because you've convinced me, over the years, that we have to spend at least some or our money in an image campaign to set up our local advertising and make our local use of the overall image line more meaningful. But 30 percent of the total is just too much. I know we argue about this every year, but why not cut the image budget in half this year and see if it has any effect?

I sense that there will be some conversation about outdoor this year. Just for the record, I'm opposed to outdoor. It doesn't have the capability to transmit a meaningful message: not more than one destination, no schedules, no fares. Just a pretty picture and more "we go all the way for you." That kind of stuff simply isn't going to do the job for us up here in the Eastern division. We know it and feel strongly about it; and Tom, you know it in your heart of hearts, too.

---

# MAA SYSTEM

Internal Communication

August 16, 1980

To: Thomas Eldridge
From: Adam Clagge, Western Division

I know I'm the new boy in this group. [Clagge had been promoted to vice-president, western sales-marketing, from the Administrative Division in late 1978. He was a 1965 graduate of a large middle-western graduate business school, and it appeared that he was being moved from division to division under a systematic plan to prepare him for an eventual senior management role.] I've only been through this annual advertising planning process once before, last year; and I may have missed something as I listened to the discussions. But I really think that all the arguments are old-fashioned and that we are missing the real point about media in the annual deliberations.

1. There was a lot of rhetoric last year about what one medium or another can do for us. As far as I know, media don't accomplish the selling job—they deliver messages; and it is the message that creates awareness, or delivers specific schedule and destination information, or whatever. I believe, therefore, that we should be talking about the relative ability of individual media to reach our market, rather than arguing about the nature of the selling job that we have to perform, in media discussions.
2. The first implication of this is that all of the media that we use are local media. We buy local newspapers, we buy local radio, and we buy local or spot television. The key point about this is that we don't advertise in any non-MAA market. We have never used any medium that was not purchased in a local MAA market. Perhaps we should be debating whether we should broaden the geographic reach of our media program. Is it to our advantage to use network television to reach a national audience? Or should we think about national magazines? We know, at least, that magazines can be selective—they can be chosen to reach upscale males who have responsible corporate jobs and are frequent travelers, for example.

   I understand Mr. Freiquist has expressed the opinion that you can't sell airline travel in magazines and that, at one time, he expressly forbade the use of magazines for Mid American Airlines. If this is the rule we must follow, well and good; but perhaps we should marshall the facts, present the case to him, and see if he still feels as strongly about the matter now as he once did.
3. The next issue we should address is whether to continue buying media on the basis of our subjective impressions of the kind of message they are best equipped to deliver, or whether we should shift our emphasis away from messages and toward audience coverage.

   The one thing we know absolutely about our market is that it is relatively small and that it is middle-aged, upper income, professional-managerial, and in major markets. The hard core of the market is all of these things, as well as predominantly male. Nobody talked about these facts in last year's planning meeting. I think we should talk about them this year.

   The most selective local media we now use is radio, primarily because there are so many stations and each station tends to have its own following. If we use a lot of stations in a market, we will tend to get fairly broad coverage. We typically use only one or two stations in a market, if we use radio at all. But as far as I can determine, no radio station in any market does a good job in reaching that small, very concentrated group that our advertising must reach. There may be an exceptional station here or there, but they do not prove the rule.

   Newspapers are not really selective in any sense of the word. They undoubtedly reach our market but with considerable waste circulation. We may have to use them, however, while recognizing their inefficiencies.

   Outdoor and television are mass media. They may provide specific selling opportunities for us; but we must recognize that they are inefficient as media, relative to our target audience.

4. I believe that we have been overlooking an ideal medium for MAA. This is direct mail. I've talked at some length to Mr. Dukes about this, and he has expressed the reservation that it is very difficult to find out exactly to whom you should be sending direct-mail messages. He pointed out that the media we have been using are essentially impersonal. We know they reach particular population groups; but we do not know the names and addresses of the members of those groups, nor do we have to know them. He went on to emphasize that the effective use of direct mail requires that you know the identity of the people whom you wish to reach. He continued, saying that we have no idea who our customers are, nor who our heavy users are.

   My rejoinder to this is: If we don't know, we should find out. List brokers are in business to identify specific kinds of individuals. We should find the five best list brokers in the country and see what they have to say. Furthermore, we know the names of twenty-one thousand hard-core users of the MAA system: They pay $25.00 a year to belong to the MAA Badger Club and use our Badger Hole lounges in the top twelve markets in our system. Can't the market managers identify other heavy MAA users? If they don't know one-hundred people who regularly fly our airline, they aren't doing their job.
5. Finally, why do we settle all this with opinion? Why not let the advertising agency in on our deliberations? Shouldn't they know more about this than we do? If they don't, let's get an agency that does. Furthermore, why don't we test some alternative approaches? If we don't know how to run such tests, the agency should.

To summarize, I think we ought to do media planning on media grounds, not on the basis of subjective feelings about the kinds of advertising messages that do our selling objectives the most good. Furthermore, if we don't know the answers, I believe we ought to find an advertising agency that does; and if such an agency doesn't exist, we should find one that at least knows how to run tests to get the answers.

---

Thomas Eldridge considered these memoranda at some length. He was particularly concerned with the points of view expressed by Adam Clagge. Eldridge believed the annual planning meetings had been an effective management device for reconciling the divergent views of strong-minded, competent people. Clagge did not seem to doubt the value of the meetings as such. Rather, he appeared to feel that the meetings had not discussed the right topics. And, Eldridge had about come to the conclusion Clagge might be right in suggesting that the advance media-planning meetings had not looked at media issues in a particularly professional way. Finally, he decided that the advertising agency should have the responsibility of contributing to the advance media-planning meetings for 1981. On the basis of this conclusion, he wrote the following letter:

# MID AMERICAN AIRLINES

8346 Airway Plaza
Kansas City, Missouri 64139

August 29, 1980

Alan W. Lingenfelder, President
Bennington, Bartley, and Avignon
389 Madison Avenue
New York, New York 10017

Dear Alan:

I am writing this letter directly to you rather than to Eddy LaRonde here in Kansas City, because it concerns a matter that is of fundamental concern to the relationship between our companies.

For some years now I have met each September with our divisional sales-marketing people to discuss media matters prior to the development of the marketing budget for the succeeding year. Although the agency has not been asked to participate in these meetings in any formal way, I am sure that your people have been fully aware of the meetings and have briefed our people thoroughly on the media matters that are likely to be discussed.

It has been my habit each year to request a media position paper from each of our divisional vice-presidents some time before the meetings, and I have developed the meeting agendas from the topics covered in these position papers. I am enclosing herewith the three position papers that have been prepared in anticipation of this year's media-planning season.

As I have reflected about the position papers this year, I have concluded that your agency has let us down badly on media-planning questions. We have simply not had adequate input from the agency. You should, for example, have been analyzing national magazines and direct mail for us. You should have been clarifying the coverage characteristics of television, radio, and newspapers for us. You should, in summary, have been making your professional presence felt in our deliberations.

Quite frankly, Alan, the agency has been nowhere to be seen in media matters; and it is imperative that your media service to us be improved, and improved immediately.

Also, I am interested to know whether you have had any experience in market testing of advertising and whether such experience is available to Mid American?

I certainly hope that I sense an improvement in agency performance in this year's planning meetings. I hope that I won't have to write you on this topic again.

Very truly yours,

[s]

Thomas Eldridge
Executive Vice-President
Sales and Marketing

## *QUESTIONS FOR CASE 6*

1. On what basis should funds be allocated between the Mid American image and local fare-destination-schedule advertising programs? Make a specific proposal for a change in the current arbitrary allocation of 30 percent to image advertising and 70 percent to local fare-destination-schedule advertising.

2. Define and describe the audience that Mid American Airlines advertising should reach.
   a. How would Elizabeth Grayson define and describe the audience that Mid American Airlines advertising should reach? How would Irving Duffy and Adam Clagge define and describe the audience?
   b. Which of the divisional vice-presidents, in your opinion, does the best job of defining and describing the audience that Mid American Airlines advertising should reach?
   c. Should an image campaign for Mid American Airlines use media that reach an audience with different characteristics than the audience reached by local advertising designed to convey information about fares-destination-scheduling? Why or why not?

3. Describe the message-dispersion strategy that Mid American Airlines should follow in selecting media. What frequency goals should Mid-American set for: (a) an image campaign and (b) a local fare-destination-schedule effort?

4. What seasonal, regional, or other special considerations affect the selection of Mid American media?

5. What qualitative requirements affect the selection of Mid American media?

6. Are there any advertising-message peculiarities that affect the selection of Mid American media?

7. Write a media-strategy statement for Mid American Airlines.

8. Develop a media planning guide* for Mid American Airlines.

9. Compare the outdoor and direct-mail media. Should either or both of these media be used by Mid American? Tell why.

10. Comment on Thomas Eldridge's letter to A. W. Lingenfelder. How has the advertising agency failed to serve Mid American Airlines? Has Mid American Airlines created an environment in which the agency can serve them easily and well? Explain.

11. Should Mid American Airlines have an advertising manager? Why? If you agree that Mid American Airlines should have an advertising manager, describe the duties the manager would perform.

12. On page 139 Adam Clagge makes the following statement, "We may have to use . . . [newspapers], however, while recognizing their inefficiencies." Explain this statement. Why might Mid American "have" to use newspapers? Why are newspapers inefficient for Mid American?

* Media planning guides are described in: William M. Weilbacher, *Advertising* (New York: Macmillan, 1979), pps. 401–408.

# Case 7

# Developing the Advertising Program

*ALLGOOD DRUG COMPANY INTRODUCES SINUGUARD, PART 1*

The Allgood Drug Company is an important manufacturer of staple and branded proprietary drugs. Although it ranks 348 in the Fortune list of the leading five-hundred American manufacturing companies, it is the third largest company in its own industry. Its proprietary drug sales in 1979 were $439,716,000; and its net profit, after tax, from proprietary drug operations was $37,243,000.

The Allgood Drug Company is regarded by its competitors and by those who are familiar with its industry as a well-managed company with a highly professional approach to the business of producing and marketing proprietary drugs. The company's success is based upon the strong sales performance of a group of eleven well-established proprietary brands. These brands were introduced between the late 1920s and 1961 and include a leading analgesic (Painout Analgesic Compound); a leading laxative (Monolax Laxative Tablets); a leading cough syrup (Cherry-Lime Cough Compound); a unique hangover remedy (Gong Gong Hangover Draught); an outstanding hemorrhoid remedy (H I Ointment); and two leading cold tablets (Histofull Cold Tablets and Super Histofull Cold Tablets). Four other less important proprietary items are also included in the Allgood line of over-the-counter medicines. In addition, Allgood also manufactures a line of generic drug items known in the trade as "wets and drys," which includes products such as boric acid, epsom salts, potassium permanganate, mineral oil, bicarbonate of soda, witch hazel, aspirin, calomine lotion, and so on. This line of generic products also makes a substantial contribution to the sales-and-profits success of Allgood.

Allgood has introduced relatively few new products in the last twenty years, compared with the new-product activities of competitive proprietary drug companies. For example, Allgood introduced 5 new products between 1960 and 1979. In the same period, Sure Pure Drug introduced 18 new products and Alton Whitney Drug Company introduced a total of 42 new product entries. Yet those new products that have been introduced by Allgood—an athlete's foot medicine, a liquid cold product, a sleep inducer, and two antacid products—were successful in four instances out of five. In contrast Sure Pure had 3 successes out of its 18 new product attempts and Alton Whitney had 6 successes out of its 42 new product introductions.

The Allgood success in the marketing of new products depends upon solid product-development work; good basic market appraisal and planning; and a dedication to slow and careful market testing before full national introduction. If Allgood's new product methods can be characterized in one or two words, perhaps they would be called "brilliant" yet "plodding." The company is like the proverbial tortoise in its new-product work; excruciatingly slow in developing and testing, yet inevitably at or near the winner's circle when the race for success is finally accounted.

New Allgood drug products are almost always different from those in the particular market segment in which the new Allgood product is to be introduced. This is the essence of the Allgood product-development philosophy. The company prides itself on introducing new products that are distinctly different from those against which they will compete. And inherent in this product distinctiveness is always some tangible consumer benefit. Allgood new products serve the consumer better, either through greater or more effective symptomatic relief, through more pleasant dosage characteristics, or through improved product form.

During the mid- and late-1970s, the Allgood Drug Company focused its product-development attention on the sinus-remedy market. In many respects this market was a relatively difficult one to define with accuracy. A variety of products containing more or less the same active ingredients were available to consumers in the marketplace. All of these products could be used, because of the similarity of their chemical composition, to achieve symptomatic relief from sinus infection. Some of these products were promoted to consumers as sinus-infection remedies. Others with virtually the same chemical composition were promoted to consumers as remedies useful in the treatment of the common cold or for the relief of allergic reaction. Finally, some of the products in this market were presented to consumers as effective in the treatment of all three—sinus headache, common cold, and allergic reaction.

This unusual state of affairs exists because the symptoms of sinus infection, common cold, and allergic reaction are frequently the same. Thus, for example, congestion and runny nose are common to sinus infection, allergic reactions, and simple colds alike. Similarly, headache frequently accompanies the simple cold, is almost always associated with sinus infection, and may characterize some allergic reactions. Yet, although sufferers of all three of these common ailments often experience similar symptoms, the symptoms of one ailment might differ considerably in degree when compared to another.

As it happens, a relatively limited group of chemical compounds are effective decongestants. Antihistamines are believed to be effective in reducing "runny nose" symptoms and watery eyes. And aspirin or acetaminophen are commonly prescribed analgesics for the relief of headache. Even though a particular product might be advertised and promoted to the consumer for either colds, sinus infection, or allergies, it is likely to be more or less effective for all three because it is certain to contain an analgesic, a decongestant, and would probably contain an antihistamine, as well.

As a result of this crossover situation in symptoms and treatments, it is difficult to determine just how large the market for sinus remedies is in dollar terms, or for that matter, to determine the dollar size of the markets for cold or allergy remedies. Allgood Director of Marketing Research Barbara M. Courtney (see the Allgood Drug Company Organization Chart, Exhibit 7-1), reasoned that it was improper to assume that simply because a product was advertised as a sinus-infection remedy, or whatever, that it was used only as a remedy for that specific ailment. There was a good deal of survey evidence suggesting that many consumers used these products to cure symptoms without bothering to figure out exactly what ailment—sinus, cold or allergy—their symptoms were indicative of.

Ms. Courtney decided that since she could not build up an estimate of symptom usage by adding the sales of individual brands together, that she must develop her estimate in some other way. She had some data, accumulated in a variety of surveys, that suggested the monthly incidence of simple colds, sinus infection, and allergic reaction in the population; and the average length of time each of these ailments was treated. On the basis of these data Ms. Courtney estimated the total number of doses of proprietary medicines that consumers devoted to each of these three ailments in the course of a month. Because, as we shall see, the different ailments have different seasonal patterns of incidence, it was necessary to make such an estimate of doses by ailments for each of the twelve months of the year. Ms. Courtney then aggregated monthly dosage estimates into an annual dose estimate for each of the ailments. She assumed that the proportion of total sales of sinus, allergy, and simple cold remedies devoted to each of these ailments was roughly equal to her estimate of the annual portion of proprietary medicine doses consumed for each of these ailments.

Exhibit 7-2 shows total sales for cold, sinus and allergy remedies from 1970 to 1979. The growth in dollar sales for the total market for these remedies was 87 percent between 1970 and 1979. Exhibit 7-3 shows Ms. Courtney's breakdown of these totals on the basis of the assumptions described above. The growth in dollar sales for sinus remedies for the 1970-79 period was 191 percent; for cold remedies, 53 percent; and for allergy remedies, 134 percent. A good deal of these apparent sales gains was, of course, due to the illusion of inflation. Ms. Courtney estimated that inflationary gains in the value of the dollar amounted to 93 percent in the period 1970 through 1979. Thus, she concluded that the total dollar sales for products in these categories had not quite kept pace with inflation. The major growth lag was, evidently, in the cold-remedy market. Both allergy remedies and, particularly, sinus remedies had registered sales gains that were well ahead of inflation and significantly ahead of dollar-sales gains in the total market.

It was this sales analysis that was instrumental in directing the attention of Allgood Vice-President of New Product Development Quincy Cornbusher toward the sinus-remedy market. Cornbusher knew that there was little chance that the Allgood product-development team could develop a new nonprescription chemical ingredient that would be more effective than those already available for the relief of the congestion, pressure and pain of infected sinuses. And, even if it were possible to develop a new chemical for superior treatment of these symptoms, Cornbusher knew it could only be made available for consumer marketing many years into the future. This was so not only because such breakthroughs inevitably took a long time to achieve, if they were achievable at all, but

**EXHIBIT 7-1**
**Allgood Drug Company Organization Chart, January 1, 1980**

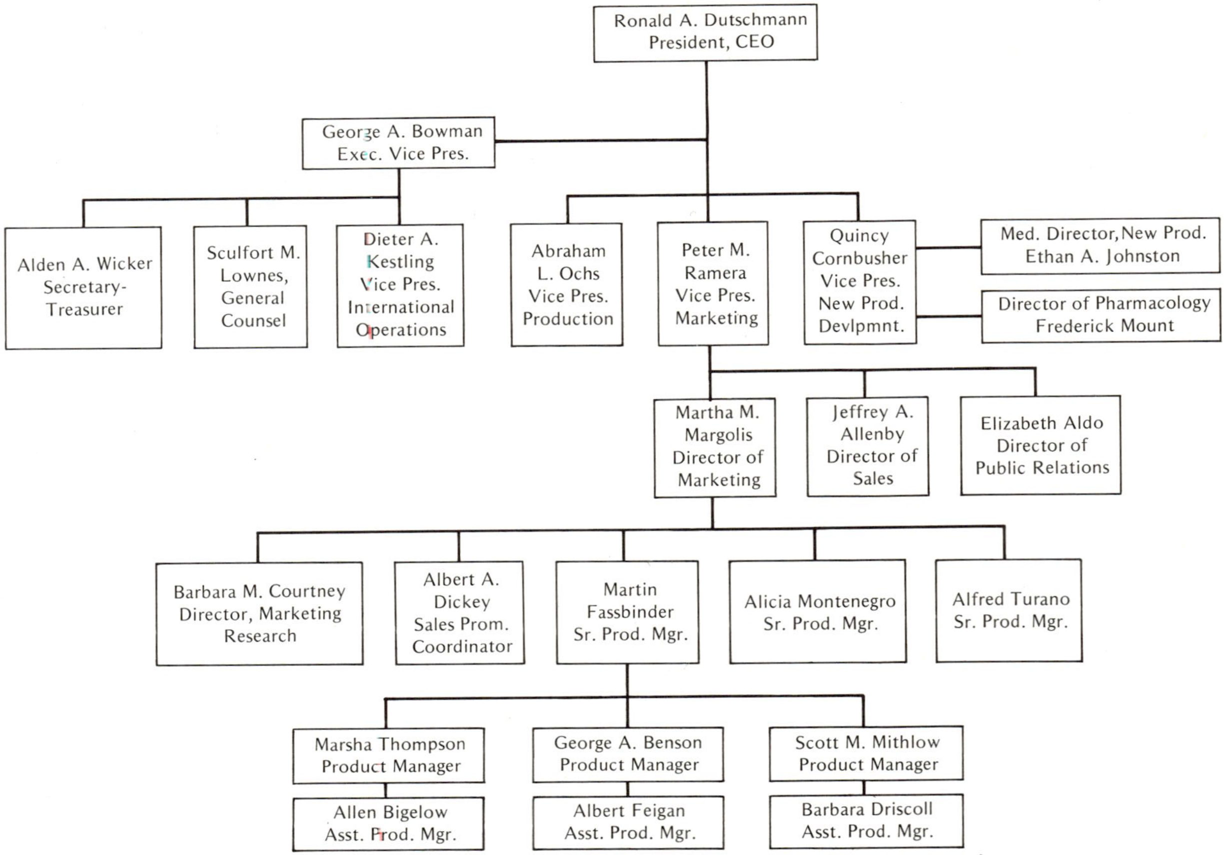

**EXHIBIT 7–2**
**Specimen Data: Estimated Total Annual Dollar Sales of Sinus Infection, Allergy, and Cold Proprietary Medicines***

| Year | Estimated* Annual Sales (Millions of Dollars) |
|---|---|
| 1970 | 298.6 |
| 1972 | 307.8 |
| 1974 | 346.3 |
| 1976 | 396.7 |
| 1977 | 419.8 |
| 1978 | 491.9 |
| 1979 | 559.3 |

*Modeled on reports from the A. C. Nielsen Company including Sinus Headache Remedies, Cold Tablets, Nasal Sprays, Allergy Remedies, and Liquid Cold Remedies.

also, especially, because of the rules of the Federal Food and Drug Administration governing the development and testing of new drug products to be marketed in the United States. If Quincy Cornbusher realized that these FDA rules and procedures had been established to insure that every new drug developed in the United States was truly safe and truly effective before its release to the consuming public, he also knew that the process of testing and approval required by the FDA could go on for years; even then the testing could end in rejection of the new drug on grounds that might be either reasonable and rational or might seem to be merely quixotic.

**EXHIBIT 7–3**
**Specimen Data: Estimated Annual Dollar Sales of Sinus, Allergy, and Cold Proprietary Medicines by Type of Product†**

| Year | Estimated* Cold-Remedy Sales (Millions of Dollars) | Estimated* Sinus-Infection-Remedy Sales (Millions of Dollars) | Estimated* Allergy-Remedy Sales (Millions of Dollars) | Total Sales (Millions of Dollars) |
|---|---|---|---|---|
| 1970 | 209.0 | 53.8 | 35.8 | 298.6 |
| 1972 | 209.3 | 61.6 | 36.9 | 307.8 |
| 1974 | 221.6 | 79.7 | 45.0 | 346.3 |
| 1976 | 238.0 | 103.2 | 55.5 | 396.7 |
| 1977 | 247.7 | 113.3 | 58.8 | 419.8 |
| 1978 | 285.3 | 137.7 | 68.9 | 491.9 |
| 1979 | 318.8 | 156.6 | 83.9 | 559.3 |

*Source: Estimates based on the projected proportion of doses consumed by ailment type, prepared by Allgood Market Research Department.
†Modeled on reports from the A. C. Nielsen Company including Sinus Headache Remedies, Cold Tablets, Nasal Sprays, Allergy Remedies and Liquid Cold Remedies.

So, in approaching the question of how to develop a successful new entry in the sinus-remedy field, Cornbusher tended to ignore the possibility of a new chemical development and to concentrate, instead, upon questions of product form. In addition, Cornbusher believed it worthwhile to explore the development of advertising that could make the Allgood sinus remedy seem more efficacious than other products, even though there was no significant difference in its symptom relief efficacy.

Cornbusher directed his own people to look into the possibility of changing the traditional tablet form of sinus-remedy medications into some form that would be superior in consumer terms. At first, this direction elicited no response at all from the Allgood director of pharmacology, Frederick Mount. Mount was not entirely sure that Cornbusher could be serious in his request. After all, a tablet was a tablet, wasn't it? Furthermore, in Mount's view, the existing sinus-relief products, possessing as they did an analgesic, a decongestant, and, in some formulations, an antihistamine, had already achieved an unwieldy tablet size. In his less sober moments, Mount referred to some of these competitive tablets as "horse pills." He couldn't understand how consumers could bring themselves to choke down tablets of that size. Where, in this situation, wondered Mount, was there a possibility of changing sinus-remedy form in order to deliver a consumer benefit?

As Mount pondered Cornbusher's request, all he could think of was the possibility of reducing tablet size, and thus to increase the number of tablets in the standard dose. Under this approach, the consumer would have a smaller tablet but would be required to take more of them, every four hours.

When he discussed this approach with Cornbusher, Mount was appalled to discover that Cornbusher was thinking in terms of a time-release dosage form. A time-release tablet would contain, under Cornbusher's conception, twice or three times as much of the active chemicals, and the tablet would be constructed in such a way that these active ingredients would be gradually released into the bloodstream over an extended period of time, perhaps eight hours, or, even more desirably, twelve hours.

Mount was quick to point out that there was simply too great a bulk of analgesic, decongestant and antihistamine chemicals involved to accomplish such an end. He pointed out that the four-hour tablets containing these three ingredients and now available in the marketplace were, in his judgment, too large.* He objected that Cornbusher was now proposing to increase the size of these already too large tablets by two or three times, plus the addition of whatever bulk would be required to encapsulate the ingredients so that they would time release.

Cornbusher's response to this objection was classic in its objective simplicity. "Yup, Fred, you understand the problem. Now all that's left is for you and your folks to solve it."

In the end, Mount discovered an obscure manufacturing process that achieved time-release through the compacting of chemicals. In this process, the chemical constituents of a medicine were packed rather loosely in the core of the tablet, but were packed more and more densely from the core outwards to the periphery. A gradual release of the product ingredients was achieved at first as the gastric juices broke down the hardened outer layer of this tablet. As the tablet began to dissolve, its physical mass gradually reduced, and, coincidentally, the degree of tablet compaction became less. Thus, the smaller the tablet became, as the process of deterioration proceeded, the more rapidly

* Time release products like CONTAC and A.R.M. contain no analgesic.

it disintegrated, and an even flow of chemicals into the bloodstream was guaranteed over an extended period of time.

Mount began to experiment with this process. His first discovery was that the chemicals that he proposed to use in the Allgood sinus-relief product—a standard nonaspirin analgesic and a standard decongestant—were compactible to an extraordinary degree. Thus, Mount learned that it was totally possible to produce a time-release tablet that contained an eight-hour dose of ingredients, in a size that was slightly smaller than the standard competitive four-hour tablet.

In due course, after considerable additional experimentation, Mount reported his success to Cornbusher. Cornbusher was, of course, elated to have, as he had directed, a superior form of sinus remedy. But he was concerned with one aspect of Mount's formulation. He asked Mount why there was no antihistamine in the product he proposed.

Mount responded: "For three reasons, Quincy. First of all, Ethan [Ethan Johnston, medical director for new products] really doesn't think there is any medical reason to include an antihistamine in a sinus-relief product. There may be a case to put an antihistamine in a cold tablet, or particularly, in an allergy remedy where runny nose and eyes are so much a part of the symptoms, but Ethan doesn't think the medical case for including an antihistamine in a sinus remedy is very compelling. Secondly, there is mounting concern in the Food and Drug Administration about using antihistamines in any of these products. There has been a recall on methapyrilene, and there is plenty of heavy heat on all these ingredients. Why get into the middle of that one? Finally, we all know that the antihistamines may cause drowsiness and that we have to use the warning about operating machinery and so forth when we include an antihistamine in a product. I thought it might be a competitive plus from an advertising standpoint *not* to have an antihistamine in the product."

And so, in due course, the New Products Director, Quincy Cornbusher turned over the new time-release sinus-remedy product to Vice-President of Marketing Peter M. Ramera and the marketing department of Allgood Drug Company. Under Allgood procedure, it was up to Ramera to decide whether the new product should finally be marketed; and if so, how.

Although the formal procedure was that the finished new product simply be turned over to the marketing department, there was in actuality a good deal more to it than that. Cornbusher and Ramera maintained a close and affable working relationship. Ramera always knew what Cornbusher was working on, and it was their informal understanding that Cornbusher and his people should not waste their time trying to develop products that Ramera had no interest in from a marketing standpoint. Furthermore, all of the marketing-analysis work that preceded a new product-development program was initiated and conducted within the marketing department because Director of Marketing Research Barbara Courtney reported, not to Cornbusher, but through Director of Marketing Martha Margolis, to Ramera. Finally, before any new-product-development program was initiated, it required the approval of the new-products committee. Since this committee consisted of Cornbusher, Ramera, and company President Ronald Dutschmann, it was almost a foregone conclusion that Cornbusher and Ramera would be in agreement before the committee ever had a formal meeting.

Thus, it was correct to think of the Allgood product-development activities as being thoroughly integrated with the Allgood marketing department. Over the years, the system had worked very well indeed. There was no residual animosity on the other side; rather the relationship between the two departments could best be described as straightforward and very professional.

Peter Ramera assigned the new sinus remedy—code named Athena—to Senior Product Manager Martin Fassbinder, who in turn assigned the project to Product Manager George A. Benson. It was Fassbinder and Benson's job to develop a detailed analysis of the marketing feasibility of Athena. In Allgood Drug practice this meant that these two men would focus, at the beginning, on the key marketing issues. The first had to do with the competitive performance of the product when used by sufferers under normal usage conditions. The second issue concerned the advertisability of the proposed new brand. That is, given the performance characteristics of the product as determined by its inherent nature and its performance in consumer use tests, the question was whether advertising could be developed that would convince consumers that the new product was sufficiently different from its competition and potentially superior in performance to justify its purchase. Finally, Fassbinder and Martin had to develop sales projections and pro forma cost estimates that would indicate the commercial and profit potential that existed for the proposed product. In addition, it was Benson's responsibility to develop a name for the new product.

In Case 7 we will be primarily concerned with the first two of these matters—product performance and advertisability—as well as the naming of Athena. In Case 8 the matter of the commercial and profit potential for Athena will be considered.

George Benson's first task after formally taking on the Athena assignment was to meet with Cornbusher and Mount and determine the availability of Athena tablets for consumer testing. As it turned out, Mount had developed a small pilot production capability, primarily because he was anxious to assure himself that the untried—by Allgood—compaction procedures would work for the Athena ingredients and that they would, in fact, yield a tablet that contained a full eight-hour dose of medication, in time-release form and of a size that was no larger than the competitors' four-hour tablets. This pilot production capability was fully operational, and Mount assured Benson that he could have as much Athena product available as necessary for the consumer-testing program.

With this assurance, Benson met with Allgood Director of Marketing Research Barbara Courtney and asked that she initiate a standard Allgood consumer-product test for Athena. A group of about two hundred and fifty consumers would be recruited to participate in the test. For this test consumers were recruited who claimed that they had suffered a sinus infection within the past year. They were then given a supply of Athena and a leading competitive product. They were instructed, when they again suffered the symptoms of sinus infection, to use these products on alternate days. In addition, they were asked to fill out a brief questionnaire on each day of use so that they would be able to recapture their experience with each of the products when the interviewer returned to administer a more formal and final questionnaire. Each respondent was asked to phone the interviewer when they began to treat the new sinus infection with the test products and to phone again after the infection had run its course. An appointment to return for the concluding interview was made during the second phone call. If the interviewer had not received a second phone call after a two-week period, the interviewer called the respondent to check progress and to make an appointment for the final interview.

Benson and Ms. Courtney discussed at some length the time frame within which they would like to receive the final test results. Ms. Courtney pointed out that the test procedure required a waiting period of unpredictable length for each respondent until he or she began to suffer from a sinus infection. Ms. Courtney commented that, because of the need to wait for consumer infection, it was customary to make considerably more test medicine placements than the number of completed questionnaires needed to constitute the finished study. She believed that if 400 placements were made, 250 completed questionnaires would be in hand within two to two-and-one-half months. She was not certain about this, but based her estimate upon previous test experience in a variety of product tests with proprietary medicines, and upon her suspicion that most sinus infection sufferers tended to have periodic bouts with the disease. Thus, she expected that anyone who claimed to have recently suffered from a sinus infection was quite likely to soon suffer from it again.

George Benson was concerned about the length of time that this testing procedure required. He also seemed nervous because it was impossible to be sure that the needed 250 questionnaires would be completed at any firm future date. Would it not be possible, he asked Barbara Courtney, to recruit consumers who where currently suffering from sinus infection and ask them to participate in the test? Benson believed that such a recruitment procedure would speed up the accumulation of test results without, at the same time, confounding them in any significant way. Ms. Courtney replied that if they were to do this, that it was likely that the respondents would already have been using some proprietary medicine to achieve symptomatic relief. She pointed out that it would therefore be difficult to control the use of the test products and interpret the results based on their use since the test products would not be used in a uniform fashion starting at the beginning of the sinus infection. In addition, she pointed out that less than two people out of a hundred were likely to be suffering from a sinus infection at any given time. Thus, it would be relatively expensive to find current sufferers; it would be much less expensive to find people who had suffered from one or more sinus infections over the past year. Thus, Barbara Courtney very strongly recommended that the standard Allgood product test procedure be followed because she believed that it would produce more results, at lower cost, in only a slightly longer period of time.

The choice of Sinucedin as the competitive standard against which to test also evoked considerable discussion. As it happened, the four leading brands of sinus remedies all held about 20 percent of the total cold-allergy-sinus-remedy market. Of these four brands, two, including Sinucedin, were advertised only for the relief of the symptoms of sinus infection, whereas the other two were advertised for the relief of cold and allergy and/or sinus-infection symptoms. Yet the formulation of Sinucedin was considerably different from that proposed for Athena. In fact, the Athena formulation was closest to that of the leading cold tablet. In the end, it was decided that it would be best to compare Athena to Sinucedin since it was Sinucedin against which Athena must perform effectively to gain consumer allegiance in the marketplace. In addition, it was assumed that Athena would perform more or less similarly to a product with a similar formulation, and that it was particularly important to test it against a product with a relatively dissimilar formulation, like Sinucedin.

In due course, the results of the product test became available to George Benson. The highlights of the test results are summarized in Exhibits 7-4 through 7-8. As these exhibits indicate, Athena was a very strong winner against Sinucedin. This was true overall:

**EXHIBIT 7-4**
**Specimen Data: Product Test of Product Athena versus Sinucedin**

Overall Preferences:

| | Base: | Total Testers |
|---|---|---|
| | Number | 248 |
| | Percent | 100 |
| Prefer Athena | | 68 |
| Prefer Sinucedin | | 30 |
| No Preference | | 2 |

*Source:* Allgood Market Research Department, 1978 (Report 78-421).

**EXHIBIT 7-5**
**Specimen Data: Product Test of Product Athena versus Sinucedin**

Reasons for Preferring Each Test Product:

| | Prefer Athena | Prefer Sinucedin |
|---|---|---|
| Base: Those preferring each product: | | |
| Number | 169 | 74 |
| Percent | 100 | 100 |
| Like time-released feature, prefer longer acting tablet | 72 | – |
| Works best on congestion | 6 | 42 |
| Works best on headache | 32 | 40 |
| Prefer to take four-hour tablets, rather take less medicine per dose | – | 39 |
| Prefer tablet size | 17 | 6 |
| All other reasons (not over 5%) | 4 | 2 |

*Source:* Allgood Market Research Department, 1978 (Report 78-421).

**EXHIBIT 7-6**
**Specimen Data: Product Test of Product Athena versus Sinucedin, by Frequency of Sinus-Remedy Use***

Overall Preference:

| Testers | Total | Frequent Users* of Sinus Remedies | Occasional Users* of Sinus Remedies |
|---|---|---|---|
| Number | 248 | 96 | 152 |
| Percent | 100 | 100 | 100 |
| Prefer Athena | 68 | 51 | 79 |
| Prefer Sinucedin | 30 | 47 | 19 |
| No Preference | 2 | 2 | 2 |

*A frequent sinus-remedy user claims usage once a month or more often. An occasional sinus-remedy user claims usage less often than once a month.
Source: Allgood Market Research Department, 1978 (Report 78-421).

**EXHIBIT 7-7**
**Specimen Data: Product Test of Product Athena versus Sinucedin, by Age**

| Overall Preference: | | | | |
|---|---|---|---|---|
| Testers | Total | Under 35 years | 35–49 years | 50 years and older |
| Number | 248 | 79 | 88 | 81 |
| Percent | 100 | 100 | 100 | 100 |
| Prefer Athena | 68 | 65 | 68 | 73 |
| Prefer Sinucedin | 30 | 34 | 31 | 24 |
| No Preference | 2 | 1 | 1 | 3 |

*Source:* Allgood Market Research Department, 1978 (Report 78–421).

Consumer preference was better than two to one in favor of Athena (Exhibit 7-4). It was also true when the results were analyzed by age (Exhibit 7-7) and by sex (Exhibit 7-8). Occasional users of sinus remedies were much more likely to prefer Athena to Sinucedin, however, than were frequent users of these remedies (Exhibit 7-6).

The basic reason for preferring Athena to Sinucedin was because of Athena's product form. Almost three out of four of those respondents who preferred Athena did so because they "liked the time-release feature," and/or "prefer longer acting tablet." Among the minority who preferred Sinucedin, there was a preference for four-hour tablets and a preference for Sinucedin's relief of congestion. Sinucedin was also slightly preferred, among this minority, for its headache relief (Exhibit 7-5).

While the Athena product test had been in the field, George Benson had also authorized the Allgood market research department to proceed with a standard qualitative study of consumer attitudes toward and perceptions of sinus infections and the proprietary medicines available to them for the treatment of sinus infections. The purpose of this work was to develop some sense of how consumers might respond to a new product in this product category and to determine the areas in which current proprietary medicines were deficient in the eyes of consumers.

The focused group-interview procedure was used in this study. In this research procedure, groups of consumers are gathered together for informal yet rigorously directed group discussions under the leadership of a specially trained social psychologist. Each

**EXHIBIT 7-8**
**Specimen Data: Product Test of Product Athena versus Sinucedin, by Sex**

| Overall Preference: | | | |
|---|---|---|---|
| Testers | Total | Female | Male |
| Number | 248 | 126 | 122 |
| Percent | 100 | 100 | 100 |
| Prefer Athena | 68 | 67 | 70 |
| Prefer Sinucedin | 30 | 31 | 29 |
| No Preference | 2 | 2 | 1 |

*Source:* Allgood Market Research Department, 1978 (Report 78–421).

such group consists of ten or twelve consumers with those consumption and demographic characteristics that are relevant to the subject under investigation. In this study four groups of female consumers between the ages of twenty-five and forty who had suffered from sinus infection one or more times in the past year, and four groups of male consumers with the same age and sinus-infection history were interviewed.

During the actual focused group sessions, consumers are encouraged to relax and interact with each other. The group leader tries to foster this relaxed atmosphere, giving it gentle yet purposeful direction. He follows a prepared topic guide but allows considerable flexibility. The topic outline for this particular investigation covered three basic areas:

1. A general discussion of sinus infections, the symptoms of sinus infection, and the medications commonly used by the respondent consumers in dealing with their sinus infections.
2. An evaluative discussion concerning the effectiveness of available sinus-infection remedies and a discussion of the relative strengths and weaknesses of individual sinus-remedy brands used by the consumer respondents.
3. A description of the proposed new Allgood sinus-infection remedy and a probe for consumer reactions to this proposed new product.

This research was conducted by Heather M. Allenby, an employee of the Allgood market research department who specialized in conducting such qualitative consumer studies. The summary-of-findings section of the Allenby report is shown in Exhibit 7-9.

George Benson attended all of the group sessions that were conducted by Miss Allenby as she carried out her investigation of the sinus-headache-remedy market. After the individual sessions they would discuss what had happened in them; what marketing implications seemed to be emerging from the sessions as they unfolded; and what topics seemed vague or unclear and needed special additional probing in subsequent group sessions. Thus, the final report, written by Miss Allenby, reflected this continuing professional interaction between the marketing researcher and the product manager. When the report was completed, Benson agreed completely with the summary of findings and felt confident that he could depend upon them in his subsequent development of advertising strategy for Athena. Yet both he and Miss Allenby were quick to point out that such a research-marketing consensus did not always develop as a result of such qualitative studies. Both knew that differences in interpretation and in the weight accorded to individual conclusions could easily develop in this process. The reduction of focused group discussions down to conclusions was, after all, a highly subjective and impressionistic process. When differences of opinion did develop between the marketer and the researcher they were duly noted in the research report because it was, ultimately, the responsibility of the researcher to render the final appraisal of research conducted under the aegis of the Allgood market research department. All of the Allgood market research personnel agreed that it was important to have Allgood marketing personnel involved in such qualitative research projects, than for them to be uninvolved and indifferent. The possibility that a research department report would circulate with an explicit marketing department exception to its findings was little enough price to pay for the active participation of the marketing department in the qualitative research process.

George Benson now had the results of both the Athena product test and the qualitative research study on sinus remedies in hand. He composed the following memorandum to Martin Fassbinder to summarize his progress to date and to indicate what he, Benson, believed the next steps should be.

## EXHIBIT 7-9

**Specimen Data: Summary Findings from a Qualitative Study of Consumer Perceptions of Sinus-Infection Remedies**

1. Sinus infections are a continuing, always annoying, and frequently painful problem for those who suffer from this condition. Yet it seems that most sufferers do not consider their sinus problem to be one of major medical import, nor an ailment that requires a doctor's care.
2. Those who suffer from sinus infection usually have done so for an extended period of time. They, typically, do not believe that their condition will ever be cured.
3. Thus, the typical sufferer is dependent upon available medications for symptomatic relief. This study was limited to the very large group of sufferers who depend upon over-the-counter or proprietary medicines for relief from the symptoms of sinus infection. Not one of the respondents in this study expressed total satisfaction with available nonprescription remedies. They are constantly on the lookout for new products with the hope that these new products may give greater relief than those they have previously used.
4. Sinus infections manifest themselves in two major ways: through sinus headaches and through congestion and pressure in the sinus passages. Although most sufferers understand these symptoms to be interconnected, they nevertheless think and speak of them as separate problems. It appears that, for most sufferers, sinus headaches are the most aggravating and painful aspect of sinus infection. Yet, there is a significant minority who believe congestion and pressure to be the primary symptoms that should be treated. In spite of these differences of perception, none of our respondents disagree that the ideal sinus medication is one that treats and relieves both of these symptoms equally.
5. The respondents seemed to feel that available sinus-headache-remedy brands were indistinguishable, one from the other. Although some respondents expressed strong allegiance to one brand or another, there were always several other respondents who had tried that brand and found it wanting in one or more critical aspects. As the conversations about individual brands developed, it quickly became clear that most of our respondents had had experience with most or all of the leading brands at one time or another. As these respondents mulled over their experience with each other, a consensus gradually emerged that the available brands were all, in fact, about the same as far as symptom relief was concerned.
6. Many of our respondents welcomed the notion of a time-release eight-hour dosage form for a sinus-infection remedy. They believed that such a dosage form would be very much more convenient than those now available. Some also expressed the (wishful) opinion that such a product might be stronger than other sinus-infection remedies that are now available.
7. Other respondents acknowledge the convenience of the eight-hour time-release dosage form, but did not believe that it would be of major significance to them. Some were distinctly hostile to the idea because they do not wish to take more medicine at one time than is absolutely necessary. They see no reason for eight-hour dosage if their headache congestion may be relieved with the standard four-hour tablets.

   Other responndents were not hostile to the new-product idea but were more interested in its efficacy in relieving headache and/or congestion than in the dosage form. To them the eight-hour, time-release tablet is little more than an attractive gimmick.
8. Some respondents expressed interest in whether the new product would contain aspirin or an effective aspirin substitute that would not irritate their stomach. It appears that at least a minority of consumers definitely prefer nonaspirin sinus remedies and that the remainder are indifferent as long as any aspirin substitute included is fully effective as a pain reliever.

# ALLGOOD MEMORANDUM

To: Martin Fassbinder
From: George A. Benson
Subject: Athena Progress Report

Two market research projects have now been completed in behalf of Athena. The purpose of this memorandum is to summarize these studies and to use them as a basis for developing a statement of marketing opportunity for Athena and an advertising creative strategy based on this Athena marketing opportunity.

1. Athena has significant market potential. The product-test results are very favorable. If there is a weakness in the product-test performance of Athena, it is that consumer preference seems to spring from the time-release, eight-hour form of the product rather than from the symptomatic relief that it delivers. Thus, the product fails, relative to Sinucedin, in effectiveness of decongestion activity and it loses to Sinucedin in respect to analgesia effect.
2. Part of these product-efficacy problems spring from the fact that the product-test format tends to draw consumer's attention to those product characteristics that are most distinguishable. Thus, those who prefer the product tend to say they do so for reasons that reflect the differentiating characteristics of the product. But, in spite of this methodological flaw, the product-test results should direct our attention to the possibility of product efficacy problems. There are, I believe, two ways in which the potential product efficacy problems should be addressed.

   First of all, I have asked Fred Mount to review the possibility of product reformulation. If Sinucedin has the potential capacity to beat us on decongestion, should we not at least consider switching from the decongestant ingredient that is now used in Athena and substituting that decongestant ingredient that is used in Sinucedin? Similarly we should review the analgesic that we now use in Athena. If aspirin (used in Sinucedin) is more efficacious than acetaminophen (used by us), then we should consider switching to aspirin.

   (Incidentally, we must also weigh the potential advantage to us of using acetaminophen in our product in preference to aspirin. The qualitative research suggests that consumers may prefer nonstomach-irritating acetaminophen to aspirin. This may be true, but it may be the kind of gratuitous consumer response that we so often seem to get in focused group sessions and must constantly guard against. I am skeptical of the "contains an aspirin substitute that can not irritate your stomach" approach to market opportunity in this product category. My suspicion is that this positioning suggests that the product is not as strong or efficacious as those which contain aspirin. The last thing we want in Athena advertising is any implication, no matter how remote, that Athena is weak or not strong. I am concerned about this because several non-aspirin analgesic products have used this approach to market opportunity—that is, "contains an aspirin substitute" —and have failed in the marketplace. The only aspirin-substitute product that has succeeded, as an aspirin substitute, is Tylenol. But the acetaminophen mystique seems to break down in products that only contain an aspirin substitute as one of several ingredients.)

Secondly, I believe that our advertising must assert the effectiveness of Athena for the relief of symptoms. The reason for marketing Athena is not solely that it is an eight-hour, time-release product. That is its distinctive feature, of course, but there is no competitive product more effective than Athena in reducing the miseries of symptoms of sinus infection. We know that Athena will have parity with our competitors in efficacy of symptom relief and we must make a virtue of this parity in our advertising. We're as good at relieving the symptoms of sinus infection as anyone else, and we are an eight-hour, time-release tablet besides. The other products are, at best, pie. Athena is pie a la mode.

3. But, in addition to defending ourselves in respect to efficacy, we must go beyond this and differentiate our product from all those indistinguishable competitors. This is why the whole matter of what we say in our advertising is so crucial. No competitive brand has developed a hammer lock on this market. If we can establish the fact that we are at least as efficacious as the competitors and have an added consumer benefit, we will give consumers a tangible reason for preferring Athena. The advertising challenge is to establish efficacy while differentiating Athena as the unique eight-hour, time-release tablet.
4. My preliminary discussions with Fred Mount indicate that Athena will be priced competitively with the market leaders on a dose-for-dose basis. Thus, a standard two-tablet dose of our product will cost about the same as the equivalent dosage of four competitive tablets. Our product may even cost somewhat less on a dose basis. So we foresee no product pricing problem on Athena.
5. The sales organization assures me that there will be little or no difficulty in achieving retail distribution for Athena. True, there are at least four major competitors in the marketplace and, true, this is a rather murky and ill-defined product category spilling over as it does into the allergy and cold-tablet areas. But we will have the only really distinctive product in the category with our eight-hour, time-release feature and this distinctiveness plus an advertising appropriation of significant size will virtually guarantee high levels of distribution.
6. We will defer all discussion of the advertising appropriation for the time being (see Case 8). We have completed a preliminary analysis of Athena sales goals, the advertising appropriation that we believe will accomplish those sales goals, and the product cost–advertising expense –profit arithmetic underlying those projections. The resulting appropriation estimates exceed current advertising expenditures of the competitive brands by very significant amounts. So for purposes of this discussion, we can assure that Athena economics and Athena market prospects are such that the Athena advertising appropriation will be competitive while it also will meet standard corporate profit requirements.
7. There are three names on the list of company-controlled product names that seem ideal for Athena. They are Sinuguard, Sinus-Relief Medicine and Calibrex. Of the three we prefer Sinuguard. It is certainly not ambiguous (as Calibrex may be); it is not too generic nor easily

confused with other competitive sinus-relief medicine remedies; and it projects a feeling of straightforwardness and protectiveness that we like very much indeed. We cannot, frankly, think of any consumer-research procedure that would make us more confident in our choice of this name for Athena than our own disciplined judgment. Therefore, with your approval, we would like to finalize the name as Sinuguard and authorize our packaging people to begin developing package designs on this basis.

8. As the preceding paragraphs suggest, we see no overwhelming marketing problems for Sinuguard except that it remains to develop successful advertising for this brand.

As the discussion above in paragraphs 1, 2, and 3 indicates, the marketing opportunity for Sinuguard can be defined in several different ways. These are indicated in the following paragraphs. Each of the possible definitions of marketing opportunity can be satisfied by Sinuguard as it is now formulated. A reformulated product along the lines suggested above in paragraph 2 would be consistent with all of the definitions of marketing opportunity given below, except marketing opportunity D which is based upon the assumption Sinuguard will contain an aspirin substitute. Here are the definitions of marketing opportunity that we believe to be inherent in Sinuguard:

A. Sinuguard offers the consumer highly effective relief from the headache, pressure, and congestion of sinus infection in a new and convenient eight-hour, time-release form.

B. Sinuguard offers the consumer the convenience of a new eight-hour, time-release tablet plus highly effective relief from the headache, pressure, and congestion of sinus infection.

(The difference between market opportunity A and market opportunity B is in whether the primary emphasis is given to the eight-hour, time-release feature or to completeness of symptomatic relief.)

C. Sinuguard offers highly effective relief from the pain of sinus headache in a convenient eight-hour, time-release tablet.

D. Sinuguard offers highly effective relief from the pain of sinus headache yet contains no aspirin and thus cannot irritate the stomach, and comes in a convenient eight-hour, time-release tablet.

E. Sinuguard offers highly effective relief from the pressure and congestion of sinus infection in a convenient eight-hour, time-release tablet.

I believe that the first step that we must take is to eliminate two or three of these statements of marketing opportunity so that we may give the advertising agency clear, focused direction as they proceed to develop advertising strategy and executions for Sinuguard.

As we have discussed in the past, statements of marketing opportunity based on a product like Sinuguard frequently seem to overlap each other and often seem to be based on differences that are, especially from the standpoint of the consumer, irrelevant and overexaggerated. Of course, all our market experience is to the contrary. We know that very slight variations in a statement of marketing opportunity may reflect very significant variation in potential consumer response to the same basic product.

With this knowledge, it is potentially dangerous to eliminate one or more statements of marketing opportunity on the basis of judgment alone. Yet unless we do eliminate some on judgment, we will be left with four or five statements that are difficult or impossible to sort out with any consumer research because they are so conceptually similar to each other. Worse yet, we will be left with a handful of statements that are potentially confusing to both us and the advertising agency. Therefore, I prefer to eliminate as many of the marketing opportunity statements as possible on the basis of logic, before we meet with the advertising agency. Once these eliminations are made, we should then meet with the agency, transform the surviving statements of marketing opportunity into advertising creative strategies and ask the agency to prepare rough advertising executions on the basis of these strategies.

Which of the statements of marketing opportunity do I believe should be eliminated on the basis of judgment? As I have indicated above, I would eliminate statement D because I do not believe that the "aspirin-substitute" assertion will lead to marketplace success. I would also eliminate statement B. Both the qualitative research and the product-test research indicate that it is necessary to promise symptomatic relief. I believe that this promise must be strongly established before the eight-hour, time-release product form can be expected to be meaningful to consumers. Consumers take sinus-relief medicine in order to alleviate the pain and discomfort of sinus infections. They do not take these medicines because they last longer or have a time-release feature. If the product is clearly established as efficacious in the relief of sinus-infection symptoms, then, and only then, can the convenience of the product form become a compelling reason to buy the product. I eliminate market opportunity statement B on the grounds, therefore, that it puts the cart before the horse. The first thing that a sinus-infection sufferer wants to know about a sinus-relief medicine is whether it will relieve his symptoms and this is not the emphasis that is reflected in statement B.

At this point, I would be inclined to proceed with statements A, C, and E. Statement A should be retained because it describes the product, and because its descriptive elements are presented in an order that is properly aligned with consumer concerns. Statements C and E emphasize only one of the symptom elements, that is, sinus headache (statement C) and the pressure and congestion of sinus infection (statement E). There was some evidence in the qualitative research that consumers think of these two symptoms of sinus infection as quite separate entities. We see in the product-test results that sinus-infection medicines are evaluated separately by consumers in respect to their efficacy in relieving sinus-headache pain, on the one hand, and sinus pressure and congestion, on the other. In addition, consumers are able to evaluate individual products in respect to their effectiveness in relieving these two individual symptoms: Recall that Sinucedin was much more effective in relieving congestion than in relieving headache pain when it was compared with Athena (Sinuguard) in the paired-comparison product test.

For all these reasons, therefore, I am inclined to recommend that creative development be undertaken on statements C and E as well as on statement A. It may well be that an advertising promise of relief for one or the other of the symptoms of sinus infection is more understandable and credible to consumers than a promise that the product will provide effective relief for both symptoms at once.

In addition, it appears medically correct that pressure and congestion normally precede headache pain. That is, the sinus cavities must become swollen and congested before a sinus headache develops. No competitive product uses this fact as a basis for current advertising. And, on the basis of the qualitative research, there is certainly no evidence that consumers are aware of this chain of causal circumstances or are interested in it. Nevertheless, it would, in my judgment, be a mistake to ignore statement E on the off-chance that it may, when properly executed into advertising, become a very powerful claim.

Here are the steps that I believe we should now take:

First of all, I believe that you and I should meet, after you have digested the contents of this memorandum, and work out any problems or questions or disagreements that you have with it.

Secondly, I believe that we should meet with the appropriate representatives of the advertising agency and review with them the contents of this memorandum, amended as necessary on the basis of our meeting.

Third, I believe, we should work with the agency in the development of advertising strategies based upon statements of market opportunity A, C, and E above.

Fourth, the agency should be directed to work up advertising executions based upon those developed advertising strategies.

Finally, the executed advertising strategies should be copy tested on the basis or our standard Allgood Day-after Recall Copy Test Procedure, and a decision made as to which of the marketing opportunities for Sinuguard holds the greatest promise.

May I meet with you at your earliest convenience to review this action plan and start its implementation?

---

Benson and Fassbinder met a few days later to review the Benson memorandum. Fassbinder was genuinely interested in the contents of the memorandum and impressed by them. He did not let these feelings, however, stand in the way of an intensive and abrasive questioning of Benson concerning his conclusions about and plans for Allgood Sinuguard.

Finally, after about three hours, Fassbinder seemed to relax. He said, "Okay, George. I'm satisfied. One thing that you should have looked at, though, is the demographic characteristics of the market. But I doubt there are surprises there, are there? I suppose we're looking at brand usage and purchasing dominated by females like so many other proprietary drugs. Anyway, get Barbara to work those figures up. Aside from that, if I had written that memorandum, I'm pretty sure it would have differed in tone and style from yours. But the content would have been almost identical. I come out exactly where you do. I think you've hit this one pretty much on the button. Tell you what you do, call up Andrew Procope over at the agency and tell him to get his Athena team together. We're ready to go and he should be, too."

And so, on the following Monday a meeting of Allgood Drug personnel and representatives from the advertising agency, Belton and Baldwin, assigned to the Athena project, convened in the main conference room at Allgood.

Belton and Baldwin had been an Allgood drug advertising agency since 1948. It had been assigned the advertising account for Painout Analgesic Compound then. The work that it did on that brand was very favorably received by Allgood executives and as Painout grew and prospered, Belton and Baldwin had received additional brand assignments from Allgood including Gong Gong Hangover Draught and the Histofull cold-tablet products. In 1979 Belton and Baldwin billed $24,250,000 on its Allgood accounts. This represented about 59 percent of the total Allgood Drug Company advertising expenditures in behalf of its proprietary medicines. The balance of the Allgood advertised brands were assigned to Ellington, Brown, and Halloran. Because Allgood was satisfied with the work of its two advertising agencies and because it could see no good business reason for hiring additional agencies, the custom had developed that Allgood split up its newly developed products between the incumbents. The assignment of new products was made more or less on an alternating basis, although this procedure was not followed when a product directly competitive to a proposed Allgood product was already handled by one of the agencies. In the case of Sinuguard, both agencies had products that were more or less competitive. Belton and Baldwin handled the Histofull cold-tablet line and Ellington, Brown, and Halloran handled the new liquid cold product and an allergy-relief product that was under development. The best disposition of the Sinuguard advertising account seemed, to Marketing Director Martha Margolis and to Martin Fassbinder, to be to assign it to Belton and Baldwin.

At the first Sinuguard meeting with the agency, Allgood Drug was represented by Martha M. Margolis, Martin Fassbinder, Frederick Mount, George Benson, his assistant Albert Feigan, and Barbara M. Courtney. The agency was represented by Andrew Procope, management director on the Allgood account; Roger Hodges, account supervisor; Henrietta Carney, account executive; Mary Gonsalves, creative group head; and Alton Hamilton, director of research.

Prior to the meeting itself, the agency had received copies of the Qualitative Research Study on Sinus Infection; copies of the final report on the Athena versus Sinucedin product test; copies of a demographic profile of sinus-infection-remedy usage (see Exhibit 7-10), and copies of the Benson-to-Fassbinder memorandum.

Martin Fassbinder served as the chairman of the first meeting with the agency. He asked Barbara Courtney to briefly review the results of the two research studies and then asked Benson to repeat the conclusions and implications that he had drawn for the marketing of Sinuguard.

Then Fassbinder asked: "Does anyone disagree with our interpretations of these research studies, or the implications that we have drawn from them?"

This was a hard question for the agency to answer in any substantive way because its people had essentially received the research reports and their interpretation as accomplished facts, fully agreed to by all of the Allgood personnel who were present in this meeting.

In preparing for the Allgood meeting, the Belton and Baldwin people had been somewhat concerned about this, because they did not totally agree with two of the interpretations that Benson had made of the research findings. Research Director Alton Hamilton had been most outspoken about his reservations at the internal agency meeting which occurred on the preceding Friday.

"Darn it, Andrew," Hamilton had said, addressing his remarks to Procope, "there isn't a shred of evidence in this research to substantiate two of Benson's conclusions. First, nowhere does the research indicate that consumers won't be receptive to an acetaminophen-sinus remedy. In fact, the qualitative research absolutely suggests that they will be highly receptive to a product with an aspirin substitute rather than aspirin. He's nervous about the kind of results that you get from group interviews and that consumers sometimes mislead you in those sessions; and of course he's right that that happens sometimes; but I'll stake my reputation on the fact that this isn't one of those times.

**EXHIBIT 7-10**
**Specimen Data: Demographic Characteristics of Users of Sinus Remedies, 1979**

| | |
|---|---|
| Incidence of Use in Population in Past Year | 42% |
| Male | 21 |
| Female | 62 |

| | Male % of Users | Index* | Female % of Users | Index* |
|---|---|---|---|---|
| By Age: | | | | |
| 18-24 | 24.9 | 132 | 17.9 | 102 |
| 25-34 | 25.9 | 113 | 28.4 | 137 |
| 35-44 | 17.4 | 108 | 21.7 | 145 |
| 45-54 | 16.7 | 102 | 16.9 | 107 |
| 55-64 | 8.1 | 62 | 8.8 | 65 |
| 65 and over | 7.0 | 54 | 6.3 | 38 |
| By Education: | | | | |
| Attended/Graduated College | 29.8 | 92 | 30.7 | 123 |
| Graduated High School | 41.6 | 119 | 45.8 | 113 |
| Did Not Graduate High School | 28.6 | 90 | 23.5 | 72 |
| By Household Income:† | | | | |
| $20,000 & over | 36.4 | 112 | 32.2 | 125 |
| $10,000-$19,999 | 21.7 | 122 | 15.3 | 89 |
| Under $10,000 | 35.3 | 87 | 41.2 | 99 |

*100 Equals the population percentage in the demographic group.
† Percent of users add to less than 100% because some households refused to provide income figures.
*Source:* Allgood Drug Market Research Department.

"I don't know how Barbara Courtney lets him get away with this kind of stuff. The point I'm making is that if we handle this aspirin-substitute issue properly in the advertising, there may be a really substantial marketing opportunity. We really ought to work with that marketing opportunity and see if we can exploit it, instead of just letting it go without even a try because that's how Benson chooses to interpret a research finding."

"Okay, Alton," responded Andrew Procope, "I get your point. I think the way we play that is for you to express your reservation. I wouldn't be quite as ah, ah, . . . vehement about it with our friends at Allgood as you have been here with us, but get the issue out on the table. Keep an eye on Fred Mount when you do it. He may be on our side, and if he is–it's his product formulation, after all–then I think we'll have a very good chance to keep the issue open and at least do some creative exploration on it. But if Mount doesn't support us, I can't see how we are going to get anywhere unless Benson all of a sudden rolls over and plays dead just because of the brilliance of your rhetoric. Think he's going to roll over, Roger? You know him a lot better than we do."

"Are you kidding, Andrew?" responded Roger Hodges. "He is one stubborn cat; and when he gets old Fassbinder lined up behind him, there is just no way that George Andrew Benson is going to roll over."

"Okay, then that's how we handle it," said Procope. "You put the ball in play and keep it going until we get a response from Fred Mount. Then let him carry the major burden. I don't want to have this meeting deteriorate into an argument right in the beginning that we can't win. You understand what I'm saying, Alton?" Then Procope proceeded immediately, without giving Hamilton any opportunity to state that he understood. Clearly Procope expected that Hamilton not only understood, but would follow Procope's instruction to the letter. "Now you said you had two reservations, Alton. What's the other?"

"I think," said Alton, "and Mary agrees with me from a creative standpoint that we ought to stress the eight-hour, time-release feature when we write creative strategies and develop copy. We wouldn't be bringing this product out unless it cured the symptoms that it's designed to cure. The real difference is that it gives eight-hour relief and is time-released, which makes it sound modern and not old-fashioned like all the competitive products."

"Gee, Andy, do I think Alton is right about that!" gushed Mary Gonsalves. "I mean, I know that you proprietary-drug people tend to stay on the basics when you write copy for these products, and I certainly don't have your experience in this kind of work, but I'll tell you that the real consumer benefit in this product is that it works a long time and you don't have to run back to the medicine chest every four hours and choke down two more of those big, ugly tablets, because our product works for eight hours, and the medicine is time-released into your system gradually, yet scientifically. Gosh, Andy, I can hear the commercials already! It's a natural, this eight-hour business, and everyone knows that these products will work okay, and we don't really, Alton and I agree about this—we really don't have to waste a lot of time, especially up front, reassuring consumers about something they already know."

Finally, Mary Gonsalves stopped talking, almost gasping for breath as if the longer she talked and the more words she said fast, the more likely she was to convince Andrew Procope of the correctness of her point of view.

"Okay, Mary, and you too, Alton, I want you to cool this one," said Procope slowly and without any emotion. He might just as well have been discussing the outcome of a dull professional football game. "Cool it. Not a word about relying on the eight-hour, time-release mumbo-jumbo and forgetting about symptomatic relief. That is a position that this agency is not going to take, not going to take, ever.

"We believe that the basis of selling proprietary drugs is to emphasize the relief that they deliver. Consumers buy these products because they are sick, and they hurt, and they want to stop hurting. I think Benson is absolutely right when he says that the eight-hour, time-release feature is not the basis upon which to sell Sinuguard. It's frosting, but it's not the cake. So when we get into the meeting, let's just not argue about it, okay?"

It was on this note that the meeting of the Belton and Baldwin personnel ended. Had this meeting not been held, there would have been no agency viewpoint about how to respond to the Allgood research studies and interpretation made of them by George Benson. But, with this preparatory meeting behind them and with the basic decisions about how the agency should react established by Andrew Procope, it was easy enough for the Belton and Baldwin people to react in concert when, on the following Monday, Martin Fassbinder asked: "Does anyone disagree with our interpretation of these research studies or the implications that we have drawn from them?"

Alton Hamilton then spoke: "Martin, we think these studies are first rate, and we believe they give us excellent direction. There is just one question of interpretation—nothing important—that we would like to raise just to be sure that everything has been thoroughly discussed. It's the matter of market opportunity for an acetaminophen-based sinus-relief product. Uh, that would be George Benson's market opportunity statement *D*. It seemed to us that the qualitative study indicated there might be some considerable consumer responsiveness to that idea."

"Okay, Alton," said George Benson. "You know that I don't trust those qualitative research findings every time. The difficulty with them is that one person in a group interview will state strongly some attitude or feeling that sounds rational and all the rest of the group participants chime in. We know that acetaminophen simply is not as effective against headache pain as aspirin, and we're pretty sure that consumers are beginning to know it, too."

"Hold on, George," said Frederick Mount. "What you know, and what you're sure that consumers know, is unknown in the medical community. There are plenty of clinical tests that prove, and prove, I might add, unequivocally, that acetaminophen is every bit as effective as aspirin against pain. I think the problem is how you describe the acetaminophen ingredient in advertising. Maybe if you call it an "aspirin substitute" it does suggest that it is ersatz and perhaps weaker or not as effective as aspirin. But that is an advertising problem and we shouldn't let it get confused with a product-formulation problem. I mean it is an advertising problem because it seems to me that you have to find words that convey that acetaminophen is at least as effective in reducing pain as aspirin. There's no question about the medical facts of the matter.

"George Benson," Mount continued, now addressing the entire group, "has asked me if we can reformulate Sinuguard with aspirin. The answer is 'yes' to that question. But I don't believe an aspirin-based product will time-release as well, and I'm not sure that we can claim eight-hour relief. Aspirin doesn't compact as easily or as thoroughly as acetaminophen, and it's harder to control the time-release capabilities of the tablet."

The conversation continued on this point for another twenty minutes or so. Almost everyone in the room expressed themselves in one way or another, until, finally, Andrew Procope spoke: "I think we ought to develop Sinuguard advertising based on George's market opportunity statement *D*. If Fred Mount is right, and if we can solve the problem of how to get around the "aspirin substitute" issue, we may have a winner. Maybe not, too. But, on the basis of what I've heard here, I think it's premature to eliminate the "contains no aspirin" statement of marketing opportunity. How do you feel about it, Martha?"

Now, for the first time, Martha Margolis, director of marketing, spoke: "I'm going to assume that Fred Mount knows more about the pharmacology of this product than anyone in the marketing department or at the agency," she said. "It sounds to me as if Fred can make a tablet that performs better if he uses acetaminophen as the pain-relieving ingredient rather than aspirin. It seems, therefore, that it's up to us in marketing, and particularly to the agency, to sell that better tablet.

"George," Ms. Margolis continued, addressing herself to Benson, "I judge that you feel strongly about this. If you want to pursue it, that's fine with me. I should think the way to do it is to repeat the product test, only use two versions of Sinuguard, one with aspirin and one with acetaminophen and see if consumers can tell the difference when they use the products for their sinus infections. But meanwhile, let's develop creative strategies for each of the four marketing opportunities we've discussed, and then let the agency develop advertising for them." On this note, the meeting turned to the development of creative strategies for each of the designated marketing opportunities.

About four weeks later the agency, represented by the same five people who were present in the previous meeting, presented a series of advertising executions based on the advertising creative strategies. In all, the agency presented a total of thirteen story boards to the Allgood team, including George Benson, Al Feigan, Martin Fassbinder, Barbara Courtney, Martha Margolis and Peter Ramera. Four story boards were executions of the creative strategy written to marketing opportunity statement A and three story boards each executed creative strategies derived from marketing opportunity statements *C, D,* and *E.*

Exhibits 7-11 and 7-12 present two of the commercials created to exploit marketing opportunity A. The commercial shown in Exhibit 7-12 was chosen from among the four commercials presented as the best of the group and the one that would be produced for test in the marketplace by comsumers. The commercial shown in Exhibit 7-11 was rejected on the basis of the group's collective judgment as a candidate for development and testing, as were the other two commercials (not shown here) presented as executions intended to exploit marketing opportunity *A*.

Exhibit 7-13 shows the commercial that was judged by the group the best of those presented in connection with marketing opportunity *C*. Similarly, Exhibits 7-14 and 7-15 show the commercials that the group judged best able to exploit marketing opportunities *D* and *E*. The commercials shown in Exhibits 7-13, 7-14, and 7-15 were also approved for further development and market testing.

Each of the commercials were then produced as finished commercials, and were tested using the day-after recall procedure. (For a description of this procedure see Exhibit 13-3, page 299.)

The results of these commercial tests are presented in Exhibits 7-16, 7-17, 7-18, 7-19. On the basis of these test results it was decided to develop an advertising campaign based on the commercials shown in 7-12 and 7-15 and to test market Sinuguard in two sets of the test markets. One of these sets of test markets would be exposed to the advertising campaign derived from Exhibit 7-12 and one set of test markets would be exposed to the advertising campaign derived from Exhibit 7-15.

## *QUESTIONS FOR CASE 7*

1. Why do you believe that two advertising campaigns were selected for test marketing? Is it possible that the question of whether or not to test market one or two advertising campaigns might have been resolved by a second product test, as suggested by Martha Margolis on page 164? What information is lacking in the case which, if available, might have helped to resolve George Benson's concern about marketing opportunity D? If you had been Martin Fassbinder, what steps, if any, would you have taken to avoid the expense of running two test markets to choose the best advertising campaign?

2. Would you depend upon the day-after-recall copy-testing procedure to determine the relative strengths of advertising campaigns for Sinuguard? If your answer is "yes," tell why. If your answer is "no," describe the kind of copy research and/or copy testing that you believe should have been undertaken by Allgood.

# EXHIBIT 7-11

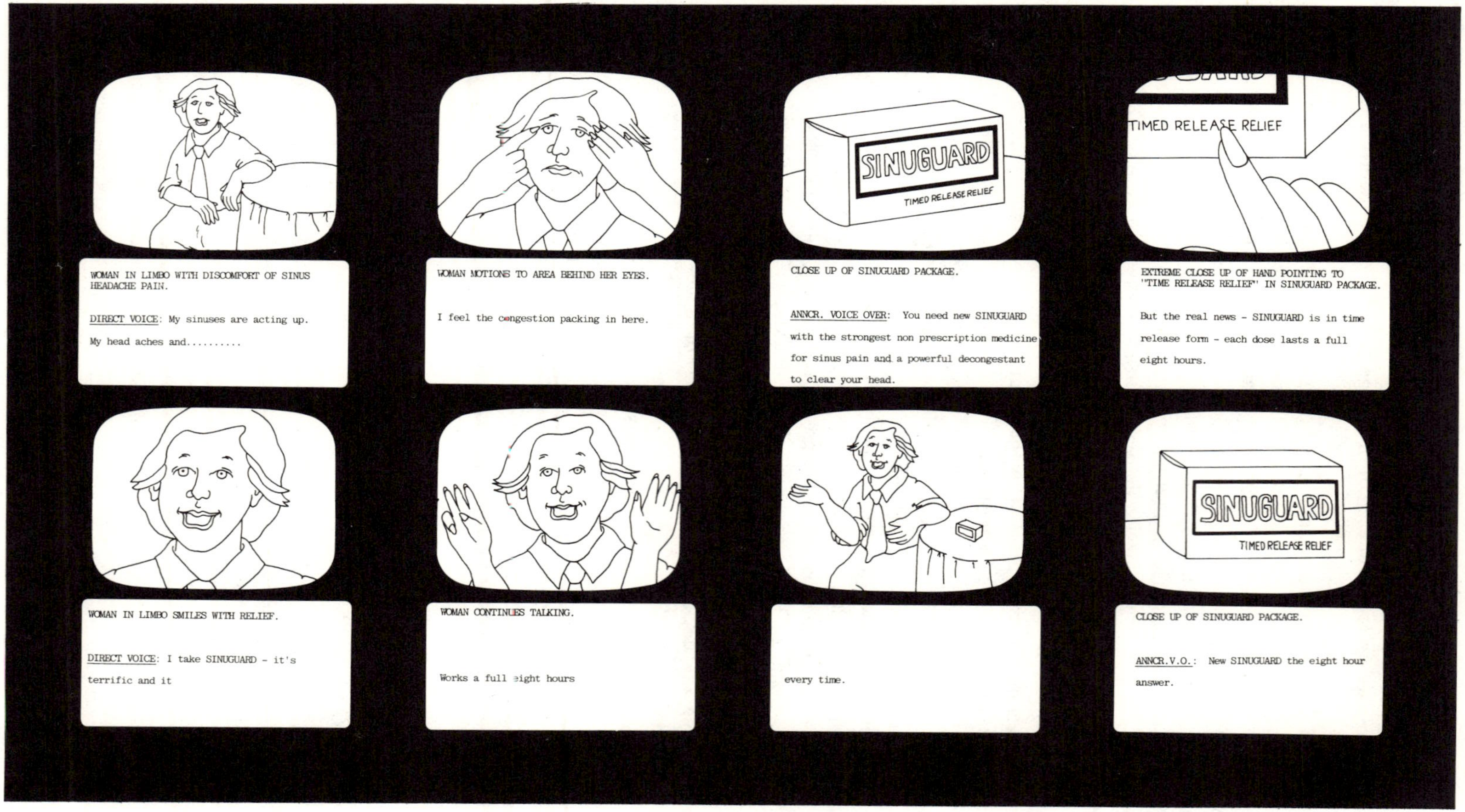
WOMAN IN LIMBO WITH DISCOMFORT OF SINUS HEADACHE PAIN.
DIRECT VOICE: My sinuses are acting up.
My head aches and..........
WOMAN MOTIONS TO AREA BEHIND HER EYES.
I feel the congestion packing in here.
SINUGUARD
TIMED RELEASE RELIEF
CLOSE UP OF SINUGUARD PACKAGE.
ANNCR. VOICE OVER: You need new SINUGUARD with the strongest non prescription medicine for sinus pain and a powerful decongestant to clear your head.
TIMED RELEASE RELIEF
EXTREME CLOSE UP OF HAND POINTING TO "TIME RELEASE RELIEF" IN SINUGUARD PACKAGE.
But the real news - SINUGUARD is in time release form - each dose lasts a full eight hours.
WOMAN IN LIMBO SMILES WITH RELIEF.
DIRECT VOICE: I take SINUGUARD - it's terrific and it
WOMAN CONTINUES TALKING.
Works a full eight hours
every time.
SINUGUARD
TIMED RELEASE RELIEF
CLOSE UP OF SINUGUARD PACKAGE.
ANNCR.V.O.: New SINUGUARD the eight hour answer.

**EXHIBIT 7-12**

CARTOON MAN IS TALKING TO HIS CARTOON SINUS CAVITIES.
DIRECT VOICE: Sinus cavities - why do you keep filling up with congestion and its pain?
CARTOON SINUS CAVITIES RESPOND.
DIRECT VOICE: Because you don't know what's good for us, dummy.
CARTOON MAN SPEAKS TO HIS CARTOON SINUS CAVITIES.
DIRECT VOICE: What's good for you and good for me?
SINUGUARD
TIMED RELEASE RELIEF
CLOSE UP OF SINUGUARD PACKAGE.
CARTOON CAVITIES VOICE OVER: New SINUGUARD is good for us - powerful pain reliever and potent decongestant.
TIMED RELEASE RELIEF
EXTREME CLOSE UP: CARTOON CAVITIES POINTS TO "TIMED RELEASE RELIEF" IN SINUGUARD PACKAGE.
CARTOON CAVITIES VOICE OVER: And, what's good for you, each dose lasts a full eight hours.
CARTOON MAN SPEAKS TO HIS CARTOON CAVITIES.
DIRECT VOICE: You mean all that relief and eight hour dosage too?
CARTOON CAVITIES, DRAWING.
DIRECT VOICE: Yup - drains us right down to nothing.
SINUGUARD
TIMED RELEASE RELIEF
CLOSE UP OF SINUGUARD PACKAGE.
CARTOON CAVITIES AND VOICE OVER: SINUGUARD - good for us, good for you.

## EXHIBIT 7-13

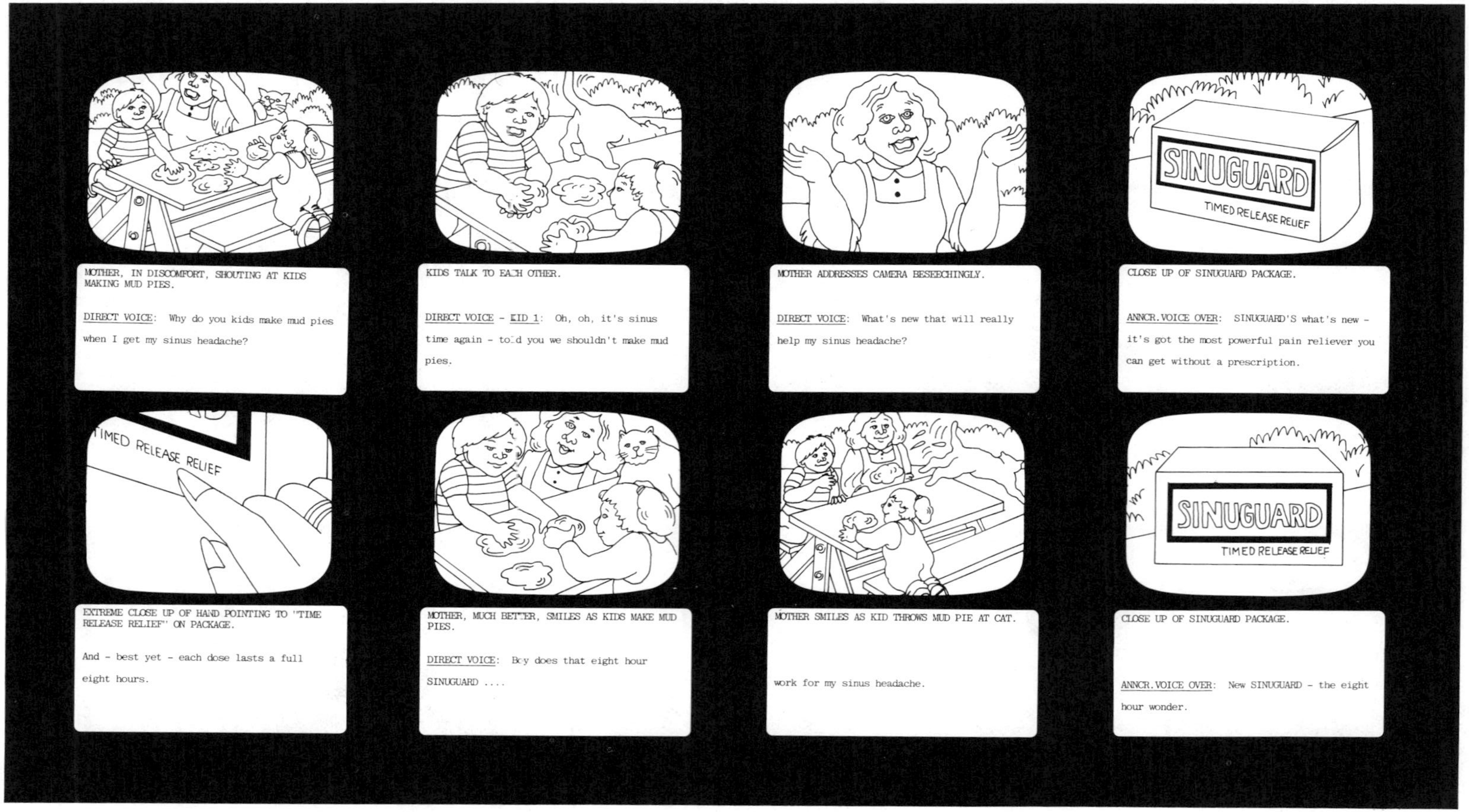
MOTHER, IN DISCOMFORT, SHOUTING AT KIDS MAKING MUD PIES.
DIRECT VOICE: Why do you kids make mud pies when I get my sinus headache?
KIDS TALK TO EACH OTHER.
DIRECT VOICE - KID 1: Oh, oh, it's sinus time again - told you we shouldn't make mud pies.
MOTHER ADDRESSES CAMERA BESEECHINGLY.
DIRECT VOICE: What's new that will really help my sinus headache?
SINUGUARD
TIMED RELEASE RELIEF
CLOSE UP OF SINUGUARD PACKAGE.
ANNCR. VOICE OVER: SINUGUARD'S what's new - it's got the most powerful pain reliever you can get without a prescription.
TIMED RELEASE RELIEF
EXTREME CLOSE UP OF HAND POINTING TO "TIME RELEASE RELIEF" ON PACKAGE.
And - best yet - each dose lasts a full eight hours.
MOTHER, MUCH BETTER, SMILES AS KIDS MAKE MUD PIES.
DIRECT VOICE: Boy does that eight hour SINUGUARD ....
MOTHER SMILES AS KID THROWS MUD PIE AT CAT.
work for my sinus headache.
SINUGUARD
TIMED RELEASE RELIEF
CLOSE UP OF SINUGUARD PACKAGE.
ANNCR. VOICE OVER: New SINUGUARD - the eight hour wonder.

# EXHIBIT 7-14

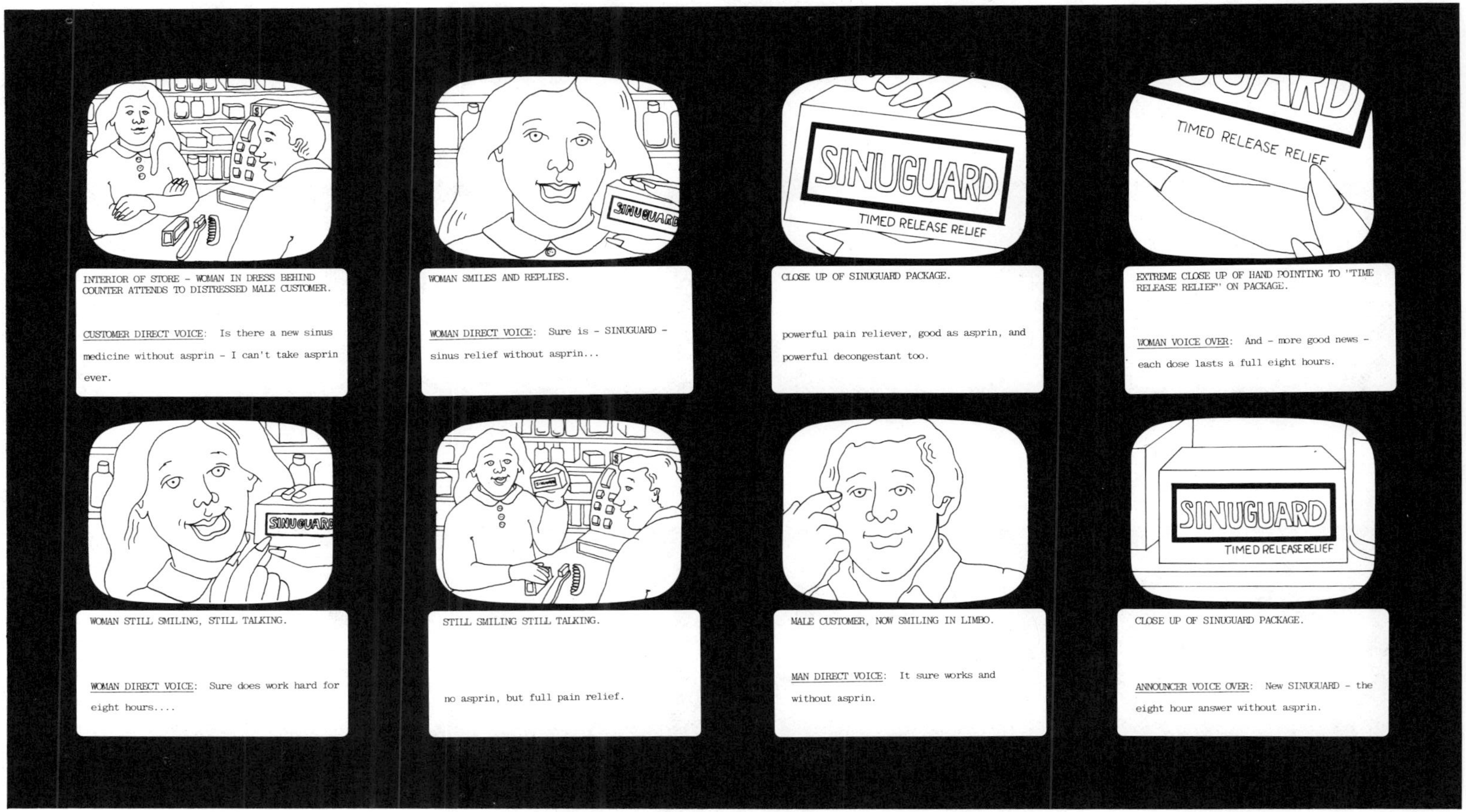
INTERIOR OF STORE - WOMAN IN DRESS BEHIND COUNTER ATTENDS TO DISTRESSED MALE CUSTOMER.
CUSTOMER DIRECT VOICE: Is there a new sinus medicine without asprin - I can't take asprin ever.
SINUGUARD
WOMAN SMILES AND REPLIES.
WOMAN DIRECT VOICE: Sure is - SINUGUARD - sinus relief without asprin...
SINUGUARD
TIMED RELEASE RELIEF
CLOSE UP OF SINUGUARD PACKAGE.
powerful pain reliever, good as asprin, and powerful decongestant too.
TIMED RELEASE RELIEF
EXTREME CLOSE UP OF HAND POINTING TO "TIME RELEASE RELIEF" ON PACKAGE.
WOMAN VOICE OVER: And - more good news - each dose lasts a full eight hours.
SINUGUARD
WOMAN STILL SMILING, STILL TALKING.
WOMAN DIRECT VOICE: Sure does work hard for eight hours....
STILL SMILING STILL TALKING.
no asprin, but full pain relief.
MALE CUSTOMER, NOW SMILING IN LIMBO.
MAN DIRECT VOICE: It sure works and without asprin.
SINUGUARD
TIMED RELEASE RELIEF
CLOSE UP OF SINUGUARD PACKAGE.
ANNOUNCER VOICE OVER: New SINUGUARD - the eight hour answer without asprin.

## EXHIBIT 7-15

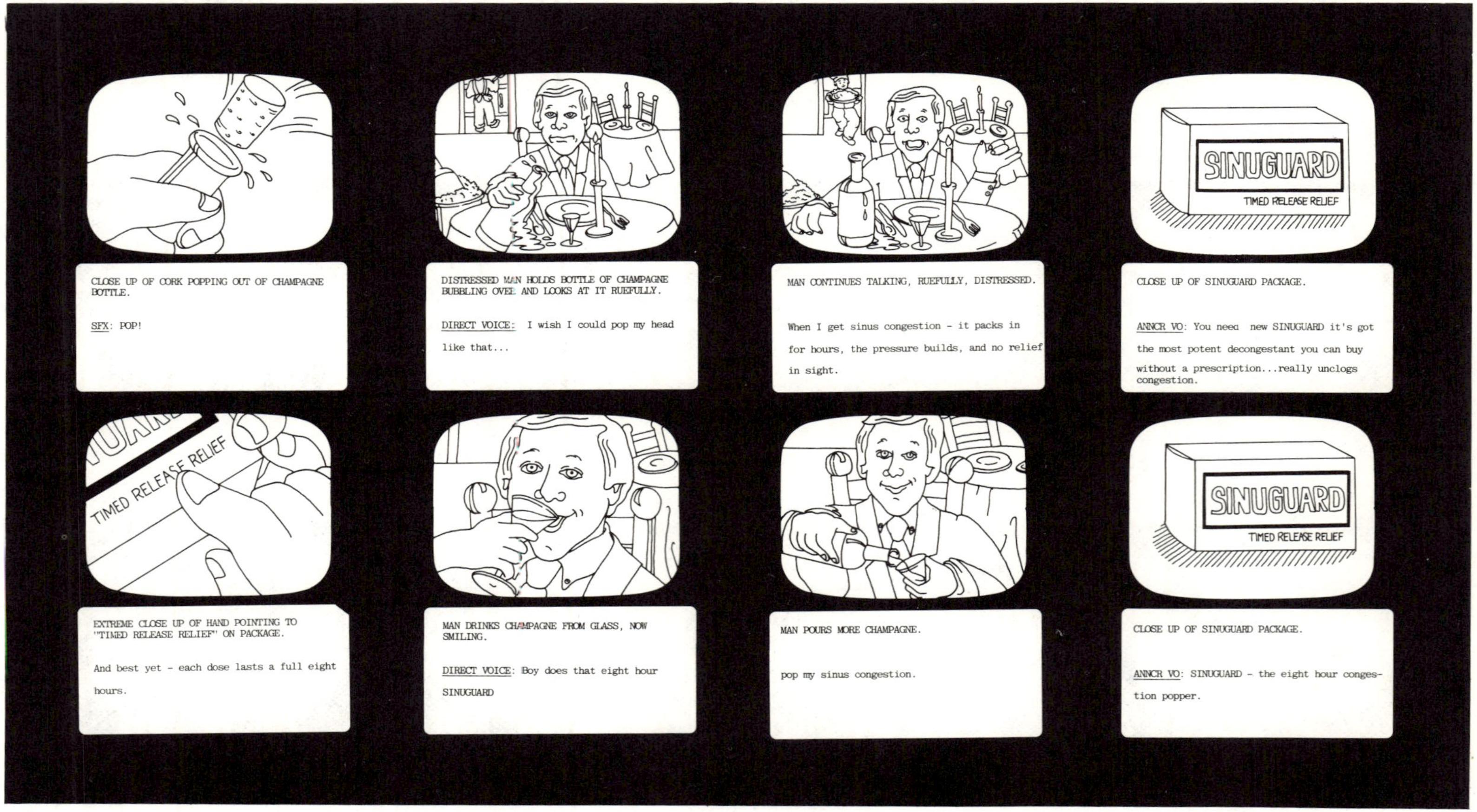

CLOSE UP OF CORK POPPING OUT OF CHAMPAGNE BOTTLE.
SFX: POP!
DISTRESSED MAN HOLDS BOTTLE OF CHAMPAGNE BUBBLING OVER AND LOOKS AT IT RUEFULLY.
DIRECT VOICE: I wish I could pop my head like that...
MAN CONTINUES TALKING, RUEFULLY, DISTRESSED.
When I get sinus congestion - it packs in for hours, the pressure builds, and no relief in sight.
SINUGUARD
TIMED RELEASE RELIEF
CLOSE UP OF SINUGUARD PACKAGE.
ANNCR VO: You need new SINUGUARD it's got the most potent decongestant you can buy without a prescription...really unclogs congestion.
TIMED RELEASE RELIEF
EXTREME CLOSE UP OF HAND POINTING TO "TIMED RELEASE RELIEF" ON PACKAGE.
And best yet - each dose lasts a full eight hours.
MAN DRINKS CHAMPAGNE FROM GLASS, NOW SMILING.
DIRECT VOICE: Boy does that eight hour SINUGUARD
MAN POURS MORE CHAMPAGNE.
pop my sinus congestion.
SINUGUARD
TIMED RELEASE RELIEF
CLOSE UP OF SINUGUARD PACKAGE.
ANNCR VO: SINUGUARD - the eight hour congestion popper.

**EXHIBIT 7-16**
**Specimen Data: Summary Results* from Day-After-Recall Copy Test, Sinuguard "Cartoons" Television Commercial**

| | | |
|---|---|---|
| Commercial Audience: | Number | 172 |
| | Percent | 100 |
| Gave Related Recall | | 41 |
| Sales Messages (Net)† | | |
| Relieves sinus congestion and pain | | 27 |
| Relieves sinus congestion (no pain mention) | | 3 |
| Relieves sinus pain (No congestion mention) | | 6 |
| Time-release over eight hours | | 22 |
| Best for sinus cavities | | 18 |
| Best for sinus sufferer | | 4 |
| All other | | 2 |
| Visual Mentions (Net)† | | 36 |

(Average related recall for thirty-second commercials: 24)
*Modeled on the Day after Recall results from copy tests conducted by Burke Marketing Research, Inc.
†Some respondents gave more than one answer.

**EXHIBIT 7-17**
**Specimen Data: Summary Results* from Day-After-Recall Copy Test, Sinuguard "Mud Pies" Television Commercial**

| | | |
|---|---|---|
| Commercial Audience: | Number | 181 |
| | Percent | 100 |
| Gave Related Recall | | 16 |
| Sales Messages (Net)† | | |
| Relieves sinus headache | | 12 |
| Relieves tension headache | | 10 |
| Time release over eight hours | | 6 |
| Pain reliever is powerful | | 2 |
| All other | | 4 |
| Visual Mentions (Net)† | | 6 |

(Average related recall for thirty-second commercials: 24)
*Modeled on the Day after Recall results from copy tests conducted by Burke Marketing Research, Inc.
†Some respondents gave more than one answer.

**EXHIBIT 7-18**

**Specimen Data: Summary Results* from Day-After-Recall Copy Test, "Without Aspirin" Television Commercial**

| | | |
|---|---|---|
| Commercial Audience: | Number | 169 |
| | Percent | 100 |
| Gave Related Recall | | 48 |
| Sales Messages (Net)† | | |
| Contains no aspirin | | 31 |
| Doesn't upset the stomach | | 14 |
| Time-release over eight hours | | 16 |
| Pain reliever is as good as aspirin | | 12 |
| All other | | 6 |
| Video Mentions (Net)† | | 14 |

(Average related recall for thirty-second commercials: 24)

*Modeled on the Day-after Recall results from copy tests conducted by Burke Marketing Research, Inc.

†Some respondents gave more than one answer.

**EXHIBIT 7-19**

**Specimen Data: Summary Results* from Day-After-Recall Copy Test, Sinuguard "Cork" Television Commercial**

| | | |
|---|---|---|
| Commercial Audience: | Number | 156 |
| | Percent | 100 |
| Gave Related Recall | | 29 |
| Sales Messages (Net)† | | |
| Unclogs congestion | | 12 |
| Time-release over eight hours | | 10 |
| Decongestant is powerful | | 2 |
| All other | | 7 |
| Video Mention (Net)† | | 27 |

(Average related recall for thirty-second commercials: 24)

*Modeled on the Day-after Recall results from copy tests conducted by Burke Marketing Research, Inc.

†Some respondents gave more than one answer.

3. Write advertising strategy statements that are derived from marketing opportunity statements A, C, D, and E.

4. Evaluate the strengths of the commercials presented in Exhibits 7-11 and 7-12. On what basis do you believe that Exhibit 7-12 was judged superior to Exhibit 7-11 as an advertising execution based on marketing opportunity statement A? Do you agree with this judgment? Tell why or why not.

5. In two instances, George Benson seems to ignore or modify research findings and thus modify their implications for advertising. For example, on page 156 he finds the product test methodology "flawed" and suggests that its results overstate consumer preferences for the eight-hour, time-release feature of Athena. And, on page 156 he also states that the apparent consumer receptiveness to aspirin substitutes "may be the kind of gratuitous consumer response that we so often seem to get in focused group sessions and must constantly guard against." Do such modifications of research findings make any difference as far as advertising strategy is concerned? Should the product manager have the authority to make research-procedure-based evaluations of research findings? What role should the research department play in such circumstances?

6. Of what value are the demographic data presented in Exhibit 7–10? They seem to have had little impact upon the deliberations of the Allgood marketing group and the agency. Of what significance would such data have in the formulation of advertising creative strategy; of advertising media strategy; of brand-marketing strategy?

7. What does the senior advertising agency account executive—in this case, Management Director Andrew Procope—do? What function does he fulfill? If you were Procope would you have acted as he is portrayed in the Case? Why or why not?

8. Analyze the copy-test results presented on Exhibits 7–16, 7–17, 7–18, 7–19. What have you learned about each of the test commercials? What have you not learned about each of the test commercials?

# Case 8

# The Advertising Appropriation and Media Plan

*ALLGOOD DRUG COMPANY INTRODUCES SINUGUARD, PART 2*

As work progressed on advertising copy for Sinuguard (see Case 7), Product Manager George A. Benson turned his attention to the development of an advertising appropriation recommendation for the brand.

Allgood Drug Company had, over the years, been guided by a relatively strict philosophy about how advertising appropriations for the company brands were to be developed by Allgood product managers. This philosophy contained several elements.

1. First, the company believed it to be improper from a marketing standpoint for Allgood to introduce a brand in any product category that could not be supported by an advertising appropriation larger than the advertising appropriation of leading competitive brands. This rule of competitive superiority was applied as follows:
   a. When a new Allgood product was introduced into the marketplace, its advertising appropriation for the introductory year should exceed, in total dollars expended in media, the advertising appropriation of that brand in the category with the largest advertising appropriation.
   b. In marketing years following the introductory year, the Allgood brands advertising-to-sales ratio should exceed the advertising-to-sales ratio of that brand in the category with the highest advertising-to-sales ratio.

In practical terms these rules meant that, when introduced, a new Allgood brand would be supported by more advertising dollars than any other brand in the category and that, in subsequent years, the Allgood brand would advertise at a higher rate than any other brand in the category.

The rule of competitive superiority was designed to build upon and amplify the basic Allgood philosophy of new-product development. Allgood would only introduce new products that were, in some way, superior, in consumer terms, to those that were already available in the marketplace. Allgood believed that if such superior products were, in turn, supported by a higher level of advertising than that enjoyed by competitive brands, the success of the new Allgood brand would be inevitable. This Allgood philosophy did not depend solely on superior products and higher advertising appropriations. It was also assumed by Allgood, as we have seen in Case 7, that a compelling statement of brand superiority had been developed in advertising copy.

2. The actual computation of the advertising appropriation for a new Allgood product depends upon the interrelation of three factors. These three factors are:
   a. The projected factory price of the new Allgood product. Although Allgood product pricing depends to some extent on the actual costs inherent in the manufacture of the product, the single most important factor in price determination is the competitive price structure that already exists in the marketplace. Allgood almost always trys to market their superior products at roughly the same price as those competitive products currently available to the consumer. Occasionally, if the new Allgood product appears to be significantly superior to available competitive brands, the company policy permits a premium pricing strategy for the Allgood product. Under usual circumstances, however, a strategy of competitive price parity is imposed upon newly developed Allgood brands.
   b. Once the factory price is established, relevant cost factors are then computed. The first of the costs is the actual cost of producing the product. This cost is determined by the Allgood manufacturing department. Three other "costs" are determined by the Allgood accounting department. These costs are standard percentages of the established factory selling price. The first standard percentage reflects company sales, distribution, and administrative costs. This percentage stood at 9.24 percent in 1979 and reflected a standard allocation applied to all company brands by the accounting department. It is designed to recoup actual expenses for these functions from individual brands during each fiscal year. The second standard percentage reflects corporate overhead and was 18.72 percent for 1979. Finally, the marketing research allocated cost was 1.75 percent for 1979.
   c. Dollars "available" for profit, promotion, and advertising are then computed by subtracting the sum of these four costs from estimated factory sales.
3. Special rules apply, as follows, to the division of these "available" dollars between promotion, profit, and advertising.
   a. In the introductory year, company policy permits all "available" dollars to be devoted to advertising. The company philosophy is simplicity itself: Advertising expenditures are maximized in the introductory year as a means to build a broad-scale consumer-product trial. If the Allgood product is, in fact, superior to that of the competitors, this broad-scale trial will build an enduring con-

sumer franchise. Company policy permits new products to yield zero profit in the introductory year. It is understood and expected that profits from each new product will be forthcoming in marketing year two and thereafter.

b. Company experience indicates that advertising is considerably more efficient in generating consumer trial of new products in the proprietary-drug category in the introductory year than any kind of consumer or trade promotion. Thus, company policy dictates that there will be no consumer promotion for new Allgood brands. The promotional activity for new brands is limited to standard trade price promotions and advertising allowances. These permitted promotional expenditures should not exceed 20 percent of the total allocation for brand advertising. This promotional policy holds both for the introductory marketing year and for subsequent marketing years.

c. In post-introductory marketing years it is expected that each Allgood new product will contribute approximately 40 percent of funds "available" for promotion, profit, and advertising to profit.

These several assumptions and rules interact so that no new Allgood product can be introduced in the market unless costs and potential sales guarantee, at least on an arithmetical basis, competitive advertising expenditures and potential profitability. The way these rules are applied to Sinuguard is illustrated in Exhibits 8-1 through 8-6.

Exhibit 8-1 shows sales of sinus-infection remedies from 1970 to 1979 and projected sales for 1980, 1981, 1982, and 1983. These sales data are based, as you will recall from Case 7, on Allgood market research department analyses of the actual number of medication doses devoted to sinus infections, regardless of the advertised use of individual remedies.

Exhibit 8-2 presents sales and advertising data for those products that currently dominate the sinus-remedy market. Market shares and two sets of dollar-sales figures are presented for the four leading brands of sinus-infection remedies: Sinucedin, Tradist,

**EXHIBIT 8-1**

**Specimen Data: Sinus-Infection-Remedy Sales, Selected Years and Projections through 1983, Consumer Dollars (000 Omitted)**

| Year | Sinus-Infection-Remedy Sales |
|---|---|
| 1970 | $ 53,800 |
| 1972 | 61,600 |
| 1974 | 79,700 |
| 1976 | 103,200 |
| 1977 | 113,300 |
| 1978 | 137,700 |
| 1979 | 156,600 |
| 1980 (estimated) | 167,000 |
| 1981 (estimated) | 178,000 |
| 1982 (estimated) | 191,000 |
| 1983 (estimated) | 201,000 |

*Source:* Estimates based on projected proportion of doses consumed by ailment type made by Allgood Market Research Department.

**EXHIBIT 8-2**
**Specimen Data: Sales and Advertising Expenditures of Leading Sinus-Infection Remedies, 1979**

| | Sinucedin | Tradist | Sinufoil | Colduban |
|---|---|---|---|---|
| Market Share* | 18% | 22% | 20% | 19% |
| Brand Sales, Consumer† | $28,188,000 | $34,452,000 | $31,320,000 | $29,754,000 |
| Brand Sales, Factory | 18,886,000 | 23,083,000 | 20,984,000 | 19,935,000 |
| Advertising‡ | 3,211,000 | 5,540,000 | 3,777,000 | 4,186,000 |
| Advertising/ Factory Sales Ratio | .17 | .24 | .18 | .21 |
| Network Television | 1,800,000 | 3,620,000 | 2,266,000 | 3,000,000 |
| Spot Television | 1,411,000 | 920,000 | | |
| Consumer Magazines | | 1,000,000 | | |
| Network Radio | | | | 1,186,000 |
| Spot Radio | | | 1,511,000 | |

*Source:* Allgood Marketing Research Department.
*Market share estimates are based on the projected proportion of brand doses consumed by ailment types.
†Sales by brand are computed by multiplying market shares by total estimated sinus-remedy sales for 1979.
‡Sinus-infection-remedy advertising appropriations for Tradist and Colduban are estimated from advertising agency analysis of brand advertising copy directed to sinus-infection relief.

Sinufoil, and Colduban. "Consumer" sales represent the dollars spent by consumers, at retail, for sinus-infection relief for each of the leading brands as computed by the Allgood market research department. "Factory" sales represent returns to the manufacturers from each product. "Consumer" sales exceed "factory" sales since they include costs generated by elements in the distribution system (wholesalers, retailers, jobbers, etc.) and included in the consumer price.

Exhibit 8-2 also shows advertising expenditures made by the leading brands. The advertising-expenditure estimates are compiled from publicly available reports of advertising-expenditure activity. The distribution of these expenditures by advertising media is also shown, along with the advertising-to-sales ratio relating advertising expenditures to factory-sales dollars.

Exhibit 8-3 shows sales estimates for Sinuguard for its first three marketing years. The table is based upon assumptions about the market shares which this new product will

**EXHIBIT 8-3**
**Specimen Data: Sales Estimates for SINUGUARD*: National Basis**
**Introductory Year, Year 2, Year 3**

| | Introductory Year (1981) | Year 2 (1982) | Year 3 (1983) |
|---|---|---|---|
| Total Market, Consumer Dollars | $178,000,000 | $191,000,000 | $201,000,000 |
| Total Market, Factory Dollars | $119,000,000 | $128,000,000 | $135,000,000 |
| Estimated Market Shares for Sinuguard | 15% | 20% | 25% |
| Estimated Factory Sales for Sinuguard | $17,850,000 | 25,600,000 | 33,750,000 |
| Pipeline | $3,570,000 | – | – |
| Total Factory Sales | $21,420,000 | 25,600,000 | 33,750,000 |
| Twelve-Count Cases | 1,500,000 | 1,793,000 | 2,363,000 |

*Assumptions: (1) Consumer sales in 1979 are used as a base in projecting consumer sales in 1981, 1982, and 1983. (2) The product will be sold at a suggested retail price of $1.79 for each package containing 24 tablets. The product will be sold to the trade in twelve-count cases yielding $1.19 per package and $14.28 per case in factory sales.

achieve in each of these three years. Market-share estimates are, of course, little more than educated guesses. They are based upon the experience of the marketing executives in Allgood Drug Company and reflect their assessment of the sales potential of a product like Sinuguard with its known product-test performance, projected advertising expenditures, and particular product characteristics. If these sales estimates are correct, they can serve as a basis for determining the viability of Sinuguard. If they are incorrect, then all of the computations for which they subsequently serve as a basis will also be incorrect.

"Pipeline" sales are one-time, nonrecurring sales to establish product stocks in wholesale and retail outlets. Allgood experience indicates that such retail stocks for a product to be sold in a single size in drugstore, food supermarkets, and mass merchandisers will account for approximately 20 percent of total first-year sales.

Factory dollar sales are converted to total sales in twelve-count cases on the basis of the logic and arithmetic described in the footnote to Exhibit 8-3.

Exhibit 8-4 shows the various costs that are incurred in the production of Sinuguard and allocated to it on the basis of standard Allgood accounting-department procedures. The cost to produce the product ($3.6357 per case of twelve units) is provided by the Allgood production department. All of the remaining, allocated costs are computed by applying the standard accounting percentages to the factory-sales dollar yield per case.

Exhibit 8-5 shows extensions of these cost figures to total estimated sales for Sinuguard. Estimated factory sales for each marketing year are drawn from Exhibit 8-3, and costs are computed by multiplying per-case cost estimates by estimated case sales in each year. The dollar amounts available for promotion, profit, and advertising are then computed by subtracting total cost of goods from total factory sales.

Exhibit 8-6 shows the allocation of available dollars to promotion, profit, and advertising for each of the three marketing years. This exhibit demonstrates that:

a. Sinuguard will spend $7,602,000 on advertising in its introductory marketing year. An advertising expenditure at this level exceeds 1979 advertising expenditures of each of the leading competitive brands (see Exhibit 8-2).
b. The *Sinuguard* advertising-to-factory-sales ratio of .25 for the second and third marketing years will exceed the 1979 advertising-to-sales ratios of each of the leading competitors.

On paper, at least, it appears that Sinuguard will be a marketing success. The real question that is raised by Exhibits 8-4 through 8-6 is whether or not the sales estimates upon which they are based can actually be achieved in the marketplace. The exhibits demonstrate that all of the Allgood rules and assumptions for new-product marketing do, in fact, hold in the case of Sinuguard. That is, the exhibits demonstrate that the pricing structure of Sinuguard is such that, at anticipated sales levels, the product will generate adequate advertising funds and prove profitable after a twelve-month introductory period.

Demonstrating that Sinuguard can become a viable marketing entity under the constraints developed by Allgood Drug Company for new products does not, however, guarantee that the new product will become a success.

It is for this reason that most companies test the viability of new products like Sinuguard on a small scale before making a final commitment to national marketing. Such small-scale market tests simulate the national marketing and advertising programs in several test markets.

The planning for test marketing of Sinuguard proceeded in two distinct steps. First, it was necessary to identify the markets in which the product would be test marketed.

**EXHIBIT 8-4**
**Specimen Data: Computation of Standard Costs for Sinuguard, Twelve-Count Case Basis***

| | |
|---|---|
| Factory dollars received per case | $14.2800 |
| Costs per case: | |
| Manufacturing costs estimated by Allgood Drug production department* | 3.6357 |
| Sales, distribution, and administrative costs (standard percentage from Allgood accounting department: 9.24%) | 1.3195 |
| Overhead (standard percentage from Allgood accounting department: 18.72%) | 2.6732 |
| Market research (standard percentage from Allgood accounting department: 1.75%) | .2499 |
| Total cost per case | $7.8783 |
| Available for profit, promotion, and advertising, per case | $6.4017 |

*Production Department states that this estimated production cost per standard case will remain constant at volumes up to and including 7,500,000 cases per year.

**EXHIBIT 8-5**
**Specimen Data: Computation of Funds Available for Sinuguard Profit, Promotion, and Advertising: Introductory Year, Year 2, and Year 3**

| | Introductory Year (1981) | Year 2 (1982) | Year 3 (1983) |
|---|---|---|---|
| Factory Sales: | | | |
| Dollars | $21,420,000 | 25,600,000 | 33,750,000 |
| Cases | 1,500,000 | 1,793,000 | 2,363,000 |
| Direct and Indirect Cost of Goods: | | | |
| Manufacturing Costs | $5,454,000 | $6,520,000 | $8,591,000 |
| Sales, etc. Costs | 1,979,000 | 2,366,000 | 3,118,000 |
| Overhead | 4,010,000 | 4,793,000 | 6,317,000 |
| Market Research | 375,000 | 448,000 | 591,000 |
| Total Cost of Goods | $11,818,000 | $14,127,000 | $18,617,000 |
| Available for Profit, Promotion, and Advertising | $9,602,000 | $11,473,000 | $15,133,000 |

Second, it was necessary to design the advertising program to be followed in these designated test markets.

Allgood Drug Company had formulated guidelines in respect to the selection of markets for testing the introduction of totally new brands and for testing variations in marketing programs of established brands. The rules for test-market selection are summarized in the following paragraphs.

1. Each market test is to be based upon three distinct test markets. A test market is defined as a television market which is, in turn, defined as the "area of dominant influence" of television stations originating in the market.

**EXHIBIT 8-6**
**Specimen Data: Projected Advertising and Promotion Expenditures and Sinuguard Profits: Introductory Year, Year 2 and Year 3**

| | Introductory Year (1981) | Year 2 (1982) | Year 3 (1983) |
|---|---|---|---|
| Factory Sales | $21,420,000 | $25,600,000 | $33,750,000 |
| Available for Profit, Promotion and Advertising | 9,602,000 | 11,473,000 | 15,133,000 |
| Advertising | 7,602,000 | 6,400,000 | 8,438,000 |
| Promotion | 2,000,000 | 1,000,000 | 1,000,000 |
| Profit | – | 4,073,000 | 5,695,000 |
| Advertising/ Sales Ratio | .35 | .25 | .25 |

2. The test markets will be geographically dispersed.
3. The markets will, collectively, account for not less than 2.0 percent of U.S. television homes and not more than 4.0 percent of U.S. television homes.
4. The test markets should be typical U.S. media markets. Typicality is defined as the presence of these media features:
   a. There should be three-network television coverage;
   b. There should be no single dominant radio station;
   c. A local newspaper Sunday supplement offering four-color reproduction should be available;
   d. Local media rates should be at reasonable levels. (This factor must be appraised in terms of recent buying experience in the market.)
   e. Test markets should not receive dominant broadcast coverage from media facilities outside the market area (there should be minimum broadcast media "spill-in" into the market). Conversely, the bulk of total listening/viewing to broadcast stations originating within the market should come from homes within the market (there should be minimum broadcast media "spill-out" out of the market.)
5. The test markets should also be "typical" in various marketing characteristics:
   a. The markets should be reasonably close to U.S. averages in regard to income distribution and population distribution.
   b. Retail-distribution facilities and coverage patterns should be reasonably typical of national retail-distribution facilities and coverage patterns.
   c. Test markets should have close to average product development for the product category which includes the Allgood test brand.
   d. Test markets should be average in respect to total Allgood Company sales. That is, markets in which Allgood Drug has had outstanding success or markets in which Allgood Drug does not make a particularly good showing should not be considered for test-market use.
   e. No test market should be the site of more than two Allgood Drug Company market tests at any given time.

Based on these several criteria, the Allgood Drug Company marketing research department had developed a list of seventy-four television markets that were suitable for use as Allgood test markets. George Benson met with representatives of the market research department to determine the availability of specific markets for the test of Sinuguard. Benson required a total of six markets for the market test of Sinuguard because, as Case 7 detailed, two alternative creative approaches were to be subjected to market test. As Allgood market test rules specify, each distinct market test requires three test markets. Since Sinuguard would have two market tests, a total of six test market areas is required.

As a result of Benson's meeting with the research people, it was decided that Seattle-Tacoma, Washington; Rochester, New York; and New Orleans, Louisiana would be used by Sinuguard in testing the cartoon advertising campaign. Together, these markets contained 1,725,000 television homes and accounted for 2.34 percent of total U.S. television homes. In addition, it was decided that Atlanta, Georgia; Denver, Colorado; and Albany-Schenectady-Troy, New York would be used in the test of the aspirin substitute advertising campaign. Together, these three markets contained 2,172,000 television homes and accounted for 2.95 percent of total U.S. television homes.

Meanwhile, Benson had been working with representatives of the media department of Belton and Baldwin advertising agency to develop a media plan for Sinuguard. Two steps were involved in this media-planning process. First, a national media plan was formulated. Second, this national plan was scaled down to the individual test markets. In formulating a media plan for any of its clients, it was customary for the Belton and Baldwin agency to address itself to five fundamental media-planning questions. Once the answers to these five questions had been worked out in nearly complete detail, the actual media-planning process was instituted. It was customary for media-department personnel to work out their own answers to these five questions, consulting with the account group and the client as they went along. The answers and supporting documentation were then committed to writing and subsequently served as a basis for all media-planning discussions and media presentations. In the following pages we present the five fundamental media-planning questions of Belton and Baldwin and describe the answers developed for each for Sinuguard.

1. *What kinds of consumers does the advertiser wish to reach?* Consumers may be described in a variety of ways. They may be described in standard demographic terms such as age, sex, household income, education, marital status, presence or absence of children, geographic region, and so forth. They may be described in terms of psychographic data such as life-style characteristics, personality needs and values, and desired product benefits. Finally, demographic and psychographic data may be combined into a statistical overview that segments consumers into groups relevant to the consumption of specific product categories.

Demographic data are most broadly used in determining the consumer characteristics relevant to media planning for individual products. The reason is that these data are generally available for both the product category for which the media plan is to be developed and for a very broad range of media vehicles. The availability of such data for product categories and media vehicles permits the matching of media vehicles to product-consumption characteristics.

Psychographic data tends to be available to some extent for media audiences and is available for particular product groupings and brands, if a special study of that group or brand has been undertaken by the advertiser.

Similarly, market-segmentation studies are typically undertaken on a custom basis for individual advertisers. Media audience data may or may not be included in such studies by their sponsors. Market-segmentation studies are of significant *specific* value in media planning *only* if they also include media-audience data for the identified segments.

As it happens, neither psychographic nor market-segmentation data are available to media planners for either the sinus-remedy market nor for Sinuguard. Of course, in the case of a new product like Sinuguard that has not yet been introduced into the market, it is impossible to have either psychographic or segmentation data available for it, *as a brand.* Psychographic and market-segmentation data might be very helpful in media planning for Sinuguard if available for the existing sinus-remedy market and brands within it. There was however, little inclination on the part of the Sinuguard brand group nor Belton and Baldwin personnel to spend the time or the money to develop such data. All of their experience indicated that available demographic data would be satisfactory for media-planning purposes. Available demographic data for the sinus-remedy market are presented in Exhibit 8-7.

Before leaving the subject of consumer characteristics in the sinus-remedy market, one additional study should be described. Allgood Drug Company has studied the market for over-the-counter medicines as a whole and identified specific usage segments within

**EXHIBIT 8-7**
**Specimen Data: Demographic Characteristics of Users of Sinus Remedies, 1979**

| | |
|---|---|
| Incidence of Use in Population in Past Year | 42% |
| Male Use | 21 |
| Female Use | 62 |

| | Male | | Female | |
|---|---|---|---|---|
| | % of Users | Index* | % of Users | Index* |
| By Age: | | | | |
| 18–24 | 24.9 | 132 | 17.9 | 102 |
| 25–34 | 25.9 | 113 | 28.4 | 137 |
| 35–44 | 17.4 | 108 | 21.7 | 145 |
| 45–54 | 16.7 | 102 | 16.9 | 107 |
| 55–64 | 8.1 | 62 | 8.8 | 65 |
| 65 & Over | 7.0 | 54 | 6.3 | 38 |
| By Education: | | | | |
| Attended/ Graduated College | 29.8 | 92 | 30.7 | 123 |
| Graduated High School | 41.6 | 119 | 45.8 | 113 |
| Did Not Graduate High School | 28.6 | 90 | 23.5 | 72 |
| By Household Income:† | | | | |
| $20,000 or over | 36.4 | 112 | 32.2 | 125 |
| $10,000–$19,999 | 21.7 | 122 | 15.3 | 89 |
| Less than $10,000 | 35.3 | 87 | 41.2 | 99 |

*100 equals the population percentage in the demographic group.
†Percent of users adds to less than 100% because some households refused to provide income figures.
*Source:* Allgood Drug Market Research Department.

this market. This Allgood study covers five proprietary medicine categories: analgesics, cold remedies, laxatives, antacids, and sleeping medicines. It is estimated that these five proprietary-medicine categories account for approximately 75 percent of the dollar volume of all proprietary drugs. Respondents in a nationally projectable sample of 1,000 were questioned about their usage of each of these proprietary medicines; about their demographic characteristics; and about their media-usage habits.

These data were then analyzed so that the respondent group was divided into three subgroups according to the intensity with which they used the measured proprietary medicines. Thus, a group of heavy proprietary-medicine users was identified as well as a group of moderate users and a group of light or nonusers. The study showed that proprietary-medicine usage is disproportionately concentrated among that third of the population classified as heavy users of proprietary medicines. In fact, some 72 percent of all proprietary-drug consumption occurs in this heavy-user group. Summary data for this heavy-user group is presented in Exhibit 8-8 and 8-9.

The major contribution of these data to Allgood media planning has been to reinforce

**EXHIBIT 8-8**
**Specimen Data: Characteristics of Total Population and Heavy Users of Proprietary Medicines, 1976**

| | Total Population | Heavy Users of Proprietary Medicines |
|---|---|---|
| Base | 1006 | 338 |
| Percent | 100 | 100 |
| Age: | | |
| 18–34 | 40.3 | 21.6 |
| 35–49 | 23.2 | 24.3 |
| 50–64 | 21.1 | 36.5 |
| 65 & over | 15.4 | 17.6 |
| Household Income: | | |
| Under \$7,500 | 21.6 | 27.6 |
| \$7,500–14,999 | 39.4 | 40.4 |
| \$15,000–24,999 | 26.5 | 21.7 |
| \$25,000 & over | 12.5 | 10.3 |
| Resident County Size: | | |
| A | 24.7 | 22.1 |
| B | 28.9 | 26.4 |
| C | 26.6 | 30.3 |
| D | 19.8 | 21.2 |
| Education: | | |
| Grade School Only | 12.7 | 14.8 |
| Some High School | 18.9 | 22.7 |
| Graduated High School | 37.6 | 35.9 |
| Some College or More | 30.8 | 26.6 |
| Sex: | | |
| Male | 48.6 | 31.7 |
| Female | 51.4 | 68.3 |
| Visits to an MD per Annum: | | |
| 3 or more | 26.2 | 34.6 |
| 1–2 | 31.7 | 46.7 |
| 1 or none | 42.1 | 18.7 |
| Smoking Behavior: | | |
| Smoke Cigarettes | 40.8 | 26.3 |
| Do Not Smoke Cigarettes | 59.2 | 73.7 |
| Alcoholic Consumption: | | |
| Drinks two or more days a week | 10.2 | 6.5 |
| Drinks on one or fewer days a week | 13.4 | 8.1 |
| Do not drink | 76.4 | 85.4 |
| Sports Participation: | | |
| Participates in one or more sports | 52.4 | 32.6 |
| Do not participate in sports | 47.6 | 67.4 |

**EXHIBIT 8-9**
**Specimen Data: Media Exposure of Total Population and Heavy Users of Proprietary Medicines, by sex; 1976**

| | Total Population | | Heavy Users of Proprietary Medicines | |
|---|---|---|---|---|
| | Male | Female | Male | Female |
| Base | 490 | 516 | 107 | 231 |
| Percent | 100 | 100 | 100 | 100 |
| Television Viewing: | | | | |
| 3 or more hours per day | 29.2 | 40.6 | 38.4 | 51.6 |
| 1-2 hours per day | 39.8 | 28.5 | 40.6 | 39.4 |
| Less than one hour per day | 31.0 | 30.9 | 21.0 | 9.0 |
| Radio Listening: | | | | |
| 3 or more hours per day | 19.6 | 26.2 | 24.6 | 27.3 |
| 1-2 hours per day | 40.7 | 30.4 | 41.8 | 32.7 |
| Less than one hour per day | 39.7 | 43.4 | 33.6 | 40.0 |
| Magazine Readership: | | | | |
| Have read in past month: | | | | |
| *Reader's Digest* | 20.6 | 27.8 | 24.3 | 31.3 |
| *TV Guide* | 22.8 | 31.3 | 26.2 | 35.7 |
| Any woman's service magazine | 6.2 | 47.8 | 4.1 | 27.3 |
| Any news magazine | 19.6 | 16.4 | 11.6 | 14.2 |
| Newspaper Readership: | | | | |
| Read any newspaper yesterday | 42.6 | 31.7 | 39.2 | 26.7 |

the company's confidence in the importance of television to the marketing of proprietary-drug products. The data also suggest that proprietary-drug users as a group are somewhat older, with lower household incomes, and are less well-educated and somewhat less urban than the United States population as a whole. The demographic data (Exhibit 8-7) for sinus remedies suggests a subpopulation of proprietary-drug users that is much less like the total population than like heavy users of proprietary drugs.

2. *What kind of message dispersion is required?* The general principle that Belton and Baldwin follows in designing media plans for proprietary medicines has been to develop a broad media-coverage pattern throughout the adult population. Frequency objectives always include an emphasis on frequency against female consumers because they are so much more likely to be heavy users of proprietary medicines and because they are usually the principal purchasing agents for these products in most households. In addition, emphasized frequency is against those other demographic groupings, if any, that are of particular importance for a particular kind of proprietary medicine. For Sinuguard it is

determined that coverage and frequency should be maximized among women in the 18-49 year age group. If possible, coverage and frequency should also be maximized in the upper-income categories.

3. *What kind of seasonal and/or regional concentration is required for advertising?* There is no evidence that there is any significant regional concentration in purchases of sinus remedies. Allgood Drug Company purchased from the A. C. Nielsen Company an analysis of product-category sales by county size and by Nielsen geographic areas and these data suggest that consumption of these products is a more or less national phenomenon with little regional or county size variation.

Allgood also purchased a Nielsen analysis of product-category sales by Nielsen bimonthly reporting periods. Once again there is no evidence in these data that sinus-remedy consumption varies significantly by season of the year.

4. *What qualities should be inherent in the media selected?* There was considerable discussion within Belton and Baldwin Media Department as to whether or not the introduction of Sinuguard might be enhanced through the use of special or unusual media opportunities. Some members of the Department felt strongly that the introduction of a new Allgood product was an event and that media vehicles should be chosen that would possess some unusual and/or outstanding content characteristics. The uniqueness of the new product should, in this view, be reflected and enhanced in consumer perception through its association with the media vehicle or vehicles in which its advertising was placed. The proponents of this view suggested, for example, that a network television "special" might be purchased in order to introduce Sinuguard to the consuming public. This special program would be selected on the basis both of its ability to attract a wide audience and the ability of its content to reflect back positively on Sinuguard. The introduction of Sinuguard would thus be enhanced since it would be associated with an unusual media event. Others at Belton and Baldwin objected to the use of Sinuguard advertising funds in such a way. They were ready to admit that a Sinuguard introduction in a popular television special would create a good deal of additional excitement and that the news that Sinuguard existed would be quickly disseminated to a very large audience. But they objected to a television special for Sinuguard for a number of reasons.

First, they pointed out that television specials were relatively expensive. It would cost Allgood almost twice as much to reach one-thousand adults or women with a special as it would with a normal night-time television commercial appearance, and almost five times as much to reach one-thousand women with a special as with a day-time commercial appearance.

Secondly, they pointed out that a one-hour night-time television special contains six minutes of commercial announcements. It was likely that only three thirty-second television commercials would be produced for Sinuguard and each of these would be designed to convey the same basic message about the product. Thus, it would be ludicrous to introduce Sinuguard in a television special: There would simply not be that much to say about Sinuguard, and it would be wasteful in the extreme to broadcast three perceptually equivalent commercial messages four times each within the same one-hour time span. If, on the other hand, Sinuguard were to purchase only two or three commercial participations in a special, the very excitement that such sponsorship of a television special could be expected to generate would be largely dissipated.

The critics also pointed out that a normal media plan could be expected to deliver very broad coverage of the actual consumer market within a relatively short period of time. And that broad coverage could be particularly extended to those groups of consumers that offered greatest opportunity for Sinuguard. Thus, if, for example, Sinuguard could be expected to achieve higher sales among adult women aged 18-49 than among adult men of the same age, the Sinuguard media program could be designed to emphasize adult women 18-49. It would be relatively harder to find a television special that was certain to deliver more adult women of this age than men. The point was that specials were designed to reach broad, nonselective audiences. The more successful the special, the less likely it was to select out a particular audience segment.

Finally, those who preferred the more traditional media approach argued that not all sinus sufferers suffered from sinus at the same time. There was, then, a good marketing reason to spread out the flow of media messages. The objective would be to repeat the message to an ever increasing audience in order to maximize the probability that each sufferer would be exposed to a Sinuguard message when it was most likely to be of interest and importance to him or her. Thus, the concentration of media expenditures in a single relatively inefficient vehicle, like a television special, was inherently unsound because it reduced the even flow of Sinuguard messages across time. In the event, it was decided not to recommend a television special or other commercial media exposure opportunity for the introduction of Sinuguard.

5. *What implication does the advertising message content have for the media plan, if any?* The final consideration in the development of media strategy is whether the advertising messages will have characteristics that require that a particular medium be used as their carrying vehicle. Some fine advertising judgments are involved here. For example, many packaged-goods advertisers have concluded that television messages are more effective and more efficient in increasing the probability that the consumer will act or think as the advertiser wishes, than are messages in any other medium. But even though this generalization may hold true in most advertising situations, it probably does not always hold true. The question that is thus often faced by the practitioner is to decide whether, in a particular advertising situation, the requirements of the advertising message are such as to dictate the choice of a particular advertising medium.

As representatives of the Belton and Baldwin media department began to discuss this question, they received a copy of the following memorandum from Mary Gonsalves, creative group head to Andrew Procope, management director.

---

## BELTON and BALDWIN

### Internal Communication

To: Andrew Procope
From: Mary Gonsalves

As we work through the creative solution to the Sinuguard introduction, it becomes increasingly apparent to me that print must be part of the Sinuguard campaign. I write this with full knowledge that Allgood is almost totally a television advertiser and with the understanding that you personally feel that television is by far the superior medium for use in promoting proprietary-drug products.

Why then am I determined to be a heretic on this question? Let me give you three reasons why I believe that magazine advertising should be part of the Sinuguard advertising program.

First, I agree with you when you say that proprietary-medicine advertising should be serious in intent and tone. People use proprietary drugs because they are hurting and they come to our advertising in search of help and relief. Magazine advertising is rational and thoughtful. It is the one advertising medium, along with newspapers, that really permits the advertiser to tell a long, full story about the advertised product. Properly handled, long, closely reasoned advertising copy can create tremendous credibility for the product. Only in magazines can we make the Sinuguard story long enough and thorough enough to give it maximum credibility and convey a real feeling of sincere concern for the consumer.

Secondly, we have more than we can tell about Sinuguard in a thirty-second commercial. You know I believe that we should give plenty of emphasis to the time-release, eight-hour aspect of Sinuguard. It is very difficult to do this in television—especially in thirty-second commercials, but even in a sixty-second commercial—because television must be so single-minded to be effective. In print we do not have to abandon the secondary story of importance. Of course, the primary copy story will dominate the magazine advertisement just as it will dominate the thirty-second television commercials. But in print it is still possible to treat the secondary story with the time and detail that it really deserves.

The Sinuguard package is a knockout. In television we should certainly show the package and give it as much emphasis as we are able. But I believe that it should be the focal point of at least some of our advertising, especially in the introductory period when it is so important to make sure that consumers will recognize Sinuguard immediately and certainly in the stores. Commercials that show only the product package for thirty unrelieved seconds make for dull television. But magazine advertisements that make a brilliantly conceived and executed package the center of full-color attention become very dramatic and memorable statements in behalf of the product.

To sum up, the Creative Department believes in four-color magazine advertising for Sinuguard!

---

Exhibits 8-10, 8-11, 8-12, 8-13, 8-14, 8-15, 8-16, and 8-17 present a variety of introductory-year media plans that might be considered for Sinuguard. Each of these media plans was developed on the basis of the conclusions reached in response to the five basic media-planning questions of the Belton and Baldwin media department.

There are six television plans and two print plans. We have assumed that the total media budget for Sinuguard will be approximately $7,300,000. (The "available" advertising funds amount to $7,602,000—see Exhibit 8-6—and it is assumed that approximately $300,000 of these funds will be required for television production, including the production of four commercials for testing purposes.)

Two of the television plans (plans A and B—Exhibits 8-10, 8-11) are television-only plans and involve no print expenditures. Two of the television plans (plans C and D—Exhibits 8-12, 8-13) are high-level television plans ($6,500,000) and assume a low level of print expenditure.

Two of the television plans (plans E and F—Exhibits 8-14, 8-15) involve a relatively lower expenditure for television ($5,500,000) and a higher expenditure for print. Finally, there are two print plans (plans E and F—Exhibits 8-16, 8-17) which detail low-level print

**EXHIBIT 8-10**
**Specimen Data: An Analysis of Proposed Television Advertising for Sinuguard, PLAN A**

| | | |
|---|---|---|
| **Proposed Television Budget:** | **$7,300,000** | |
| **Proposed Television Usage:*** | **Daytime** | **$4,000,000** |
| | **Nighttime** | **3,300,000** |
| **Proposed Weekly Schedule (30-second commercials):** | **Daytime** | **6½ weekly network appearances** |
| | **Nighttime** | **1¼ weekly network appearances** |

| | 4 Weeks | | |
|---|---|---|---|
| Audience Analysis | GRP | Coverage | Frequency |
| Total Adults | 298 | 82 | 3.6 |
| Women: Total | 343 | 84 | 4.1 |
| 18–49 | 373 | 86 | 4.3 |
| 50+ | 220 | 82 | 2.7 |
| Men: Total | 250 | 79 | 3.2 |
| 18–49 | 262 | 81 | 3.2 |
| 50+ | 234 | 75 | 3.1 |
| Household Income: | | | |
| Under $10,000 | 308 | 87 | 3.5 |
| $10,000–$14,999 | 300 | 83 | 3.6 |
| $15,000 & over | 274 | 74 | 3.7 |

*Assumes that the average network night time 30-second television commercial appearance will cost approximately $55,000 and that the average network day time 30-second television commercial appearance will cost approximately $12,000.
*Source:* Belton and Baldwin Media Research Department estimates.

expenditures ($800,000) and high-level print expenditures ($1,800,000), respectively.

It is assumed that the lower level print plan will run in conjunction with either television plan C or D and that the higher level print plan will run in conjunction with either television plan E or F. The television and print segments are analyzed separately in the exhibits for two reasons.

First, the basic media-research measurements that generate the television data (as supplied by the A. C. Nielsen Company) are different from and incompatible with the basic media-research measurements that generate the print data (as supplied by W. R. Simmons Media Studies). Because of this measurement incompatibility, it is improper to mix or meld these two different kinds of data.

Secondly, the schedules to be used in the two media plans differ in the relative continuity with which media vehicles are to be used. Thus, the television exposures are planned to be more or less continuous throughout the year with the same intensity of

**EXHIBIT 8-11**
**Specimen Data: An Analysis of Proposed Television Advertising for Sinuguard, PLAN B**

| | | |
|---|---|---|
| **Proposed Television Budget:** | **$7,300,000** | |
| **Proposed Television Usage:*** | **Daytime** | **$7,300,000** |
| | **Nighttime** | **-0-** |
| **Proposed Weekly Schedule (30-second commercials):** | **Daytime** | **11½ weekly network appearances** |
| | **Nighttime** | **0 weekly network appearances** |

| | 4 Weeks | | |
|---|---|---|---|
| Audience Analysis | GRP | Coverage | Frequency |
| Total Adults | 368 | 67 | 5.5 |
| Women: Total | 518 | 72 | 7.2 |
| 18–49 | 528 | 73 | 7.2 |
| 50+ | 508 | 71 | 7.3 |
| Men: Total | 218 | 60 | 3.6 |
| 18–49 | 223 | 62 | 3.6 |
| 50+ | 213 | 58 | 3.7 |
| Household Income: | | | |
| Under $10,000 | 408 | 69 | 5.9 |
| $10,000–14,999 | 373 | 68 | 5.5 |
| $15,000 + over | 343 | 67 | 5.1 |

*Assumes that the average network daytime 30-second television commercial appearance will cost approximately $12,000.
*Source:* Belton and Baldwin Media Research Department estimates.

exposure planned for each four-week period. Print insertions are, however, intensified during the month in which Sinuguard is introduced, maintained at a lower level in the next month or two, and sustained at an even lower level throughout the year. To average these insertion levels would achieve no good purpose, since there is a good reason for varying the print intensity throughout the introductory year. But the incompatibility of the continuity schedules makes it difficult to make direct comparisons of the television and print programs.

Therefore, the print and television plans are presented separately in the exhibits and analyzed for cost efficiency and audience delivery in Exhibit 8-18.

In the television-plan exhibits, 8-10 through 8-15, the advertising appropriation is presented with its allocation for daytime or nighttime television appearances. As we have seen, it has been decided to spend the television appropriation evenly across the year, with the same schedule of commercial appearances in each week of the year.

It is assumed in the exhibits that a typical thirty-second daytime television commer-

**EXHIBIT 8-12**
**Specimen Data: An Analysis of Proposed Television Advertising for Sinuguard, PLAN C**

| | | |
|---|---|---|
| **Proposed Television Budget:** | **$6,500,000** | |
| **Proposed Television Usage:*** | **Daytime** | **$4,000,000** |
| | **Nighttime** | **2,500,000** |
| **Proposed Weekly Schedule (30-second commercials):** | **Daytime** | **6½ weekly network appearances** |
| | **Nighttime** | **4/5 weekly network appearances** |
| | **(i.e. 4 commercials in every five weeks)** | |

| | 4 Weeks | | |
|---|---|---|---|
| Audience Analysis | GRP | Coverage | Frequency |
| Total Adults | 266 | 74 | 3.6 |
| Women: Total | 306 | 76 | 4.0 |
| 18–49 | 333 | 78 | 4.3 |
| 50+ | 197 | 74 | 2.7 |
| Men: Total | 223 | 71 | 3.1 |
| 18–49 | 234 | 75 | 3.1 |
| 50+ | 210 | 67 | 3.1 |
| Household Income: | | | |
| Under $10,000 | 274 | 79 | 3.5 |
| $10,000–14,999 | 269 | 75 | 3.6 |
| $15,000 & over | 245 | 66 | 3.7 |

*Assumes that the average nighttime 30-second television spot will cost approximately $55,000 and that the average daytime 30 second television spot will cost approximately $12,000.
*Source:* Belton and Baldwin Media Research Department estimates.

cial appearance will cost $12,000 and will achieve a rating of 8 percent among total adults. Thus, for example, in Exhibit 8-10, an appropriation of $4,000,000 is allocated for daytime television:

$$\frac{\$4{,}000{,}000}{\$12{,}000} = 333 \text{ daytime television appearances per year}$$

$$\frac{333}{52} = 6.4 \text{ daytime television appearances per week, rounded to 6.5 daytime appearances per week.}$$

Each daytime television appearance reaches 8 percent of total adults. In one week, 6.5 appearances will aggregate 52 percentage points (6.5 × 8) or 52 percentage or gross rating points against total adults. In four weeks, the daytime schedule will aggregate 208 gross rating points (52 × 4).

**EXHIBIT 8-13**
**Specimen Data: An Analysis of Proposed Television Advertising for Sinuguard, PLAN D**

| | | |
|---|---|---|
| **Proposed Television Budget:** | **$6,500,000** | |
| **Proposed Television Usage:*** | **Daytime** | **$6,500,000** |
| | **Nighttime** | **-0-** |
| **Proposed Weekly Schedule (30-second commercials):** | **Daytime** | **10½ weekly network appearances** |
| | **Nighttime** | **0 weekly network appearances** |

| | 4 Weeks | | |
|---|---|---|---|
| Audience Analysis | GRP | Coverage | Frequency |
| Total Adults | 336 | 64 | 5.3 |
| Women: Total | 474 | 69 | 6.9 |
| 18-49 | 480 | 70 | 6.9 |
| 50+ | 464 | 68 | 6.8 |
| Men: Total | 198 | 57 | 3.5 |
| 18-49 | 205 | 59 | 3.5 |
| 50+ | 195 | 55 | 3.5 |
| Household Income: | | | |
| Under $10,000 | 373 | 66 | 5.7 |
| $10,000-14,999 | 339 | 65 | 5.2 |
| $15,000 & over | 312 | 64 | 4.9 |

*Assumes that the average network daytime 30-second television commercial appearance will cost approximately $12,000.
*Source:* Belton and Baldwin Media Research Department estimates.

It is assumed that a typical thirty-second nighttime television commercial will cost $55,000 and will achieve a rating of 18 percent among total adults. Thus, for example, in Exhibit 8-10, an appropriation of $3,300,000 is allocated to nighttime television.

$$\frac{\$3,300,000}{\$55,000} = 60 \text{ nighttime television appearances per year}$$

$$\frac{60}{52} = 1.15 \text{ nighttime television appearances per week, rounded to 1.25 nighttime appearances per week.}$$

Each nighttime television appearance reaches 18 percent of total adults. In one week, 1.25 appearances will aggregate 22.5 percentage points (1.25 × 18) or 22.5 percentage or gross rating points against total adults. In four weeks, the nighttime schedule will aggregate 90 gross rating points (22.5 × 4).

The total schedule will generate a total of 298 gross rating points in a four-week

**EXHIBIT 8-14**
**Specimen Data: An Analysis of Proposed Television Advertising for Sinuguard, PLAN E**

| | | |
|---|---|---|
| **Proposed Television Budget:** | **$5,500,000** | |
| **Proposed Television Usage:*** | **Daytime** | **$3,000,000** |
| | **Nighttime** | **2,500,000** |
| **Proposed Weekly Schedule (30-second commercials):** | **Daytime** | **5 weekly network appearances** |
| | **Nighttime** | **4/5 weekly network appearances** |
| | **(i.e. 4 commercials every five weeks)** | |

| Audience Analysis | 4 Weeks | | |
|---|---|---|---|
| | GRP | Coverage | Frequency |
| Total Adults | 218 | 70 | 3.1 |
| Women: Total | 251 | 72 | 3.5 |
| 18–49 | 273 | 74 | 3.7 |
| 50+ | 161 | 70 | 2.3 |
| Men: Total | 183 | 67 | 2.7 |
| 18–49 | 192 | 71 | 2.7 |
| 50+ | 172 | 63 | 2.7 |
| Household Income: | | | |
| Under $10,000 | 225 | 75 | 3.0 |
| $10,000–14,999 | 220 | 71 | 3.1 |
| $15,000 & over | 201 | 62 | 3.2 |

*Assumes that the average network nighttime 30-second television commercial appearance will cost $55,000 and that the average network daytime 30 second television commercial appearance will cost $12,000.
*Source:* Belton and Baldwin Media Research Department estimates.

period among total adults. The coverage and frequency data for this combination of day and night television appearances is estimated using formulae that have been developed from detailed study of the way in which daytime and nighttime television audiences accumulate. The formula-derived estimates for this schedule is a coverage of 82 percent of all adults in a four-week period, with a resulting frequency of 3.6 impressions per adult per four-week period. The interrelation between gross rating points, coverage, and frequency is shown by the formula:

$$\text{Frequency} = \frac{\text{Gross rating points}}{\text{Coverage}} \text{ or } 3.6 = \frac{298}{82}$$

The balance of Exhibit 8-10 has been developed on the basis of rating estimates for typical daytime and nighttime programs for each of the demographic groups shown.

**EXHIBIT 8-15**
**Specimen Data: An Analysis of Proposed Television Advertising for Sinuguard, PLAN F**

| | | |
|---|---|---|
| **Proposed Television Budget:** | **$5,500,000** | |
| **Proposed Television Usage:*** | **Daytime** | **$5,500,000** |
| | **Nighttime** | **-0-** |
| **Proposed Weekly Schedule (30-second commercials):** | **Daytime** | **8¾ weekly network appearances** |
| | **Nighttime** | **0 weekly network appearances** |

| | 4 Weeks | | |
|---|---|---|---|
| Audience Analysis | GRP | Coverage | Frequency |
| Total Adults | 280 | 58 | 4.8 |
| Women: Total | 395 | 63 | 6.3 |
| 18–49 | 400 | 64 | 6.3 |
| 50+ | 386 | 62 | 6.2 |
| Men: Total | 165 | 51 | 3.2 |
| 18–49 | 171 | 53 | 3.2 |
| 50+ | 162 | 49 | 3.3 |
| Household Income: | | | |
| Under $10,000 | 311 | 60 | 5.2 |
| $10,000–14,999 | 283 | 59 | 4.8 |
| $15,000 & over | 260 | 58 | 4.5 |

*Assumes that the average network daytime 30-second television commercial appearance will cost approximately $12,000.
*Source:* Belton and Baldwin Media Research Department estimates.

The print plan exhibits, 8-16 and 8-17, show the advertising appropriation, the magazines that are proposed for use at that budget level, and the proposed insertion schedule. The costs are given based on the use of four-color, one-page insertions.

In Exhibit 8-16 (Plan G) $800,000 is allocated to print, and it is planned to spend this appropriation for eight four-color, full-page insertions in the *Reader's Digest* (at an assumed cost of $77,500 per insertion) and three four-color, full-page insertions in *TV Guide* (at an assumed cost of $66,500 per insertion).

The costs in Exhibit 8-16 are based on one-time costs according to current rate cards. In fact, the insertions shown in Exhibit 8-16 add up to $819,500 or $19,500 over the established budget. The *Reader's Digest* eight-insertion schedule will earn at least a 5 percent discount from the one-time rates, and additional discounts may also be earned as a result of other Allgood corporate buys. The Belton and Baldwin media department uses one-time rates as estimated costs for preliminary plans on the assumption that earned discounts will absorb overages.

**EXHIBIT 8-16**
**Specimen Data: An Analysis of Proposed Magazine Advertising For Sinuguard, PLAN G**

| | |
|---|---|
| **Proposed Magazine Budget:** | **$800,000** |
| **Proposed Magazine Usage:** | *Reader's Digest** |
| | **8 four-color insertions** |
| | *TV Guide** |
| | **3 four color insertions** |

**Proposed Schedule:**

| | | Months | | | | | | | | | | |
|---|---|---|---|---|---|---|---|---|---|---|---|---|
| **Month of Introduction** | | **2** | **3** | **4** | **5** | **6** | **7** | **8** | **9** | **10** | **11** | **12** |
| **RD** | | **RD** | **RD** | **RD** | | **RD** | | **RD** | | **RD** | | **RD** |
| **TV** | **TV** | **TV** | | | | | | | | | | |

| | Issue Audience | | | |
|---|---|---|---|---|
| | | | *Reader's Digest & TV Guide* | |
| | *Reader's Digest* | *TV Guide* | Coverage | Frequency |
| Total Adults | 27.0 | 28.1 | 45.5 | 1.2 |
| Women: Total | 29.7 | 29.3 | 48.5 | 1.2 |
| 18–49 | 27.8 | 33.7 | 50.2 | 1.2 |
| 50+ | 32.9 | 22.2 | 45.7 | 1.2 |
| Men: Total | 24.0 | 26.8 | 42.3 | 1.2 |
| 18–49 | 20.5 | 30.9 | 45.7 | 1.2 |
| 50+ | 31.1 | 18.9 | 41.5 | 1.2 |
| Household Income: | | | | |
| Under $10,000 | 22.3 | 25.7 | 36.9 | 1.3 |
| $10,000–14,999 | 25.4 | 30.5 | 46.6 | 1.2 |
| $15,000 & over | 30.5 | 28.6 | 48.5 | 1.2 |

*One-time, full-page, four-color costs are assumed to be:
*Reader's Digest* – $77,500
*TV Guide* – $66,500
*Source:* Belton and Baldwin Media Research Department estimates.

The *Reader's Digest* insertions are run each month during the first four months of the introductory year and every other month during the balance of the year. The three *TV Guide* insertions are bunched at the beginning of the introductory year.

Media-research data indicate that a single issue of *Reader's Digest* reaches 27.0 percent of all adults and that a single issue of *TV Guide* reaches 28.1 percent of all adults. Studies of the duplication of readership between *Reader's Digest* and *TV Guide* indicate that the audiences of the two magazines are relatively unduplicated. Thus, one issue of *TV Guide* and one issue of *Reader's Digest* will reach, unduplicated, 45.5 percent of all adults, with a frequency of 1.2 exposures per adult.

**EXHIBIT 8-17**
**Specimen Data: An Analysis of Proposed Magazine Advertising for Sinuguard, PLAN H**

**Proposed Magazine Budget:** **$1,800,000**

**Proposed Magazine Usage:**
*Reader's Digest:**
**6 four color insertions**
*TV Guide:**
**2 four color insertions**
*Ladies' Home Journal:**
**6 four color insertions**
*McCall's:**
**6 four color insertions**
*Good Housekeeping:**
**6 four color insertions**
*Woman's Day:**
**6 four color insertions**
*Family Circle:**
**6 four color insertions**

**Proposed Schedule:**

| Month of Introduction | Months: 2 | 3 | 4 | 5 | 6 | 7 | 8 | 9 | 10 | 11 | 12 |
|---|---|---|---|---|---|---|---|---|---|---|---|
| RD | RD | RD | | | RD | | | RD | | | RD |
| TV | TV | | | | | | | | | | |
| LHJ | LHJ | LHJ | | LHJ | | | LHJ | | | LHJ | |
| McC | McC | McC | McC | | | McC | | | McC | | |
| GH | GH | GH | | | GH | | | GH | | | GH |
| WD | WD | WD | | WD | | | WD | | | WD | |
| FC | FC | FC | FC | | | RC | | | FC | | |

| | Issue Audience: *Reader's Digest* | *TV Guide* | *Ladies' Home Journal* | *McCall's* | *Good House-keeping* | *Woman's Day* | *Family Circle* |
|---|---|---|---|---|---|---|---|
| Total Adults | 27.0 | 28.1 | 9.9 | 12.9 | 13.2 | 12.5 | 13.4 |
| Women: Total | 29.7 | 29.3 | 16.4 | 20.9 | 21.3 | 21.9 | 22.2 |
| 18–49 | 27.8 | 33.7 | 16.5 | 22.3 | 22.9 | 24.0 | 24.9 |
| 50+ | 32.9 | 22.2 | 16.2 | 18.7 | 18.8 | 18.6 | 17.9 |
| Men: Total | 24.0 | 26.8 | 2.9 | 4.3 | 4.3 | 2.6 | 3.8 |
| 18–49 | 20.5 | 30.9 | 2.6 | 3.9 | 4.5 | 2.5 | 3.7 |
| 50+ | 31.1 | 18.9 | 3.7 | 5.0 | 3.9 | 2.7 | 4.1 |
| Household Income: | | | | | | | |
| Under $10,000 | 22.3 | 25.7 | 7.8 | 11.7 | 10.7 | 10.2 | 10.3 |
| $10,000–14,999 | 25.4 | 30.5 | 9.3 | 12.4 | 13.4 | 12.7 | 13.0 |
| $15,000 & over | 30.5 | 28.6 | 11.5 | 13.9 | 14.5 | 14.1 | 15.4 |

**EXHIBIT 8-17 (Continued)**

| | Two Issues Net Unduplicated Audiences | | | | | |
|---|---|---|---|---|---|---|
| | *McCall's* and *Family Cir.* | | *Ladies' Home* and *Woman's Day* | | *Reader's Digest* and *Good Housekeeping* | |
| | Cov. | Freq. | Cov. | Freq. | Cov. | Freq. |
| Total Adults | 21.9 | 1.2 | 19.0 | 1.2 | 34.2 | 1.2 |
| Women: Total | 35.4 | 1.2 | 34.9 | 1.1 | 48.5 | 1.1 |
| 18–49 | 38.4 | 1.2 | 33.4 | 1.2 | 50.2 | 1.0 |
| 50+ | 30.6 | 1.2 | 31.0 | 1.1 | 45.7 | 1.1 |
| Men: Total | 7.2 | 1.1 | 5.1 | 1.1 | 26.2 | 1.1 |
| 18–49 | 6.7 | 1.1 | 4.7 | 1.1 | 23.0 | 1.1 |
| 50+ | 8.2 | 1.1 | 5.9 | 1.1 | 32.6 | 1.1 |
| Household Income: | | | | | | |
| Under $10,000 | 18.6 | 1.2 | 15.5 | 1.2 | 28.1 | 1.2 |
| $10,000–14,999 | 20.7 | 1.2 | 18.5 | 1.2 | 32.9 | 1.2 |
| $15,000 & over | 24.4 | 1.2 | 21.3 | 1.2 | 38.4 | 1.2 |

*One-time, full-page, four-color costs are assumed to be:

| | |
|---|---|
| *Reader's Digest* | $77,500 |
| *TV Guide* | 66,500 |
| *Ladies' Home Journal* | 37,500 |
| *McCall's* | 47,500 |
| *Good Housekeeping* | 41,575 |
| *Woman's Day* | 53,700 |
| *Family Circle* | 53,800 |

*Source:* Belton and Baldwin Media Research Department estimates.

The media research department of Belton and Baldwin estimates that the gross four-week coverage of total adults achieved by Plan C (television at the $6,500,000 level, with daytime and nighttime) plus Plan G (print at the $800,000 level) is 86 percent. Similarly, it is estimated that the gross four-week coverage of Plan D (television at the $6,500,000 level, daytime only) plus Plan G (print at the $800,000 level) is 79 percent.

In Exhibit 8-17 (Plan H) $1,800,000 is allocated to print, and it is planned to spend this appropriation for four-color, full-page advertisements in a total of seven magazines. *Reader's Digest* receives six insertions (at $77,500 per insertion); *TV Guide* receives two insertions (at $66,500 per insertion); *Ladies' Home Journal* receives six insertions (at $37,500 per insertion); *McCall's* receives six insertions (at $47,500 per insertion); *Good Housekeeping* receives six insertions (at $41,575 per insertion); *Woman's Day* receives six insertions (at $53,700 per insertion); and *Family Circle* receives six insertions (at $53,800 per insertion).

The print appropriation under Plan H is set at $1,800,000. The gross cost of the insertions in seven magazines detailed in the plan is $2,002,000. The costs in Exhibit 8-17 are based on one-time costs at current rate card levels. In fact, insertion schedules at the six-time per year level will earn discounts from the one-time rate of about 5 percent. In addition, Sinuguard will benefit from corporate discounts earned by Allgood by aggregating insertions for all Allgood brands in each magazine. For preliminary planning purposes, Belton and Baldwin media department assumes that Sinuguard will earn discounts amounting to about 10 percent if Plan H is implemented; and it is this assumption that is reflected in Exhibit 8-17.

Exhibit 8-17 shows how the insertion in each of the magazines will be scheduled throughout the year. In the introductory month there will be one insertion in every magazine on the list and two insertions in *TV Guide.* In months two and three, there will be one insertion in every magazine on the list except *TV Guide.* In the remaining nine months of the year all magazines except *TV Guide* are used three times each. With six magazines, this means that there are a total of two insertions per month. The magazine insertions are rotated throughout the nine-month period as indicated in the exhibit.

Exhibit 8-17 also shows audience data for the individual magazines and for combinations of magazines. The description and interpretation of these data is the same as that given above for Exhibit 8-16 for *Reader's Digest* and *TV Guide.*

The media research department of Belton and Baldwin estimates that the gross four-week coverage of total adults achieved by Plan E (television at the $5,500,000 level, with daytime and nighttime) plus print at the $1,800,000 level (Plan H) is 84 percent. Similarly, it is estimated that the gross four-week coverage of Plan F (television at the $5,500,000 level, all daytime) plus print at the $1,800,000 level (Plan H) is 76 percent.

Exhibit 8-18 presents an analysis of the audience delivery and cost efficiency for each of the eight media plans. Media exposures are computed by multiplying the gross rating points delivered against an audience segment in a four-week period times the number of individuals in that segment.

For example, there are 153,244,000 adults eighteen years and older in the United States. Under media Plan D, a total of 326 gross rating points will be delivered against total adults in a four-week period:

$$153{,}244{,}000 \times 336 = 51{,}489{,}984{,}000$$

But, gross rating points are expressed as percentages. Thus, two decimal places are dropped:

$$153{,}244{,}000 \times 3.36 = 514{,}899{,}840 \text{ media exposures}$$

Cost efficiency is computed as:

$$\frac{\text{Cost of media vehicles}}{\text{Media exposures delivered by media vehicles}}$$

The cost of television in Plan D is $6,500,000 per year. In four weeks the cost is:

$$\frac{\$6{,}500{,}000.}{13} = \$500{,}000$$

since there are thirteen four-week periods per year. Thus, the cost per thousand media exposures against total adults in Plan D is:

$$\frac{\$500{,}000.}{514{,}899.8} = \$0.97$$

**EXHIBIT 8-18**
**Specimen Data: An Analysis of the Audience Delivery and Cost Efficiency of Eight Media Plans**

| | Plan A | Plan B | Plan C | Plan D |
|---|---|---|---|---|
| Total Adults | | | | |
| Media Exposure in four weeks | 456,667,120 | 563,937,920 | 407,629,040 | 514,899,840 |
| Cost per thousand | $1.23 | $1.00 | $1.23 | $0.97 |
| Women 18–49 | | | | |
| Media Exposure in four weeks | 184,082,960 | 260,578,560 | 164,342,160 | 236,889,600 |
| Cost per thousand | $3.05 | $2.15 | $3.04 | $2.11 |
| | **Plan E** | **Plan F** | **Plan G*** | **Plan H†** |
| Total Adults | | | | |
| Medial Exposure in four weeks | 334,071,920 | 429,083,200 | 84,437,444 | 179,295,480 |
| Cost per thousand | $1.27 | $0.99 | $1.71 | $2.11 |
| Women 18–49 | | | | |
| Media Exposure in four weeks | 134,730,960 | 197,408,000 | 30,351,480 | 84,934,792 |
| Cost per thousand | $3.14 | $2.14 | $4.74 | $4.45 |

*One insertion each in *Reader's Digest* and *TV Guide.*
†One insertion each in *Reader's Digest, TV Guide, Ladies' Home Journal, McCall's, Good Housekeeping, Woman's Day* and *Family Circle.*

(514,899,840 media exposure is converted to thousands of media exposures—514,899.8—in order to compute *cost per thousand* media exposures).

The print cost per thousands are computed in the same way. The percentage of total audience segment covered by a particular magazine is aggregated across the entire magazine list to yield a gross rating print delivery for one insertion of each magazine on the list. The gross rating points are then multiplied by the number of individuals in the audience segment to determine total media exposures in a four week period. The appropriate cost is divided by media exposures to determine cost per thousand.

For example, to determine audience delivery and cost efficiency for the magazine list in Plan H against women 18–49, the following computations would be made:

Gross rating points: *Reader's Digest* - 27.8 + *TV Guide* - 33.7 + *Ladies' Home Journal* - 16.5 + *McCall's* - 22.3 + *Good Housekeeping* - 22.9 + *Woman's Day* - 24.0 + *Family Circle* - 24.9 = 172.1

Total Women 18–49 = 49,352,000

49,352,000 X 172.1 = 8,493,479,200.0

Percentage conversion: 49,352,000 X 1.721 = 84,934,792
Cost of schedule, single insertion = $378,075

$$\text{Cost per thousand} = \frac{378{,}075}{84{,}934.8} = \$4.45$$

## *QUESTIONS FOR CASE 8*

1. What media plan should be used to introduce Sinuguard? Why should this plan be selected in preference to others?

2. Are the sales estimates for Sinuguard shown in Exhibit 8-3 reasonable? If you believe them to be reasonable, tell why; and if you believe them to be too high or low, tell how you would amend them.

3. It is estimated that a market test of Sinuguard involving six separate test markets will:
   a. cost $850,000
   b. delay the national introduction of Sinuguard at least a year
   c. reveal Sinuguard and its formulation to Allgood competitors at least a year before its national introduction.

   Under these circumstances, do you believe it to be worthwhile to market test Sinuguard? Tell why or why not.

4. The decision has been made in Case 7 to subject two alternative advertising campaigns (Cartoons and Without Aspirin) to market test. In Case 8, several alternative media plans are developed for consideration for Sinuguard. Should there be a market test of two or three alternative media plans in addition to the market tests of the alternative advertising campaigns? Why or why not? Should there be a market test of two or three alternative media plans instead of the market tests of the alternative advertising campaigns? Why or why not?

5. Will the rule of competitive superiority be achieved for Sinuguard if competitive sales and advertising data are projected to estimated category sales for 1981, 1982, and 1983? Is there an inherent fallacy in Exhibit 8-6? What is that fallacy?

6. What is the implication of Allgood Drug Company cost of goods of the rules outlined in the case pages 175 and 176 for determining advertising appropriations? Are the rules sound? Are the rules practical?

   The Allgood Drug manufacturing department estimates the cost of manufacturing a twelve-unit case of Sinuguard to be $3.6357. Does this cost seem relatively high or low? Explain. Do you think competitive products have higher production costs or are more profitable, or both? Explain.

7. Compute the cost efficiencies that Media Plans A, B, G, and H achieve in reaching total adult women. Assume that the total number of adult women in the United States is 79,687,000 and that the total number of women aged fifty and over is 30,335,000.

8. On pages 185 and 186, the following statement is made: "For Sinuguard it is determined that coverage and frequency should be maximized among women in the 18–49 year age group. If possible, coverage and frequency should also be maximized

in the upper-income categories." On what basis was such a conclusion reached? Refer to statistical material presented in the case in preparing your answers.

9. On pages 189 and 190, it is indicated that print and television-audience data cannot be comingled in estimating the reach, frequency, and efficiency of media plans. Yet on page 198 estimates for gross coverage of the print-plus-television plan are presented. How can this be justified? How meaningful are these estimates?

10. Do you agree with the conclusion that a television special should not be used in the introduction of Sinuguard? Tell why. What problems in test marketing would be introduced by the decision to use a television special in the introduction of Sinuguard? What implications does this have for the concept of test marketing?

# Case 9

# Testing Advertising Campaigns in the Marketplace

*ALLGOOD DRUG COMPANY INTRODUCES SINUGUARD, PART 3; A, B, C, D, E*

Market testing of Sinuguard was now imminent. As we have seen, two Sinuguard advertising campaigns, called Cartoon and Without Aspirin had been selected for in-market testing (Case 7). And final decisions had been reached about the prototype national media plan for Sinuguard, based on the materials presented in Case 8. It was now time for George Benson, the Sinuguard product manager, to complete the final steps prior to the actual implementation of test marketing for Sinuguard. These last steps include:

1. Determination of the method by which the national media program will be translated into the six test markets that have been selected in Case 8.
2. Calculation of Sinuguard introductory-year dollar-sales goals for those test markets.
3. Determination of the research measurements that will be made to assess the success or failure of each of the proposed advertising campaigns for Sinuguard.
4. Final clearance of the Sinuguard television commercials with the appropriate network broadcast-standards personnel.

Case 9 covers all of these matters and will, in addition, present test-market sales results for Sinuguard in its introductory marketing year.

## *CASE 9: PART A*

George Benson was concerned that the traditional procedures followed by Allgood Drug Company in translating new-product media plans into test markets did not accurately reflect the media delivery of the same media plan when the product was nationally launched. The standard Allgood practice was to follow the "Little America" approach in translating national new-product media plans for test markets. Under the Little America approach, the media plan is translated directly on a rating-point-for-rating-point or print-insertion-for-print-insertion basis into available local media. It is simply assumed that the results of the national plan run in the test market will precisely reflect the results to be achieved when the same plan is run nationally.

On the face of it, the logic of Little America seems incontrovertible. How better to translate a national plan in a local test market than by simply implementing it in the test market? What bothered George Benson about this was his experience that, in actuality, national media plans almost always varied in their total message delivery from market to market. Thus, if one translates a national media plan so that the average national expectation is achieved in a test market, it is almost certain that the achieved message delivery will be different in the test market than it would be if the same plan were to run nationally.

There are many reasons for this phenomenon. The basic reasons are that advertising media vehicles are not equally popular or available in all markets. Some magazines have greater circulation per thousand population in some markets than others. Local newspaper penetration varies from market to market depending upon the inherent popularity of the newspaper medium in the markets. The distribution of the radio audience among available stations varies significantly from market to market, as does the number of available radio stations. Finally, the popularity of television programs varies from market to market, as does the physical signal strength of network affiliates in the different markets. Thus, it is almost certain that a national media plan if translated directly into a market will yield a different media delivery than if the same plan were actively in effect nationally.

At Allgood, the responsibility for determining policy in respect to the translation of national media plans into test markets rested with the marketing research department. Accordingly, before approving the advertising agency proposal for the Sinuguard media-plan translation, George Benson wrote the following memorandum to Barbara M. Courtney, director of marketing research:

---

# ALLGOOD MEMORANDUM

To: Barbara M. Courtney
From: George A. Benson
Subject: Translation of the Sinuguard Media Plan

I have real concerns about using the "Little America" translation procedure in developing test-market media plans for Sinuguard. As we have discussed in the past, I believe that Little America does exactly the opposite of what a correct media-plan translation should do: It is almost certain to provide a test-market media plan which is different—often radically different—from the average delivery of the national media plan which it sets out to simulate!

What I believe we should do is to adopt the "As It Falls" media-plan translation procedure. Under this procedure as I understand it, the agency attempts to predict exactly what the national plan will deliver in the individual test market and then recreates the actual delivery in translating the national media plan.

Under this scheme, the test market will be subjected to the same advertising that it would get if Sinuguard were national. If this happens to mean 15 percent more media impressions in one market, and 7 percent fewer media impressions in another, then so be it: This is exactly what As It Falls means. And this is, as far as I'm concerned, exactly what we are attempting to do when we subject a brand like Sinuguard to the test-market process.

Can't we direct the agency to follow the As It Falls procedure for the Sinuguard test market?

---

Immediately upon receiving this memorandum, Barbara Courtney telephoned George Benson:

*Courtney:* George, it's Barbara Courtney.

*Benson:* Hello, Barbara. Did you get my little note?

*C:* Come on, George. You know we've been over this ground at least a dozen times in the past three years. You know why we insist on using Little America.

*B:* Refresh my memory, Barbara.

*C:* The trouble with Little America is just what you say it is, George. A national plan never runs just like it's laid out in any individual market. Everybody knows that. But what everybody—except you, apparently—also knows is that no one, including the media experts over at the agency, can predict exactly how a national plan will actually work out in individual markets. Take network television, for example. The agency is going to buy some daytime for Sinuguard, right?

*B:* Right, quite a bit of it, as a matter of fact.

*C:* Okay, but they won't tell you now what programs or what networks they'll buy a year from now when you go national, because they don't know. Isn't that right, too?

*B:* But, Barbara, they know *about* what they're going to buy and they can predict how it will fall based on the averages.

*C:* That's where you're wrong, George. Maybe they *say* that they can do that, but they really can't with any accuracy. Your whole point with Little America is that you can't predict how a national plan will play in individual markets. You know that it will vary from market to market from experience. But that's after-the-fact experience, George. If we could predict exact media deliveries in individual markets, we might modify our Little America translation and then you'd have your As It Falls translation; but we can't, and we don't.

*B:* Okay, Barbara, you win. I still can't believe that Little America is the best way to do this, but what you say about the agency not even knowing what exact shows it will buy a year from now makes sense. Let's consider the subject closed.

*C:* Okay, George. Do you want me to put all this in writing as a response to your memorandum?

*B:* No, I guess not, Barbara. Let it slide. I'll tell the agency to go ahead with Little America.

And so Belton and Baldwin proceeded to translate the Sinuguard media plan into specific individual test-market media plans using the Little America translation principle. Wherever possible the agency translated media units on a direct unit-for-unit basis. Thus, for example, a daytime television spot in an audience-participation program was translated directly for a daytime spot in an audience-participation program, if such a spot were available in the local market. If a unit-for-unit translation was not possible, a substitution was made. For example, a daytime spot *between* audience-participation programs might be purchased in one or more individual markets, to replace a spot *within* an audience-participation program. Sometimes it was judged by the agency that the overall advertising effect of the substitute spot was somewhat less (or greater) than the overall advertising effect of the planned spot for which it was substituted. Frequently these judgments are made based on the average day-after-copy-test recall performance of advertising appearing in alternative media locations or, as in this example, the average-recall performance of an advertisement appearing within network daytime programming compared with the average-recall performance of advertising appearing in isolated positions between network daytime programs. When the agency judged that there was such a difference in advertising effect, it would buy proportionately more (or less) of the substitute time. For example, if the average day after copy test recall data indicated that between-program announcements averaged only 80 percent of the recall achieved by within-program announcements, the agency would buy 20 percent more gross rating points in spot announcements to compensate for this deficiency. Similar judgments and adjustments would also be made for nighttime network television appearances, if required, and for the print elements in the national plan, if any.

## *CASE 9: PART B*

Benson then proceeded to compute the introductory-year sales goals for each of the individual test markets. He did this, as was the custom at Allgood, on a direct percentage-of television home population basis. Thus, Benson used total television homes as the base and total television homes in the test market to determine the proportion of television homes in each test market. He then assumed that Sinuguard would achieve the same fraction of its national sales projection in that test market. The computations and sales goals are indicated in Exhibit 9-1.

## *CASE 9: PART C*

The next question to be answered by Benson was how test-market success was to be evaluated. It was a long-standing Allgood viewpoint that in marketing there is no substitute for sales. Thus, Benson accepted without question the principle that the success or failure of Sinuguard in test markets would depend upon some kind of sales measurement.

**EXHIBIT 9-1**

**Specimen Data: Computation of Consumer and Factory-Sales Goals for Sinuguard in Introductory-Year Test Markets**

| | Cartoons | | | Without aspirin | | |
|---|---|---|---|---|---|---|
| | Seattle/ Tacoma | Rochester | New Orleans | Atlanta | Denver | Albany/Troy Schenectady |
| Market-Area TV Homes (000) | 877.6 | 324.8 | 522.6 | 944.6 | 733.8 | 493.6 |
| Percent total U.S. | 1.192% | 0.441% | 0.710% | 1.283% | 0.997% | 0.671% |
| U.S. Sinuguard Consumer-Sales Estimate: Introductory Year | $26,700,000 | $26,700,000 | $26,700,000 | $26,700,000 | $26,700,000 | $26,700,000 |
| Test Market Sinuguard Consumer-Sales Estimate: Introductory Year | $318,264 | $117,747 | $189,570 | $342,561 | $266,199 | $179,157 |
| U.S. Sinuguard Factory-Sales Estimate:* Introductory Year | $21,420,000 | $21,420,000 | $21,420,000 | $21,420,000 | $21,420,000 | $21,420,000 |
| Test Market Sinuguard Factory-Sales Estimate:* Introductory Year | $255,326 | $94,462 | $152,082 | $274,819 | $213,557 | $143,728 |

*Includes pipeline sales.

In fact, Benson knew that he would have two kinds of sales data available to him for appraising Sinuguard test-market performance. First, he would have direct factory sales. These data, less returns, represented the actual sales that were made by the company: that is, the cash that actually passed into company hands as a result of Sinuguard sales. Benson knew that factory sales in the introductory year would be composed of two elements: sales made to establish Sinuguard stocks throughout the distribution system (i.e., "Pipeline" sales) and sales made to replenish items stocked as a result of actual sales from the distribution system to consumers.

Benson also knew that he would have no way of distinguishing between these two sources of sales in the factory-sales data. This fact reflected the basic shortcoming of factory sales as a measure of the success or failure of a particular marketing program. The fact that Sinuguard would be promoted to consumers through a very sizeable advertising expenditure would in itself tend to generate demand from the distribution system and inflate trade inventories above the level that would be held by the trade if advertising appropriations were lower. But, in addition Benson would, through a variety of trade promotions, do his best to force the trade to load up inventory-distribution channels in anticipation of subsequent consumer demand. The presumption was, of course, that the impact of advertising plus favorable word-of-mouth based upon superior product performance would combine to move such inflated inventories quickly into consumer hands. This result would, in turn, tend to lead the trade to sustain higher inventory levels in the expectation that consumer sales would hold at a relatively high level or even increase as time passed.

But this happy sequence of events might not, in fact, occur. Sales to consumers might well lag behind the level that the trade had anticipated based upon Sinuguard advertising plans and stimulated by trade promotions for the brand. Perhaps, in addition, consumers would conclude that Sinuguard was no more efficacious than other leading sinus remedies, in spite of the fact that it contains no aspirin and/or has an eight-hour, time-release dosage feature. Under these circumstances, there would be no need for the trade to maintain inventories at relatively high levels since consumer sales were not high enough to justify them. In addition, the trade response would be to reduce overall inventory levels back to a point where the consumer sales volume that had been generated could be sustained. As the trade "worked off" excess inventories, factory sales would fall off even further, even though consumer sales might be holding up reasonably well, even if at a lower level than initially hoped.

Ultimately, consumer sales would determine the level of factory sales, but the upward and downward manipulation of trade inventories because of these other factors could well mask immediate consumer sales and mislead Product Manager Benson as he tried to determine precisely what was happening in the marketplace.

It was for exactly this reason that Allgood also subscribed to the food and drug consumer-sales audit service, provided by the A. C. Nielsen Company. The Nielsen service measures actual consumer sales out of food and drug stores. Just as factory sales are a measure of sales made into the distribution system, A. C. Nielsen measures sales made at the other end of the system on the retail level, to consumers. Exactly what was happening to inventories within the distribution system could then be inferred by a comparison of these two sets of data, if it remained an issue; but George Benson and other Allgood product managers tended to concentrate instead upon the Nielsen reports because they believed them to reflect the final impact of marketing programs, where they counted—with the ultimate consumer.

At the same time, Benson and his fellow product managers at Allgood knew that they could not ignore the factory-sales reports. If these factory sales reports were ambiguous in a marketing sense, they were not at all ambiguous to those who account corporate success and failure. Factory sales are, after all, factory sales. From the standpoint of corporate cash income they are the ultimate determinant of the success or failure of Allgood advertising programs. Even if the senior executives in the Allgood accounting office could understand the importance of sales to ultimate consumers and could thus condone the expenditures of corporate funds for the purchase of Nielsen sales-audit reports, they would not ignore faltering factory sales for any extended period of time *no matter what* the Nielsen report suggested about consumer sales. And thus, Benson and his colleagues learned to keep a wary eye on factory-sales reports, whatever they knew their analytic shortcomings to be. Benson arranged to receive daily factory-sales reports on Sinuguard from the accounting department and contracted to receive bimonthly sales-audit reports from the test markets from the A. C. Nielsen Company. Shortly after he placed his order for Nielsen reports through the Allgood marketing research department, he received the following memorandum from Barbara Courtney.

---

# ALLGOOD MEMORANDUM

To: George Benson
From: Barbara Courtney
Subject: Assessing Sinuguard Success

We have now placed a firm order with the Nielsen Company for Sinuguard consumer-sales audits in the six test markets. We will begin receiving bimonthly reports from Nielsen about April 15 of next year. The first report will cover consumer sales in the first two months of test marketing, January and February.

The marketing research department would like to suggest that in addition to the sales data that you will be receiving for Sinuguard you also give consideration to the possibility of undertaking advertising-tracking studies in the test markets in order to monitor trends in consumer awareness of Sinuguard and the advertising claims made for it.

This seems especially appropriate to us because of the nature of the market test that you are undertaking for this product, involving as it does variations in advertising copy. We think that you should want to know more about the impact of your advertising messages among consumers than simply that one campaign, or the other, happened to be running in markets where one sales result, or another, is observed. This kind of information would be particularly useful, it would seem to us, in the event that the sales results in the two sets of test markets are more or less the same.

We know that it is more normal in this company to infer the relative effectiveness of advertising copy from achieved sales results, but in this particular case, it occurs to us that there may be good reason to augment the sales data with solid measurements of the new consumer knowledge and attitudes that the advertising campaigns create.

---

Shortly thereafter Benson received a second memorandum on the subject of advertising-tracking studies for Sinuguard. This one was written by Martha M. Margolis, director of marketing.

---

# ALLGOOD MEMORANDUM

To: George Benson
From: Martha M. Margolis
Subject: Advertising Tracking for Sinuguard

I have seen Barbara Courtney's memorandum on advertising-tracking studies for Sinuguard, and I believe that this proposal has some merit. Barbara, you, and I should meet to discuss this subject next Tuesday afternoon at three o'clock, in my office, if that is convenient for the two of you.

---

And, so, it came to pass, that Martha Margolis, Barbara Courtney, and George Benson met to discuss advertising-tracking studies for Sinuguard.

Martha Margolis opened the discussion. "George," she said, "this is your brand, you're responsible for it, and I think we should know what you think about advertising tracking for Sinuguard."

"I think it's a waste of money, Martha," responded Benson, "and I'm dead set against it. I'll let the sales results make up my mind about which campaign to run for Sinuguard. I'm frankly not interested in what consumers can remember about my advertising. All I care about is what they do as a result. And, if we get a tie between the two campaigns—which I'd bet a lot of dough we won't—then I'll decide which to run on judgment."

"But, George," said Barbara Courtney, "you know that you won't know a thing about the *communications* effect of your advertising if you just depend upon sales results. Sales results are all right, but . . ."

"Wait a minute, Barbara," broke in Martha Margolis, "before you tell us what's lacking in the sales data, I'd like you to be a bit more specific about just what the 'communication' effects' of advertising are. We haven't done much advertising-tracking work on our brands, as you perfectly well know, and I think you have the responsibility to tell us what it is that we've been missing."

"Okay, Martha, fair enough," said Barbara Courtney. "I think that we would want to measure five aspects of advertising accomplishment for Sinuguard. First, we would want to know how many people are aware of the brand on an unaided basis: that is, the numbers of people who give us Sinuguard as an answer when we ask them to name all the sinus remedies that they can think of. Second, we will want to know how many people, over and above those that give unaided recall, are familiar with the brand name when they hear it. We would group the total of those who name Sinuguard without aid and those who know the name when they hear it under *brand recognition.* Third, we would want to know what facts these people know about Sinuguard: How many are aware of the eight-hour, time-release feature; how many are aware of the nonaspirin analgesic that this product contains; how many know that Sinuguard is as efficacious for sinus infection as any other over-the-counter remedy one can buy? And so on. Fourth, we would determine people's attitudes toward Sinuguard. How many people believe that Sinuguard is an effective remedy for sinus infection; how many people believe that the eight hour time release feature is important to them; how many people believe that the nonaspirin analgesic ingredient is important to them? And so on. Finally, we would want to use our standard buying-intention scale to measure interest in purchase. We know that this measure does not reflect actual buying intention, but we have had enough experience using the measure to know what constitutes a good score and what does not."

"All of this information has value in and of itself, we think, but it should be especially valuable in comparing the two advertising campaigns–Cartoons and Without Aspirin –in their separate test markets. We really think this is the thing to do, Martha."

"Okay, Barbara," said Martha Margolis. "What would all this cost, and how would you schedule the studies?"

"Well, since Sinuguard is a totally new product," responded Barbara Courtney, "there is no need to do a wave of interviews prior to the introduction of the product, as far as I can see. I mean, no one should be aware of it or recognize the name, or have knowledge or attitudes about it or have any purchase intent before the product is in the stores or before the advertising starts, should they? So, I would think we should do two waves of interviews: one about two months after the start of advertising to measure its immediate impact and a second about eight or nine months after introduction so that we'll have a progress report at about the time you are making a final evaluation of the sales results. We'd do about two-hundred completed interviews per market, per wave; so this would be about twenty-four hundred interviews in total. The interviewing would be done by telephone and we should have a top-line report about two weeks after the completion of the interviewing and a final report in, say, six weeks. The whole job would run about $30,000 or $35,000 out of pocket, and, of course, there would be internal time charges against your research budget. You've got plenty of money in that budget, incidentally, to cover the works; so no need to worry about that."

"Okay, Barbara," said Martha Margolis, "that's a very clear statement; and I certainly feel that we now know exactly where we are on this and have a good basis for figuring out what we should do. What should we do, George?"

George Benson was rather puzzled by the question. As far as he could tell, he had already made his views on advertising-tracking studies for Sinuguard perfectly clear. And he knew Martha Margolis well enough to know that it was very unlikely that she had not understood exactly what he had said and exactly what he had meant. "Either she thinks we really should do this and is trying to make it easy for me to back off from what I said and change my tune," Benson thought quickly, "or she is trying to let Barbara down gently. I've got to figure out a way to find out where she stands before I get in too deep, or I may end up with Martha annoyed at me as well as having to agree to the dumb study."

"Ah, Barbara, ah, what would we do," started George Benson, "if we, ah, got different results in the tracking study and the Neilsen reports? I mean, suppose we see very good consumer take-away on Sinuguard, good enough to exceed our sales goals, and your tracking study showed low awareness, low recognition, low knowledge, negative attitudes, and low purchase intent. What would we do then, Barbara?" Benson looked at Martha Margolis as he asked this question and was pleased to see a slight frown come across her face.

"Why, George," said Barbara Courtney, somewhat sharply, "that just couldn't happen. You know that and I know that, don't we, Martha?"

Martha Margolis remained silent.

George Benson responded: "Couldn't happen, or wouldn't happen, Barbara? There's a big difference. But whether it could happen or not is, in a funny way, really beside the point. The point is that regardless of how the tracking study turns out, it doesn't make any difference. If the tracking study results follow the sales results, we haven't gained anything and if they contradict the sales results, we're going to ignore them."

George Benson stopped talking then. No one said anything for a minute or two, although George sensed that Barbara Courtney was seething behind what appeared to be a relatively placid exterior. Benson glanced at Martha Margolis expecting her to break in, to say something that would resolve what seemed to him to be a perfectly clear-cut and resolvable issue. But she didn't.

As the silence continued, Benson decided that he must continue on the offensive.

"Martha," he said, looking directly at Martha Margolis, ignoring Barbara Courtney, "I guess it comes down to whether I run Sinuguard or not. I haven't the slightest interest in an advertising-tracking study and I've told you why. I think I'm right. But if you think we should do it, say so and I'll go along and go along willingly."

Martha Margolis looked at Barbara Courtney and said, "Okay, Barbara, what have you got to say?"

Barbara Courtney was mad as a boil—not so much because she could see the advertising-tracking study for Sinuguard gradually slipping away but rather because she sensed that George Benson had outmaneuvered her, and she didn't know how to recover.

"Well," she said, quietly, trying through a feigned calmness to suggest control of a situation in which she had lost all control, "I'm not sure there's much more to say. It seems to me that the more knowledge a marketing manager has"—she avoided looking at Benson as she said this—"the better decisions he'll make over the long haul. You may be right, George, that the advertising-tracking study may not be decisive for Sinuguard. But, if I were you, I'd like to have it. Everyone around here seems to be operating on the assumption"—she was looking right at Benson now, ignoring the marketing director completely—"that Sinuguard will be a howling success and maybe it will be. Frankly, on the research evidence that I've seen, I have my doubts. But I guess that being optimistic is really part of your job, isn't it, George?" In spite of her resolve to remain calm, Barbara Courtney had become quite heated by now. It was beginning to show as she spoke just how strongly she felt and just how sure she was that George Benson was wrong. "If you have a winner in Sinuguard, George," she continued, "you may be right, a tracking study may not make any difference at all, one way or the other. But if you don't have a winner, if Sinuguard bombs, or if it is marginal with very suspect factory sales, you're going to need more than your Nielsen store audits. And by then, it probably will be too late."

Once again, no one said anything. Both Benson and Ms. Courtney looked at Martha Margolis. They both realized that neither had left each other much ground upon which to compromise. The question had to be resolved as far as the advertising-tracking study was concerned, and only the director of marketing could make the final decision.

Finally, Martha Margolis said, "Okay, Barbara, you've made your case, and frankly I think it's a strong one. But the way we run things around here, it's up to the product manager to decide what he needs to know to run his business. George feels pretty strongly about this, as far as I can tell."

George Benson groaned to himself and nodded at this.

"And," Martha Margolis continued, "I'm not going to force a tracking study down his throat if he doesn't want one. It could be an expensive luxury. If that's the way George feels, $35,000 out of pocket is a big chunk of cash. But, George," she now looked directly at Benson, "if Sinuguard falls on its face or begins to look doubtful, we're all going to be back in here trying to figure out what to do next; and I'll want to be very sure that you understand then that I think you're making a mistake now. What I mean, George, is that you may find it a lot easier to lose Sinuguard later if you don't have a tracking study in your hand to tell me why we should continue a project that isn't doing well enough saleswise. But that's a hypothetical risk, isn't it, George? And if you're willing to discount it in your optimism for Sinuguard, well I guess it has to be all right with me. That's the kind of risk we expect our product managers to take."

The meeting ended on that note. Barbara Courtney felt somewhat vindicated, as she considered Martha Margolis's closing remarks. "She really thinks that I'm right," Barbara thought to herself. "She knows that marketing research made the right recommendation; and either way Sinuguard turns out, we've made ground with her, not lost it."

George Benson didn't like the tone of Martha Margolis's final comments very much, but he wasn't very upset by them either. Benson had a tough, cynical streak in him and he rarely got upset in business situations in which he won his own way. "She has to make Barbara think that she's on her side," thought Benson. "But what did she really do? She told me that I was on the spot with Sinuguard and if it flops, I'm going to have some rough sailing. So what else is new?" he thought, smiling to himself. "I still don't need any tracking study to bring this brand in as a success and Martha Margolis knows that just as well as I do."

Probably Martha was more upset than either of the other two, as she sat in her office, musing, immediately after Benson and Courtney had left. "Somehow, that decision didn't get made on the merits of the case," she thought. "Benson never really brought himself to consider a tracking study for Sinuguard in an objective way. As far as he's concerned, Barbara Courtney was trying to move in on his turf and made a decision for him. And he just couldn't stand for that. I guess Barbara left here happy, or as happy as I could make her, and I did have to back the product manager on his judgment. But it really ended up a display of product-manager power, rather than a clear decision made on the basis of the facts. We'll have to keep an eye on Benson, I suppose," she concluded her thoughts. "But, after all, he just showed the kind of toughness that we look for when we hire these people."

## *CASE 9, PART D*

While all of this was going on, George Benson was carrying out another task for Sinuguard. Benson, along with Sinuguard Account Supervisor Roger Hodges from Belton and Baldwin, was engaged in securing clearance of the advertising copy that was to be run in behalf of Sinuguard in its test markets. As we have seen in Case 7, two advertising campaigns are to be tested. One, represented by a television commercial called Cartoons (Exhibit 7-12) is to be tested in Seattle-Tacoma, Rochester, and New Orleans. A second, represented by a television commercial called Without Aspirin (Exhibit 7-14) is to be tested in Atlanta, Denver, and Albany-Schenectady-Troy.

The process of advertising clearance involves two steps. First there is an internal clearance process which is designed to insure that all of the relevant individuals and viewpoints within the Allgood Drug Company have formally reviewed and approved advertising to be run by an Allgood brand. Second, there is an external approval process which, for Allgood, involves the submission of each commercial proposed for an Allgood brand to the Broadcast Standards Department of each of the leading television networks. This second step is taken even in the case of test brands that do not appear on national network television, at least right away, because it is imperative that the test-market results be based upon advertising copy that is acceptable for possible national use. In addition, it has been the company's experience that the television networks provide the toughest advertising-copy review of any of the media. To pass the acceptance standards of all three television networks usually means that the advertising copy in question can pass muster with any other media that may be used. It also provides at least some assurance that the copy will not later be challenged by the National Advertising Review Board or any of the federal government regulatory agencies.

The internal review at Allgood involves five steps. First, the product manager and the director of marketing are required to "sign off" on the proposed advertising. Their approval implies that they are satisfied with the advertising from a marketing standpoint and believe it to be true and in no way deceptive.

The second step requires the approval of Elwood Locker, Allgood director of medical affairs. Locker reviews the advertising from the medical standpoint. Locker's office is totally divorced, organizationally, from that of company medical officers such as Frederick Mount, directory of pharmacology, who is responsible for the development of new products. Locker's office has been separated from the line medical and pharmacological development work as a final check on the integrity of that work. The thought was that Locker, and his associates, could review dispassionately the medical bases for Allgood advertising claims, because they had not personally been involved in developing the medical rationalizations for such claims in the first place.

Next, the approved copy proceeds to the office of Sculfort M. Lownes, general counsel of Allgood Drug Company. It is the responsibility of the office of the general counsel to review all advertising copy from the standpoint of applicable statutes, regulatory agency policies, and the relevant policies of Allgood Drug Company. Approval of advertising copy by the office of the general counsel implies that it would not, as far as could be foreseen, become the basis of future legal actions involving the company. Sculfort Lownes is a busy man within the company. Lownes discovered early in his career that he did not have much interest in the narrow, convoluted legal arguments frequently involved in the appraisal of advertising copy. Thus, Lownes has delegated this work to Alben Stearns, a young lawyer who was, for reasons obscure to Lownes, vitally interested in advertising matters and who loved the peculiar and tightly drawn legal arguments of advertising legal work. Stearns prides himself on his understanding of the marketing implications of advertising copy and believes that his legal judgments are always delivered with an understanding of the impact they will have upon a brand's marketing programs.

Allgood product managers do not share Stearns's enthusiasm for his own marketing wisdom. Their experience is that Stearns's copy decisions are often, at least from the standpoint of the product manager, shortsighted and totally lacking in basic marketing insight. To the product managers, Stearns seems a dilettante in marketing; and his nickname among them, but never of course to his face, is "the Knife." The dissatisfaction of the product managers with Stearns's legal judgment avails them nothing. Stearns has been delegated absolute authority in this area by Sculfort Lownes, and his final decisions are unappealable.

Finally, all advertising copy is reviewed by Ronald A. Dutschmann, president and chief executive officer of Allgood Drug Company. Dutschmann rarely gives more than a cursory glance to the advertising copy that is presented to him for approval. When he does make comments, they are almost always in the area of what he considers to be "good taste." Most of the Allgood marketing people who have participated in copy review sessions with Dutschmann agree that he has little interest in the advertising itself but wants to be able to say that he has a hand in its review if the matter comes up at an annual stockholders' meeting. Some of the more cynical Allgood employees also assume that Dutschmann wants to look copy over on taste grounds to protect himself from subsequent criticisms of the copy by his wife, who is known throughout the company to keep a close eye on Allgood advertising.

Altogether, the individuals involved in advertising review for Allgood are formidable. Probably some of the best brains in the company are involved in this process, and certainly all of the power that the company affords can be brought to bear on any advertising question that may arise. To Andrew Procope, management supervisor for the Allgood account at Belton and Baldwin, this review process poses the greatest single threat to the work of the agency. He believes that Belton and Baldwin employees assigned to the Allgood account are as good as any in the advertising business at assessing the marketing implications for advertising that are inherent in brands assigned to Belton and Baldwin by Allgood. He also believes that his people are excellent at the process of transforming those marketing implications into advertising copy that is truthful, in good taste, and, almost inevitably, commercially effective. And Procope is proud of the way in which his people sell the agency creative product to successive layers of Allgood marketing personnel, compromising and backtracking when necessary but almost always emerging from the interaction with the marketing people with advertising that will be effective for Allgood and reflect creditably upon the agency itself.

But all of this can be lost precipitously and permanently in the review process. Changes are made in this process, especially by the medical and legal people, who arbitrarily and, from Procope's viewpoint, capriciously emasculate the work of the agency. Procope admits to himself that the Allgood people involved in the advertising review are well intentioned. He doesn't believe them to be malicious or vindictive when they reject specific portions or all of proposed advertisements. But he knows that the effect of their review on advertising is often injurious to Allgood, and he believes that the revisions that sap the effectiveness of the advertising copy are usually of no other practical importance to the well-being of Allgood.

However, although he thinks about all of this a great deal, he says very little about it. He has, as Martha Margolis once remarked to him in a conversation about the review process, "nothing to gain by griping about the advertising review, because it will never change and, if anything, it's bound to get more stringent in the years ahead as the Allgood executives collectively respond to government and consumer pressures."

The Allgood internal review for the Sinuguard commercial was relatively typical of the process. George Benson and Martha Margolis signed off on the commercials immediately after they had reached final agreement with the agency about them. Director of Medical Affairs Elwood Locker had the following comments:

# ALLGOOD MEMORANDUM

To: George Benson
From: Elwood Locker
Subject: Sinuguard Advertising

cc: Martha Margolis

I have reviewed the proposed television commercials for Sinuguard and have the following observations to make about them:

1. We cannot guarantee eight hours of symptomatic relief. Relief will vary from individual to individual. The duration of Sinuguard symptomatic relief must be referred to as "up to eight hours."
2. In Cartoons, I believe it improper to state that Sinuguard "drains me right down to nothing." The sinus cavities themselves remain, after they have been decongested. They do not become "nothing." This misconception must be corrected.
3. In Without Aspirin, the phrase "sinus relief" is medically meaningless. What Sinuguard does is to relieve the symptoms associated with sinus infection. This must be changed to "relief of sinus symptoms without aspirin."
4. I question the inherent good taste of a man represented as talking to his sinuses. The sinus cavities are, after all, internal components of an individual's head. I think of them as the complex site of an annoying and often chronic disease condition. I don't find them amusing in any sense of that word, nor do I believe it to be in the best interest of Allgood to portray the sinus cavities in a lighthearted or frivolous way. I cannot, within the terms of reference that apply to the medical review of advertising copy, reject the Cartoons commercial on the grounds of good taste. But I can express most urgently my own personal opinion that this commercial is in bad taste and will reflect negatively upon our company.

As a result of Elwood Locker's comments, the two commercials were revised and the new audio scripts for the commercials are shown in Exhibits 9-2 and 9-3.

George Benson, Martha Margolis, Roger Hodges, and Andrew Procope met to discuss Locker's fourth criticism, concerning the relative taste of the Cartoons commercial. Martha Margolis expressed the opinion that the Cartoons commercial was not in bad taste and that, in fact, it was one of the freshest and most interesting television commercials for a proprietary-drug product that she had seen in years. There was no disagreement with this point of view from the other members of the group and they decided to ignore Locker's objections, at least for the time being.

The meeting ended with this exchange:

Andrew Procope said, "Martha, as far as I can tell, Ronald Dutschmann is the final arbiter on taste in this company. I think we should prepare ourselves to argue the taste question with him when he reviews this commercial. We can show him the version that was produced for day-after recall testing, so that he won't be passing judgment that is based only on a storyboard, like Locker. I don't think we'll have any trouble."

**EXHIBIT 9-2**
**Revised Audio Script for the Sinuguard Cartoons Commercial**

| | |
|---|---|
| Frame 1 | Direct Voice:<br>Sinus cavities, why do you keep filling up with congestion and its pain? |
| Frame 2 | Direct Voice:<br>Because you don't know what's good for me, dummy. |
| Frame 3 | Direct Voice:<br>What's good for you and good for me? |
| Frame 4 | Cartoon Cavities Voice-Over:<br>New Sinuguard is good for me—powerful pain reliever and potent decongestant. |
| Frame 5 | Cartoon Cavities Voice-over:<br>And, what's good for you, each dose lasts up to a full eight hours. |
| Frame 6 | Direct Voice:<br>You mean all that relief and for up to eight hours, too? |
| Frame 7 | Cartoon Cavities Voice-over:<br>Yup, drains me out completely, too. |
| Frame 8 | Cartoon Cavities Voice-over:<br>Sinuguard—good for me, good for you. |

**EXHIBIT 9-3**
**Revised Audio Script for the Sinuguard Without Aspirin Commercial**

| | |
|---|---|
| Frame 1 | Customer Direct Voice:<br>Is there a new sinus medicine without aspirin? I can't take aspirin, ever. |
| Frame 2 | Woman Direct Voice:<br>Sure is—Sinuguard—relieves sinus symptoms without aspirin . . . |
| Frame 3 | Powerful pain reliever, good as aspirin, and powerful decongestant, too. |
| Frame 4 | Woman Voice-over:<br>And—now good news—each dose lasts up to a full eight hours. |
| Frame 5 | Woman Direct Voice:<br>Sure does work hard for up to eight hours . . . |
| Frame 6 | No aspirin, but full pain relief. |
| Frame 7 | Customer Direct Voice:<br>It sure works, and without aspirin. |
| Frame 8 | Announcer Voice-over:<br>New Sinuguard—the eight-hour answer—without aspirin. |

"Okay, Andrew," said Martha Margolis, "I agree that it's a waste of time arguing about this with Locker and the Knife, if he brings it up, or with anyone else, for that matter. You're right. We're going to win it or lose it with Mr. Dutschmann, and we'd better have pretty good arguments in hand when we get to him."

Shortly thereafter, Alben Stearns in the Legal Department completed his review of the commercials. He sent the following memorandum:

---

# ALLGOOD MEMORANDUM

To: George Benson cc: Martha Margolis
From: Alben Stearns
Subject: Review of Sinuguard Commercials

I have now subjected two Sinuguard commercials to legal review. I assume that the commercials I have looked over have received medical approval, although Elwood Locker's initials do not appear on either of the attached routing slips. Here are my comments:

1. I am concerned with Frames 4 and 6 in the Cartoons commercial. The phrases "powerful pain reliever and potent decongestant" and "all that relief" imply to me that Sinuguard provides a higher level of analgesic and decongestant action and thus provides more relief than its competition. I don't mean to be arbitrary about this, but I do have some concern and would like to discuss the matter with you, Elwood Locker, and your associates.
2. I have the same problem in Frame 3 of Without Aspirin—"powerful pain reliever" . . . "powerful decongestant, too."
3. In Frame 7 of Without Aspirin, "it sure works" is unacceptable. We cannot promise complete symptomatic relief, as this phrase implies. We can say: "it sure is effective for me," which I prefer, or "it sure works for me," if you prefer the vernacular construction.
4. In Without Aspirin, you have gone to great lengths to qualify the eight-hour feature of Sinuguard by saying "lasts up to a full eight hours" or "sure does work hard for up to eight hours." I presume that this was done as a result of medical advice. You cannot, however, end the commercial with the phrase "the eight-hour answer." This must be changed to suggest that the product may work for as long as eight hours for at least some consumers.

---

George Benson, Martha Margolis, Roger Hodges, and Andrew Procope met to discuss Stearns's review of the Sinuguard commercials. They agreed the use of phrases like "powerful pain reliever" and "potent decongestant" were very important to the commercials because they suggested the overall effectiveness of Sinuguard in delivering symptomatic relief. Without such phrases they feared the product might seem no better than at parity with competition.

They agreed that a defense of the commercials would be undertaken in writing by George Benson. They talked for some time about the grounds that could be used to defend the portrayal of the ingredients in Sinuguard as "powerful" and "potent." As a result of this discussion and the agreements reached during it, Benson prepared the following memorandum:

---

## ALLGOOD MEMORANDUM

To: Alben Stearns
From: George Benson
Subject: Powerful and Potent Sinuguard

cc: Martha Margolis
Andrew Procope

We have given very careful consideration to your point that the Sinuguard commercials imply that Sinuguard provides a higher level of analgesic and decongestant action and thus provides more symptomatic relief than does its competitors.

We do not agree that such an implication can be drawn from these commercials. There is no comparative thrust in either of these commercials; they simply describe Sinuguard. And they do so with language that accurately describes the action of the ingredients in the products.

Acetaminophen is a powerful pain reliever, a fact that has been clinically substantiated. There is no other analgesic available for inclusion in over-the-counter products that is more potent than the acetaminophen used in Sinuguard.

The decongestant in Sinuguard has the potential to decongest. It decongests in a totally efficient and thorough way. It certainly can be called a "potent" or "powerful" decongestant. There is no other decongestant available for inclusion in over-the-counter products that is more potent than ours.

We therefore urge that these commercials be left unchanged in respect to the words "powerful" and "potent" as they appear in Frames 4 and 6 in Cartoons and in Frame 3 of Without Aspirin.

---

Two days later, George Benson received the following memorandum from Alben Stearns:

---

## ALLGOOD MEMORANDUM

To: George Benson
From: Alben Stearns
Subject: Powerful and Potent Sinuguard

cc: Martha Margolis
Andrew Procope

Thank you for your prompt and thoughtful response to my memorandum concerning advertising copy for Sinuguard. The solution to the problem is to be found in your memorandum. The key is that there is no over-the-counter analgesic or decongestant more potent or powerful than those contained in Sinuguard. This must be explicitly stated in the commercials. As the commercials stand, they may imply that Sinuguard contains ingredients more potent or powerful than those contained in other remedies sold over-the-counter.

Therefore, in Cartoons, Frame 4, the phrase should be "most powerful pain reliever and potent decongestant that you can take without a prescription." In Without Aspirin, a similar change should be made in Frame 3.

---

When he received his copy of the memorandum, Andrew Procope was annoyed. "This really is the final straw," he thought to himself. "We deliver two commercials with clear, succinct, and compelling language that will be understood by consumers and motivate them to buy. But by the time the commercials go through review, they are filled with hedges and weak words, and with stilted language that the consumer understands means that the product you are advertising is just the same as everyone else's, or maybe a little worse. Now, the way our luck is running, old Dutschmann will decree that Cartoons is in bad taste."

Martha Margolis and Andrew Procope met with Ronald Dutschmann later in the week for his consideration of the two Sinuguard television commercials. George Benson and Roger Hodges were not included in this meeting with Dutschmann for two reasons. First, Martha Margolis believed that it was easier to have a relatively successful, from her viewpoint, meeting with Dutschmann when only a few people were involved. The more people, the more Dutschmann seemed to feel that he must appear "presidential." Thus, he was likely to talk longer when more people attended meetings with him and he was likely to want to appear more profound. Long talk and profound talk could have a disastrous effect upon television commercials, especially when Dutschmann was evaluating them for tastefulness. More than once Martha Margolis had literally seen Dutschmann talk himself into the conviction that a particular commercial was in bad taste as he rambled on, pontifically, before a roomful of attentive Allgood and Belton and Baldwin employees.

The second reason was that neither Martha Margolis nor Andrew Procope wished to dilute the impact of their own professional personalities upon the president of Allgood. Dutschmann, after all, held ultimate power to control the professional destinies of Martha Margolis and Andrew Procope. They were highly motivated to make a favorable impression upon Dutschmann and to do so as often as they were able. Thus, both preferred to meet with him with as few other people as possible to avoid the possibility that his attention might be distracted from their own display of professional competence. This was especially important in meetings in which Dutschmann reviewed proposed advertising. He was in no sense a professional advertising man and would neither review advertising in an objective, professional way nor respond easily to arguments in defense of the presented advertising that were those of the objective professional. Dutschmann tended to react to advertising in an irrational, almost naive way. Thus, it was more through strength of personality rather than strength of professional argument that Ms. Margolis and Procope had to entreat, cajole, and hesitantly insist that the proffered advertising had excellence. This was a risky, subtle manipulation of a company president through the acuity of quick-witted response and through pure power of personality. Ms. Margolis and Procope worked well together as a team in selling advertising to Dutschmann. But they had no need for helpers in the process and genuinely believed that their juniors simply did not have the skills that were needed to bring Dutschmann into agreement with the advertising that was presented.

In the meeting with Dutschmann, Martha Margolis made the opening remark:

"Well, Mr. Dutschmann, you've had an opportunity to see the new Sinuguard commercials, I guess." (The rule was that Ronald Dutschmann had an opportunity to see advertising that he was to comment upon at least twenty-four hours before any meeting in which he was to deliver his comments upon it.) "Andrew and I," Martha Margolis continued, "certainly hope that you're as enthusiastic about it as we are."

Ronald Dutschmann was uncomfortable in his meetings with the advertising and marketing people. He was almost always uncertain when he criticized the advertising they brought to him, yet he was certain that he had the responsibility to do so. And he was somehow intimidated by Ms. Margolis and Procope with their facile way with words, their easy self-assurance, and their quick and felicitous arguments against any point he made. In these circumstances, he often fell back upon criticisms based on taste because, as he once remarked to his wife, "they can't easily argue with me about what good taste is. I'm the one who is going to say what it is for Allgood Drug Company, and no one else. Anyway, after Locker and Stearns get done working that advertising over, there really is relatively little left for me to say from an objective standpoint, if those guys are doing what we pay them to do."

In the Sinuguard meeting, Dutschmann responded immediately to Martha Margolis's opening remarks: "Well, Martha," he stated, "I am inclined not to dislike this advertising. I have the same problem with it, ah, Andrew," he said, turning to Procope, "that I have with so much of the work that comes out of your agency. The language seems to me to be kind of sterile and stilted—almost predictable. I know," he said, raising his hand to stop Procope from breaking in. "You tell me that much of this is due to the constraints our medical and legal people—very able people, incidentally—and the government, as well, impose on you. But isn't that just what we pay you for? I mean, isn't your job to find fresh and appealing ways—with words particularly—to present our products to Mrs. Consumer? We've worked with you people a good long time, Andrew, and we like your work; but candor becomes the relations of old friends and business associates, and I would be less than candid if I didn't say to you that I think your people are coming up short in the area of language."

Procope was visibly affected by this. He cleared his throat and began to say, "But, Ronald," when Dutschmann cut him off.

"No, no, Andrew, don't say anything. As far as I can see you really have nothing to say, unless that is, you start bringing commercials in here that say something other than hedges like 'up to eight-hours of symptomatic relief' or 'there's no ingredient that's stronger that you can buy without a prescription.' Anyway, let's move on. I've said what I have to say about language.

"How can you, the two of you, seriously propose advertising based on a cartoon representation of a person's sinus cavities? We just can't have Allgood or its products represented by attempts to make light of very serious internal organs. I know you know that this kind of thing is in execrable taste, and I know that you are bright and sensitive people. Therefore, I wonder why I am sitting here talking with you about the possibility of putting on a cartoon representation of the sinus cavities. You must have a reason, but I can't for the life of me figure out what it is."

"Mr. Dutschmann," responded Martha Margolis, "I want you to think about this rough commercial you've just seen. I think the *idea* of representing the sinus cavities in cartoon form is an audacious one, one that does go to the margin of tastefulness. But I think that our *execution* of that idea is totally tasteful. Please try to separate in your mind the difference between an idea that could be executed in bad taste and an execution that totally avoids that potential problem."

"Okay, Martha," said Dutschmann, "you make a good point. I must confess, when I think about it, I really did almost like those sinus cavities, as they were portrayed. I guess that 'charming' is not the right word to use to describe them, but they were charming in a sense. I still don't see, though, no matter how, uh, charmingly you have presented sinus cavities in your commercial, how *anyone* and particularly Allgood can bring a representation of an internal organ onto the home television screen. The next thing you'll do is bring in dancing small intestines and tell me that they're in good taste, because I let you get away with cartoon sinus cavities."

"We won't do that, Mr. Dutschmann," sighed Martha Margolis with just a suggestion of a smile. You know we won't do that because you won't let us do it. It will be a long day before Andrew or I come in here with dancing small intestines or anything else like that and try to get you to go for it—especially on the basis that you once approved a commercial showing with a rather whimsical cartoon representation of the sinus cavities how one of our products worked."

"But they don't even look like sinus cavities," retorted Dutschmann.

"That's just the point," smiled Martha Margolis. "We're not trying for medical exactitude. We're trying to say something meaningful to consumers in a compelling yet totally inoffensive way. And we really have succeeded."

"There's another point to be made, Mr. Dutschmann," said Andrew Procope, speaking for the first time. "You say to me that it's the agency's job to bring you fresh, appealing, and innovative advertising. Then we do it: We bring you an introductory commercial based on the hyperbole of a man talking to his sinus cavities. Never before has anyone done this. It's a genuinely creative idea. It's fresh. It'll attract attention. It'll sell Sinuguard. But you object to it because it may be in bad taste. I agree with Martha that the idea of a sinus cavity *may* be in bad taste but that our execution of it isn't. I believe you agree, too. It's almost charming, as you said. Now, what I'm suggesting is that we must forget the taste issue, because it really isn't there at all. The issue is whether we have the courage of our convictions to run genuinely unusual advertising for Sinuguard."

For practical purposes, the meeting was now over, although the discussion continued for another twenty minutes. Dutschmann agreed that the Cartoons commercial should run, that although it might offend some, its inherent originality outweighed that risk. He resented, however, that, once again, he, the president of Allgood had been argued out of a position by Martha Margolis and Andrew Procope. He refused to acknowledge to them the completeness with which he had finally come to accept their arguments. In the end, all he would say was, "Okay, run your sinus-cavity commercial. I won't forbid it. But I'll watch the mail. If we begin getting letters from consumers who think it's in bad taste, off the air it comes."

As they walked away from the president's office, Andrew Procope said, "I'll tell you something, Martha. Every one of these that we win just makes the next one harder. He's a tough boy and we're going to push him around just so much; then we're not going to be able to do it anymore."

"You're right, Andrew," she said. "I sure hope his wife likes that commercial."

Two weeks later George Benson had received approval from all the television networks to run Without Aspirin and Cartoons. One of the networks noted the possibility of a taste problem in showing a cartoon representation of sinus cavities. But it approved the commercial on the basis of the test version of Cartoons, with the proviso that the final version must portray the sinus cavities in substantially the same manner as had the test version.

## *CASE 9: PART E*

Exhibits 9-4 through 9-9 present sales results from the market tests of Sinuguard.

## *QUESTIONS FOR CASE 9*

*Part A*

1. What is the purpose of the test-marketing program for Sinuguard? What will constitute a successful test of Sinuguard? What will constitute an unsuccessful test of Sinuguard?

2. Do you believe that the Little America principle should be used in the translation of the Sinuguard media plan? Why or why not? Suppose a media plan that was closely comparable to the Sinuguard media plan was currently being used by a second Allgood Drug Company brand? Could the media experience of this second Allgood brand be used as the basis for an As It Falls translation for Sinuguard? Would this be preferable to the Little America translation? Why or why not?

*Part B*

3. The proportion of television homes in Sinuguard test markets is used as a basis for determining Sinuguard sales goals in these test markets. Is this the only reasonable basis for determining Sinuguard sales goals? If you believe it to be the only reasonable basis, tell why. If you believe there to be other reasonable bases for such sales-goals determination, list three or four.

*Part C*

4. Do you believe that factory-sales data are inadequate to assess the effectiveness of an advertising campaign? Tell why or why not.

5. When Barbara Courtney says, "We think that you should want to know more about the impact of your advertising messages among consumers than simply that one campaign, or the other, happened to be running in markets where one sales result, or another, is observed," what does she mean? What does her statement imply about how advertising works?

6. Do you believe that Sinuguard progress should be measured through an advertising-tracking study? If you believe that it should, give at least three reasons why. If you believe that it should not, give at least three reasons why not.

*Part D*

7. Revise the audio script for the Sinuguard television commercials on the basis of Alben Stearn's memoranda appearing on pages 218 and 219.

8. Do you believe that the Sinuguard television commercials have been "arbitrarily and capriciously emasculated" in the Allgood review process? If you believe this to be the case, give specific examples of how the sales effectiveness of the commercials has been reduced. If you believe the commercials to have been unaffected by the review process, tell why.

9. Does the Allgood review process have implications for the "creativity" of the advertising presented to Allgood by its advertising agency? Is Andrew Procope correct

when he says, on page 214, that the Allgood review process is "the greatest single threat to the work of the agency?" Is it reasonable that the final decision as to advertising content be left in the hands of people such as Elwood Locker, Alben Stearns, and Ronald Dutschmann, who are not advertising professionals and have no training or practice in advertising?

10. Define good taste in advertising. Who should be responsible for the good taste of Allgood advertising? Is the determination of good taste limited to Allgood advertising personnel, or is it also the responsibility of employees of Belton and Baldwin?

11. Do you agree that the Cartoons commercial is in good taste? If your answer is "yes," tell why. If your answer is "no," tell why not.

*Part E*

12. Evaluate the sales results for Sinuguard presented in Exhibits 9-4 through 9-9. What decision about the national marketing of Sinuguard would you make on the basis of these exhibits?

13. On the basis of the sales results presented in Exhibit 9-4 through 9-9, what comments do you have to make about the copy research results presented in Case 7, Exhibits 7-16 through 7-19?

**EXHIBIT 9-4**

**Specimen Data: Sales Results for Sinuguard in the Seattle-Tacoma Test Market (Cartoons)**

| | | |
|---|---|---|
| Factory Sales | January | $49,642 |
| | February | 18,736 |
| | March | 20,824 |
| | April | 24,777 |
| | May | 23,824 |
| | June | 21,723 |
| | July | 26,321 |
| | August | 24,427 |
| | September | 21,339 |
| | October | 27,242 |
| | November | 26,344 |
| | December | 28,421 |
| Nielsen Sales | January–February | $54,279 |
| | March–April | 62,799 |
| | May–June | 70,842 |
| | July–August | 84,322 |
| | September–October | 86,724 |
| | November–December | 91,824 |

| Computed Market Share* | | | |
|---|---|---|---|
| January–February | 16% | July–August | 25% |
| March–April | 18% | September–October | 26% |
| May–June | 21% | November–December | 27% |

*As computed by Allgood Marketing Research Department.

**EXHIBIT 9-5**
**Specimen Data: Sales Results for Sinuguard in the Rochester Test Market (Cartoons)**

| | | |
|---|---|---|
| Factory Sales | January | $ 8,439 |
| | February | 4,266 |
| | March | 5,729 |
| | April | 6,824 |
| | May | 5,979 |
| | June | 8,432 |
| | July | 7,642 |
| | August | 9,827 |
| | September | 8,629 |
| | October | 9,437 |
| | November | 10,821 |
| | December | 9,972 |
| Nielsen Sales | January-February | $10,731 |
| | March-April | 15,432 |
| | May-June | 17,539 |
| | July-August | 24,872 |
| | September-October | 27,988 |
| | November-December | 30,841 |

Computed Market Share*

| | | | |
|---|---|---|---|
| January-February | 9% | July-August | 20% |
| March-April | 14% | September-October | 25% |
| May-June | 15% | November-December | 26% |

*As computed by Allgood Marketing Research Department.

**EXHIBIT 9-6**
**Specimen Data: Sales Results for Sinuguard in the New Orleans Test Market (Cartoons)**

| | | |
|---|---|---|
| Factory Sales | January | $22,796 |
| | February | 12,824 |
| | March | 14,729 |
| | April | 17,824 |
| | May | 13,631 |
| | June | 14,724 |
| | July | 10,926 |
| | August | 8,429 |
| | September | 11,562 |
| | October | 12,723 |
| | November | 9,767 |
| | December | 14,824 |
| Nielsen Sales | January-February | $12,241 |
| | March-April | 18,732 |
| | May-June | 26,843 |
| | July-August | 35,942 |
| | September-October | 38,241 |
| | November-December | 43,821 |

Computed Market Share*

| | | | |
|---|---|---|---|
| January-February | 6% | July-August | 18% |
| March-April | 9% | September-October | 19% |
| May-June | 13% | November-December | 22% |

*As computed by Allgood Marketing Research Department.

**EXHIBIT 9-7**
**Specimen Data: Sales Results for Sinuguard in the Atlanta Test Market (Without Aspirin)**

| | | |
|---|---|---|
| Factory Sales | January | $34,935 |
| | February | 9,242 |
| | March | 12,731 |
| | April | 16,422 |
| | May | 14,321 |
| | June | 18,624 |
| | July | 11,513 |
| | August | 18,624 |
| | September | 17,231 |
| | October | 12,299 |
| | November | 10,763 |
| | December | 11,532 |
| Nielsen Sales | January-February | $37,231 |
| | March-April | 41,242 |
| | May-June | 39,639 |
| | July-August | 37,322 |
| | September-October | 34,612 |
| | November-December | 29,731 |

Computed Market Share*

| | | | |
|---|---|---|---|
| January-February | 13% | July-August | 13% |
| March-April | 14% | September-October | 12% |
| May-June | 14% | November-December | 10% |

*As computed by Allgood Marketing Research Department.

**EXHIBIT 9-8**
**Specimen Data: Sales Results for Sinuguard in the Denver Test Market (Without Aspirin)**

| | | |
|---|---|---|
| Factory Sales | January | $32,927 |
| | February | 26,824 |
| | March | 8,423 |
| | April | 12,613 |
| | May | 13,242 |
| | June | 9,641 |
| | July | 14,231 |
| | August | 14,229 |
| | September | 10,385 |
| | October | 8,763 |
| | November | 14,921 |
| | December | 12,769 |
| Nielsen Sales | January–February | $47,932 |
| | March–April | 38,421 |
| | May–June | 37,639 |
| | July–August | 30,132 |
| | September–October | 32,433 |
| | November–December | 33,729 |

Computed Market Share*

| | | | |
|---|---|---|---|
| January–February | 22% | July–August | 14% |
| March–April | 18% | September–October | 15% |
| May–June | 17% | November–December | 15% |

*As computed by Allgood Marketing Research Department.

**EXHIBIT 9-9**
**Specimen Data: Sales Results for Sinuguard in the Albany-Schenectady-Troy Test Market (Without Aspirin)**

| | | |
|---|---|---|
| Factory Sales | January | $24,242 |
| | February | 8,649 |
| | March | 9,724 |
| | April | 10,823 |
| | May | 12,962 |
| | June | 11,977 |
| | July | 10,624 |
| | August | 12,429 |
| | September | 13,927 |
| | October | 9,684 |
| | November | 11,729 |
| | December | 10,429 |
| Nielsen Sales | January–February | $24,292 |
| | March–April | 21,724 |
| | May–June | 23,823 |
| | July–August | 28,629 |
| | September–October | 31,731 |
| | November–December | 26,042 |

Computed Market Share*

| | | | |
|---|---|---|---|
| January–February | 16% | July–August | 19% |
| March–April | 14% | September–October | 21% |
| May–June | 16% | November–December | 17% |

*As computed by Allgood Marketing Research Department.

# Case 10

# Institutional Advertising

## *THE COMPUEL DIVISION OF UNITED ELECTRONICS, LTD. LAUNCHES AN ADVERTISING CAMPAIGN*

United Electronics, Ltd., is the corporate name of a far-flung conglomerate of operating divisions and subsidiary companies. The company was formed in 1947 when the Southern and Pacific Independent Telephone Company was acquired by the Commodore Radio Corporation. The resulting company was then called United Electronics, Ltd., and came to be known as UEL. By 1980 it was the fourteenth largest company in America and was comprised of seventeen operating divisions and twenty-two subsidiary companies.

The UEL operating divisions had grown from the original base of technological expertise and previously developed markets that the two founding firms had provided. There was thus the Apex Television Division, the Microwave Communications Division, the Altoona Semi-Conductor Division, and so on.

Companies acquired by UEL were generally run as autonomous subsidiaries under the management in place at the time these companies were acquired. The subsidiary companies were usually acquired because of their individual profitability and growth potential rather than because of any fundamental affinity with the mainstream activities of United Electronics, Ltd. itself. Thus, the subsidiary companies included such diverse businesses as a hotel chain; a phonograph-record-producing company; a chain of Italian pizza restaurants; a home appliance company; several television stations; and a chain of suburban weekly newspapers.

As long as these subsidiaries maintained sales and operating costs at UEL standards, the parent company was normally content to let them go about their business without interference. If a subsidiary company faltered, a team of UEL house consultants was shortly to be found working within the subsidiary to find solutions to the problems of sluggish sales and profits, as we have seen in the instance of UEL subsidiary Atlas Home-Appliance Company, described in Case 3.

UEL involvement with and control over its operating divisions tended to be more direct and intense than with the subsidiary companies. This was because the divisions were involved in activities in the traditional mainstream of the company and were closely related to the background of the UEL top management team. All of the top management at UEL had come to corporate headquarters only after extensive training and experience in one or more of the operating divisions.

The Compuel division of UEL was formed in 1958. Its purpose was to develop a line of business computers with attendant software that would have particular application in consumer service industries, such as hotels and airlines, and in industries that dealt with their customers on a continuing, monthly basis, such as utility companies and local department stores. This particular orientation for Compuel reflected several of the basic businesses that UEL already managed. For example, UEL owned the thirty-six local independent telephone companies in the United States that had once formed the Southern and Pacific Independent Telephone Company. In addition, since the formation of UEL, the company had been very active in soliciting contracts for the installation and maintenance of telephone systems in many foreign countries, especially in South America and in Southeast Asia. A major expense in these companies was customer billing, not only because it was all done by hand but also because the process was exceptionally subject to human error; and an immense amount of time and expense was needed to reconcile billing discrepancies.

In addition, UEL's Hillcrest Hotels Division spent an extraordinary amount of time and money in handling interchain reservations. As a basic policy, the Hillcrest chain emphasized its willingness to make reservations for its customers at any of the hotels throughout its system. These communications were handled at special rates by Western Union, but it was, in spite of the lower cost of late-night transmission, an expensive affair and also very prone to error. In addition, the hotels kept all their guest bills by hand and this process, also, was time consuming, expensive, and error-prone.

As a result of such billing and reservations needs within UEL operating divisions and subsidiaries, Compuel was given firm direction and the opportunity for pragmatic exposure to operating problems that urgently required solid long-term solutions. In this environment the Compuel division flourished. At first the products of the division tended to be more like office machines than computers, yet they were always based on that level of computer technology that the current state of the art permitted. As basic computer technology evolved, so too did the capabilities of the Compuel hardware. By the mid-1960s, Compuel had completely automated systems for both hotel-guest billing and for utility billing services. These systems were then adapted to a wide variety of retail enterprises and to credit-card billing operations. In later years, customer-billing systems were integrated with inventory-control systems, especially for department, hardware, and soft-goods retail stores, and for direct-response retailers.

Meanwhile, working with the UEL Microwave Communications Division, the company developed an interconnected communications network in the Hillcrest system, which by 1969 consisted of more than one-hundred hotels, motor inns and Fiesta Resorts. The heart of the interconnected communications network was a computer reservations bank that stored information on room availabilities within the system for a period of six months in advance. A single phone call to any Hillcrest facility or to a central 800 number, day or night, was all that was required to obtain a confirmed reservation at any international Hillcrest facility. The computers and software that permitted this reservation service were subsequently sold to other hotel chains and, in addition, by 1973 had been adapted to the needs of airlines, railroads, and car-rental firms. By the late 1970s, John McPherson, a sales statistician of Compuel, estimated that the average consumer was served about twenty-one times a year by a Compuel computer system. This unusual statistic had been developed by McPherson at the request of Compuel President and Chief Executive Officer Lincoln L. Rehnquist.

Rehnquist, a long-term UEL employee had been appointed president of Compuel when the division was formed in 1958. He was then forty-one years old, and had been, immediately prior to his appointment as president, executive vice-president for operations of the Hillcrest Hotels Division. An electrical engineer by training, Rehnquist had joined Southern and Pacific Independent Telephone Company in 1946 after service in the Marines in World War II, and had quickly risen to vice-president in charge of system design and installation. He was transferred to the hotel company in 1954 because he had, by then, been identified as a potential corporate manager. Under the UEL management-development program, people of strong potential were shifted into various divisions and subsidiaries of the company in order to develop a broadly based, corporate view of the management process.

Rehnquist was ideally qualified to head the new Compuel division in 1958 because he was an electrical engineer and thus could be expected to understand and master applications of the rapidly developing technology of electronic computers; because he had operating experience in the two UEL enterprises that Compuel was intended to service directly; and because it was now clear that Rehnquist was a superb manager. During the first fifteen years of his presidency, Rehnquist was largely concerned with the development of superior computer hardware and practical systems that would solve the problems in billing and reservations that had plagued the telephone companies and the hotel chains. By 1975 the engineering and systems-development tasks at Compuel had largely been completed. The future of the division now rested with its ability to market its capabilities to those firms that could gain advantages from their use.

"We can think of our future business as coming from one of two sources." Rehnquist said to sales statistician John McPherson in a meeting in Rehnquist's office, early in 1977. "We can sell more computers and systems to companies like the ones with which we are now doing business. Or we can identify other industries in which our products are not now used but could be, either as they now stand or with suitable adaptation. We have done a pretty thorough job in the industries where we are currently making sales. Our sales force has done well in identifying the companies in those industries that have real potential, and the sales people have put heavy pressure on those that are attractive prospects. The companies that we haven't yet sold seem to be well satisfied with competitive equipment and programming—usually either IBM or NCR. It's hard to find a reason to convert a potential customer who is satisfied with the machines and systems that he has in place: It's just too disruptive to make a change. So I would imagine that we are not going to be getting much new business out of those industries. Our real future has to be in identifying companies in the industries that we are not now selling, but where our machines and systems can be easily adapted.

"You tell me that the average consumer in this country is involved in twenty-one transactions per year that are handled by our machines. What I want to know is how many additional transactions there would be if we add in things that our products could do but have never been adapted to do."

"I don't want to be negative, Mr. Rehnquist," replied McPherson to what seemed to him to be a request for service from himself as sales statistician, "but I'll be goldarned if I can figure out how to estimate potential figures like that. I can tell you the number of transactions that we're now involved in because I know where our machines are and what they're doing and because when we license a program, we get a pretty good idea about its utilization in specific applications. But I don't know where our competitor's machines are or what they're doing, let alone what they're doing that our machines aren't doing."

"Okay, John," said Rehnquist, "I figured that you might not be able to put those numbers together for me. But that doesn't mean I can't think of this business in terms of increasing the number of transactions we make between consumers and our customers—does it?"

"Of course not, Mr. Rehnquist," replied McPherson.

"Okay, John," said Rehnquist, "and meantime let's set up a system in which I get that transaction per consumer number updated every month—can you do that?"

"You bet," said McPherson. And on that note their meeting ended.

The basic problem that faced UEL was how to compete more effectively against the giants in the computer field like IBM, General Electric, Control Data, and National Cash Register. While many of these firms in the 1950s and 1960s had developed a broad-scale approach to the design and utilization of computer products, Compuel had limited itself to the two basic applications of billing and reservations handling for a relatively small group of consumer-oriented industries. Thus Compuel had, by design, eliminated itself from competition with the larger firms in many of the areas in which computers and computer technology had made their most significant inroads. This had two implications for Compuel.

First, it meant that it was not really a computer company in the same sense that IBM, for example, was. IBM had developed a long line of computers and then had specialized in finding applications for that hardware wherever they might conceivably appear. Compuel, on the other hand, had developed a relatively limited line of highly specialized computers that were, by design, only useful in two basic ways. IBM could be thought of as a horizontal computer firm, whereas Compuel might be thought of as a vertical firm.

Second, Compuel was virtually unknown as a computer manufacturer, except among those industries in which it had specialized. It was difficult for Compuel to seek new applications for its specialized products outside these industries because most industries were already served by the more broadly based computer firms such as IBM, GE, and others. And just as IBM, for example, got business in the first place because of its reputation for facility in developing new applications for its computers, Compuel tended to be stymied in its expansion attempts because of it historic policy of specialization. Any business executive who looked into the matter would find that Compuel had a reputation, if it had reputation at all, for specialized rather than general expertise. Thus, even though some businesses might well have computer requirements for which Compuel would be particularly well suited, it was unlikely that it would even occur to their executives to get in touch with a Compuel representative.

Although Rehnquist brooded about this, he was, nevertheless, quite realistic. "We don't want to be an IBM, and what's more there is no way that we can ever become an IBM," he thought. "But the truth is that there are lots of things that our machines can do without any modification at all. It's just that we don't know what they are. Then there's the problem of familiarity. Most businesses have never heard of us, and the ones who have are pretty sure that we aren't for them. If we ourselves could only get over the notion that we specialize in computers that handle the same kinds of transactions day after day, week after week, and month after month, then we might begin to uncover opportunities for ourselves."

Rehnquist gradually evolved a plan to improve the competitive position of Compuel. It involved two aspects: a reorganization and redefinition of the Compuel sales organization, on the one hand, and the development of an institutional advertising program for Compuel, on the other.

The Compuel sales organization had from the beginning been thought of more as a sales-service activity rather than as a straight sales activity. Compuel had developed most of its computers and computer services in the first instance for other UEL divisions or subsidiaries. As Compuel pioneered the systems for UEL, it was easy enough to license them to UEL division and subsidiary competitors because of the service improvements and cost savings that the systems had already delivered to UEL.

Compuel was willing to do business with competitors for three reasons. First, as Rehnquist put it, "If we license our systems to our competition, we can make our systems the standard in the industry. This will tend to keep us in the picture and others out. Second, we don't compete with other hotel chains because our reservations system is better; we compete with them on the basis of our hotel services. We may get a hotel customer with our reservation system the first time but we'll never keep him, no matter how easy it is to get a reservation, unless our hotels themselves deliver a superior product." Finally, Compuel could make money by licensing their systems and broadening the base of their own operations at the same time. The more companies that used Compuel systems, the more profitable Compuel would become and the stronger its competitive position would be against the more broadly based, horizontal firms.

With its dependence upon direct competitors of UEL subsidiaries and divisions for increased sales, Compuel had little need for an aggressive sales organization. The most likely prospects for Compuel services were obvious, if not to Compuel staff, at least to the UEL divisions and subsidiaries for which they provided computer service. And the superiority of Compuel systems was already apparent to these prospects as they observed their UEL competitors' own operations. Thus, no attempt had been made in the history of Compuel to ferret out other, less obvious sources of business, nor had any tradition of imaginative salesmanship been developed within the company.

So Rehnquist became convinced that he must change the basic character of the Compuel sales organization. It would, as a result of his planned reorganization, be geared to identifying new prospects in industries not now served by Compuel and to pursuing agressively these prospects until Compuel hardware and systems had been adapted within the prospect firms.

In addition, Rehnquist also believed that an institutional advertising program in behalf of Compuel would serve the very worthwhile purpose of creating a general awareness of Compuel in the business community at large, as well as an understanding of what Compuel was capable of doing. Such awareness and knowledge would, in turn, help the revitalized sales department as it went about the business of bringing new customers into the Compuel fold.

Rehnquist discussed his plan for a Compuel advertising program with Charles D. Gelson, director of marketing for Compuel. Over the years Gelson, as director of marketing, had done just about anything that Rehnquist wanted that was not involved with the technical side of the business. When Rehnquist had given him the title in 1962, Gelson had already been working for UEL for twelve years and for Rehnquist, in one capacity or another, for ten. An electrical engineer by training, he had been hired into the Southern and Pacific training program, spotted by Rehnquist shortly thereafter, and become his de facto assistant in 1951. By 1955 he had nearly become Rehnquist's alter ego. The two men worked very well together; and Gelson was content to follow Rehnquist, whom he knew to be brilliant and believed to be as good a possibility as anyone in the company to end up as chairman of UEL in a reasonable number of years.

"I don't know what marketing will amount to in Compuel, Charlie," Rehnquist remarked to Gelson when he made him director of marketing in 1962, but we'll worry about that some other time. For now, let's make you director of marketing because it's a title that crops up in most of the divisions and the subsidiaries and no one at UEL headquarters will ever question whether we should have one in Compuel. Meanwhile, marketing people get paid pretty well. I'll be able to compensate you better with that title than I can with "assistant to the president," which some of the UEL people think is an affectation for me rather than a job for you."

"Okay, Linc," replied Gelson, "whatever you say." And that was that. Gelson supervised the sales-service operation, talked to the press whenever necessary, supplied speakers to local community groups upon request, and generally was to be found at Rehnquist's side doing whatever was asked, without raising a question.

And so, the two men now found themselves talking about an advertising program for Compuel.

"We have to find some way of telling the business community who we are," said Rehnquist. "If anybody who doesn't do business with us has ever heard of us, and they probably haven't, they think we do billing applications and design reservations networks and reservation holding capabilities.

"What do you think, Linc?" asked Gelson. "There must be plenty of reservations and billing business out there but in industries that no one in UEL competes with. So we run ads to tell them about our successful applications in those fields, is that what you think?"

"No, that's not what I think, Charlie," responded Rehnquist. "We'd like more reservations and billing business but it's going to be tough to get, and I don't want to stress that in advertisements. We don't want to say that we are just a specialist company and if we only advertise about reservations and billings, that is exactly what we are going to be saying. I want to go after that business, but the real future for us is with industries we've never made a sale in. Johnnie McPherson came in the other day and told me something that just fascinates me, even though I'll be darned if I know what do about it. The average adult in this country has contact twenty-one times every year with a Compuel system. I've thought about that for days and I simply can't get it out of my mind.

"That's the business we're in, Charlie. We're not in the business of selling hardware and systems to airlines and utility companies and retail chains and what not. We're in the business of performing transactions for consumers and the businesses that serve them. We're in between a business and its customers—we're the interface. Our long-term potential is to increase the number of transactions that Compuel is a party to, the number of business/customer interfaces."

"I don't get it, Linc," responded Gelson. "I mean, what we do is make computers that are practically foolproof and adapt them to billing problems and reservations problems. That's the business we're in. That's what you're aware of around here. You go into the shop and you can touch our XL9206 computer or the RR720. And you go up to

Connecticut where the systems people are and you see the systems they work up to make those machines operate. That's what our business is. I don't know from interfaces, consumer transactions, twenty-one times a year, or any of that."

"But, darn it, Charlie," said Rehnquist, now getting heated and seemingly impatient with his director of marketing, "it's a mistake to think about the hardware and software in only a 'literal' way. If we made dump trucks, we wouldn't think that our business was dump trucks, would we? We'd think that it was helping companies move dirt."

"You're out there beyond me again, Linc," replied Gelson. "I don't know anything about dump trucks, and frankly I can't see any connection at all between dump trucks and our computers. But I'll tell you this. You think that I'm dense—I don't get all this interface business, wait until you pull that on the boys up at UEL in Chicago.

"I mean, those guys there don't much believe in advertising—which you know just as well as I do—even when it just gives straightforward information and hard-case sell about your products. But you go over there and tell them you want to spend millions of their profit dollars talking to businessmen—not consumers where you can be a little nutty, but businessmen like them—about twenty-one interfaces and transaction levels and all, and they are going to have a fit. They think you're good Linc; and you are, and they'll probably let you get away with it; but, believe me, they'll never forget. If you can't prove that it gets you new business—and I don't see how you'll be able to do that, ever—then they'll hold it against you. Linc, you want to get ahead at UEL, you don't want those guys there, holding anything against you, let alone some dumb advertising business."

Finally Gelson ran out of breath. Rehnquist had listened to his monologue with considerable patience, used as he was to such nonstop outbursts whenever Gelson disapproved of some plan of his and could not find the words or perhaps the courage to simply say something simple like "You shouldn't do that, Linc, because it's stupid and it'll get you into trouble over at UEL."

"Okay, Charlie, cool down," responded Rehnquist. "First of all, nobody said anything about millions of dollars except you. Second, it's my profits, not theirs; and as long as I meet their profit goals, I can spend money any way I want. And finally, Charlie, I'm beginning to think you don't understand about advertising as a way to change the preconceived ideas and opinions about our company of businessmen who aren't our customers." On that note, the meeting between the two men ended. But a week later, Rehnquist and Gelson were talking about advertising again.

"We've got to get going on this advertising program, Charlie," said Rehnquist, over lunch. "I've thought about our conversation of last week, and I'm more convinced than ever that we've got to present our company as the one that specializes in machines and programs that handle repetitive transactions. If the boys at UEL think that that is ridiculous, they'll just have to hold their peace; because I'm responsible for Compuel in the long run. They're not.

"You did make one good point, Charlie," Rehnquist continued, "about measuring the effect our advertising program actually has on sales. Once we get into the planning phase, we are absolutely going to have to figure out how to measure what our advertising is accomplishing in terms of increased sales. You were right to bring it up, and I'm not going to forget it. But what do we do next? How do we get some advertising experts into the picture? Have you given any thought to that?"

"One of two ways, Linc," answered Gelson. "We can call up some advertising agencies, tell them what we think our problem is, and have them make presentations on how they would go about solving it. Then we pick the best one and appoint them our advertising agency. The other way is to ask what's-his-name—the guy who is corporate communications director up at UEL, uh, Whitney Sandemar—if there is an agency already working within the UEL system that is qualified to deal with the kind of problem we've got; and would he be good enough to get us together. If we find our own agency, we'll probably get a bunch of people we like better, who may do the job better, too. But from a political standpoint, I think it would be a *lot* smarter to let Sandemar put us in touch with an agency that he chooses. It probably won't make much difference in the end as far as the finished advertising work is concerned, but it will tend to give us a pal at UEL if the heat comes on up there."

"Okay," said Rehnquist. "I think you're absolutely right about that, Charlie. Call up Sandemar and butter him up. Get him involved in our problem. Good idea."

And so it came to pass that Humboldt Aesop, chairman and founder of the Aesop and Acton advertising agency, came to meet Lincoln Rehnquist and Charles Gelson and to hear about Compuel and its advertising problem.

"So," said Aesop, after hearing Rehnquist out, "let me see if I've got this right. You believe what the business community—even your current customers—doesn't know about Compuel is that you're really in the business of providing computers and expertise to companies that have many repetitive transactions of one kind or another, is that right?"

"Yup, that's right, Hum" said Rehnquist. "And what we want is an advertising campaign that will convince companies with those kinds of transactions that they have to talk to us if they want to get the real expertise in this field. And furthermore, we want an ironclad measurement of the extra sales we get from that advertising campaign."

"Okay, I've got it," said Aesop. "Let me respond to what you've just said in two ways. First of all, we can create the kind of advertising you have in mind. What you say makes a lot of sense to me on first hearing, but I want to think about it some more and talk to some of our people who are experienced in this field. Maybe we'll want to recommend that you do some research to be sure that the portrayal of your company as the computer company that specializes in repetitive-transaction applications is meaningful to the business community, or at least the most meaningful thing that you can say about Compuel. But anyway, we would be delighted to take on this advertising assignment. We do a lot of this kind of work, and we do it well. We'd love to have your assignment, too.

"Now about measuring the results of a campaign of this kind in sales terms: The easy way for me to respond is to say we'll think about it and it should be possible to make such measurements, and we'll develop a plan and come back to you with it, and so forth and so on. But if you're going to work with our agency, you might as well get to know what we're like right away. We tend to be pretty candid with our clients, Linc and Charlie; and sometimes we may be a little too candid. But anyway, I have to tell you right away that I think it's mighty unlikely we'll be able to relate a campaign of the type we're discussing, with the objectives that you've been talking about, directly to sales.

"I get the impression that you're going to undertake a major overhaul of your sales organization, of its methods, objectives, and personnel, and of the tone of its operation at the same time that you're starting this advertising program. Am I right?" Aesop paused and looked expectantly at Rehnquist.

Gelson said quickly, "Yes, Humboldt, that's right; but what of it?"

Aesop continued. "Okay. If that's right, then my impression—and we've had quite a bit of experience with this kind of thing—is that you'll never be able to separate the effects of the changes in the sales organization from the effects of the advertising. It'll be hard to tell which causes the increased sales. Let me put it another way: You will know how many inquiries about Compuel you get from the advertising campaign. We'll build that right into the advertising itself. But when a salesman makes a sale on a lead, we won't know whether he was the persuader or whether the advertising had the sale virtually made before the salesman got into the picture. Or, if the salesman doesn't make the sale after he's given a lead from the advertising, we won't know if the salesman blew it or if the advertising caused false expectations."

"Okay, Hum," interjected Rehnquist. "I think I get the point you're making. But does this mean I can't measure the effect of the advertising at all? Am I just going to be left high and dry?"

"Well, in my judgment," said Aesop, "you're going to be left high and dry as far as sales are concerned. What you can do is measure the number of inquiries that the campaign generates. That would certainly reflect pure advertising effect, wouldn't it? And the number of sales that come from such inquiries would be a measure of the joint effectiveness of the advertising in conjunction with the revitalized selling effort."

"Okay, Hum," said Rehnquist "that's fine. Charlie and I certainly appreciate your candor and all of the thoughtful and responsive comments you've made today. You've been very helpful and we're grateful to you for your time. If we do decide to go forward on this project, I'd be interested in the answers to two additional questions. First of all, how would you like to be compensated for this work; and, second, just what relation would you want with the folks at UEL, if we were to proceed with you in this project?"

"Right, Linc, I want very much to talk about both of those points," answered Aesop. "In the first place, we would want to handle the assignment on a fee basis. Its very hard to know just how much of our time will be required to get this project going; and of course you don't know when you'll start placing the advertising in the media, or on what scale. We'll prefer, therefore, not to depend on commissions, rather just to bill you net for media when you begin to incur media costs. In the meantime, I'll talk to my people and we'll try to give you an estimate of our costs on a quarter-by-quarter basis for the first year. My guess is that our work will run about $25,000 a month for the first six months and about $15,000 a month for the second six months, after the basic creative work has been done and approved by you. But these are just guesses right now, Linc. We'll be back to you with firm figures. And, once we're off and running, we'll review our costs with you every month or every quarter, if you wish. If we come in under estimate, the money is yours. If we come in above estimate, it means you've required more service than we anticipated; and we'll ask you to make up the difference. Incidentally, we bill raw salary costs and multiply them by three to cover salary followers like social security and health insurance, our overhead, and our agency profit.

"Now, with respect to UEL. It's time to be candid again. We do a lot of work for divisions and subsidiaries of UEL. Taken together, they make UEL our third-largest client. And we enjoy cordial relations with Whit Sandemar, even though he is not our client on any of the business that we have that originates with UEL. Another agency handles his corporate institutional program. When we deal with a UEL division or a UEL subsidiary, the division or subsidiary is our client, not UEL, I've been very frank with Whit about this: Aesop and Acton doesn't want to get caught in the middle between UEL and one of its divisions. I've asked Whit, if he has a problem with one of the division or subsidiary advertising programs, to take it up directly with the division or subsidiary rather than with us. We're not trying to ditch our responsibility, but when we develop an advertising solution for one of our clients, we do it in concert with them. It's a joint solution and we usually can't defend it properly unless the division or subsidiary is involved in that defense. Does that answer your question, Linc?"

"Yes, thanks Humboldt," said Rehnquist, "that's very responsive, and frankly it's exactly what I wanted to hear. A fee is the fair way to compensate an agency under any circumstance, I think. You'll make more money off us this year and probably considerably less after we get this advertising rolling. It will reflect what you actually have earned, not some arbitrary number of dollars that just happens to get thrown off by the commissions the media kick back to the agencies."

(Humboldt Aesop shuddered at this, thinking that it reflected a very real and potentially disastrous misconception about the system of agency compensation based on media commissions, but said nothing. He continued to attend closely to what Rehnquist was saying, an attentive smile on his face.)

"As far as your attitude toward UEL and its divisions and subsidiaries is concerned," continued Rehnquist, "I think you're exactly right; and, frankly, we would want nothing to do with an agency that had any other attitude.

"Okay. That's all that's on my mind for now," concluded Rehnquist. After a pause, he changed expression, breaking the previous mood of frank exchange of views. Looking over at Charles Gelson, he asked, "Anything you want to say, Charlie?" Gelson said nothing, shaking his head negatively ever so slightly. "All right then, Hum," Rehnquist concluded, "the ball's in our court; and it's up to us to figure out what we'll finally do. We'll be back to you within the week.

Rehnquist and Gelson met briefly the next morning and quickly decided that the Compuel advertising account should be awarded to the Aesop and Acton advertising agency.

When representatives of Aesop and Acton returned to Compuel eleven days later, they were led by Humboldt Aesop and included Charles Abelson, account management supervisor, and Isabelle Greene, senior copywriter. They brought with them a memorandum written by Abelson, which they intended to use as the basis of the discussion of advertising for Compuel. This document is reproduced below.

---

# AESOP AND ACTON

Client Memorandum

May 17, 1979

To: Lincoln Rehnquist
From: Charles R. Abelson

cc: C. D. Gelson
H. Aesop
I. Greene

The purpose of this memorandum is to review the agency's preliminary thinking about an advertising program for Compuel and to present agency recommendations for the steps that should now be taken to further that advertising program.

1. There is one aspect of the marketing of Compuel computers and Compuel computer programs that seems to us to be very elusive. That is the identification of the best new prospects for your products. We

agree that there must be corporations "out there" that have a very significant need for your products because of your very extensive expertise in multiple-transaction computer applications. As far as we are able to determine, no other computer firm, including IBM, has developed expertise in such applications to nearly the extent that you have. This means that a market of new or unidentified prospects *should* exist for your products; but it is also almost impossible to define that new market.

We assume that one of the first things you will want to do when the sales department has been reorganized is to attempt to define the new market in very concrete terms. This will not be an easy task because you are already servicing most of the industries that have an obvious need for Compuel machines and programs. Of course, Compuel does not sell its machines and services to every firm in those industries in which you have achieved sales penetration. But you have identified the firms in these penetrated industries, and they are already subject to direct-sales pressures. As we understand it, the purpose of the proposed Compuel advertising campaign is to reach unidentified prospects in industries in which Compuel has, so far, made no sales at all.

2. The problem of new prospect definition has two quite distinct implications for the advertising program.
   a. In the first place, it has a great deal to do with the formulation of media strategy. If we don't know the specific industries in which your best prospects are to be found, it's impossible to tailor a selective media program to Compuel needs. This disturbs us, because all of our experience indicates that the most effective business advertising campaigns are based on tight market definitions and intensive use of those media—usually business papers—that do the best job of reaching into those identified markets.

      Now, of course, we can use generalized business media like *Fortune, Forbes, Business Week, Time* "B", and the executive edition of *Newsweek*. But these tend to be expensive absolutely and expensive because they deliver so much circulation to industries in which there will be no application at all for Compuel products. We usually recommend one or two generalized business magazines for advertising programs like that of Compuel but only after primary coverage of the prospect market has been achieved by the selective media.
   b. The second problem that arises when markets have not been closely defined has to do with message content. If we don't know who the prospects are, we will have a good deal of trouble knowing just what to say about Compuel that will be most compelling. We can write advertising that will be of general interest to the general business community; but it will not be as specifically meaningful to real prospects as it might have been if we had known exactly who these prospects were in the first place.
3. All this leads us to the conclusion that an advertising campaign for Compuel undertaken in the absence of precise market definition will have to be quite general in character, both in respect to the audience delivered, and in respect to the message delivered. This will be advertising that is really institutional in nature; advertising that describes

Compuel in general terms; advertising that cannot deliver specific messages particularly crafted to stimulate sales on a prospect-industry by prospect-industry basis.

4. The thought that such advertising should be based on Compuel's expertise in repetitive-transaction computing in the interface between a firm and its customers is totally compatible with this conclusion. This is a general statement about Compuel which does describe its expertise. Once again, we must emphasize that this is not the kind of advertising for Compuel that we would instinctively prefer; but it undoubtedly, at this stage of the development of Compuel marketing, is exactly the right thing to do.
5. On the basis of this analysis we have the following recommendations to make:
   a. Aesop and Acton should now prepare advertising campaigns for Compuel based upon the following advertising strategy:
      Compuel is a computer firm that specializes in machines and systems to facilitate and routinize large volumes of repetitive transactions between companies and their customers.
   b. It is understood that this advertising will have, in addition to its general communication objective, the specific objective of generating leads for the Compuel sales organization.
   c. Once this advertising has been prepared in rough form, we recommend that it be tested with a random sample of 200 *Business Week* subscribers to determine whether it is comprehensible and to determine the reaction of these general business-audience executives.

---

Rehnquist and Gelson studied this memorandum for several minutes after it had been presented to them by the Aesop and Acton group. Finally, Rehnquist said, "Okay, I guess I understand what this is all about, and I guess I agree with it. I see that you have built in the prospect-generator idea that we discussed when you were here before, Hum. That's fine because we really should build up evidence that this advertising is productive in some sales-related way.

"Let me ask you one question. When you get all done with your copywriting and researching etcetera, what happens then?

Ableson responded immediately, "You get an advertising-campaign recommendation from the agency that is based upon the best expertise we can bring to bear upon the Compuel problem; *and* you get the reassurance through the research results that the general business audience understands what your advertising is trying to say and responds favorably to it."

"Do we get just one campaign," asked Gelson, "that we more or less have to accept? Why can't we see several campaigns *before* we do any research at all and then confirm, through the research, that the campaigns we like on judgment are understandable and generate positive response?"

"Yes, that's right, Charlie," broke in Rehnquist, "now you're getting at the thing that I'm confused about. I sense in your memorandum, uh, Charlie or Chuck or Charles—what is it, Mr. Ableson?"

"I prefer Charles, Mr. Rehnquist," responded Ableson.

"Okay. In your memorandum, Charles, I felt that you were saying, more or less between the lines, that you would really prefer to approach our problem after we have our markets defined, say a year or so from now. But you don't want to wait around that long with nothing to do and no money coming in, so you gave us a kind of second-best recommendation that you're only halfheartedly in favor of. Am I right?"

Humboldt Aesop immediately broke in, sensing real trouble. "No, that's not it at all, Linc. We wholeheartedly back this recommendation. We believe—and we talked about this a lot, Charles, but it doesn't seem to have surfaced in the final draft of this memorandum you've written—we believe that this advertising will tell the business community who Compuel is, exactly, and that the leads the advertising generates will help you define your markets with precision. We think, in other words, that this advertising campaign will be an integral part of the development of your marketing program in the year ahead. If you get responses from five industries that you had never thought might be able to use your company's products, the campaign will repay itself many times over."

"All right, Hum, I agree with that and have from the very beginning," said Rehnquist. I'm glad to hear that the agency is in agreement with that, too; because I sure didn't get it from this memorandum. Now let's get back to Charlie's question about more than one campaign.

"Let me pose a hypothetical situation. First of all, I assume that you can write more than one advertisement that will express the strategy you have outlined in this memorandum. Am I right, Charles?"

"Yes, that's right, Mr. Rehnquist," responded Abelson. "Quite a few more than just one, I would think in this case."

"Okay," continued Rehnquist. "Suppose you come in here, as Charlie suggests, and show us several campaigns before we do this research. And suppose there are three or four campaigns that we really like a lot. We research them and find that, let's say two of them, really score very strongly on the research, okay? Now, you admit that it's going to be hard to predict just what this advertising will do because it is going to be general, right? Not aimed at specific markets? Now we come up with two winners we like equally well. Are we going to make that decision on judgment?"

For a moment the agency contingent was silent. Then Charles Abelson cleared his throat and began to talk, slowly at first, then with growing conviction. "Well, uh, Mr. Rehnquist, I, uh, don't know that we'll ever find ourselves in just exactly that spot. We could of course, I suppose. Okay, let's accept your hypothetical situation, just as you've laid it out. Let's make the assumption that when we get done with all the creative and research work, we end up with two different campaigns we can't choose between.

"One thing we could do in that situation, unlikely as it is, is to take typical advertisements from the two campaigns and use them in a split-run test in one of the magazines that will be on the final media list. I should explain what a "split run" is. Some magazines offer the capability of printing different advertisements in every other copy of the magazine that they print. This is called a split run. Thus, half the copies of the magazine issue are printed with advertisement "A" and half with advertisement "B." It's not the first half of the press run with "A" and the second half of the press run with "B"; it's every other copy throughout the entire press run. What this does is to expose an advertisement that is representative of one campaign to a randomly selected half of the magazine's circulation and an advertisement representative of the second campaign to the other half. To find out which campaign is better, we would just count up the number of inquiries that have been generated by each campaign." (The coupons in the advertisements are keyed to indicate which campaign they have been generated by, and for direct calls each advertisement contains a different telephone number.)

The meeting then ended. Rehnquist and Gelson agreed that the agency presentation was satisfactory and that the agency should prepare advertising for their review. The following step would be the initiation of comprehension and reaction testing on the advertisements.

Over the next few weeks there were several meetings between Compuel and Aesop and Acton representatives. In the first meeting a total of six proposed advertising campaigns were presented by Aesop and Acton. After much discussion, it was decided, on judgment, that three of these campaigns were superior to the remaining three. All of the presented campaigns were in an all-type format, without illustrations of any kind. The body copy in each of the proposed advertisements was more or less the same; the major differences among the advertisements were in the headlines of each.

"What Compuel has to sell is a serious, no-nonsense line of computers and applications," said Isabelle Greene as she presented the proposed advertising to Rehnquist and Gelson. "We have gone out of our way to make these advertisements stark, declarative statements of information that should have interest and import throughout the business community. This is a no-frills approach to a no-frills story of efficient accomplishment by a leading but too little-known firm of computer experts."

The headlines on the three advertisements that were selected by Rehnquist and Gelson, with the complete concurrence of the advertising agency representatives were:

*CAMPAIGN #1*

If your business is based upon massive numbers of repetitive transactions with your customers, Compuel is the computer firm for you.

*CAMPAIGN #2*

Every American citizen will participate in 27 Compuel transactions in 1980. Shouldn't you know more about the computer firm that accomplishes this?

*CAMPAIGN #3*

Compuel can increase the profitability of one American company out of three. You should find out if your firm is one of them.

Campaigns #1 and #2 came through the comprehension and reaction research with flying colors. A very high proportion of the businessmen interviewed about the advertisements that represented these campaigns understood them and reacted favorably to their content.

The campaign #3 comprehension and reaction study results were, however, another matter entirely. There was no trouble in businessmen understanding the message—almost everyone who was exposed to the test advertisement understood exactly what it intended to convey. The difficulty was in the area of credibility. Three out of four of the exposed respondents did not believe that any computer company, let alone Compuel, could increase the profitability of one out of three of all American companies.

On the basis of these results, and because neither Rehnquist or Gelson, nor the representatives of Aesop and Acton could find any compelling judgmental basis upon which to choose between the two surviving advertising campaigns, it was decided to run each in a split-run test in an early January 1980 issue of *Business Week* magazine.

Shortly after this advertising appeared in *Business Week*, Lincoln L. Rehnquist received the following letter from Whitney Sandemar, vice-president and director of corporate communications of United Electronics, Ltd.

# UNITED ELECTRONICS, LTD.

-UEL-

January 23, 1980

Lincoln A. Rehnquist
Compuel Division of United Electronics, Ltd.
29868 Shawnee Boulevard
Topeka, Kansas

Dear Linc:

I have now seen the split run advertisements that Compuel is running in *Business Week.*

I must say that they do not seem to me to have been designed to produce sales for Compuel. Why have you settled on a strategy that brags about the Compuel capability in executing multiple transactions?

It seems to me that Compuel has plenty of opportunity to increase its sales by going after firms in industries in which Compuel has a proven record of success—such as airlines and motel chains—that are still using competitive systems. If you were to follow such a strategy, you could sell hard in your advertising and expect to see specific sales results immediately. Furthermore, we are interested to know why you and your agency have undertaken a split-run test of advertisements based on your brag-and-boast strategy. The "MASSIVE REPETITIVE TRANSACTIONS" approach is clearly superior. We can't understand what twenty-seven transactions per year conceivably has to do with any businessman's decision to explore new computer transactions.

When you are in Chicago within the next week or two, I hope you will drop in and chat about this. Incidentally, Russ Todd, our board chairman, indicated an interest in sitting in when we discuss this matter.

Best wishes,

[s]
A. Whitney Sandemar

## *QUESTIONS FOR CASE 10*

1. Has Lincoln Rehnquist made prudent decisions about Compuel advertising in this case? Specifically, do you think Compuel has adopted the correct advertising strategy? Has Compuel followed the right course in split-run testing the two alternative campaigns?

2. The case materials suggest that the results of an institutional advertising campaign might be measured directly by sales results, or by inquiries generated. What other kinds of results might an institutional advertising campaign be expected to produce? How would such results be measured?

3. On what basis would an inquiry generated by an institutional advertisement be evaluated? Would cost per thousand inquiries be an adequate measure? Would dollar sales produced per inquiry be an adequate measure? What other measures of the quality of each inquiry would be useful in your evaluation?

4. Define institutional advertising. Describe three situations in which an institutional advertising campaign should be used by a corporation.

5. What does Humboldt Aesop mean when he thinks that Renhquists's view reflects "a very real and potentially disastrous misconception about the system of agency compensation based on media commissions"? Do you agree with Aesop's view? If you do, tell why. If you do not, tell what alternative viewpoint you endorse and why.

6. When one talks about the "politics" of a company or corporation, what is meant? Do any of the people in this case make decisions on the basis of political considerations? Give at least two examples of such politically based decisions. Do you agree with these decisions, or do you believe that politics should not have been permitted to affect them? Tell why.

7. Are media programs for institutional advertising campaigns actually based upon vertical business publications, or are they usually based upon horizontal business publications such as *Fortune, Business Week,* etc? Explain your answer.

8. What judgmental criteria would Rehnquist and Gelson use in deciding to eliminate three of the six advertisements presented to them by the advertising agency? List six or seven such criteria.

9. Consider the following results from the split-run test:

| | Repetitive Transaction Campaign | Twenty-seven Transactions in 1980 Campaign |
|---|---|---|
| Number of Inquiries generated | 26 | 49 |
| (i) What interpretation would you place on the results? | | |
| (ii) What action would you take based on these results? | | |
| Number of inquiries generated | 26 | 24 |
| (i) What interpretation would you place on these results? | | |
| (ii) What action would you take based on these results? | | |

# Case 11

# Retail Advertising

***THE ACKEROYD COMPANY PLANS EXPANDED OPERATIONS***

Edmund C. Ackeroyd has been president and chief executive officer of The Ackeroyd Store of Albany, New York, since 1966. He is the third Ackeroyd to hold this position, having been preceded in it by his father Preston O. Ackeroyd, who served from 1932 to 1966, and Elwood O. Ackeroyd, his grandfather, the founder of The Ackeroyd Store.

The Ackeroyd Store was the first general merchandise "department store" to open in Albany. Elwood O. Ackeroyd started the store, on North Pearl Street, in 1908, when he was thirty-two years old. He had previously run a men's ready-to-wear store that he had, in turn, inherited from his father, which had also been called The Ackeroyd Store. Elwood Ackeroyd always dated the beginning of the Ackeroyd (department) store in 1908, even though he might have been excused some little license had he dated its founding in 1868 when his father opened the ready-to-wear Ackeroyd Store. His insistence on the 1908 date was less a reflection of his integrity in such matters than a competitive ploy. Owens and Kilroy was the second department store to open in Albany. It started as a department store in 1917, but dated its establishment back to 1863 when its progenitor company had entered the yard-goods business. So Elwood Ackeroyd clung to 1908 as the date on which his department store had been established and always portrayed The Ackeroyd Store in advertising as "Albany's oldest department store–since 1908." Frank Owens and Elmer Kilroy did not dispute this claim. Rather they blithely ignored it in their own advertising which announced simply that Owens and Kilroy was "Founded in 1863."

Those Albanians who read the advertisements of the competing firms thoroughly enough to be aware of their inconsistency on this point ignored it, assuming it to be merely yet another manifestation of the rivalry that existed between the two stores. Both stores advertised their merchandise with great intensity in the morning *Times Union* and in the evening *Knickerbocker News.* The advertising of both stores emphasized the merchandise that was currently being featured by each. Both stores were committed to a traditional policy of merchandising. Each sought out goods they believed would have particular appeal to its customers, usually national brands; and each tried to feature this merchandise at an attractive price, based on volume discounts granted by the manufacturer. Thus, on any given day, the advertisements of The Ackeroyd Store and of Owens and Kilroy were unlikely to feature identical goods; yet the advertised merchandise of one store often paralleled that of the competitor because of seasonal merchandising traditions. When the two competing stores presented nationally advertised merchandise at an attractive price, both seemed to feel that the merchandising and advertising job had been done. Because neither store tried to meet the merchandise offerings of the other head-on with a lower price, there were almost no competitive price or value claims in the advertising of either store.

In fact, with the exception of the Ackeroyd claim "Albany's oldest department store—since 1908" and the Owens and Kilroy statement "Founded in 1863," no attempt was made in the advertising to impart other character or qualities to the individual stores. Each seemed content to rest on their representations as competing merchants with attractive merchandise offerings. This had been the way each of the stores had approached advertising since they had begun to use it as a tool to attract customers fifty or sixty years before.

The management of both stores recognized that they competed with each other for the same group of consumers. Although the stores knew little enough about their own customers and nothing about those of their competitors, they believed that basically the same people divided their purchases between The Ackeroyd Store and Owens and Kilroy in rough proportion to the success of the merchandising programs followed by the individual stores.

Neither store had made any overt attempt over the years to differentiate itself from the other, except through its cumulative merchandising skill and the reflection of that skill in the store's advertising program. As a result, and as might be expected, throughout the twenties, thirties, forties, and fifties neither store had gained a distinct advantage over the other. There were brief periods—perhaps a year or two—during which one or the other would, because of especially shrewd merchandise purchases and features, gain an upper hand for a time. Traffic in the more successful store would perceptibly increase for the relatively brief period of ascendancy, while traffic in its competitor would seem to slack off. But inevitably this imbalance would prove temporary; the store which seemed three or four months before to be slowing down would gradually reverse the trend through its own merchandising coups and, suddenly, an equilibrium would be reestablished.

Meanwhile, the stores competed in other ways, as well. Each sponsored teams in the Twilight League semiprofessional baseball program during the summer months. Fashion shows were sponsored on the stages of the leading local movie houses in conjunction with local charities: The Ackeroyd Company at Warner Brothers Strand and Owens and Kilroy at the more modern and larger RKO Palace. Bowling teams were supported in several of the city leagues. The two stores vied in their support of local parades and booster events, and so on.

The overall image held by consumers of the individual stores probably depended more on these nonstore activities and sponsorships than upon the stores or their advertising. A winning team in the Twilight League, a successful charity fashion show, or a particularly spectacular parade float seemed to lend more individual personality to the sponsoring stores than did the stores themselves. Certainly, the relentlessly unimaginative advertising programs of the two stores added no perceptible dimension to the images held by consumers. Knowing Albanians when talking about the stores and the nature of their competition would amuse each other with visions of waking up in one of the two stores and not being able to determine which store they were in.

Eventually, of course, this competitive equilibrium had to come to an end. The beginning of this end heaved into view in 1962, unbeknownst to either Preston Ackeroyd or to Richard Owens and Edward Kilroy, the successors to the founders of the Owens and Kilroy department store. In March of 1962 Harrison B. Weston, vice-president for special projects of Staley's Department Store in New York, checked into the Ten Eyck Hotel for a stay that continued sporadically for the next seven months.

Staley's was the largest department store in New York City. Its name was synonymous with sophisticated merchandising. In addition, the Staley advertising program, with its slogan "No one sells for less than Staley's," had built a clear consumer perception of the store as the source of ultimate value among New York department stores. Shortly after World War II, Staley's had determined upon a policy of expansion into major metropolitan markets throughout the United States. Harrison B. Weston was appointed Staley's "vice-president for special projects" in 1949 and given the job of identifying those markets that represented superior potential opportunity for Staley's. Weston had taken Staley's to San Francisco, Kansas City, Dallas, Atlanta, and several other major cities in the years between his appointment to this job and his arrival at the Ten Eyck in Albany.

When Weston visited a city, it was far from foregone that Staley's would open a branch in that city. What *was* certain, however, was that the city represented apparent potential for Staley's. It was Weston's job to determine whether or not that potential was real. He tended to select cities with solid potential for economic growth, with stodgy or underdeveloped local department stores, with no major chain department-store competition, and with a population minimum of at least 350,000 homes. Albany was, from Weston's viewpoint, a sleeper. On its surface, the city was too small to support Staley's operations. Yet a glance at a map told Weston that Albany, with its companion cities of Schenectady and Troy, adjacent towns like Cohoes, Rensselaer, and Menands, and the smaller suburbs might collectively be large enough to support a Staley's store. The question in Weston's mind when he went to Albany was whether it was conceivable that these three cities might be drawn together into a single market area. Could Staley's convert these moderately sized and bustling upstate towns into one integrated metropolitan area for department-store retailing purposes?

Here is a summary excerpt from Harrison B. Weston's report (dated January 26, 1963) to the Staley's executive management committee:

"On first glance we have no business in Albany. The city is simply too small with its 60,000 homes. But if we combine Albany, Schenectady, Troy and the towns and hamlets that surround and interconnect them, we are looking at a consolidated population area in excess of 300,000 homes. This is still somewhat small from the standpoint of population. But since all other factors seem favorable, I am inclined to consider the consolidated market size to be large enough.

"What about these other factors?"

"In the three-city area there is a very diversified base of economic enterprise. In Albany itself there is the state government with its bureaucracy and the service industries that government tends to attract. There is also the state university. As we all acknowledge, government appears to be one of the solid growth industries in this country and its presence in a community tends to guarantee a well-educated, value-conscious middle class. Albany is also a communications center (Delaware and Hudson Railroad, New York Telephone Company, etc.). In addition, it has a nice mix of predominantly light industry —publishing, printing, felt manufacture, meatpacking, paper manufacturing, machine tool manufacturing, electronics manufacturing, etc.

"Schenectady has light and heavy industry. General Electric turns out everything from locomotives to jet aircraft engines, and it is a main supplier of electrical motors for industrial applications. In addition, there are manufacturers of electrical insulating materials; printing machinery; synthetic resins and varnishes; concrete products; and meat packing, dairy, and bakery enterprises.

"Troy is a center for the production of building materials, such as stone, glass, and clay, as well as the manufacture of machine tools and textiles. There is also some food packing, printing, and publishing there.

"All in all, there is very widely diversified economic activity in the area—much more than we are accustomed to finding in much larger middle western and southern cities which are so often dominated by one or two industries. This means, of course, that the consolidated Albany-Schenectady-Troy area is much less vulnerable to local economic downturns than are many of the cities in which we now operate. The presence of state government in the area also lends a good deal of economic stability. Although some of the industries in these cities may be stagnant—felt, printing, glass, and clay—there is so much diversity that there is a very strong basis for vibrant economic growth.

"Each of the three cities has an old, decaying downtown shopping sector. Walking around in these downtown areas, one can almost sense their inevitable death. We know from experience that these downtown shopping areas must gradually decline and decay as the old city population moves into the suburbs. There has been some movement to the suburbs in all three communities, but it has been nowhere nearly as abrupt and widespread as in other old-line cities. Thus, the downtown shopping centers of Albany, Schenectady, and Troy continue along seemingly unaware of their impending fate.

"There are two nice small-scale department stores in Albany—The Ackeroyd Store and Owens and Kilroy. The Schenectady department store is called Claughson's, and the Troy department store is the Bon Ton. All these stores are right out of the 1920s. Each is oriented totally to its own community: It's as if they have never heard of the adjacent cities and do not know they exist. They thus render a community service, and they appear to merchandise well; but beyond this they are totally indistinguishable. They have a standard assortment of national brands in all their departments and seem to depend heavily on manufacturer-supported price promotions. There is no store-brand merchandise; no value emphasis; no quality emphasis; no fashion emphasis; very little professionally trained sales personnel; no direct-mail activity; no professional image advertising. In short, these stores are vulnerable to Staley's. We should have very little trouble competing with them effectively; and our programs are so sophisticated and well founded that these stores will have a great deal of trouble catching up with us once we start.

"Each of the communities has its own newspaper coverage. In Albany there is the morning *Times Union* and the evening *Knickerbocker News*; in Schenectady there is the morning *Gazette*; and in Troy there is the evening *Times Record.* Each of the department stores is a heavy user of the local newspaper. This is especially true in Albany where the relatively intense competition between The Ackeroyd Store and Owens and Kilroy seems to express itself in an abnormally high level of newspaper advertising for both stores.

"Each city has its own originating radio stations, although listening to each of these appears to occur throughout the coverage area of each station, which usually includes all three cities. There is virtually no use of the radio stations by the four department stores.

"Albany-Schenectady-Troy is a single market as far as television is concerned. There are three VHF television stations. One of these is situated in Schenectady (WRGB, Channel 6–NBC affiliate) and two are physically located in Albany (WTEN, Channel 10–ABC affiliate; and WAST, Channel 13–CBS affiliate). This is one unified television area. No use of these television facilities has ever been made by any of the department stores, dependent as they are upon the local newspapers.

"Where would we locate a Staley's, if we were to decide to enter this market? Not in Albany. Not in Schenectady. Not in Troy. Somewhere in between. In my judgment, this is where great opportunity lies, but it is also where a very significant risk also lies.

"What kind of risks would we face if we were to move 'somewhere in between' Albany, Troy, and Schenectady? We would, in essence, have to make three correct assumptions.

"First, we must be correct when we assume that, in due course, a large shopping center will be developed adjacent to the three cities and their suburbs, as they grow in the years ahead. This is an easy prediction to make. It has been happening all over the country. It is beginning to happen in the Albany-Schenectady-Troy area, as small, almost innocent shopping centers are popping up adjacent to some of the larger suburbs and just beyond city limits. These are not shopping centers as we customarily think of them—there are no major retailers involved; no department stores; no variety stores; no auto-service centers; no movie theaters; no chain-drug installations; no Sears or Penney's or Montgomery Wards. These minishopping centers cluster around a single food supermarket and typically include an appliance store or two, a book store, a barber shop, a haberdasher, and other insignificant enterprises. But they are a harbinger of things to come!

"Second, we must be correct when we predict where the first major shopping center will be. I am almost certain that I can make this prediction with accuracy, as you will shortly see. But I could be wrong; and if I am, a disaster could shortly follow for us.

"Third, we must be correct when we assume that we can start a major shopping center by announcing our intention to open a full-service Staley's branch at a particular location. We know that there is plenty of insurance-company money for financing. We also know that, just as they are in touch with us, most of the insurance companies are in close touch with other major potential shopping-center occupants: occupants who, in conjunction with Staley's, will generate the kind of broad-scale synergistic consumer-service energy that is the key to shopping-center success. We've seen how these centers come to fruition time and again. We have the financial and retailer contacts to put a very powerful group together without any commitment on our part beyond Staley's own store. I believe that we *can* create a major shopping center, if we wish to do so.

"So, we're back to the question of location. The key phrase to keep in mind is 'between Albany, Schenectady, and Troy.' No major shopping center will ever be successful if it is placed on the far side of one of the three cities: that is, in a location that would

**EXHIBIT 11-1**
**The Albany-Schenectady-Troy Area**

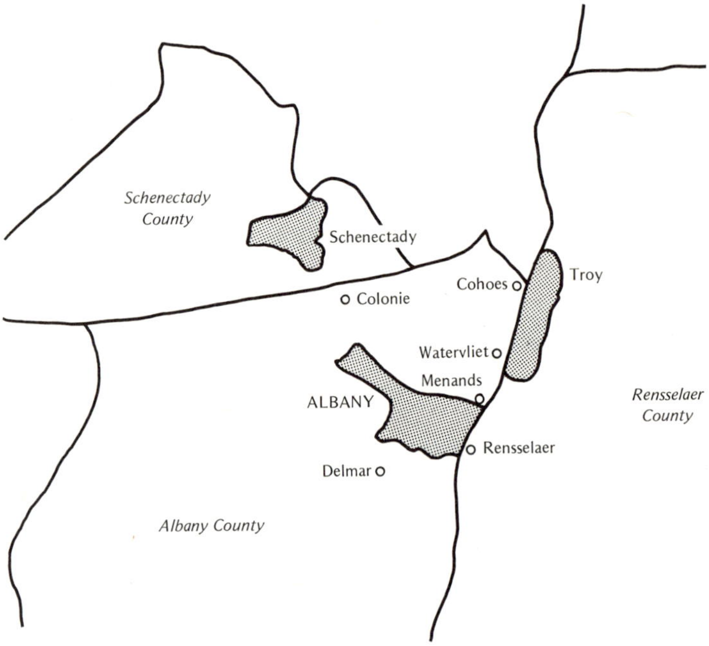


require residents of two of the cities to drive through the third city to reach the shopping center.

"A glance at the map (Exhibit 11-1) shows that the shopping center must be north of Albany, west of Troy, and south and east of Schenectady. The ideal location and, in my judgment, the inevitable location is in the area adjacent to the hamlet of Colonie. It is easily accessible to all three cities; it is relatively uninhabited and underdeveloped; it satisfies all of the normal criteria of our real-estate people. It is, in a word, a 'natural.'

"My recommendation is, therefore, that we immediately authorize the real estate people to move into the Colonie area and find and option a suitable tract or tracts of land for the development of a major new shopping center.

"One additional issue must be considered as you decide whether or not we should enter the Albany-Schenectady-Troy market. That is the reponse we may expect from the local stores. My strong intuition is that there will be no response at all in the foreseeable future. Perhaps one of these stores will come to its senses in eight or ten years, as the decay of the downtown center intensifies and as they realize that the center of retail trade in the area has shifted to the environs (I presume) of Colonie. But this realization will dawn long after we have had our run and are either firmly entrenched or defeated. These local merchants will simply perceive a Staley's in Colonie as having absolutely nothing to do with them. They will wonder idly why we indulge in such folly, but they will totally miss the point that the retailing center for this area will, and must, move from the downtown shopping areas and into the dominant central location.

"We will have much more to worry about from the likes of Sears, J. C. Penney and perhaps some other metropolitan chains such as Filene's or Jordan Marsh from Boston.

They, like ourselves, are looking ever more broadly for new fields to conquer. But we have taken on competition of this kind in the past and we have rarely lost to it."

The executive management committee of Staley's voted unanimously to initiate a site search in the Colonie, New York, market when they met to consider Harrison Weston's report on February 17, 1963.

A suitable site was located and optioned in the fall of 1963. A consortium of experienced shopping-center retailers was brought together by a major Hartford insurance company in the winter of 1963-64, and ground was broken for the new Staley's Department Store, destined to become the centerpiece of this new shopping center, in March of 1964. The grand opening of the shopping center took place in the second week of April of 1965.

Preston Ackeroyd was vaguely aware that some major retailers were involved in the building of a shopping center in the Colonie area. As Weston had correctly foreseen, Ackeroyd had little interest in this turn of events. He wondered lazily why "anyone would want to put up a department store out in the sticks there in Colonie."

His son Edmund was somewhat more alert to the development and considerably more intrigued by it.

"What do you think Staley's is up to out there in Colonie?" Edmund asked his father at lunch one day in February of 1964.

"You got me, Edmund," replied his father. "I expect they think they can get business away from Claughson's up in Schenectady and maybe Bon Ton over in Troy. But I don't see how it can affect us much. I mean Albany folks will never go way out to Colonie to shop in a congested shopping center."

"I wouldn't be too sure about that, Dad," replied Edmund. "A lot of them are going out to Monkey Wards in Menands (between Albany and Troy) and have been for years."

"But those people who go to Wards simply are not our class of trade, Edmund, and you know it," responded his father, rather sharply. "Our customers expect a quality of merchandise, and a level of service that Ward's neither can nor will supply. We've got enough to worry about with Owens and Kilroy. That's our competition, not some bunch of New York sharpies who've made a mistake starting a big store in Colonie with a population of 2,500 households."

There the matter rested for the next year or so. It still continued to be of concern to Edmund, but he knew the subject irritated his father. The two men had plenty on their hands, anyway; because in the spring and summer of 1964, Owens and Kilroy seemed to be pulling slightly away from The Ackeroyd Store. So the two men spent all of their active hours trying to redress their competitive imbalance.

Edmund Ackeroyd entered his father's office on Friday morning in mid-July of 1965. "Were you watching television last night, Dad?" he asked his father.

"Nope. I was reading," came the reply. "I don't watch television much, and that's a fact. It's really for kids and teenagers, isn't it? I mean all those cowboy shows and commercials. I watch the sports some and the news, and that's about all."

With this, Preston Ackeroyd returned intently to the mail that was heaped on his desk. He was oblivious to Edmund, who, like it or not, still stood before him with something having to do with last night's television very much on his mind.

Edmund patiently waited for his father to finish. He was determined to have the conversation that he intended, whatever his father's idiosyncrasy might be on this particular day. Finally his father looked up again and, realizing that his son was still there, cocked his head in an encouraging, if not apologetic, manner. The younger man began to speak.

"It's Staley's," Edmund said.

"What do you mean, "It's Staley's'?"

"I mean," said Edmund, "that they're advertising on television. They're having a white sale this weekend on their own Staley's brand dry goods. They're saying that their merchandise is superior to all the advertised brands we carry and that they have proved it in their testing laboratories. Furthermore, this merchandise of theirs, on sale, is up to one-third less expensive than the leading national brands, and Staley's says they'll never be undersold on equal quality. I'd say this is trouble for us, and we'd better start thinking about it."

"Won't attract our class of trade," his father replied. "All they'll get out to Colonie this weekend are the lower-income groups looking for a bargain and willing to take some brand they've never heard of to save fifty cents or whatever. They've been out there in Colonie for three months now, and we haven't felt it at all. And what's more we won't. If our sales are off it's because of Owens and Kilroy, not those Johnny-come-latelies out there in the woods.

"Edmund," his father continued, "you know I'll be sixty-four in November. You know I intend to retire on the first of the year and that you'll be president then. Until January first, I intend to run this store according to what I think is important. What's important now is the same thing that's always been important—beating Owens and Kilroy, particularly at Christmas. What's not important is what Staley's is doing up in Colonie."

That ended the conversation, but not the subject, as far as Edmund Ackeroyd was concerned. He went to his own office and asked his secretary to get Suzanne Whitney, general merchandise manager for The Ackeroyd Store, and Radford M. Myers, its treasurer. When Suzanne and Myers came into his office, Edmund outlined his concerns about the Staley store in Colonie to them. He described his father's reaction and his essential indifference to the Staley's thrust. He then asked the other two what they thought.

Radford M. Myers was fifty-four years old, and had been with The Ackeroyd Store in accounting work since he had graduated from the Wharton School in Philadelphia in 1935. He had been a loyal and competent employee and had been well rewarded for it, finally having been appointed treasurer of the company in 1958. Myers was Preston Ackeroyd's man. He had been appointed to the treasurer's post when he was because Preston Ackeroyd knew he would retire in 1966 and wanted to have an experienced financial man in place to guide and even restrain Edmund's enthusiasm during his first years as the new president. It had never occurred to Preston Ackeroyd or to anyone else in Albany that anyone besides Edmund would succeed him when he retired in 1966.

But if Radford Myers was loyal to Preston Ackeroyd, he was not a toady to his ideas. Myers listened to Edmund patiently. When he was finished, Myers thought for some time while Suzanne Whitney deferred to his seniority, before replying.

"Well, Edmund, I'm glad you've brought this subject up. If you hadn't, I was going to. I know how your father feels about this because I've asked him about it, and I respect his judgment. If he doesn't know about department-store retailing in Albany, who does? But I'll tell you this. The boys down at the banks—the National Commercial, the Albany Trust Company, and City and County Savings and the others—they are paying close attention to this one because of the way it's financed. Staley's came in here—some bird by the name of Weston was the advance man—and studied the situation, and then they quietly bought up options on land in Colonie. When they had the land they wanted on option—some say more than four-hundred acres—they went over to Hartford to one of the insurance companies with the options and some tentative plans. Between them they put together a package with fourteen other big retail operations, with the insurance company managing the deal and putting up as much as 75 percent of the money in exchange for twenty-year leases, something like that. The local banks are mad as a boil because they think they should have been invited in, and they don't like to see that kind of business go outside the city or the area." Myers paused.

Edmund Ackeroyd interrupted to ask a question. "Are any of the local banks big enough, sophisticated enough, or courageous enough to play that kind of game? How much money was involved for the insurance company, anyway?"

"That's an interesting question, Edmund," responded Myers. "No one in town really knows how many dollars the insurance company put up, or the retail companies either for that matter. My guess would be between twenty and thirty million from the insurance company, and maybe another ten or fifteen from the retailers.

"But you make the right point about the local boys at the banks. They moan and groan about this, as they absolutely must, because it does take the play out of their hands. But I'll tell you there isn't a banker north of New York or west of Boston that can operate this kind of deal, and I'm not even sure many of the New York or Boston vultures would want to try to handle one of these things. They are complicated and risky, and the insurance companies have been doing them for fifteen years and have gotten awfully good at them.

"But, the real point of all this is not that our banking brethren are mad and frustrated but that this is a professional operation. These people have been doing the same thing all over the country. They know what they are about. There is big money and smart money involved. And it's not just Staley's that's involved but a whole lot of other very smart retailers. Edmund, this isn't going to go away. This is trouble for us of absolutely the worst kind. I respect your father, admire him, love him for what he is; but he's wrong about this and you're right to bring it up and to think about doing something about it."

He's right, Edmund," said Suzanne Whitney. "Oh, is he right! I know because I've competed with Staley's. No one else in this place has, as far as I know. I mean they are wild! They have their own brands; and insistence on quality and value and comparison shopping all the time. They build this incredible image of never being undersold, and then they go to work with the direct mail against your customers. Now they're using television besides! Wow, I mean that is the end! They never did that while I was at Wimpel's in New York beating my brains out trying to figure out how to get a third of a step ahead of them—or just to stay even some of the time. Edmund, what are we going to do about this?"

Suzanne Whitney had come to The Ackeroyd Company in 1961. She had had ten good merchandising years at Wimpel's in New York and had been judged the best of thirty-odd candidates for the Ackeroyd job by the executive search firm hired by the Ackeroyd Company to find a replacement for Anders A. Knoll who retired in 1961 after forty years with The Ackeroyd Company.

Edmund Ackeroyd had convinced his father that they should find someone with New York training and fresh New York ideas to succeed Knoll as merchandise manager. His father acceded to this point of view but Edmund did not know whether it was because of the strength of his arguments; because Owens and Kilroy had just hired a younger man as general merchandise manager from Fanstalls in Boston; or because his father believed that Edmund should have his own way in this matter as he moved toward the presidency of The Ackeroyd Store. So an executive-search firm was retained; and in due course Suzanne Whitney was identified as the most qualified candidate, wooed by Ackeroyd, and hired.

Edmund Ackeroyd listened to Myers and Whitney with interest and enthusiasm as they confirmed, in their different ways, his own judgment about the threat posed to The Ackeroyd Company by Staley's. But he was not overwhelmed by the advice they offered him about what should be done in the circumstances.

"They don't know what to do, anymore than I do," Edmund reflected to himself, "and I guess what I'll have to get used to as president is that it will be up to me to figure out what to do, right or wrong, when no one else has the foggiest idea."

Edmund looked at Myers and Whitney for a minute or two, hoping that he appeared to be reflective rather than merely dumb. Finally, he asked, "Have either of you ever been out to Staley's in Colonie?"

It turned out that neither of them had. Edmund then admitted that he had not been there, either. He suggested that before they could begin to think about how to meet the threat imposed by Staley's, they should spend Saturday looking over the competition.

"My father thinks that Staley's won't appeal to our customers. He says that only lower-income people and the folks from the farming communities will take the trouble. I think we ought to go out and look around the parking lots and see how many new cars with Albany plates* we can see. Then we should go inside and see what kind of business they are really doing–see if we can get some kind of idea of their class of trade and whether they seem likely to hurt us or not. Okay?"

And so it came to pass that Edmund Ackeroyd, Suzanne Whitney, and Radford Myers spent the next Saturday observing what was going on at Staley's department store in the new Colonie shopping center. They found the parking lots crowded with prosperous-looking cars bearing license plates from Albany, Rensselaer (Troy), and Schenectady counties, as well as other surrounding counties. They couldn't be sure that all the car owners were shopping in Staley's, for, by now, most of the other retail chain stores in the shopping center were also open for business. Yet, it seemed reasonable to believe that Staley's was attracting its share of the Albany residents who had come to the shopping center.

Inside Staley's the shoppers were indistinguishable from those who would be seen inside The Ackeroyd Store or Owens and Kilroy on a typical midsummer Saturday. Business was generally brisk in Staley's and was downright hectic in those sections of the store in which the white sale was in progress.

Ackeroyd, Myers, and Whitney hung around the shopping center most of the day,

* At this time it was still possible to discern the residence of a New York car owner from the state license plates on his or her automobile. For example, most Albany County residents' license plates had the letter A, or AA incorporated in a sequence such as 1A 7499 or AA 8264.

taking in the events unfolding before them and discussing and confirming each other's views as to what they were seeing.

At the end of the day, while driving home together, the three seemed not to have much more to say. Finally, Radford Myers broke the somewhat stony silence.

"Well, I don't think we learned much there today that we hadn't already suspected, did we? Those shoppers might just as well have been in our store, as far as outward appearances are concerned; and Staley's is sure doing business out there, isn't it?"

No one responded to this observation by Myers; and as the miles seemed to speed by, silence settled in, reflecting a glumness that was rapidly becoming oppressive. Finally, as he approached Suzanne Whitney's residence, Edmund Ackeroyd interrupted their thoughts.

"Well, I guess I've told you both, or you've figured it out, that my Dad isn't going to be bothered with this while he's still president. I gathered, Rad, from what you said the other day, that he'd told you about the same thing. What that means is that The Ackeroyd Store can't do anything *overt* about this Staley's business until the first of the year. But we must begin to prepare ourselves to handle this problem when I take over in January. And when I say 'we', I mean 'we'—the three of us. There aren't any buyers who are competent to deal with this, and there aren't really any other executives around our place who can do it; so it boils down to us."

"Okay, Edmund, I accept what you say and agree with it, too," said Radford Myers. "But your father is not just going to walk away from The Ackeroyd Store on the first of the year, is he? I mean, he's been president since, whenever it was, 1932; and that's all he's ever done with his life. He's going to have a say in this even when he isn't president, if for no other reason than that he and Carolyn own more stock in the store than anyone else. How are you going to handle that, Edmund? Understand, I'm not questioning your authority or that you're right. I'm with you 100 percent. But the thing I can't figure out is how your father will say okay after January first, when he's so opposed to doing anything about Staley's now."

"You're right, of course, Rad," replied Edmund. "I'm going to bet on two things—first, that Staley's is going to begin hurting us so clearly that there won't be any argument about it. I think we're in for a rough Christmas. Second, no matter how much they hurt us, I think I can talk my father into doing what we believe should be done, especially if I have the unswerving support of both of you. Let's try to enjoy the rest of the weekend and then meet on Monday to figure out what we can do to prepare ourselves to compete with these people."

On Monday morning, Radford Myers arrived in Edmund Ackeroyd's office with a memorandum that he had spent most of Saturday night and a good deal of Sunday writing.

"Edmund," said Myers, "I put my thoughts about this Staley's business into writing. I thought it might be helpful to you to have some ideas in a more or less organized form."

Ackeroyd thanked Myers for that, took the memorandum from him, and suggested that they meet with Miss Whitney at 10:30 to discuss next steps.

"She has a copy of this, does she?" asked Edmund Ackeroyd, waving the Myers memorandum in the air.

"Yes, I'm on my way to give her one right now," said Myers.

"Okay, then I'll see you both back here at 10:30," said Edmund Ackeroyd. Here is the Myers memorandum:

# THE ACKEROYD STORE

-Internal Communication-
Personal and Confidential

To: Edmund Ackeroyd
cc: Ms. Suzanne Whitney
From: Radford M. Myers
Subject: Staley's and Beyond

We all agree that Staley's is a definite threat to The Ackeroyd Store. At best, it is probable that they will hurt our sales and profits very seriously. At worst they may threaten the very existence of our store.

I believe we must distinguish two elements in this situation.

First, Staley's is a very strong competitor. If they had set up a store across North Pearl Street from our present location, they would have posed a very considerable threat to The Ackeroyd Store. This is because they have developed a very potent merchandising program. It works in the toughest department-store market in the world—New York City—and it has worked in virtually every market into which they've expanded. (But they're not all powerful. The one market where they seem to be having trouble, San Francisco, is the only market where they opened a downtown store, rather than a suburban store in a shopping center.)

The elements in their success seem to be these:

1. Strong emphasis on store-brand merchandise.
2. Insistence that the store-brand merchandise be of quality equal or superior to nationally advertised brand merchandise.
3. Consequent dependence on a price-value image. "We will not be undersold," says their advertising.
4. There are many product categories in which Staley's either cannot develop their own store brands or chooses not to do so. In these product categories they depend upon comparison shoppers to confirm that they are not undersold.
5. Finally, Staley's integrates all these elements into very potent merchandising programs that are heavily supported by advertising. As we have just seen, when Staley's has a white sale, they really have a white sale. I can hardly wait for Back-to-School time, Columbus Day, and Christmas.

These people are professionals in the best sense of the word. We would be hard pressed to compete with them if they opened a store across the street, but we have a few tricks of our own. We are old Albany and what works in New York doesn't always work out here in the sticks.

But, there is a second, complicating factor, in this situation. Staley's hasn't come to Albany to compete with us. Nor have they gone to Schenectady to compete with Claughson's, nor to Troy to compete with Bon Ton. They are taking us all on at once! They have redefined the Albany-Schenectady-Troy retail trading area under our noses. Television is part of this, because each of the local television stations covers the area that Staley's wants to service. But Staley's is still using a lot of newspaper, at least here in Albany, and I would assume in Schenectady and Troy, too. So television may not turn out to be too important in the picture. We'll have to wait and see.

The choice which confronts us is to stay in downtown Albany and hope that we can maintain our clientele or to go to Colonie ourselves and compete with Staley's directly, throughout the entire Albany-Schenectady-Troy area. They appear to be betting that the downtown shopping areas will ultimately decline and that shrewdly placed and managed shopping centers like the one in Colonie will merely accelerate this process. This insight has, I must add, proven correct for them in many of the other markets that they have entered since the war. And, of course, there are many markets in which the strong department stores have moved to the suburbs and established their own branch operations. The thing that makes our situation unique is that Staley's has now moved to consolidate our retail trading area with those of Schenectady and Troy.

What that means, from our standpoint, is that if we follow them to Colonie, we will be operating on a much broader scale than we ever have in Albany. This will not be a "branch" operation for us. In fact, to do this right, the North Pearl Street store will become the Albany branch, as long as it can survive, of our Colonie operation!

---

Radford Myers and Suzanne Whitney met with Edmund Ackeroyd in his office late that morning.

Edmund Ackeroyd said, glancing in Suzanne Whitney's direction: "I presume you've read this memorandum that Radford has been good enough to prepare."

"Uh, huh," she replied, neutrally, neither with approval or reservation.

"What do you think of it, Suzanne?" asked Edmund Ackeroyd.

"Oh," she replied, "he's absolutely right, isn't he? I mean, I absolutely shudder to think about this store being a branch store to something way out there in Colonie, but that's what it would become, wouldn't it? Yes, Radford's right, we have to go after them and really give them a run for their money."

"Okay," said Edmund, "I agree with you Suzanne and with you Radford.

"Now," he continued, looking at Myers, "let's suppose we want to build a store in Colonie, perhaps in that center that Staley's is in—they can't keep us out, can they. And let's say that our store would be as big or bigger than theirs. Would your local banker pals support us? Say a $20,000,000 nut; and, what could we handle ourselves, $8,000,000? Would they swing for $12,000,000?"

Radford Myers looked at Edmund Ackeroyd with a reflective light in his eye. "If he can get this past his father," thought Myers, "he's a better man than I am." But he said, "They'd consider it a risk, and you know that. They moan and groan when out-of-town money comes in, and they are not the most courageous group in the world. But, yes, I think they would support you in the ten to twelve million range. I don't think that they'd have a choice.

"Staley's can't keep you out of that center if there is space available. And they probably wouldn't want to do it. They like to be right next door to their competition, always have been next to Wimpels in New York, with their main store. Let's assume that we can get in there somewhere close, and let's assume that the banks will support us."

"All right, Radford," said Edmund, "that takes care of that. We just won't worry about it anymore. I'll call you up some morning and we'll get the money together and get the land and hire an architect; and between us, we'll build a building. I'm not trying to be facetious about this. But until the first of the year, we can't realistically begin to do anything about the store. That's why I want to concentrate on some other issues in the meantime, *if,* and I emphasize *if,* it's plausible to assume that when we want to do it, we can get a store up and operating.

"The thing that concerns me more at the moment is what that store will be. Staley's comes in here and they are big deal operators out of New York. They're world famous and consumers know more or less what to expect from them. Then they start presenting themselves in their advertising and lock up their image. It's just the way you said it was in your memorandum.

"Now Suzanne, I'm going to give you a job to do that's critical. If we move to Colonie, what kind of a store will we be? I mean, how should we present ourselves to our old customers and to the new ones we should be appealing to? We know what the Staley approach will be, and we've got to figure out what The Ackeroyd Store must become to compete effectively with Staley's.

"And, Radford," said Edmund, turning to Myers, "we've got to get into this media thing. It looks to me as if Staley's is going to try to use newspapers and television. They probably feel they have to use newspapers in most co-op programs, and maybe they'll just use television to support seasonal promotions. Who knows? We'll find out more about it as we study what they do. But I want you to study the media question and tell me whether we would use only newspapers, or only television, or both; and why. Get into the television question with our suppliers and find out on what basis they'll co-op with us. Talk to the television stations and find out what kind of rate cards they have for major local advertisers. Do they want our business, or not? And work out some kind of a basis to compare the media, so we won't be making up our minds only according to what our wives and kids think."

Exhibits 11-2 through 11-9 summarize the basic media information that Radford Myers assembled in response to Edmund Ackeroyd's request.

## *QUESTIONS FOR CASE 11*

1. Should The Ackeroyd Store attempt to compete with Staley's by opening a new store in the environs of Colonie? Why are advertising considerations important to that decision? Do you agree with the pessimistic prognosis for the North Pearl Street store presented by Radford Myers in his memorandum?

2. Prepare a memorandum in behalf of Suzanne Whitney that responds to Edmund Ackeroyd's requests about the advertising presentation of a new Ackeroyd store in Colonie. Present at least three alternative advertising creative strategies for the Ackeroyd Store. Relate each of these to the creative strategy that Staley's has pursued.

3. Prepare a memorandum in behalf of Radford Myers that responds to Edmund Ackeroyd's requests about media strategy for a new Ackeroyd Store in Colonie. What is the key unknown about the use of television? On what basis would you propose to compare television and newspapers as advertising media for the new Ackeroyd Store?

4. Is it important for Myers to know what creative strategy will be used in presenting the new Ackeroyd Store to its new and old customers before he reaches a final conclusion

about the relative strengths of television and newspapers as advertising media for the new Ackeroyd Store? Why or why not?

5. Why does Edmund Ackeroyd assume that Staley's uses newspapers *because* of manufacturer-sponsored cooperative advertising programs? What are the implications of this assumption as far as the use of television as a retail advertising medium is concerned? What effect will manufacturers' attitudes toward television in cooperative advertising programs have upon the Ackeroyd Store's ability to compete with Staley's?

6. Discuss the kinds of information available to The Ackeroyd Store about the characteristics of its customers and the customers of competing stores. In developing advertising goals and advertising media and creative strategies, what additional information should Edmund Ackeroyd have?

7. Why are manufacturers unwilling to reimburse retailers for cooperative advertising in television at a standard percentage of the television station's printed rate? What is the difference between television rates and newspaper rates that causes this manufacturer attitude? What advantages do newspapers have in obtaining advertising based on manufacturers' cooperative-advertising programs? How do available measures of newspaper and television audiences enter into this decision process?

**EXHIBIT 11–2**
**Specimen Data: Albany *Times Union/Knickerbocker News* Data and Rates**

| | Circulation* | | | | | |
|---|---|---|---|---|---|---|
| | Morning *Times Union* | | Evening *Knickerbocker News* | | Sunday *Times Union* | |
| County | Circulation | % Household Coverage | Circulation | % Household Coverage | Circulation | % Household Coverage |
| Albany | 47,671 | 46.3% | 38,048 | 36.9% | 57,540 | 55.9% |
| Columbia | 2,833 | 14.5 | † | | 5,244 | 26.8 |
| Essex | † | | † | | 1,512 | 12.5 |
| Fulton | † | | † | | 3,380 | 15.8 |
| Greene | 2,620 | 17.9 | † | | 3,791 | 26.0 |
| Hamilton | † | | † | | 342 | 17.1 |
| Montgomery | † | | † | | 3,405 | 16.1 |
| Rensselaer | 11,610 | 22.4 | 6.247 | 12.0 | 14,646 | 28.2 |
| Saratoga | 6,242 | 13.2 | † | | 13,166 | 27.8 |
| Schenectady | † | | 10,482 | 18.5 | 20,879 | 36.9 |
| Warren | † | | † | | 3,554 | 18.7 |
| Washington | † | | † | | 3,223 | 17.8 |

*For counties in which paper achieves 10 percent household coverage or better.
†County with less than 10 percent household coverage.

Household Coverage of Television Area of Dominant Influence

| | | |
|---|---|---|
| Morning *Times Union:* | 17.3% | (ADI Circulation: 77,788) |
| Evening *Knickerbocker News:* | 13.5% | (ADI Circulation: 60,522) |
| Sunday *Times Union:* | 29.5% | (ADI Circulation: 132,557) |

| | Black and White Rate Information | |
|---|---|---|
| Combination | Line Rate | Page Rate |
| Morning & evening | $ .95 | $2,573.55 (2 insertions, same advertisement, consecutive issues) |
| Sunday only | .95 | 2,573.55 (1 insertion) |
| Morning or evening, plus Sunday | 1.20 | 3,250.80 (2 insertions, same advertisement, same week) |
| Morning, evening, and Sunday | 1.25 | 3,386.25 (3 insertions, same advertisement, same week) |

The Ackeroyd Company buys full pages, 2 insertions, same advertisement, consecutive issues at a total cost of $2,573.55 per purchase. Because The Ackeroyd Store contracts for four such purchases a week for 52 weeks, it earns a discount of 25 percent. A typical Ackeroyd Store buy is, thus:

| Typical Buy: | Rate Card | Discount Rate |
|---|---|---|
| Thursday *Knickerbocker News,* full page plus Friday *Times Union,* same advertisement: | $2,573.55 | $1,930.16 |

The contractual obligation of The Ackeroyd Company in any given year is:

4 combination purchases × 52 weeks × net rate = Newspaper Advertising Budget
4 × 52 × $1,930.16 = $401,473.

**EXHIBIT 11-3**
**Specimen Data: Schenectady *Gazette* Data and Rates**

| | Circulation* Morning *Gazette* | |
|---|---|---|
| County | Circulation | % Household Coverage |
| Fulton | 2,137 | 10.0% |
| Montgomery | 3,428 | 15.9 |
| Saratoga | 9,951 | 21.0 |
| Schenectady | 42,480 | 75.1 |
| Schoharie | 1,992 | 19.9 |

*For counties in which paper achieves 10 percent household coverage or better.

Household Coverage of Television Area of Dominant Influence
Schenectady *Gazette*: 14.1% (ADI Circulation: 63,659)

Black & White Rate Information

| | Line Rate | Page Rate |
|---|---|---|
| Schenectady *Gazette* | .30 | $739.20 |

The Ackeroyd Store makes no use of the Schenectady *Gazette* and thus does not know what discounts might be available to it, if it were to become a heavy, continuing advertiser. Radford Myers has monitored the Schenectady *Gazette* and Claughson's usage of it for a four-month period. He observes that Claughson's runs five full pages of advertising in the paper in the typical week and deduces that they earn a discount of between 20 and 25 percent per insertion, at this level of use. Thus, it is Myers's guess that The Ackeroyd Store would pay between $554,40 and $591.36 per full page insertion if it were to advertise in the Schenectady *Gazette* with the same frequency as does Claughson's.

**EXHIBIT 11-4**
**Specimen Data: Troy *Times Record* Data and Rates**

| | Circulation* | | | |
|---|---|---|---|---|
| | Evening *Times Record* | | Sunday *Times Record* | |
| County | Circulation | % Household Coverage | Circulation | % Household Coverage |
| Albany | 11,576 | 11.2% | 11,261 | 10.9% |
| Rensselaer | 27,484 | 53.0 | 26,028 | 50.2 |
| Saratoga | 6,198 | 13.1 | 5,730 | 12.1 |

*For counties in which paper achieves 10 percent household coverage or better.

Household Coverage of Television Area of Dominant Influence

| | | |
|---|---|---|
| Evening *Times Record*: | 10.2% | (ADI Circulation: 45,706) |
| Sunday *Times Record*: | 9.6% | (ADI Circulation: 43,378) |

Black and White Rate Information

| | Line Rate | Page Rate |
|---|---|---|
| Daily or Sunday | .30 | $ 739.20 |
| Daily and Sunday | .54 | $1,330.56 |

The Ackeroyd Store makes no use of the Troy *Times Record* and thus does not know what discounts might be available to it, if it were to become a heavy, continuing advertiser. Radford Myers has monitored the Troy *Times Record* and the Bon Ton store's usage of it for a four-month period. He observes that Bon Ton runs six full pages of advertising in the paper in a typical week—three pages on weekdays and three on Sunday—and deduces that they earn a discount of no more than 20 percent from the daily-Sunday combination rate, at this level of use. Thus, it is Myers's guess that The Ackeroyd Store would pay about $1,064.45 per combined daily-Sunday insertion if it were to advertise in the Troy *Times Record* with the same frequency as does Bon Ton.

**EXHIBIT 11-5**
**Specimen Data: The Television Area of Dominant Influence***

| Counties Included in ADI: | Television Homes |
|---|---|
| Albany | 100,600 |
| Schenectady | 54,900 |
| Rensselaer | 49,700 |
| Greene | 15,100 |
| Columbia | 19,500 |
| Berkshire (Mass.) | 49,400 |
| Bennington (Vt.) | 11,100 |
| Washington | 17,900 |
| Saratoga | 47,300 |
| Warren | 18,700 |
| Hamilton | 1,800 |
| Fulton | 21,400 |
| Montgomery | 20,600 |
| Schoharie | 9,800 |

*As defined by The Arbitron Company.

**EXHIBIT 11-6**
**Specimen Data: Average Household Ratings of Albany-Schenectady-Troy Television Stations by Day Part and by Quarter, Monday–Friday**

| | WRGB Channel 6 NBC | WTEN Channel 10 ABC | WAST Channel 13 CBS |
|---|---|---|---|
| 7:00 A.M.–4:30 P.M. | | | |
| JAN., FEB., MARCH | 7 | 3 | 7 |
| APRIL, MAY, JUNE | 6 | 3 | 6 |
| JULY, AUG., SEPT. | 6 | 3 | 6 |
| OCT., NOV., DEC. | 6 | 4 | 6 |
| 4:30 P.M. - 7:30 P.M. | | | |
| JAN., FEB., MARCH | 19 | 10 | 16 |
| APRIL, MAY, JUNE | 16 | 7 | 11 |
| JULY, AUG., SEPT. | 14 | 7 | 11 |
| OCT., NOV., DEC. | 19 | 9 | 13 |
| 7:30 P.M. - 8:00 P.M. | | | |
| JAN., FEB., MARCH | 20 | 11 | 16 |
| APRIL, MAY, JUNE | 17 | 9 | 11 |
| JULY, AUG., SEPT. | 14 | 8 | 8 |
| OCT., NOV., DEC. | 19 | 18 | 9 |
| 8:00 P.M. - 11:00 P.M. | | | |
| JAN., FEB., MARCH | 20 | 17 | 23 |
| APRIL, MAY, JUNE | 20 | 13 | 18 |
| JULY, AUG., SEPT. | 14 | 12 | 16 |
| OCT., NOV., DEC. | 20 | 14 | 20 |
| 11:00 P.M. - 11:30 P.M. | | | |
| JAN., FEB., MARCH | 15 | 8 | 14 |
| APRIL, MAY, JUNE | 15 | 5 | 12 |
| JULY, AUG., SEPT. | 13 | 5 | 10 |
| OCT., NOV., DEC. | 14 | 5 | 12 |

**EXHIBIT 11-7**

# THE ACKEROYD STORE

-Internal Communication-

September 19, 1965

To: File
From: Radford M. Myers
Subject: Television Pricing

It is very difficult to get solid rates from the television stations. TV stations operate differently from the newspapers. In the latter case, the rates are laid out in printed form. We know the discounts we earn and thus we know what to expect. We can budget our advertising expenditures and depend on them.

The attached exhibit (11-8) shows what it costs to "deliver" one-thousand homes at different times of day on each local television station, at least as far as I have been able to develop hard numbers. Each of the stations have indicated that we might do substantially better if we were to commit $500,000 over the course of the year, and were willing to be flexible in scheduling, as long as the station "guaranteed" to reach a pre-established number of homes.

These station "guarantees" are based on statistical "ratings" surveys which are, in my judgment, of dubious validity and reliability. There is nothing analogous to the ABC-audited circulation data supplied to us by the newspapers.

Another problem is that when we start comparing newspapers and television we are comparing one-minute commercials on the one hand, and full-page newspaper advertisements on the other. Of course these aren't comparable, but what unit of space could fairly be compared to a minute of television time?

Even though any comparisons of this type seem to be absurd, the differences they reveal between television and newspapers are sufficiently large to be more than intriguing:

For example, we pay $1,930.16 to buy a full page in the Thursday *Knickerbocker News* and in the Friday *Times Union.* This advertisement reaches:

77,788 homes via the Times Union, and
60,522 homes via the Knickerbocker News

138,310 total

The cost of reaching one-thousand homes through this newspaper combination is:

$$\frac{\$1,930.16}{138,310} = \$13.96$$

The most expensive television cost to reach one thousand homes via the local stations is $5.17 in the second and fourth quarters over WAST during the prime evening hours.

**EXHIBIT 11-7 (Continued)**

If we use one-half page of newspaper space in the combination buy, on the assumption that our discount would hold, the cost per thousand for newspapers is $6.67. A quarter page, making the same assumption, is $3.33, still much higher than television costs on all stations in most day parts.

It looks as if we could reach a home with a one-minute commercial, three or four times as frequently with television as with newspaper space, for about the same money if we continue to use full-pages in newspapers.

I still have a lot of thinking to do about this. Other questions that bother me are these:

Doesn't television reach into a lot of homes that are not in our traditional class of trade? Is this good or bad? Isn't it a strength of newspapers that they tend to reach the better-educated, more affluent homes, rather than all homes?

If we are sure that newspapers do the job for us, why would we want to switch to a medium that is untried?

**EXHIBIT 11-8**
**Specimen Data: Cost per Thousand Homes Reached By Albany-Schenectady-Troy Television Stations: Planning Guides, 60 Second Commercials, 1966**

| | WRGB Channel 6 NBC | WTEN Channel 10 ABC | WAST Channel 13 CBS |
|---|---|---|---|
| 7:00 A.M. – 4:30 P.M. | | | |
| 1st & 3rd Quarters | $1.43 | $1.26 | $1.52 |
| 2nd & 4th Quarters | 1.86 | 1.64 | 1.97 |
| 4:30 P.M. – 7:30 P.M. | | | |
| 1st & 3rd Quarters | 1.74 | 1.36 | 1.81 |
| 2nd & 4th Quarters | 2.26 | 1.77 | 2.35 |
| 7:30 P.M. – 8:00 P.M. | | | |
| 1st & 3rd Quarters | 3.41 | 3.02 | 3.47 |
| 2nd & 4th Quarters | 4.43 | 3.93 | 4.51 |
| 8:00 P.M. – 11:00 P.M. | | | |
| 1st & 3rd Quarters | 3.79 | 3.41 | 3.98 |
| 2nd & 4th Quarters | 4.92 | 4.43 | 5.17 |
| 11:00 P.M. – 11:30 P.M. | | | |
| 1st & 3rd Quarters | 1.82 | 1.40 | 1.44 |
| 2nd & 4th Quarters | 2.37 | 1.82 | 1.87 |

**EXHIBIT 11-9**

# THE ACKEROYD STORE

-Internal Communication-

To: File — September 25, 1965
From: Radford M. Myers
Subject: CO-OP Money for TV

I have now discussed the availability of co-op money for television use with 16 of our leading 25 suppliers. This group contributed a total of $226,000 to our newspaper advertising budgets in 1964 and thus represents, collectively, the source of over 90 percent of total cooperative-advertising contributions to our 1964 advertising programs.

None of these companies has had any extensive experience with the use of television in their cooperative-advertising programs. Ten of the 16 have never allowed cooperative money to be contributed to television advertising programs. The remaining 6 have had isolated experience.

All of those who have had television experience confirm that fluid television rates are a problem in cooperative programs. They are reluctant to reimburse TV expenditures at 50 cents on the rate-card dollar, because it is their impression that television rates often deviate very significantly from printed rate cards and that, therefore, printed rate cards are meaningless. I would emphasize that it is the fluctuations in television rates that concern them. These companies seem unperturbed by the fact that they reimburse us at 50 cents of the open line rate while we pay only 75 percent of that rate under our discount structure.

They won't talk about it, but they seem perfectly willing to pay us what is, in effect, a premium over their 50 percent allowance on the open rate. This is a standard percentage and perhaps they feel we earn the discount because of our service in preparing advertisements. They do not want to allow a flat percentage on printed television rates that may vary, in actual practice, from 10 to 90 percent of the rate card. This just doesn't strike them as very businesslike. Yet they know that we will object to any compensation plan that is based on the invoices we pay since we are used to earning a discount on the newspaper rates paid under manufacturers' cooperative-advertising plans.

In addition, the advertisers who have tried co-op programs with TV have learned that they must provide significant help to retailers in television production. It is not simply a matter of pasting up some pictures from a mat service and letting the publication set type. So they see extra expense for them in helping us produce television commercials or in supplying commercials to us for our use with an Ackeroyd Store tag.

Everyone of these suppliers is willing to work with us on an experimental basis. My conclusions are:

1. It is possible to develop cooperative-advertising programs for television. I can't believe that Staley's hasn't worked out some sort of an arrangement with some of these same suppliers.
2. It will be difficult and expensive.
3. We will have to invest extra Ackeroyd money to learn how to use television effectively. We cannot expect to use television with the same proportion of our advertising expense funded by cooperative programs as is the case with our current use of newspapers.

# Case 12

# Specialty Market Advertising

## *THE ETHICO DIVISION OF ALLGOOD DRUG COMPANY INTRODUCES OSTEOFLEX*

The Allgood Drug Company is, as seen in Cases 7, 8 and 9, a medium-sized manufacturer of generic and branded proprietary-drug products. It was established in 1903 and during its early years specialized in the manufacture and distribution of a line of high-quality generic-drug items. In the 1920s the company began to develop and market a series of branded proprietary-drug items. It was the continuing success of these branded-drug items that made the company prosperous in the years that followed because the generic-drug market declined precipitously. By 1960 Allgood sales exceeded $200 million a year, and it had evolved as the third-largest maker of proprietary drugs in the United States.

As Allgood moved through the 1960s, J. C. McPhee, its president at that time, came to the conclusion that the company was too narrowly based. Although Allgood was prosperous and immensely profitable, McPhee was aware that two fundamental forces—extremely heightened competition and increasingly punitive government regulation—threatened the long-term growth of Allgood and companies like it whose business was limited to proprietary medicines. Accordingly, in 1968 McPhee recommended to his board of directors that the company actively seek acquisitions in fields that were compatible with the proprietary-medicine business. McPhee's presentation to the board included a detailed analysis of the kinds of companies that Allgood should seek to acquire. This analysis indicated that firms in the cosmetic industry and firms in the ethical-pharmaceutical industry seemed best suited for acquisition by Allgood. The board accepted McPhee's assessment of Allgood's position and agreed unanimously that McPhee should develop programs aimed at identifying potential acquisitions for Allgood in these industries. Thus, it came to pass that Allgood Drug Company acquired Effluvia House Cosmetics in 1970 for cash and stock and Ethico Pharmaceutical Company in 1973, also for cash and stock.

McPhee and his associates at Allgood worked with the management-consulting firm of Nork, Olsen, and Kusserow in assessing potential acquisition candidates in the ethical-pharmaceutical industry. The following criteria were established by Allgood and NO&K for the evaluation of these kinds of companies:

1. The ideal firm would be of small to medium size—sales should range from $30 million to $75 million per year.
2. It would epitomize the highest standards of ethical-pharmaceutical manufacturing and marketing practice.
3. The ideal company would enjoy a superior reputation in the medical community and with the retail and wholesale drug trades.
4. It would have a superior management team that was young enough to respond to the challenge that acquisition by Allgood would represent, yet mature enough to expand the company with minimal direct guidance from Allgood.
5. The ideal firm would have a well-established line of ethical-pharmaceutical products: that is, its current prosperity should not depend upon only one or two very successful recent ethical pharmaceutical introductions.
6. It should have superior research and development capability. Laboratory and testing facilities should be both modern and extensive. These facilities should be staffed with superior medical and pharmacological technicians with developed access to leading medical authorities in fields of company research and development activity.
7. The ideal company would have a well-developed research and development tradition in one or more medical fields. In other words, the company should be a logical source for important new pharmaceutical developments in one or more developing areas of medical practice.

It was not easy to find a company that met all of these criteria; and it was even harder to find such a company that would be amenable to the acquisition overtures of an organization that had made its own reputation and fortune in the manufacture of proprietary-drug products. Inherent in the growth of an ethical-pharmaceutical firm of superior reputation and outstanding accomplishment seemed to be a corresponding growth of contempt for those companies that merely manufactured branded medicines of dubious competitive superiority. Thus, many of the smaller, superior manufacturers of ethical pharmaceuticals were not interested in discussing their acquisition by a firm such as Allgood Drug Company.

Ethico Pharmaceutical Company was identified as an ideal candidate for acquisition by Allgood as early as 1970, but it took almost four years and much more money than Allgood had at first considered reasonable to bring Ethico into the Allgood fold. This occurred in late 1973.

Ethico sales were $59 million in 1972. The company's considerable reputation was built on several distinctive characteristics. In the first place, Ethico possessed a superior tradition in two ethical drug areas: the development of medicines for hypertension and the development of various analgesic specialty products. In 1972, the company manufactured a total of thirteen different products for the treatment of hypertension. Four of these were generic prescription drugs; three were manufactured under license from European firms; and six products had been developed in the Ethico research and development laboratories. In addition, in 1972 Ethico manufactured a total of twenty-three analgesic products; of these, six were generic, seven were manufactured under license, and ten had been developed and were completely owned by Ethico. At the time of the Ethico acquisition, the Ethico research and development laboratories had sixteen active hypertensive-drug research projects underway and twenty-eight active analgesic-drug research projects in work. In addition, Ethico Pharmaceutical had a strong manufacturing reputation. An understanding of exactly why this was so requires a good deal of background.

Drug manufacturing, proprietary or ethical, tends to be a tricky business. A finished drug product should have two characteristics: It should be both safe and effective in easing or curing specific medical conditions.

The safety of ethical-drug products dispensed under prescription is a matter of degree. In other words, the medical community and the Food and Drug Administration will countenance unpleasant side effects and modest adverse reactions in drugs that are believed to be effective against particularly severe or potentially mortal diseases; whereas they will insist that there be neither undesirable side effects nor adverse reactions of any kind in drugs that are to be widely used for less life-threatening illnesses or conditions.

The question of ethical-drug safety is customarily resolved through animal and human clinical testing, according to stringent government standards and controls. The results of such tests then serve as the basis for final Food and Drug Administration decisions.

All manufacturers are required to establish the relative safety of the drug-products they develop and abide by the government rules and restrictions in the manufacture and marketing of these products. Once a drug product has been approved for marketing and the conditions for its use and prescription established, there still remains the question of the realized effectiveness of that drug in broad-scale human use. In principle, of course, every dose of a drug should be equally effective. In practice, it is widely acknowledged that a drug dose, though constituted of exactly the ingredient or ingredients approved by government review under precisely specified conditions and/or in precisely specified combinations and meeting all of the manufacturing and safety standards, may vary to a greater or lesser degree in its effectiveness in use. The problem is one of bioavailability. The bioavailability of a drug is defined as the degree to which it is absorbed by the human patient to produce, within that patient, the expected therapeutic effect. It is generally recognized therefore, that a particular drug may conform chemically to government-approved specifications yet may fail to meet an adequate standard of bioavailability.

The Office of Technology Assessment of the Food and Drug Administration in its July 1974 report entitled *Drug Bioequivalence* has, for example, stated:

> Current Standards and regulatory practices do not assure bioequivalence for drug products. . . .
>
> Since the studies in which lack of bioequivalence was demonstrated involved marketed products that met current compendial standards, these documented instances constitute unequivocal evidence that neither the present standards for testing the finished products, nor the specifications for material, manufacturing process and controls are adequate to ensure that ostensibly equivalent drug products are, in fact, equivalent in bioavailability.

A concern with bioavailability and all of its potential therapeutic implications had marked the manufacturing operations of Ethico Pharmaceutical since its beginnings in 1938. Alton G. Swartfaegger, founder of Ethico, had stumbled upon problems of bioavailability in experiments he conducted on an analgesic preparation in 1946, a time when the issue of bioavailability was not generally recognized by either the Food and Drug Administration or the pharmaceutical-drug manufacturing industry. Swartfaeggar observed that doses of an experimental analgesic were somewhat effective in relieving the pain of migraine headache for some of his test subjects, and yet doses from other batches of the same preparation were totally ineffective for the same subject on subsequent days against migraine attacks that the subjects themselves considered to be significantly less severe. Swartfaegger further observed that it was not merely a matter of the efficacy of the drug exhausting itself for these patients; for these same subjects again achieved relief from migraine when treated with doses of the experimental drug drawn from the original batch or, sometimes, from yet a third batch.

As he continued to work with the development of analgesic products over the years, Swartfaegger became increasingly interested in bioavailability and its problems. He became convinced that drug bioavailability could generally be improved in three ways. First, it was often, but not always, possible to improve bioavailability in the basic formulation of the drug itself. Second, manufacturing practice alternatives could also lead to improved bioavailability. Swartfaegger began, therefore, to insist that all Ethico research and development projects consider bioavailability questions as well as those of therapeutic efficacy in formulating and planning the manufacture of new drug products.

The third way of improving bioavailability, at least in some instances, was through meticulous quality control in the manufacturing process. There is no ethical pharmaceutical manufacturing firm in the United States that is unaware of the importance of quality control in its operations. Yet quality control can seem to the manufacturer of pharmaceutical products like an endless road. There almost always seems to be some other check or confirmation that can be imposed upon the manufacturing process to insure its integrity—to insure that every nuance of the manufacturing process is executed with total perfection, without the compromise that the mass production of large continuous quantities seems, otherwise, to require.

It became Ethico policy always to take those extra steps in manufacturing that other pharmaceutical manufacturers might sometimes choose not to take. This did not mean that Ethico competitors did not produce drugs of high quality; for they did. It did mean that comparable Ethico products were often made with a meticulousness that their competitors held nearly in awe. As a result, Ethico developed a reputation especially in the medical community for superior manufacturing practice, as well as for products of excellent bioavailability.

A highly qualified research and development staff and modern facilities supported the company interests in hypertension and pain as well as the commitment to superior manufacturing practice. Alton Swartfaegger held a Ph.D. in biochemistry. Through the early years of Ethico he served as director of research and development. As the business expanded, he found it necessary to delegate this responsibility but continued to maintain a deep interest in holding the quality of this department at the highest affordable level. As he moved effortlessly between the worlds of pharmaceutical manufacturer and advanced academic practice and research, he found it relatively easy both to attract superior people to the Ethico research and development department and to hold Ethico in the forefront of developmental work in medicines for the relief of hypertension and pain.

Hunter Swartfaegger, M.D., succeeded his father as president of Ethico Pharmaceutical Company in 1970. "Hunty" Swartfaegger was forty-six in 1970. After graduating from medical school in 1954 with a specialization in problems of the circulatory system, he had actively pursued two careers. He joined the faculty of the local medical school, where he continued his studies of the circulatory system and carried a modest teaching load. In addition, he became executive assistant to his father at Ethico. The plan was for Hunty to develop a deep medical expertise in areas in which Ethico had a professional commitment; while, as executive assistant to his father, he also learned all there was to know about running the Ethico Pharmaceutical Company. Young Swartfaegger inherited his father's interests in hypertension, analgesia, and bioavailability. He was also interested, as was his father, in the importance of product formulation, manufacturing practice and quality control in achieving products of overall superiority.

So, it was little wonder that Ethico attracted the attention and interest of Allgood Drug Company in the late sixties. It seemed to meet all of the criteria that McPhee, his staff, and Nork, Olsen, and Kusserow had set up for the acquisition of an ethical pharmaceutical manufacturing firm. In the end, it was Allgood's guarantees of professional independence for Ethico and Hunter Swartfaegger that made the acquisition possible. It was also that J. C. McPhee and Hunter Swartfaegger grew to like and respect each other as the negotiations stretched over the years.

"I know you think we ought to go it alone, Pop," said Hunter Swartfaegger to his father as they once again discussed the possibility of the Allgood acquisition in late 1973.

"Hunter," his father responded, "I really feel that you have everything you need to make Ethico whatever you want it to be. Why let the others in? I agree with you that Jack McPhee is a swell guy and a serious executive. Keep him as a friend. But what do you need him and his people running around in your business for? You don't."

"Okay, Pop, I know what you mean and I thank you for your confidence in me," replied Hunter. "But when you retired the year before last, you agreed that I had to run the company and that it was up to me to make whatever decisions had to be made. And this is a decision that has to be made. Allgood can provide the capital that we'll need in the years ahead to keep our leadership in hypertensives and analgesics. And profitable as we are, we're going to need more capital than I believe we can comfortably generate on our own. And Allgood offers us a way to get into the proprietary markets if we neet to. I know how you feel about proprietary drugs and proprietary-drug marketing, and I certainly agree with you. But some day we may develop an analgesic that can be sold over the counter and is dramatically more effective than aspirin or acetaminophen—don't laugh, Pop, it could happen. If we were to do that, we would need someone who knows how to market proprietary medicines to consumers. We not only don't know anything about it, the people around here are just downright contemptuous of it. Allgood can and will take over all the aspects of the business that we both detest—the financial side, personnel administration, logistics management, and all that. If they acquire us, I'll be able to concentrate on making us the best Pharmaceutical house in the world in the seventies and the eighties—just as you made us the best in the world in the forties, fifties, and into the sixties. Jack McPhee is an honest guy. He'll let me run this place the way I want to because he believes in Ethico and what we stand for. We need Allgood and they need us. They know that they have to let us run it our way because we're the only ones who know how, and if they don't let us do it, they'll louse it up. So you see that this is something we *have* to do, Pop! I hope I'll have your support."

It was shortly after this discussion between father and son that the final papers were drawn up between Allgood Drug Company and the Ethico Pharmaceutical Company.

In late 1977 the Ethico Pharmaceutical Division of Allgood Drug Company received approval from the Food and Drug Administration of a new drug application for an analgesic anti-inflammatory product designed to be especially effective in relieving the pain and inflammation associated with arthritis. Extensive clinical testing demonstrated that this new drug—called Osteoflex by Ethico—provided consistently better pain relief than other analgesic products that were customarily prescribed for the relief of arthritic pain including such time-trusted remedies as plain aspirin and the most modern prescription products.

As important as the fact that clinical tests demonstrated superior pain relief was that Osteoflex had no side effects, either immediately or after extended use. The lack of side effects is particularly important for drugs used in the treatment of symptoms of arthritis. The disease is chronic and there is no known cure for it. The patient thus must seek symptomatic relief from medications that are taken more or less continuously, for life. Most arthritic medications produce side effects of one kind or another, especially if taken at high dosage levels for an extended period of time.

Finally, the Osteoflex formulation was such that it was possible to achieve very high and consistent bioavailability regardless of patient variability and regardless of patient drug sensitivity.

If Osteoflex had a disadvantage, it was that it cost about three times as much per average daily dosage as the leading prescription arthritis medication and about six times as much per average daily dosage as plain aspirin.

So, when the Food and Drug Administration released Osteoflex for marketing as a prescription drug, the Ethico Pharmaceutical Division faced the problem of how to communicate the very significant advantages of Osteoflex to the medical community.

Ethico had, of course, substantial experience in marketing ethical analgesic products to the medical community. The market research department of Ethico, for example, prepared an annual analysis of NDTI (National Disease and Therapeutic Index) data. The annual NDTI study published by Lea Incorporated provides, among a variety of data, information about prescriptions written by the United States medical community. Thus, NDTI furnishes information about prescriptions according both to the medical conditions for which they are written and to the drug categories and specific drug products named in the prescriptions written for each condition. This information is further classified by the medical specialty of the prescription writer. Thus, if one wishes to know what kinds of medical doctors write prescriptions for arthritis and the kinds of products they now prescribe for the disease, the information is available from the NDTI reports.

Analyses of NDTI data indicate that about three quarters of all prescriptions in the United States are written by four groups of doctors: general practitioners, internal medicine specialists, osteopaths, and general surgeons. The American Medical Association reported that, as of December 31, 1975, there were 340,280 doctors active in the United States. Of these, 140,450 were categorized as either general practitioners (54,557), internists (54,331), or general surgeons (31,562). Osteopaths are not recognized as a part of the medical community by the American Medical Association. In 1975 it was estimated that 12,000 osteopaths were practicing in the United States, increasing the total number of doctors to 352,180. Thus, 43 percent of all doctors (including osteopaths) write more than three quarters of total United States prescriptions.

In addition, general practitioners, internists, and general surgeons write more than 85 of the nonnarcotic analgesic prescriptions in the United States. Although aspirin is available for sale over the counter without a prescription, it is frequently formally prescribed; and the above three medical specialists plus osteopaths write more than three quarters of all aspirin prescriptions each year too.

Finally, the NTDI data reveal that in 95 percent of the instances that a patient goes to a doctor for advice about rheumatism or arthritis, the doctor will be either a general practitioner, an internist, an osteopath, or a general surgeon.

All of these data make it abundantly clear that the target audience for a prescription analgesic product like Osteoflex consists of four medical specialties and that these specialties account for somewhat less than one half (43 percent) of the active doctors and (estimated) osteopaths in the United States.

Pharmaceutical companies use a variety of means to communicate with the medical community. By far the most important means is the "detailing" of information to doctors by employees of pharmaceutical companies. It is the job of detail men and women to call on doctors and give them information about the products of the firm they represent and especially about new products of that firm. Detailers also provide product samples to doctors, usually on the written request of the doctor. It was estimated in 1977 that sixty-nine leading drug-firm members of the Pharmaceutical Manufacturer's Association (PMA) employed a total of 24,000 detail men and women and that 77 percent of these employees were college graduates.

In addition to detailing and sampling, pharmaceutical firms provide audiovisual materials for use in hospitals and physician-certification programs; direct a good deal of direct mail about their products to the medical community; sponsor medical symposia about the most recent advances in particular areas of medicine; and use journal advertising. Of all the means and media available to pharmaceutical companies for communication with the medical community, straight journal advertising is one of the least important in terms both of total effort expended and of promotional dollars allocated.

Ethico Pharmaceutical Company expended more than 12 percent of its total sales of $84,000,000 in 1977 on promotional activities. Exhibit 12-1 shows how this allocation of $10,400,000 broke down among the various promotional methods. The pharmaceutical industry's average percent of sales expended upon direct promotional activity has hovered around 9 percent in recent years. The Ethico percentage of 12.4 is thus high relative to industry average. Ethico spends at this higher level for two reasons. First of all,

**EXHIBIT 12-1**
**Specimen Data: Allocation of Ethico Pharmaceutical Promotional Expenditures, 1977**

| Total Promotional Expenditures | $10,400,000 | 100% |
|---|---|---|
| Detail Force of 127 Men and Women (including transportation, fringe benefits, expenses, and product samples) | $ 7,340,600 | 70.6% |
| Medical Symposia | 678,200 | 6.5 |
| Direct Mail | 1,240,300 | 11.9 |
| Instructional Films | 175,000 | 1.7 |
| Professional Journal Advertising | 965,900 | 9.3 |

the cost of maintaining a detail force tends to be relatively higher for small companies than for larger ones. All companies have to cover the population of prescribing doctors and for most companies this means basic coverage of the four major specialties listed above plus, depending upon the company's product line, other specialty groups. Detail coverage usually therefore requires a minimum number of people, regardless of company sales; and it thus costs smaller companies relatively more to maintain a detail force than it costs the industry giants. In addition, Ethico has, as a matter of policy, a higher-quality detail force than its immediate competitors. Ethico detailers are all college graduates: One may not work for Ethico as a detailer without a college degree. In addition, Ethico tends to pay its detail people about 20 percent more than the industry average in order to attract and hold better-quality people in its detailing force.

But Ethico expenditures for direct mail, journal advertising, medical symposia, and films are generally comparable, proportionately, to the expenditures of other competitive pharmaceutical firms.

Each year the Ethico promotional department lays out a master promotional calendar. The basic purpose of this calendar is to plan how the detail force will spend its time throughout the year. Detailer time is allocated among products each month and from month to month. Some products receive at least some detailer attention on every doctor call, whereas others receive attention only once or twice a year. In addition to the allocation of detailer time to standard-line items are allocations of time for the introduction of new products to the medical profession. Direct-mail programs and journal advertising are developed to anticipate and supplement detailer activities. These media are used to pique the doctors' curiosity about some new Ethico product or some important aspect of an existing item. The hope is that the direct mail and journal advertising will provide a basis for doctors to *want* to see the Ethico detail person and to welcome him when he arrives.

Medical symposia are usually held for leaders in a particular field of medicine about the time of introduction of a particular new product in that field. These symposia are scheduled more or less independently of the detail calendar.

The introduction of Osteoflex to the medical community was scheduled for the fall of 1978. The product was to be emphasized by the detailer force during the period October 15 through December 1, and journal advertising was authorized to appear in journal issues dated September, October, November and/or December. Journal advertising would presumably be continued into 1979, but no schedule for it was developed as part of the 1978 introductory plans. This was because calendar 1979 journal schedules for all Ethico products were customarily planned in the fall of 1978. In addition, two direct mailings on Osteoflex were to be made to target physician categories. The first of these would be posted on September 19 and the second on October 19. The journal advertising budget was set at $180,000 for the four-month period, September to December 1978.

Advertising for prescription medicines tends to be forthright and heavily factual. The devices that are common to consumer advertising are largely absent from advertising that appears in the medical journals and periodicals. This is true because of the inherent nature of ethical-pharmaceutical products themselves; because of the importance of dispersing detailed information about these products to the medical community; and because much of the content of such advertisments is specified by Food and Drug Administration standards. In addition, all advertising by the ethical-pharmaceutical industry is subject to continuing critical review by the Food and Drug Administration. In fact, the Food, Drug, and Cosmetic Act provides that the FDA may seize any ethical-pharmaceutical products that it considers to be misbranded; and for purposes of this provision of the act, advertising that fails to comply with FDA regulations is considered to be misbranding.

The development of competitive advertising for prescription products that are therapeutically equivalent tends to be extremely difficult because of this structure of government regulation. In the case of new products that are clinically unique however, a flat statement of distinctive characteristics and uses tends to be very effective and such advertisements can easily be created within the FDA strictures. Thus, the advertisements for Osteoflex were relatively easy to develop, because the product represented a significant improvement over other available medications for arthritis.

Each of the advertisements consisted of two pages. The first page, in four color, showed a picture of the Osteoflex package and several individual Osteoflex capsules. The headline said: "Osteoflex–important new medication for arthritis. Clinically effective, no major side effects, high bioequivalence. FROM ETHICO." The second page, backing the first, was in black and white and presented detailed information about the new drug under the following headings: Description; Clinical Evidence of Effectiveness; Indications; Effective for . . . ; "Probably" effective for . . . ; Contraindications; Warnings; Precautions; Adverse Reactions; Acute Overdosage; Dosage and Administration; How Supplied; Physician References in Medical Literature.

This advertising was presented to Hunter Swartfaegger on July 14, 1978, by Eldred Ebersole, director of marketing for the Ethico Pharmaceutical Company, and Randle W. McPartland of McPartland and Hildreth, medical advertising agency. McPartland and Hildreth had worked with Ethico as its advertising agency since 1953.

Swartfaegger approved the advertising as presented and was told that the agency was hard at work on an introductory media plan for the new analgesic/anti-inflammatory product.

"I hope you plan to use *American Medical News,* Randle," said Swartfaegger. "That's a dandy paper–I really like it a lot. Keeps me really up to date on what's happening in the world."

McPartland and Hunter Swartfaegger had discussed *American Medical News* on many past occasions. It was edited and distributed by the American Medical Association to all of its members. The agency usually preferred not to recommend this paper both because its advertising rates were relatively expensive and because it contained a great deal of waste circulation for advertising either analgesic or hypertension medicines. McPartland did not know now whether Swartfaegger was gently pulling his leg, or whether he genuinely believed the *American Medical News* was really appropriate as a medium to carry the introductory advertising messages for Osteoflex.

"Well, you know what our general view of *American Medical News* is, Hunty," replied McPartland. "We usually think that there are wiser ways in which to invest your advertising dollars. But, we'll give it a real, cold, hard look for Osteoflex. Maybe this will be the exception that proves the rule."

"This time, Eldred," said Swartfaegger, turning his attention ostensibly to Ebersole, yet indicating with his manner that he was really directing his comment to McPartland, "I'm really going to go over the media plan. I know that you pay a good deal of attention to the media we use, but I'm really nervous about Osteoflex. This is the most important new product that we've had in years, and I want everything about it to be perfect. So come prepared to argue. I'm really going to work you over on media—don't want us to fall into a rut."

With that, the meeting came to an end. Randle McPartland excused himself, while Ebersole remained behind to discuss other matters with Swartfaegger. Later in the day, Ebersole called McPartland on the telephone and the following exchange took place:

*Ebersole:* Randy, I thought I'd better tip you off. Hunty has got a real thing about this media plan. I know you and Al Balducci (the McPartland and Hildreth media director) do a thorough and careful job with our media plans, but he meant what he said this morning: He's in a mood to question every journal you put on the Osteoflex list.

*McPartland:* What brought this on Eeb? I mean, I didn't think Hunty cared one way or another about media. What's happened? Has some media salesman got his ear?

*E:* You got me, Randy; but that's what it sounds like. Either that or he's been playing golf with one of his president pals from some other pharmaceutical company and they've shown him a new way to be presidential. Who knows? Who cares? The important thing is the heat's on. And we have to look good.

*M:* Okay, Eeb. I got the picture. Let me tell you the criteria we've set up for this plan, Balducci and me; and see what you think of them. Okay?

*E:* Okay, yeah, that's a good idea.

*M:* Well first, we'll analyze circulation and coverage of the heavy analgesic prescription writers: the GPs, internists, general surgeons, and osteopaths, as we have in the past. We think we're solid as a rock with that, what with the NTDI data and all.

*E:* Yeah, I think that's right. But be sure you spell it out for him, Randy. He doesn't know an NTDI from a hammerhead whale and you've got to start from scratch. What else?

*M:* Well, we'll try to generate double coverage of our target group on each insertion. I mean we'll run that spread in journals that, taken together, have twice as much target circulation as the total members of our target group. And we'll make sure that each of the individual target groups—the GPs, internists, and so forth—get at least double coverage, too. No one will be slighted by this plan.

*E:* I've never understood this double-coverage business, Randy. Doesn't that mean that we're spending twice as much as we need to?

*M:* Come on, Eeb—you know better than that. The problem in this field is we have no studies of journal and magazine coverage of the various medical-specialty groups. We know that a particular portion of a specialty group receives a particular journal because it's sent to them in the mail. But we don't know whether they read the journals and magazines they get. In the consumer magazine field they measure issue readership of magazines, but we don't. About all we can do is deliver more circulation than there are specialists by using a variety of journals and hope that by overkilling with circulation, we'll get the coverage we want. In this case we want to cover all of the target group, and we believe that double-target circulation will do the job.

*E:* Okay, I guess I get it. Aren't there studies of reader reactions to these journals? Seems to me I keep hearing about research studies about ad-page readership and studies of reader evaluation of the editorial content of the journals. I mean if these doctors don't pay for these journals and magazines, why should they read them at all? Shouldn't we pay attention to these research studies?

*M:* Well, Eeb, of course you're right about that. We do keep an eye on those studies. But frankly, we're nervous about the research techniques that are used. Balducci can cover the details of that with you or with Hunty, or whomever you like.

*E:* Okay, you don't like the research, but how do you assess these publications? Or do you just double up on circulation and let it go at that?

McPartland was sweating by now. What had started out as an innocent and even lightly bantering conversation was by now a deadly serious attack on the agency's media-selection procedure. There was a lot more here than met the eye, he reflected, as he scrambled mentally to keep up with Ebersole's continuing questions.

*M:* We study the content and we study the publisher's statement about his editorial purpose. Then we try to assess just how valuable a publication is to a doctor, and in what way it is valuable. After this, we try to match up the content of the advertisement that we're placing with the editorial thrust and tone of the journal.

Let me be specific about this. Take Hunty's favorite, *American Medical News.* Nothing wrong with it editorially except it doesn't have anything to do with medicine. It talks about politics and social issues and what not. Of course Hunty likes it. He's running a pharmaceutical company and that paper is full of the kinds of issues that he *has* to be concerned with every day, all the time. There are a lot of things we would advertise in that paper but we think Osteoflex should be advertised in a serious, clinical, editorial environment that doctors read to keep up to date medically. We want to create credibility through context. That is, we want the editorial power of the journal or magazine to help us sell Osteoflex. This isn't a consumer good. These doctors are supposed to be serious about their work and we want to take advantage of it. And we don't want the whole darned AMA either—don't want to pay for all those extra doctors that aren't writing prescriptions for analgesics.

Hunty can have *American Medical News* if he wants and we wouldn't object. As I've already said, I think It's a fine editorial product and ideal for lots of advertising purposes, but not for the introduction of Osteoflex.

*E:* Okay, Randy, cool down, I really didn't mean to get you excited about this. Don't worry, either. You and Balducci do media planning well and we know it; this isn't a problem for you. You say the media plan will be ready next Thursday?

*M:* That's right Eeb and I'm sorry I got a little overheated with you, but this is important to us and *has been* important to us. I get defensive when someone questions me about an area that I know we're the best in the business in.

The medical journals and periodicals that were considered by McPartland and Hildreth as potential advertising media for Osteoflex are presented in Exhibits 12-2 through 12-18. The material in these exhibits are authentic and have been derived from *Business Publication Rates and Data,* October 24, 1978, published by Standard Rate and Data, Inc.

Terms used in the exhibits are defined as follows:

*Percent Circulation in Target Audience:* the percentage of the journal or periodical's total circulation that is delivered to general practitioners, internists, general surgeons, and osteopaths. (Calculated from circulation data.)

*Percent Coverage of Target Audience:* the percentage of all general practitioners, internists, general surgeons, and osteopaths covered by this journal or periodical. (Calculated from circulation data.)

**EXHIBIT 12-2**
*American Family Physician,* **1978**

Publisher: American Academy of Family Physicians
Method of Circulation: Unpaid, monthly.
Total Circulation: 123,720 (6-30-78)

| | |
|---|---|
| Circulation to General Practitioners | 46,311 |
| Circulation to Internists | 38,148 |
| Circulation to General Surgeons | 1,019 |
| Circulation to Osteopaths | 14,357 |
| Percent circulation in Target Audience | 80.7 |
| Percent coverage of Target Audience | 65.5 |
| Cost of single page, black & white | $2,475 |
| CPM, page, black & white, against Target Audience | $24.79 |
| Cost of single page, four color | $3,300 |
| CPM, page, four color, against Target Audience | $33.05 |

Publisher's description of the medium:

*American Family Physician* is edited for physicians in the general practice of medicine and surgery. Four or more original scientific articles, written on assignment, emphasize diagnostic and therapeutic techniques. Other editorial features include scientific abstracts plus socioeconomic and legislative information of interest to physicians in active practice. Fifty-five percent of *American Family Physicians* editorial content is devoted to scientific information. Special emphasis is placed on design and illustration.

## *QUESTIONS FOR CASE 12*

1. Prepare a media plan for Osteoflex. Choose from among the journals, magazines, and papers that are described in Exhibits 12-2 through 12-18.
2. Analyze the McPartland and Hildredth proposal to buy space with target circulation that is at least double the size of the target audience. Is this sound or wasteful? Why?
3. Should Ethico Pharmaceutical be concerned that the bulk of the journals and magazines circulated to doctors come to them either free or as a part of their membership in a professional society? What are the weaknesses of unpaid circulation? What are the strengths of paid circulation? Does it make a difference in this case? Why?
4. Is the publisher's description of the editorial content of his magazine important for specialist advertisers? Why? How does the advertiser use these descriptions in evaluating media vehicles? Would similar descriptions be important in consumer magazines with paid circulation? Why or why not?
5. Journal advertising is portrayed, in this case, as not especially important in the marketing programs for new prescription drugs. Detail men, product sampling, and direct mail are all said to be more important. Is this unique to pharmaceutical marketing or would other specialist/industrial advertisers tend to place relatively less dependence on space advertising? Explain your answer.
6. Evaluate McPartland's defense of his agency's media selection process. Do you agree with it? Would you be inclined to place heavy dependence upon advertising page

## EXHIBIT 12-3
*American Medical News*, 1978

Publisher: American Medical Association
Method of Circulation: Unpaid, weekly
Total Circulation: 278,706 (Unaudited: Publisher's sworn statement, 6-30-78)

| | |
|---|---|
| Circulation to General Practitioners | NA |
| Circulation to Internists | NA |
| Circulation to General Surgeons | NA |
| Circulation to Osteopaths | NA |
| Percent circulation in Target Audience | NA |
| Percent coverage of Target Audience | NA |
| Cost of single page, black & white | $4,390. |
| CPM, page, black & white, against Target Audience | NA |
| Cost of single page, four color | $5,750. |
| CPM, page, four color, against Target Audience | NA |

Publisher's description of the medium:

*American Medical News* publishes news and opinions on issues of political, social, and economic significance concerning the practice and delivery of medical care. Additionally, there is nontechnical reporting and discussion of medical developments, legal decisions, legislation, business trends, and tax rulings.

## EXHIBIT 12-4
*Anesthesia and Analgesia*, 1978

Publisher: The International Anesthesia Research Society
Method of Circulation: Paid, bimonthly
Total Circulation: 12,721 (Unaudited: Publisher's sworn statement, 6-30-78)

| | |
|---|---|
| Circulation to General Practitioners | NA |
| Circulation to Internists | NA |
| Circulation to General Surgeons | NA |
| Circulation to Osteopaths | NA |
| Percent circulation in Target Audience | 100.0* |
| Percent coverage of Target Audience | 8.3* |
| Cost of single page, black & white | $315. |
| CPM, page, black & white, against Target Audience | $24.76* |
| Cost of single page, four color | $765. |
| CPM, page, four color, against Target Audience | $60.14* |

Publisher's description of the medium:

*Anesthesia and Analgesia* is edited for practicing anesthesiologists and other medical personnel in the specialty. Emphasis is on practical and clinical material. Special editorial features include: Capsule Review of Articles; Something New; Questions and Answers; Book Shelf; We Salute; and "Physician and the Law." Editorial material is provided through independent researchers carried out by anesthesiologists and related specialists in medical schools and hospitals, some of which were originally presented at the Society's annual scientific congresses.

*Computed on total circulation on the assumption that readers of this journal must fall into the Target Audience.

## EXHIBIT 12-5
*Arthritis and Rheumatism*, 1978

Publisher: The Arthritis Foundation
Method of Circulation: Paid, eight times a year.
Total Circulation: 5,522 (Unaudited: Publisher's sworn statement, 6-30-78)

| | |
|---|---|
| Circulation to General Practitioners | NA |
| Circulation to Internists | NA |
| Circulation to General Surgeons | NA |
| Circulation to Osteopaths | NA |
| Percent circulation in Target Audience | 100* |
| Percent coverage of Target Audience | 3.6* |
| Cost of single page, black & white | $440. |
| CPM, page, black & white, against Target Audience | $79.68* |
| Cost of single page, four color | $1,140. |
| CPM, page, four color, against Target Audience | $206.45* |

Publisher's description of the medium:

*Arthritis and Rheumatism* is edited for the general practitioner, as well as the specialist, including those interested in the growing field of geriatrics. Original work, progress reports, clinical rounds, and review articles provide a clear exposition of clinical experience and advances made in rheumatoid arthritis, rheumatic fever, osteoarthritis, gout, nonarticular rheumatism, and the field of connective tissue diseases. Included also are case studies, reports on the efficacy of new drugs and methods of treatment, new testing methods and important new research.

*Computed on total circulation on the assumption that readers of this Journal must fall into the Target Audience.

## EXHIBIT 12-6
*Consultant*, 1978

Publisher: Consultant Publications
Method of Circulation: Unpaid, monthly.
Total Circulation: 148,957 (6-30-78)

| | |
|---|---|
| Circulation to General Practitioners | 35,532 |
| Circulation to Internists | 24,059 |
| Circulation to General Surgeons | 14,661 |
| Circulation to Osteopaths | 10,088 |
| Percent circulation in Target Audience | 56.6 |
| Percent coverage of Target Audience | 55.3 |
| Cost of single page, black & white | $2,685 |
| CPM, page, black & white, against Target Audience | $31.84 |
| Cost of single page, four color | $3,935 |
| CPM, page, four color, against Target Audience | $46.66 |

Publisher's description of the medium:

*Consultant* articles emphasize the "how to" aspects of medicine. They help the reader resolve questions common to his everyday practice and provide peer references so he can measure his own techniques against those of leading authorities. Articles are original, covering such areas as internal medicine, cardiology, gastroenterology, surgery, obstetrics and gynecology, pediatrics, psychiatry, and orthopedics. The emphasis throughout is on providing practical and immediately relevant help to clinicians.

**EXHIBIT 12-7**
*Current Prescribing,* **1978**

Publisher: Medical Economics Company
Method of Circulation: Unpaid, monthly.
Total Circulation: 120,916 (6-30-78)

| | |
|---|---|
| Circulation to General Practitioners | 42,686 |
| Circulation to Internists | 24,779 |
| Circulation to General Surgeons | 571 |
| Circulation to Osteopaths | 10,015 |
| Percent circulation in Target Audience | 64.5 |
| Percent coverage of Target Audience | 51.2 |
| Cost of single page, black & white | $2,235 |
| CPM, page, black & white, against Target Audience | $28.64 |
| Cost of single page, four color | $3,170 |
| CPM, page, four color, against Target Audience | $40.61 |

Publisher's description of the medium:

*Current Prescribing* presents clinical advice on those diseases and conditions that doctors frequently treat in their busy practices. Consulting physician-authors—each an acknowledged authority in his field—discuss relevant diagnostic considerations, recommend appropriate drugs, and offer alternative therapy guidelines for refractory conditions.

**EXHIBIT 12-8**
*Drug Therapy*—**Hospital and Office Editions, 1978**

Publisher: Biomedical Information Corp.
Method of Circulation: Unpaid, monthly.
Total Circulation: 240,564 (6-30-78)

| | |
|---|---|
| Circulation to General Practitioners | 47,840 |
| Circulation to Internists | 45,437 |
| Circulation to General Surgeons | 13,823 |
| Circulation to Osteopaths | NA |
| Percent circulation in Target Audience | 44.5 |
| Percent coverage of Target Audience | 70.3 |
| Cost of single page, black & white | $3,550 |
| CPM, page, black & white, against Target Audience | $33.15 |
| Cost of single page, four color | $4,600 |
| CPM, page, four color, against Target Audience | $42.95 |

Publisher's description of the medium:

*Drug Therapy,* hospital edition, contains original articles on the use and action of therapeutic agents. Authored by physicians, contents are edited especially for the hospital physician and resident. Special editorial features include: Case reports on Clinical Pharmacology and Self-Assessment, Drug Therapy in the Seriously Ill Patient, Controlling Drug Therapy Using Serum Levels, Clinical Drug Abstracts, Keeping Up with Prescribing Information, Using the Hospital Formulary and Drugs in Emergencies.
*Drug Therapy,* office edition, contains original articles on the use and action of therapeutic agents. Authored by physicians, contents are edited to be practical and clinically relevant. Regular departments will include Drug Interaction, Patient Instructions, Drugs and Diagnostic Tests, Drugs and Society, Drug Abstracts, Advances in Clinical Therapeutics, and Revisions in Official Prescribing Information.

## EXHIBIT 12-9
*Emergency Medicine*, 1978

Publisher: Fischer Medical Publications
Method of Circulation: Unpaid, monthly.
Total Circulation: 119,467 (6-30-78)

| | |
|---|---|
| Circulation to General Practitioners | 47,023 |
| Circulation to Internists | 43,514 |
| Circulation to General Surgeons | 512 |
| Circulation to Osteopaths | 14,816 |
| Percent circulation in Target Audience | 88.6 |
| Percent coverage of Target Audience | 69.4 |
| Cost of single page, black & white | $2,185 |
| CPM, page, black & white, against Target Audience | $20.64 |
| Cost of single page, four color | $3,035 |
| CPM, page, four color, against Target Audience | $28.67 |

Publisher's description of the medium:

*Emergency Medicine* is published for those physicians who deal with the broadest range of patients and illnesses. The publication addresses itself to the acute phases of various types of illnesses and injuries. It treats on a "how-to" level common emergencies ranging from the most routine to the most serious. Special features include: errors in emergency practice, the toxic emergency, emergency tips from the literature, and major hospital therapeutic conferences aimed at helping doctors diagnose and treat acute medical and traumatic conditions.

## EXHIBIT 12-10
*Journal of the American Medical Association (JAMA)*, 1978

Publisher: American Medical Association
Method of Circulation: Paid,* weekly
Total Circulation: 250,429 (Paid* 209,673, Unpaid 40,756, 6-30-78)

| | |
|---|---|
| Circulation to General Practitioners | 31,602 |
| Circulation to Internists | 31,621 |
| Circulation to General Surgeons | 20,615 |
| Circulation to Osteopaths | 485 |
| Percent circulation in Target Audiences | 33.7 |
| Percent coverage of Target Audience | 55.3 |
| Cost of single page, black & white | $3,180 |
| CPM, page, black & white, against Target Audience | $37.71 |
| Cost of single page, four color | $4,300 |
| CPM, page, four color, against Target Audience | $50.99 |

Publisher's description of the medium:

*JAMA* reports on progress in clinical medicine, pertinent research, and landmark evolutions in other areas as they interface with medicine. It publishes various directories, medical news items, letters, original papers, abstracts, questions and answers, obituaries, and practice opportunities.

*Included in membership dues of American Medical Association

**EXHIBIT 12-11**
*Journal of Continuing Education in Family Medicine,* **1978**

Publisher: Journals of Continuing Education
Method of Circulation: Unpaid, monthly
Total Circulation: 49,944 (Unaudited, Publisher's sworn statement, 6-30-78)

| | |
|---|---|
| Circulation to General Practitioners | NA |
| Circulation to Internists | NA |
| Circulation to General Surgeons | NA |
| Circulation to Osteopaths | NA |
| Percent circulation in Target Audience | NA |
| Percent coverage of Target Audience | NA |
| Cost of single page, black & white | $1,275 |
| CPM, page black & white, against Target Audience | NA |
| Cost of single page, four color | $2,100 |
| CPM, page, four color, against Target Audience | NA |

Publisher's description of the medium:

*Family Medicine* is edited for general practitioners and prescribing osteopaths in the United States. Each year more than 1,500 articles dealing with subjects of interest to those doctors are digested from the world's medical literature. More than 3,000 journals are reviewed each month and articles in the areas of surgery, therapeutics, medicine, gynecology, diagnosis, dermatology, obstetrics, urology, pediatrics, neurology, otolaryngology, ophthalmology, psychiatry, radiology, orthopedics, allergy, and proctology are selected by the editors for digesting. Special features include an editorial of the month, a section devoted to new drugs, and a section on legal medicine.

**EXHIBIT 12-12**
*MD, Medical Newsmagazine,* **1978**

Publisher: MD Publications, Inc.
Method of Circulation: Unpaid, monthly
Total Circulation: 188,221 (6-30-78)

| | |
|---|---|
| Circulation to General Practitioners | 37,909 |
| Circulation to Internists | 36,860 |
| Circulation to General Surgeons | 14,833 |
| Circulation to Osteopaths | 14,199 |
| Percent circulation in Target Audience | 55.1 |
| Percent coverage of Target Audience | 68.1 |
| Cost of single page, black & white | $2,875 |
| CPM, page, black & white, against Target Audience | $27.69 |
| Cost of single page, four color | $4,275 |
| CPM, page, four color, against Target Audience | $41.18 |

Publisher's description of the medium:

*MD, Medical Newsmagazine* is a cultural medical journal published for physicians. *MD* features articles on medicine, science, history, art, literature, travel, sports, biography, and various other subjects, offering physicians a total perspective of human life. Written from the point of view of the physician, each article correlates the topic's present essence, which is life, with its dimension in history, integrating these two components into a living history that is both informative and interesting for the physician in his triple role as a professional, as a member of society, and as a human being.

**EXHIBIT 12-13**

*Medical Aspects of Human Sexuality,* 1978

| | |
|---|---|
| Publisher: Hospital Publications Inc. | |
| Method of Circulation: Unpaid, monthly | |
| Total Circulation: 164,895 (6-30-78) | |
| Circulation to General Practitioners | 43,918 |
| Circulation to Internists | 36,996 |
| Circulation to General Surgeons | 574 |
| Circulation to Osteopaths | 14,039 |
| Percent circulation in Target Audience | 57.9 |
| Percent coverage of Target Audience | 62.7 |
| Cost of single page, black & white | $2,975 |
| CPM, page, black & white, against Target Audience | $31.14 |
| Cost of single page, four color | $4,415 |
| CPM, page, four color, against Target Audience | $46.22 |

Publisher's description of the medium:

*Medical Aspects of Human Sexuality* is a scientific journal for practicing physicians, covering the physical, psychological, and cultural components of human sexuality and related aspects of family life. It provides authoritative clinical information on sexual problems that affect many patients, plus pertinent current data from sociology, psychology, and other behavioral sciences. As a scientific journal, *Medical Aspects of Human Sexuality* is not designed to promulgate any particular point of view. Its content represents a variety of opinions. Special features include interviews, roundtable discussions, and a "Viewpoints" series on controversial problems.

**EXHIBIT 12-14**

*Medical Economics,* 1978

| | |
|---|---|
| Publisher: Medical Economics Company | |
| Method of Circulation: Unpaid, biweekly | |
| Total Circulation: 162,892 (6-30-78) | |
| Circulation to General Practitioners | 36,084 |
| Circulation to Internists | 21,451 |
| Circulation to General Surgeons | 13,540 |
| Circulation to Osteopaths | 7,608 |
| Percent circulation in Target Audience | 48.3 |
| Percent coverage of Target Audience | 51.6 |
| Cost of single page, black & white | $3,100 |
| CPM, page, black & white, against Target Audience | $39.40 |
| Cost of single page, four color | $4,650 |
| CPM, page, four color, against Target Audience | $59.10 |

Publisher's description of the medium:

*Medical Economics* is edited for physicians in private practice. Covers patient relations, office management, fee setting and collecting, health insurance, hospital practice, government regulation, professional liability—plus such financial subjects as personal insurance, investments tax and estate planning. Also medical ethics, medical humor, medical family life, leisure activities. Interpretive articles feature advice from experts, based on experiences of practicing physicians.

**EXHIBIT 12-15**
*Medical Times*, 1978

| | |
|---|---|
| Publisher: Romaine Pierson Publishers | |
| Method of Circulation: Unpaid, monthly | |
| Total Circulation: 80,861 (6-30-78) | |
| Circulation to General Practitioners | 43,006 |
| Circulation to Internists | 25,189 |
| Circulation to General Surgeons | 572 |
| Circulation to Osteopaths | 10,230 |
| Percent circulation in Target Audience | 97.7 |
| Percent coverage of Target Audience | 51.8 |
| Cost of single page, black & white | $2,200 |
| CPM, page, black & white, against Target Audience | $27.85 |
| Cost of single page, four color | $3,050 |
| CPM, page, four color, against Target Audience | $38.61 |

Publisher's description of the medium:

*Medical Times* contains clinical articles from teaching centers plus special departments. Special editorial features include: Patient Education Charts; Two-minute Quizzes in Dermatology, Neurology, Radiology, and Cardiology; Malpractice Decisions You Should Know About; Mediquiz; Two Minutes with Diabetes; Two Minutes with Arthritis. Desk Reference issues on: hypertension, cardiology, common cancer problems, ENT problems.

**EXHIBIT 12-16**
*Medical Tribune*, 1978

| | |
|---|---|
| Publisher: Medical Tribune, Inc. | |
| Method of Circulation: Unpaid, forty times per annum. Tabloid. | |
| Total Circulation: 157,498 (6-30-78) | |
| Circulation to General Practitioners | 42,168 |
| Circulation to Internists | 24,741 |
| Circulation to General Surgeons | 15,361 |
| Circulation to Osteopaths | 9,287 |
| Percent circulation in Target Audience | 58.1 |
| Percent coverage of Target Audience | 60.1 |
| Cost of single page, black & white | $3,155 (Standard A-size page) |
| CPM, page black & white, against Target Audience | $34.46 |
| Cost of single page, four color | $4,155 (Standard A-size page) |
| CPM, page, four color, against Target Audience | $45.38 |

Publisher's description of the medium:

*Medical Tribune* provide the physician with coverage of medical news throughout the world including clinical, experimental, national, and international meeting coverage, drug hearings, medico-legal, continuing medical education, and infection control.

**EXHIBIT 12-17**
*Modern Medicine,* **1978**

Publisher: Modern Medicine Publications
Method of Circulation: Unpaid, twenty-one times per annum
Total Circulation: 170,186 (6-30-78)

| | |
|---|---|
| Circulation to General Practitioners | 43,911 |
| Circulation to Internists | 35,864 |
| Circulation to General Surgeons | 24,149 |
| Circulation to Osteopaths | 14,255 |
| Percent circulation in Target Audience | 69.4 |
| Percent coverage of Target Audience | 77.5 |
| Cost of single page, black & white | $2,885 |
| CPM, page, black & white, against Target Audience | $24.41 |
| Cost of single page, four color | $3,980 |
| CPM, page, four color, against Target Audience | $33.68 |

Publisher's description of the medium:

*Modern Medicine* serves physicians practicing in primary care and basic medical specialties. Its content includes abstracts of original papers selected from medical and psychiatric journals, physician-written articles on diagnosis and therapy; forums on medical and surgical questions, and illustrated reports of clinical techniques; plus editorial opinion and Washington news departments. A self-test diagnostic problem and a feature on drug actions and interactions also are part of the regular editorial content.

**EXHIBIT 12-18**
*Post-graduate Medicine,* **1978**

Publisher: McGraw-Hill Publications
Method of Circulation: Unpaid, monthly.
Total Circulation: 109,887 (6-30-78)

| | |
|---|---|
| Circulation to General Practitioners | 47,197 |
| Circulation to Internists | 43,826 |
| Circulation to General Surgeons | 537 |
| Circulation to Osteopaths | 13,685 |
| Percent circulation in Target Audience | 95.8 |
| Percent coverage of Target Audience | 69.0 |
| Cost of single page, black & white | $2,100 |
| CPM, page, black & white, against Target Audience | $19.95 |
| Cost of single page, four color | $2,975 |
| CPM, page, four color, against Target Audience | $28.27 |

Publisher's description of the medium:

*Post-graduate Medicine* is edited for family doctors (GP, Internist, and DO), providing proved clinical advances to help them in their daily practice. Complete, original clinical articles stressing the diagnosis and treatment of medical problems encountered in general practice are included in each issue. Clinical symposiums in each issue are accompanied by tests which may be completed for AMA category I credits, and AAFP-prescribed credit.

readership studies and/or studies of reader evaluation of journal editorial quality, even if you knew the research procedures upon which such studies were based tended to be shaky? Why or why not?

7. Ethico Pharmaceutical Company has achieved a reputation for the quality and dependable bioavailability of their drug products. What implications does this reputation have for the Osteoflex advertising program? Would it tend to influence media selection? If you believe it would, tell how. If you believe it would have no effect on media selection, explain why not.

8. Show how the cost per thousand of $24.79 for a one-page black-and-white advertisement in *American Family Physician* (Exhibit 12–2) is computed.

# Case 13

# Evaluating Alternative Copy Research Procedures

## *MID-AMERICAN AIRLINES REVIEWS ITS ADVERTISING*

Adam Clagge is Mid American Airlines western division vice-president for sales and marketing. Clagge's role in Mid American Airlines is indicated in the company's organization chart, Exhibit 6-3; and some history of this company and its advertising program is given in Case 6. Clagge has been with Mid American since his graduation in 1965 from a large middle-western graduate business school. He was appointed to his present position in 1978 and prior to that had been moved systematically from one job to another within various divisions as he was prepared for eventual assignment to a senior management role within the company.

In Case 6 Clagge's role in reassessing Mid American's media usage was described. Clagge was not, however, content to raise fundamental questions about the media aspects of the Mid American advertising programs. He was, in addition, concerned that Mid American sales and marketing personnel were not sufficiently critical of the advertisements that were presented for their approval by Mid American advertising agency Bennington, Bartley, and Avignon.

Clagge had flown up to Kansas City one morning in early October 1980 to discuss a variety of rather routine matters with Mid American executive vice-president for sales and marketing, Thomas Eldridge. After a hard morning's work the two left the company's offices for lunch, journeying into downtown Kansas City to visit a restaurant much admired by Tom Eldridge.

"It's smart to get out of the office at lunchtime, Adam," remarked Eldridge. "Gives you a change of scene, change of pace, and it really recharges your approach to things."

"I guess that's right, Tom," responded Clagge, "and if you're used to it, I suppose it's hard not to do it. In Houston we generally have sandwiches sent in and work on through at our desks. That way we don't waste any time. But you have a point, because along about three o'clock the office does seem to get kind of oppressive; and when we work on past six or seven, it can really be deadly." Their talk proceeded along such inconsequential lines until, sometime after their entrees had been served, Clagge abruptly changed the subject.

"Tom, there's something I've been meaning to ask you for a couple of months now, and I keep forgetting to do it. It's business, and I know you don't especially like to discuss business at lunch; but make an exception with this one, okay?" Clagge did not wait for an acquiescent response from Eldridge but, rather, simply plunged ahead:

"It's about our advertising creative work. I'm thinking of the image campaign we use television for—you know, 'Mid American goes all the way for you.' How do we know whether that campaign is any good or not?"

"What do you mean, Adam?" responded Eldridge. "Of course, it's good. We've been using the same line and roughly the same format for over five years and, believe me, it means Mid American to the public. Our customers really like that advertising. Adam, we get letters about it all the time, and hardly ever a negative one. But even more important, the employees think it's terrific. It's had a very positive effect on everything we do: Our people really want to go all the way to make our customers happy. And even though I know industry awards don't mean very much, the campaign has been voted best in the airline industry three years in a row by the Association of American Travel Consultants. I mean, Adam, what more evidence do you need about an advertising campaign than that—we have a corker! Why do you bring this subject up?"

"Well, Tom, I know about the letters we get and the AATC award, of course; and I'd have to be blind not to see the effect that the campaign has had on our employees. There's no question that it's teriffic in all those ways; but I wonder has anyone, for instance at the agency, ever copy tested this campaign with consumers? I mean people who are likely to use our airline, not just the group of odd people who write us letters."

"What do you mean, the odd people who write us letters?" bristled Eldridge. "We're mighty glad to get those letters, I can tell you. Lots of times they let us know when we're doing something wrong that we can fix, and they have been really helpful to us."

"Okay, Tom, relax," responded Clagge. "I'm not trying to get you all riled up about this. You know, when you think about it, that letter writers are different from your average customer. They're different if for no other reason than that they take the time and trouble to write letters. If everybody we served did, we'd have a couple of million letters coming in here in the course of a year; and we both know that if we get two-hundred letters in a month, we're almost overwhelmed. But forget about the letters for a minute. What I'm interested in knowing is if anyone has ever objectively evaluated that advertising of ours. Run a copy test on it, I mean. Do consumers recall our commercials after they've seen them, for example; and do they recall the selling points that we make about Mid American? Does our advertising make consumers feel more favorable toward us, or not? And so on."

"But why would we want to know that, Adam? I mean if all the signals that we get about the advertising are positive and there are no negatives that we can see, why should we do—what did you call it—copy appraisals on it?"

"We should do it because it's a routine control procedure," replied Clagge. "Experienced and sophisticated advertisers routinely test their advertisements so that they will know the advertisements accomplish their purpose. That is, these advertisers make sure that their advertisements have the effect or effects upon their customers that the advertisers want them to have. Now, I assume that we really do have some other purposes in mind for the 'We go all the way' campaign beyond generating a few favorable letters or winning AATC awards, don't we, Tom?"

Eldridge quickly agreed that the Mid American image advertising certainly had specific objectives beyond generating letters and winning travel-agent association awards, even though he could not think what those specific objectives might be. He forestalled a discussion of such objectives by immediately agreeing with Clagge that an investigation of copy testing for Mid American be undertaken. It was agreed that Clagge should take the matter up with Bennington, Bartley, and Avignon's New York office and whomever directed its research department. Lunch was then concluded. Because the work of the day had been finished in the morning, Eldridge drove Clagge back to the airport in time for him to catch the 3:00 P.M. Mid American flight back to Houston.

The next morning Adam Clagge placed a telephone call to Ellwood Haswell, senior vice-president and director of research in the New York office of Bennington, Bartley, and Avignon.

Haswell had not yet arrived in the office at 9:30 A.M., New York time, when Clagge's call came in. When he did receive the message, he wondered why an executive of Mid American Airlines should be calling him, because the account was serviced out of the agency's Houston, Kansas City, and Detroit offices. Since Clagge's call had originated in Houston, Haswell called the head of the agency's Houston office, Oliver Morton.

"Oliver," inquired Haswell, once the connection was completed, "who is Adam Clagge and why would he want to talk to me?"

"He's the sales and marketing vice-president for MAA here in Houston, for their Western division," replied Morton, "But Ellwood, he's a lot more than that. He's a comer in Mid American. They keep moving him to more and more responsible jobs every year or two. We think, if he doesn't make a really horrendous mistake, he'll end up running the place. Why he wants to talk to you, I have no idea. And I won't call him to find out. As far as I'm concerned, Clagge must have direct access to any person in this agency he wants, when he wants. So please call him back, Ellwood, and be nice to him!"

Clagge and Haswell finally got together on the phone in midafternoon. Clagge explained to Ellwood that he, Clagge, was concerned about the quality of the advertising copy that was being prepared for Mid American by BB&A. He explained that he was exploring the possibility of instituting a system of copy testing of proposed new television image advertisements in order to make sure that consumer response to the advertising was as favorable, in fact, as the agency suggested it would be.

Ellwood Haswell was an excellent research technician and an able interpreter and presenter of research findings. He had a pleasant, nonthreatening air, was a good politician, and had a good record in handling client personnel as well as the creative and account people within the agency with whom it was necessary for him to deal. But he was a researcher rather than an advertising professional, and he tended to assume that he would receive advertising problems in a form that was easily amenable to available research techniques. It was not his practice, in other words, to patiently explore the ramifications of an advertising problem until he knew all of its characteristics and then develop a research solution of uniqueness or integrity. Rather, he wanted the problems stated in a form that could be solved only by one research technique, which he would then apply without other discussion or philosophical discourse. This was particularly true in the case of copy testing. Haswell did not believe that any available copy-testing system would predict the sales effectiveness of advertising, and he tended to assume that most other advertising people had the same view of available copy-testing procedures. Thus, Haswell expected to receive requests for copy testing from practitioners who used the results in a routine way to improve some aspect of their advertising. Copy tests were thus, in Haswell's view, tools to be used in the day-to-day work of advertising professionals. They were not procedures to be applied by those who were merely curious about the way an advertisement or campaign performed.

Because Clagge was new to copy testing, he did not know how to frame his request in researchable form. Thus it was inevitable that Clagge would irritate Haswell, because Clagge didn't know how to ask the research questions that Haswell was prepared to answer. And, similarly, it was inevitable that Haswell, in his intransigence, would frustrate Clagge when the latter sought general information about copy testing, rather than cut-and-dried answers.

As Clagge expressed his interest in copy testing, Haswell listened rather impatiently and then broke in when he thought that Clagge had finished speaking.

"What do you want to measure, ah, ah, is it Adam? Do you want to measure persuasion or recall?"

"I don't think I understand the question," responded Clagge.

"Well, what you want to measure in copy testing depends upon what you think is important for advertising to accomplish. We measure commercial recall, and we measure commercial persuasion. You have to decide which you want," explained Haswell.

"But, Ellwood," replied Clagge, rather hesitantly, "there must be more to it than that. I mean what are the implications of a measurement of commercial recall, and how do they compare with the implications of a measurement of commercial persuasion? I mean, how would I make that decision? Suppose I think that both persuasion and memorability are important? What do I do then?"

"Well, Adam," replied Haswell, "then you measure *both* persuasion and memorability. By the way, do you want to measure rough commercials, or finished?"

"Why would I want to measure rough commercials?" said Clagge, with mounting exasperation. "What is a rough commercial, anyway? How do you define it, and how does it differ from a finished commercial?"

"Adam," responded Haswell, "I'm a researcher; and the way I do my job I mostly make measurements and report findings. You're raising a lot of questions that I am really not qualified to answer. I think you ought to sit down with your account executive, figure out what your advertising is trying to do, and then get back to me; then we'll tell you how to measure it and when. I'm not trying to be uncooperative, Adam; but I usually come into these problems a good deal later. Why don't you call old Ollie Morton down there in Houston and have a good fat chew with him; then get back to me."

By this time Clagge was livid with anger. Before Haswell had a chance to hang up on him, he responded with a new tone of authority and control in his voice: "I'm not going to talk to your man Morton, Ellwood, because he doesn't know anything about research. That's not his job. They told me that research was your job. I want information from you about research copy testing procedures. I also intend to get that information. I want a description from you of the leading copy testing service, if there is one, that measures copy memorability. I want a description from you of the leading copy testing service, if there is one, that measures copy persuasibility. I want a description from you of the leading copy testing service, if there is one, that measures memorability and persuasibility at the same time. I want to know, for each of those services, what they measure, how they measure it, what assumptions they make as they measure it, how the measurement is used in practice, and how many people they talk to in the standard measure. And I want to know whether these services measure rough commercials, whatever they are, and whether they measure finished commercials. And I want all of this by the end of next week. Is that clear, Ellwood?"

"Yes, Adam, it's clear," replied Haswell, with humility and quietude in his voice.

"Can you do it by next week?"

"Yes, Adam," replied Haswell. "We can do it by next week, without fail." As soon as this conversation was finished, Haswell immediately phoned Alan W. Lingenfelder, president of Bennington, Bartley, and Avignon. It was not until the next day that Lingenfelder returned the call.

"I've got a hot one for you, Al," said Haswell. "You've been backstopping on Mid American, haven't you?"

Lingenfelder said "yes" abruptly, and yet expectantly.

"Well, do you know a guy named Adam Clagge down in Houston?"

"I certainly do, and he's been giving us fits in media," responded Lingenfelder. "Now what has he got his finders into?"

"It's copy testing, Al," replied Haswell.

"Ouch!" said Lingenfelder, "Well, I guess I should have been smart enough to figure out that that was inevitable. Tell me about it."

Whereupon, Haswell gave a largely straightforward description of his telephone conversation with Adam Clagge. He reported with dispassion that Clagge had gotten distinctly upset when he, Haswell, had raised questions about the kinds of information that was wanted from copy testing.

"Al," concluded Haswell, "you know as well as I do that 99 times out of 100 the client or the account and the creative people decide what kinds of copy-testing information they want to see; then they more or less order it up from us. That's what I expected that this Clagge had in mind. When it turned out that he didn't know what he wanted and kind of expected a guided tour from me, it was too late to do much more than make him mad. But, anyway, now you know all about it."

Lingenfelder was silent for several moments while he absorbed what Haswell had told him. Then he said: "Okay, Ellwood. I think you did fine. This whole thing was more or less inevitable. I suppose that we should have gotten Mid American into copy testing years ago. But we slipped up on that and now we're kind of vulnerable. You be sure to get those descriptions out on time and make sure that they are succinct and clear. I think we'll have to go down to Houston or Kansas City and have this out. But I'll work on that. I'll let you know."

Lingenfelder was not at all sure that Haswell had handled the phone conversation with Clagge as well as he might, but that was water over the dam. So he was supportive of Haswell to make sure that Haswell didn't go into a pout and let the copy-testing descriptions slide. He immediately called Ray W. Bliss, the senior BB&A account executive in the Kansas City office assigned to the Mid American account. Bliss was responsible for supervising the image television advertising conceived and developed by the creative department in Kansas City.

Lingenfelder explained the situation to Bliss and then said, "Ray, what I want you to do is to shoot up a storyboard for the new Mid American image advertising that's been approved. Have you produced it, yet?"

"No, Al," responded Bliss, "we expect to get into preproduction next week, I think. The first scheduled air date isn't until our late spring spot wave, so we're in plenty of time."

"Okay, Ray, that's fine," said Lingenfelder. "I suspect that what we should do is test a rough version of this. You and the creative people talk this over. Augie Bellano has had more experience in making roughs for commercial testing than probably anybody else in New York—get in touch with him; he works on Corn-All margarine—and have him talk to your creative people about it. We'll send him down to work with you for a day or two if you think it's desirable. Meanwhile, I'll call Clagge and suggest that we all meet in Kansas City or Houston, or wherever he wants, and talk out what we should do to test this campaign. And, Ray, call Tom Eldridge and see what he knows about this. Fill him in on what's happened, Okay? Any questions?"

"No questions, Al," responded Bliss, "except when are these guys going to stop going over my head to you people in New York? And what are we going to do about it?"

"We're not going to do anything about it until we get Clagge under control, Ray," responded Lingenfelder. "If we had a research facility in Kansas City or Houston this wouldn't have happened. But sooner or later we're going to have to come to grips with the problem. Maybe the best thing would be to move the image advertising and all the media planning to New York. But let's not try to settle that today. Let me know if Eldridge doesn't know about this, but I'm sure he does."

Shortly thereafter, Lingenfelder received a copy of the proposed extension of the basic Mid American campaign in the form of a storyboard. This storyboard is reproduced as Exhibit 13-1.

And, about a week later, Ellwood Haswell sent descriptions of three well-established television-commercial testing services to Adam Clagge. The descriptions of these services—Day-After Recall Testing (Exhibit 13-2); Tests of Brand Allegiance Shifts (Exhibit 13-3); and Recruited Audience Recall and Brand Preference Change Tests (Exhibit 13-4) were accompanied by the following letter of transmittal.

**EXHIBIT 13-1**

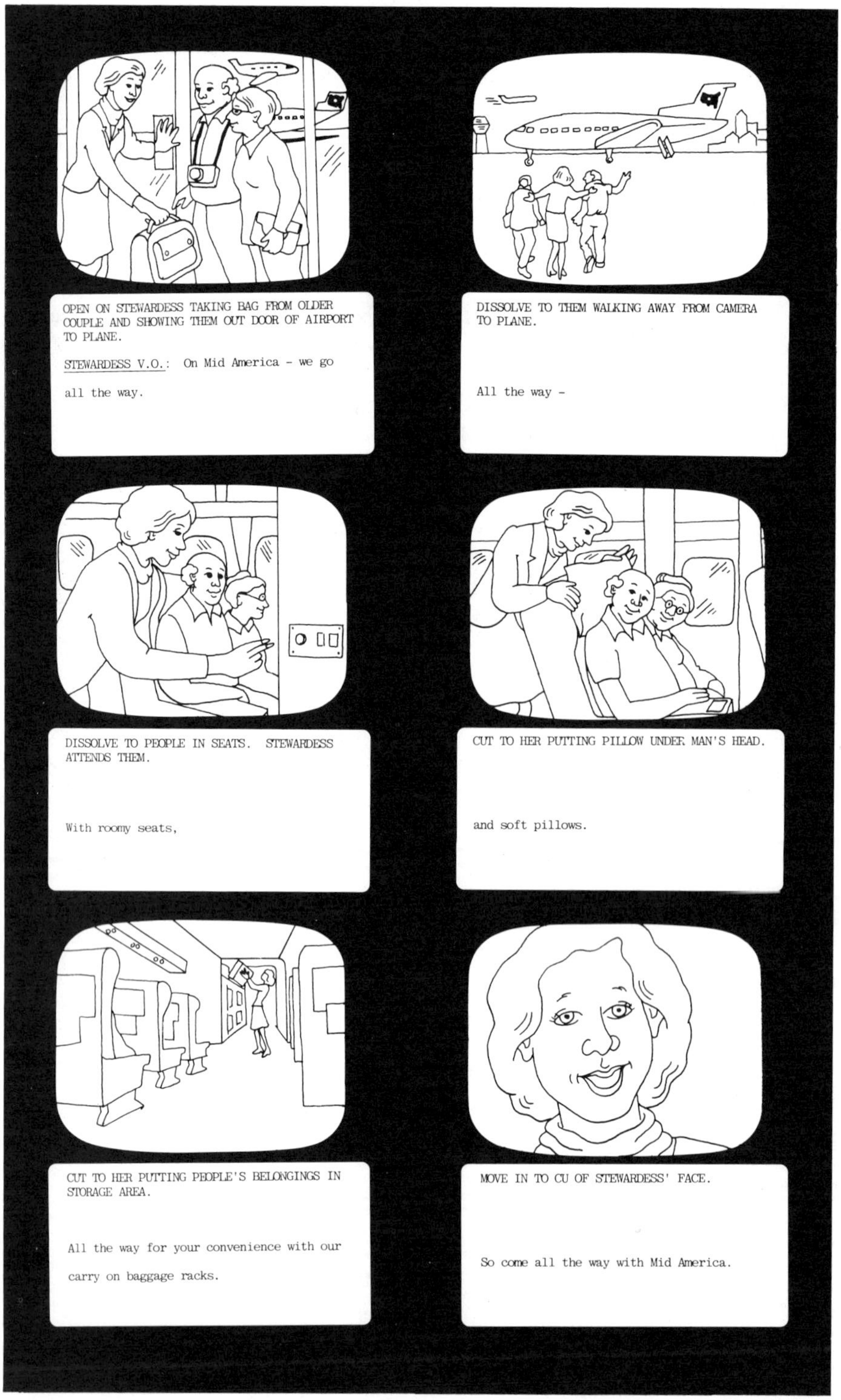
OPEN ON STEWARDESS TAKING BAG FROM OLDER COUPLE AND SHOWING THEM OUT DOOR OF AIRPORT TO PLANE.
STEWARDESS V.O.: On Mid America - we go all the way.
DISSOLVE TO THEM WALKING AWAY FROM CAMERA TO PLANE.
All the way -
DISSOLVE TO PEOPLE IN SEATS. STEWARDESS ATTENDS THEM.
With roomy seats,
CUT TO HER PUTTING PILLOW UNDER MAN'S HEAD.
and soft pillows.
CUT TO HER PUTTING PEOPLE'S BELONGINGS IN STORAGE AREA.
All the way for your convenience with our carry on baggage racks.
MOVE IN TO CU OF STEWARDESS' FACE.
So come all the way with Mid America.

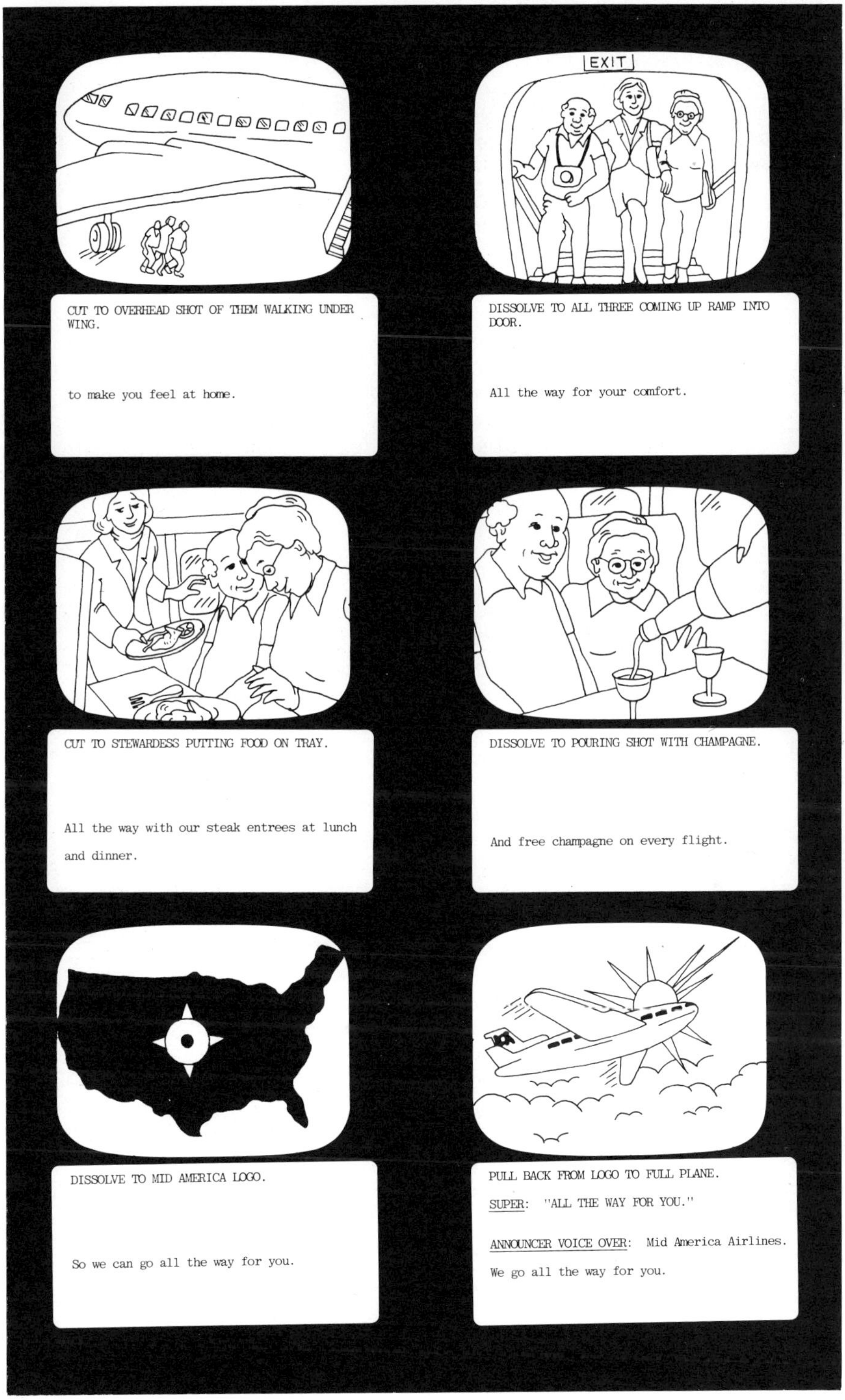
EXIT
CUT TO OVERHEAD SHOT OF THEM WALKING UNDER WING.
to make you feel at home.
DISSOLVE TO ALL THREE COMING UP RAMP INTO DOOR.
All the way for your comfort.
CUT TO STEWARDESS PUTTING FOOD ON TRAY.
All the way with our steak entrees at lunch and dinner.
DISSOLVE TO POURING SHOT WITH CHAMPAGNE.
And free champagne on every flight.
DISSOLVE TO MID AMERICA LOGO.
So we can go all the way for you.
PULL BACK FROM LOGO TO FULL PLANE.
SUPER: "ALL THE WAY FOR YOU."
ANNOUNCER VOICE OVER: Mid America Airlines.
We go all the way for you.

**EXHIBIT 13-2**

---

## DAY-AFTER-RECALL TESTS OF TELEVISION COMMERCIALS– Burke Marketing Research*

### What Is Measured?

Day-after-recall tests measure the proportion of consumers who prove they can recall specific elements of a test commercial that they have seen the day before, in their homes, during regular television viewing. This procedure yields a percentage score: the Related Recall Score. It also yields verbatim transcripts of what respondents do, in fact, recall from the test commercial.

### Research Procedure

A test television commercial is telecast on a particular television program in three or four markets. The commercial is usually cut in in place of a regularly scheduled commercial in a network program for the same product, service, or institution, or for another commercial from the same company. The next day, telephone interviews are conducted to find individuals who confirm that they watched the program in which the test commercial appeared and were physically present at the television set when the test commercial appeared. Respondents are asked whether they saw a commercial for the product, service, or institution, and then are asked to remember all that they can about the commercial. Their recall qualifies as related only if it includes material that is specific to the test commercial.

### Assumptions of the Measurement

The measurement assumes that the more people who recall a commercial, the more effective the commercial will be. It also assumes that the total effect of a commercial is the consumer's remembrance of commercial elements, and that analysis of the remembered elements can serve as a basis both for assessing the commercial's effectiveness and for improving its subsequent effectiveness.

### Major Uses of the Measurement

The day-after-recall measurement is used to assess the effectiveness of television commercials. It is also used to identify specific strengths and weaknesses in test commercials on the basis of content recall. This analysis may serve as a basis for changing the commercial with the hope of improving its subsequent performance.

### Sample Size

Burke Marketing Research bases its day-after-recall studies on a total of 200 respondents who have qualified as part of the commercial audience. These can be further qualified by product usage or demographic characteristics at the discretion of the study sponsor. Rough and finished commercials are tested with the procedure.

---

*Burke Marketing Research is not the only firm qualified to conduct day-after-recall studies of television commercials, but this firm pioneered in the use of the procedure and is the dominant supplier of this type of research.

Reprinted from William M. Weilbacher, *Advertising* (New York, Macmillan, 1979), p. 486; with the permission of the publisher.

## EXHIBIT 13-3

### TESTS OF BRAND ALLEGIANCE SHIFTS

The measurement of consumer brand-preference change as a result of controlled exposure to advertisements has a long history in advertising research. The ASI procedure* is now the dominant syndicated version of this type of measurement and it derives from a procedure developed and practiced by Horace Schwerin and his associates in the 1940s through the 1960s. Many refinements of this procedure have been developed on a custom basis by research companies and advertising agencies. A typical customized refinement of the general procedure is the Competitive Environment Test.

**What Is Measured?**

In the Competitive Environment Test, a pre-post measure of attitude change is obtained from respondents who have been exposed to a test commercial. In this procedure, however, the respondent is exposed not only to the test commercial but also to a set of commercials for brands directly competitive to the test brand. Before exposure to the test and competitive commercials, the respondent is asked to allocate ten purchases among the brands in a particular product category. They suggest the way the respondent might make the next ten purchases in the category. After commercial exposure, the respondent is asked to reallocate the same ten purchases. Brand allegiance shift is assessed by comparing the pre-allocation of votes with the post-allocation. In addition, various comprehension and reaction measures of the commercial are also made during the interview.

**The Research Procedure**

Qualified respondents are recruited in shopping centers or other heavy traffic locations. They are invited to view some television commercials and give their opinions. The commercial viewing takes place in an adjacent research facility—a storefront, or a trailer. The respondents first give demographic data, then divide their ten purchases among a group of competitive brands, are exposed to one test and two or three competitive commercials, are asked to recall commercial content and react to the commercials, and finally are asked to reallocate the ten votes or purchases among the competing brands.

This procedure creates a situation in which changes in brand allegiance are observed after exposure not only to the test commercial, but to commercials for leading competitive brands. The respondent has no idea which commercial is under test and cannot therefore bias his or her response as a result of the test situation. The test commercial can produce either a positive or a negative shift in brand allegiance, depending solely upon respondent reaction to it in a competitive context.

**Assumptions of the Measurement**

The measurement assumes that the objective of advertising is to cause a positive shift in brand allegiance under competitive conditions.

**Uses of the Measurement**

The measurement is used to assess the potential effectiveness of television commercials. The diagnostic comprehension and reaction data are used as a basis for commercial revisions when indicated. Rough and finished commercials have been tested with this procedure.

**Sample Size**

The usual sample size is 200 qualified respondents per test commercial evaluated.

---

Reprinted from William M. Weilbacher, *Advertising* (New York, Macmillan, 1979), p. 488; with the permission of the publisher.

*The ASI procedure is described in William M. Weilbacher, *Advertising,* pp. 486–487.

## EXHIBIT 13-4

### RECRUITED AUDIENCE RECALL AND BRAND PREFERENCE CHANGE TESTS OF TELEVISION COMMERCIALS—Mapes and Ross Incorporated

Standard day-after-recall tests have at least three weaknesses:

1. It is sometimes difficult to locate, by phone, viewers of the particular program in which a test commercial appeared. Some programs are not as popular as others, and individual episodes of very popular programs may not attract a large audience because of chance factors like important local events, catastrophes, exceptional competitive programming, etc.
2. The cost of running standard day-after-recall tests is escalating, and becomes particularly burdensome when particular program episodes yield an unusually low number of program viewers.
3. Standard day-after-recall tests do not easily lend themselves to research measurements other than the recall questioning itself.

For all of these reasons, there has been substantial interest in the prerecruitment of television program audiences. Under this approach, individuals in television homes are telephoned *before* a television program is aired and invited to view the particular program in which a test commercial will be included. Such audience pre-recruitment reduces day-after search costs for program viewers; permits the recruitment of audience members with particular demographic, product usage, or other characteristics; and also permits considerable flexibility in the research measurements to be made. There are several pre-recruited audience television-commercial test services available to advertising practitioners: That offered by Mapes and Ross Incorporated is one of the oldest and best established of these.

**What Is Measured?**

In the Mapes and Ross variant of recruited audience television-commercial tests, two standard measurements are made:

1. Day-after-recall: the proportion of consumers who prove they can recall specific elements of the test commercial. In addition to a proved recall score, these tests generate verbatim recall of commercial content elements; a measure of the importance of the main idea in the commercial to recallers; and a rating of the test brand on specific qualities or attributes covered in the commercial.
2. The ability of the commercial specifically and immediately to affect brand preference is measured by contrasting consumer preference for the advertised brand before and after exposure to the test commercial.

**Research Procedure**

Respondents are telephoned in each of three markets in which Mapes and Ross conduct Recruited Audience Commercial Tests. These markets are Kansas City, Missouri, Philadelphia, Pennsylvania, and Seattle, Washington. In each of these markets Mapes and Ross arranges to buy commercial time in a prime-time evening movie shown on a non-network-affiliated television station. The test commercials are then run in these purchased time slots in these movies.

Interviewers make telephone calls in these markets and invite potential respondents to

**EXHIBIT 13-4 (Continued)**

view the movie in which the test commercials will be shown, when it is aired that evening. The respondents are not told that they will participate in a test of television commercials but are told that if they do watch the movie that they will be eligible for a drawing of cash prizes.

Once a respondent has agreed to participate, the interviewer makes an appointment for a call-back interview on the next day. In addition, the respondents are asked to state their brand preferences in six product categories, some of which will—unbeknownst to the respondents—be advertised that evening in the evening movie, and some not. These brand preference questions "cover whether one brand is the very best within that product group, whether two or three brands are better than others, or whether all brands are about the same. If either of the first two choices are picked, specific brand preferences are obtained. Then, respondents are asked what other brands of the category they would like to try."

Follow-up interviews are made at the appointed time the next day. First, viewing of the movie during the period in which the test commercials are shown is confirmed. Next, the brand preference questions are repeated. Finally commercial recall is obtained, first on product-group cue basis, and finally with the aid of a brand-name cue. Commercial content recall is elicited with the use of an elaborate series of established interviewer probing questions.

**Assumptions of the Measurements**

The recall measurement assumes that the more people who recall a commercial, the more effective a commercial will be. In addition, the recall measurement in a recruited audience research study assumes that the process of recruitment will not invalidate or bias the measurement of recall.

The brand-preference change measure assumes that television commercial exposure should lead to immediate and overt change in expressed brand choice and that such changes in expressed brand choice are predictive of subsequent market place behavior. In addition, the brand preference measurement in a recruited audience research study assumes that the process of recruitment as well as brand preference questioning in the recruitment interview, will not invalidate the basic brand preference measurement.

**Major Uses of the Measurement**

The recall and brand-preference measurements are used together to assess the effectiveness of television commercials. The recall measure is used to assess the impact and memorability of the test commercial and the brand preference measurement is used to assess its persuasiveness.

**Sample Size**

Mapes and Ross Incorporated invites enough men and/or women to watch the movie containing the test commercial so that follow-up interviews can be completed with between 150 and 200 males and the same number of females who have watched the program segment within which the particular test commercials appeared.

---

# BENNINGTON, BARTLEY, AND AVIGNON

-Advertising-

Elwood C. Haswell
Senior Vice President
Director of Research

October 18, 1980

Adam Clagge
Vice President, Sales and Marketing
Western Division
Mid American Airlines
Houston, Texas 77061

Dear Adam:

As promised in our telephone conversation last week, I am attaching descriptions that have been prepared in our research department of three of the leading commercial testing services. I believe that these descriptions follow the format that you suggested in the conversation; but if anything is not clear or to your satisfaction, please don't hesitate to call me.

I understand that we are meeting in your offices next week to discuss the whole question of copy testing. I believe that that will be the appropriate time to resolve the questions of what copy testing procedure is best suited to Mid American needs and to decide whether or not to use rough or finished commercials in our testing programs.

We will be bringing a reel of "rough" commercials with us and a reel of "finished" commercials that match the roughs, at least in those instances in which a finished commercial was produced after research was completed on the rough version.

I should add that each of the three commercial-testing services that are described in the enclosed exhibits can be used with either rough or finished commercials.

We'll look forward to seeing you on the twenty-fourth.

Best wishes,

[s] Ellwood C. Haswell

---

The meeting to discuss copy testing was held in the Mid American offices in Houston, Texas, on October 24, 1979, as scheduled. Lingenfelder, Bliss, Morton, Haswell, and Stephanie Mahoney, senior vice-president and copy group head from the Kansas City office of Bennington, Bartley, and Avignon represented the advertising agency. (Ms. Mahoney was the senior creative person assigned to the Mid American account and she had coined the line "Mid American goes all the way for you" several years before. Since that time Ms. Mahoney had personally supervised the creation and production of all the television commercials based on that theme, in the image advertising campaign for Mid American.) Mid American was represented by Tom Eldridge and Adam Clagge.

The meeting opened with a brief statement by Clagge about why he had become interested in copy testing and why he believed that such research work should be carried out in behalf of Mid American Airlines.

"We're not questioning the excellence of your work, Stephanie," said Clagge. "Everyone at Mid American, from Mr. Freiquist and Mr. Dukes on down, love the 'Goes all the way' campaign. We just want to subject it to the discipline of copy research, is all. We want to make sure that it's getting across to our customers and giving them a valid reason for traveling with us."

Stephanie Mahoney didn't like copy testing, didn't like this meeting, and didn't like the idea that her superb Mid American advertising was now, suddenly, after seven wonderfully successful years to be subjected to research. She only knew one thing about copy testing: Never, in her experience, had it improved any of her advertising. The only thing that it could do and did do was to kill advertising campaigns that she believed in. She felt like asking Adam Clagge what would happen if the test "Goes all the way" commercial received a low score. She wondered if all his pious sentiments in favor of the campaign would suddenly evaporate. But she had promised Ray Bliss that she would be a good girl in the Mid American meeting; and that promise specifically included not asking Adam Clagge any smart-jack questions about what would happen to her campaign if the research results were low. So she kept her mouth shut, smiled at Clagge rather tentatively, and tried as hard as she could to pay attention to what he had to say about copy testing.

Clagge droned on: "I've studied all of the material that you sent down here, Ellwood —that was a bang-up job on short notice—and I really don't know what we should do. It seems to me that all those services measure something different and every one of them measures something that I want to know. Suppose, uh, we were to try all three services this first time so that we could get a real feel for the data they generate, Ellwood. How much money are we talking?"

It was clear that this thought was not a popular one with the agency contingent. Every agency face in the room registered concern and preoccupation as soon as Clagge hinted that he was giving consideration to subjecting Mid American advertising to three separate copy tests, at least the first time.

Every agency person reflected concern; that is, except Ellwood Haswell. Here was a cut-and-dried question and he had a cut-and-dried answer for it: "Under twelve-grand easy, Adam; maybe under ten, if we're lucky." As the answer snapped out, Stephanie Mahoney was rocking on her mental feet. "My gosh," she thought to herself "this creep is going to put my campaign under triple jeopardy. The only thing that three copy tests can do for me is give me three separate ways that I can lose."

Ray Bliss was visibly disturbed, but he kept his mouth shut. "We may never get a campaign that can score well on three copy tests," he thought futilely to himself. "But Al Lingenfelder is president of our merry band—let's see if he can get us out of this one. If not, I'll get Eldridge to lunch a couple of times and really go to work on him."

Al Lingelder was thinking fast, trying to find a way to blunt the obvious implication of Clagge's musings about copy testing. "Adam," he said promptly, after Haswell's answer about costs, "I don't think this is solely a matter of money. We should be able to figure out what this advertising is supposed to be doing to people and then go with the one copy test that reflects that agreement. Most of our clients seem to prefer day-after-recall. They figure, and we agree, that the real question is whether or not the agency has made the basic message memorable or not. Can people remember it the next day after they've seen it and heard it? That's the key question, and I'd like to suggest that we agree to that question and run a Burke day-after-recall test on this commercial. Don't you agree with that, Adam?"

"Okay, Al," replied Clagge. "That sounds reasonable. But bear with me a minute, will you? I know that advertising isn't my game. You've dedicated your life to it, Al; and you have to lead me along with you. It seems to me that recall studies only measure the attention-attracting power of a commercial. That's important all right, but haven't advertisers for years used pretty girls, and babies and puppies to attract attention? And haven't many of those advertisers discovered that attention isn't enough—it is important, but it isn't enough. Once you've got the consumers' attention, you've got to say something to them that will convince them to use your product. If you leave it solely to attention, isn't it possible that you may have lost the game? What I mean is, we might get a high day-after-recall score; and our commercial still might not be doing the job for us. So I think day-after-recall is necessary, but not sufficient."

"But Ada . . ." Haswell started to say, as Lingenfelder cut him off.

"Excuse me, Ellwood," said Lingenfelder. "I know we'll want to have your research views in a moment, but just let me give a quick response to Adam that reflects our, uh, management perspective. Adam, we don't just get a score in a day-after-recall test. We also get the consumer playback from our commercial—that is, we get consumer verbatim comments that tell exactly what consumers remember about our advertising. So you see we know whether what we intended to convey in the advertising registers or not; and if it does register, just how it registers. So when we evaluate day-after-recall testing, we must also realize that it measures message registration as well as overall attention attraction."

"Okay, Al," replied George. "I understand all that—Ellwood's good description of the various services made that crystal clear. But if I limit myself to measures of message registration and attention attraction, I still have no idea of whether my message had an effect on consumer attitudes, or consumer preference toward Mid American. I do want a sound measurement of attention attraction and message registration, and in that sense I am in total agreement with everything that you have to say. But, I want to know more. I want to know whether or not that message that has registered has really started a positive process of moving consumers toward me. Is there anything wrong with that?"

Al Lingenfelder replied: "Not a thing wrong with that, Adam; and I can't help but agree with you. One thing that we should say, and Ellwood can say it as a researcher much better than I can, is that none of these measures are perfect. I mean none of them have been proved to be predictive of marketplace performance. We know of many cases where high-scoring commercials have not seemed to produce any market effect. Lots of other things are involved in an airline's success, of course, like scheduling, on-time performance, terminal facilities, food-service quality, and on and on that may have as much or more effect on the final marketplace results as the advertising. And another thing that we know is that the results of day-after-recall testing and persuasibility testing don't necessarily correlate with each other. It's one thing to state that advertising should attract attention and register its message and, in addition, persuade the consumer. But we may waste some sales-effective campaigns if we hold each one up to both kinds of tests.

"It's our experience that we should come to depend upon one kind of test or the other and use its results to feed back into the creative process, help us find mistakes in advertisements and give us a basis for correcting them. This doesn't work well when you get contradictory results from different testing procedures. We don't always know what to do then and we think we can lose a lot of great advertising–which we've all agreed is great on judgment before the testing–in that situation. Don't you agree, Stephanie?"

Stephanie Mahoney had been following this discussion with a sinking sensation. "We're going to lose this," she thought to herself. "We have different interests in this. We want to develop superior advertising and we think that we know how to do it. We like copy testing alright, if it can help us develop and perfect great campaigns. But Clagge doesn't much care about developing great advertising campaigns, as such. He just wants an objective standard that he can apply to our work, like an accounting standard."

This reverie was interrupted by Lingenfelder's question, which Stephanie did not completely understand, having been distracted by her own musings. She knew that she could not ask to have the question repeated but sensed that it had something to do with losing great campaigns to copy testing; and she replied in this vein. "Well, yes, that's true, Al. It is better for us to work with one system, but even then we sometimes fear that superior advertising will get lost in the single-minded pursuit of a high score. Can I ask you, Adam, what would happen if in this exercise, the 'We go all the way for you' campaign got a bad score. Just what would you do?"

"That may not be a fair question for Adam, Stephanie," Lingenfelder said quickly. "I mean we haven't even seen any scores, and here you are, putting Adam on the spot. Gonna call a foul on you, Stephanie, and let Adam off the hook. No need to answer Stephanie's question, Adam."

With this a silence settled across the room for several moments with Lingenfelder looking at Clagge with a kind of forced joviality, and everyone else looking at no one else, and, mostly, down at the mahogany surface of the conference-room table.

Finally, Clagge broke the silence. "Look," he said, "I understand what you're saying. You don't want to lose what you believe to be a great advertising campaign. Neither do I. But I believe it is imperative to introduce some system of objective advertising appraisal into this company. And we're going to do it. Now, I frankly can't decide on what basis or bases we should objectively appraise this advertising. You say that you only want one system and that it should be day-after-recall. I don't agree with you at this point. Maybe I'll come to agree with it. But first I have to have some experience with alternatives. You really haven't proved to me that I shouldn't experiment with persuasion measures, too. So, Tom," he said turning to Eldridge, "what I want to do is to test this new commercial in day-after-recall tests, in a test of brand allegiance, and in a recruited audience recall and brand-preference change test. Do you agree that this is what we should do?"

Up to this point, Tom Eldridge had had nothing to say. He was a competent airline marketing man, with particular strengths in direct field selling and merchandising. He understood nothing about consumer research and had little taste for it. He had studied the materials reproduced here as Exhibits 13-2, 13-3 and 13-4 and had become merely confused. He had lost interest in the conversation generated in the meeting. He knew that Adam Clagge was a rising star to whom he would sooner or later report. He knew that the politically impeccable move to make at this point was to give full agreement and support to Clagge's position. He said, therefore, in complete ignorance of the merits of the case, "That's where I come out, Adam. Try out all three to get the feel of this animal and then let's all meet again and see where we go from there."

Adam Clagge turned to Ellwood Haswell at this point and said, "Ellwood, you are authorized to conduct each of these three tests on our new "Old Folks" commercial."

Haswell said, "Okay, Adam. But we still need to know whether or not to test in rough or finished form."

"Yes, Adam," said Al Lingenfelder, recovering at least some of his composure, "we brought down reels of rough and finished commercials for you to see."

"Al," responded Clagge, "do you have confidence in the testing of rough commercials?"

"Yes, we do, Adam. About three quarters of the agency copy-testing work is done on rough commercials that are carefully produced to simulate the finished commercial, but at lower cost. Take a look at the reels."

"Don't need to, Al. If you say rough testing is okay that's good enough for me. And, by the way, Ellwood, set the tests up so that we can look at our target group—say male flyers, thirty five years of age and older—separately from the total audience."

The meeting ended on that note. The agency had inadvertently become a full participant in a test of three copy-testing methods, whether it liked it or not.

Summaries of the copy-test results are presented in the form of specimen data in Exhibits 13-5, 13-6 and 13-7.

**EXHIBIT 13-5**
**Specimen Data: Summary Results* from Day-After-Recall Copy Test, Mid-American Airlines "Old Folks" TV Commercial**

| | Total | Men 35+ Who Fly at Least Once a Year |
|---|---|---|
| Commercial Audience | 147 | 73 |
| Percent | 100 | 100 |
| Gave Related Recall | 34 | 42 |
| Sales Messages (Net)† | 26 | 37 |
| Mid American goes all the way for you | 24 | 37 |
| Mid American has pleasant stewardesses | 14 | 10 |
| Mid American gives free champagne | 8 | 4 |
| Mid American has on-time arrivals & departures | 7 | 11 |
| Mid American is pleasant to fly | 7 | 6 |
| Mid American serves steak | 6 | 4 |
| Mid American has baggage racks on planes | 4 | 8 |
| Visual Mentions (Net)† | 18 | 14 |
| Situations in commercial | 12 | 10 |
| Older couple on plane | 10 | 7 |
| Pretty stewardesses | 4 | 8 |

(Average related recall score for thirty-second commercials: 24)

*Modeled on the Day-After-Recall results from copy tests conducted by Burke Marketing Research, Inc.

†Some respondents gave more than one answer.

**EXHIBIT 13-6**
**Specimen Data: Summary Results* from a Competitive Environment Copy Test, Mid-American Airlines "Old Folks" TV Commercial**

| | Total | Men 35+ Who Fly at Least Once a Year |
|---|---|---|
| Test Participants | 200 | 103 |
| Percent | 100 | 100 |
| Pre-Post Differences in Means (Average Competitive Environment Copy Test Result: all commercials tested: +7.4) | +6.2 | +3.1 |
| Commercial Communication | 84 | 92 |
| Sales Messages (Net)† | 68 | 87 |
| Mid American goes all the way for you | 44 | 57 |
| Mid American gives free champagne | 42 | 30 |
| Mid American serves steak | 38 | 26 |
| Mid American has on-time arrivals & departures | 26 | 47 |
| Mid American is pleasant to fly | 24 | 35 |
| Mid American has pleasant stewardesses | 22 | 37 |
| Mid American has baggage racks on planes | 18 | 31 |
| Visual Mentions (Net)† | 42 | 35 |
| Situations in commercial | 26 | 18 |
| Older couple on plane | 17 | 12 |
| Pretty stewardesses | 12 | 16 |

*Modeled on advertising-agency-supervised Competitive Environment Test.
†Some respondents gave more than one answer.

**EXHIBIT 13-7**
**Specimen Data: Summary Results* from Mapes & Ross Invited Viewing Copy Test, Mid-American Airlines "Old Folks" TV Commercial**

| | Total Audience | Men 30+ who Fly at Least Once a Year | Airline Total Audience Norm |
|---|---|---|---|
| Pre/Post Brand Preference Change | | | |
| Best/Better Measure | +10.2 | +12.6 | +9.7 |
| Like-to-try Measure | + 3.1 | + 6.9 | +4.7 |
| Proved Recall | | | |
| Communication of Ideas (Among Recallers) | 27 | 32 | 21 |
| Main idea played back (Mid-American goes all the way for you) | 72 | 74 | 62 |
| Average number of ideas per respondent | 2.6 | 2.4 | 3.2 |

*Modeled on results from Mapes & Ross Invinted Viewing Copy Tests.

## *QUESTIONS FOR CASE 13*

1. What television copy test or copy tests, if any, should Mid American Airlines adopt for routine future use?
2. The text makes no mention of creative strategy nor of research to determine creative strategy. Would your answer to Question 1 be different if creative-strategy research had indicated that the "We go all the way for you" campaign had a positive effect on consumer attitudes toward Mid-American?
3. What does this case suggest about the nature of advertiser–advertising-agency relations? How independent can an advertising agency afford to be? If you were Stephanie Mahoney, what would you think and do as a result of the meeting described on pages 302 to 306 of the case?
4. Eldridge defends the "We go all the way for you" campaign on the basis of industry awards, consumer letters, and the positive effect that he perceives the campaign to have had on Mid-American employee attitudes and performance (page 291). Evaluate these criteria as a basis for judging the excellence of Mid-American advertising.
5. Why does Clagge want to copy test the Mid-American television image campaign? Are his reasons valid?
6. Why does the agency resist multiple copy tests of the Mid-American television-image campaign? Are its reasons valid?
7. What is the purpose of copy testing? When Haswell says that in 99 cases out of 100 the creative people, and/or the account managers, and/or the client dictate what copy-testing procedure should be used, does this reflect the ideal basis for selecting a television copy test? Ideally, what role should the researcher play in the selection of copy-testing methods?
8. Why is the Mapes and Ross procedure included in the Mid American test? What practical advantages does it possess relative to the other two copy-testing procedures?
9. Is it efficient for Bennington, Bartley, and Avignon to service Mid American from three separate offices? Why do you suppose that this system of service has evolved? What would an ideal service arrangement be?
10. Of what value are average or normative commercial test scores? Should such scores be provided for rough commercial and finished commercial tests? Why or why not? Of what value is an average score for the product category under test? Why do some commercial-testing services provide such category average scores and others not?

# Case 14

# Evaluating the Effectiveness of Alternative Advertising Campaigns

*THE AMELIA ETERNAL COMPANY MEASURES ADVERTISING RESULTS IN TEST MARKETS*

The Amelia Eternal Company decided to test alternative advertising campaigns in the marketplace, commencing October 6, 1979. (See Case 1 and Case 4 for a description of the events and issues which preceded this decision.)

Basically, Morgan Harris and his associates at Amelia Eternal accepted, with one exception, the recommendations of the advertising agency Aesop and Acton, as presented in Exhibit 4-11. The exception was that in established Amelia Eternal markets it was decided to test one more campaign—based on the so-called product-line strategy (F)—than recommended by the agency.

The structure of the market tests was as follows:

**Test 1**: Strategies to be tested:

*Strategy I:* Create separate recruitment advertising to identify prospective sales representatives.

*Advertising Period:* September 1, 1979 - February 28, 1980.

*Strategy A:* Describe Amelia Eternal as direct-sales company of household and cosmetic products.

*Advertising Period:* October 6, 1979 - September 30, 1980.

*Test-Market Type:* Underdeveloped Amelia Eternal markets.

*Test Markets to Be Used:* Albany-Schenectady-Troy, New York; Birmingham, Alabama; Columbus, Ohio.

*Test-Evaluation Criteria:* 1) Basic Amelia Eternal audit of consumer awareness, knowledge, and attitudes to be conducted in weeks ending 10/1/79; 4/1/80; and 10/1/80. Sample size: 1,000 per wave, allocated equally to each market. 2) Amelia Eternal monthly sales-representative records aggregated across the test markets.

*Media Weight Level:* Local market weight projectable to $7,500,000 expenditure in defined Amelia Eternal underdeveloped markets (42 percent of U.S.): Use Little America projection basis.

**Test 2**: Strategy to be tested:

*Strategy B:* Describe Amelia Eternal as a relation between consumers and representatives.

*Advertising Period:* October 6, 1979 - September 30, 1980.

*Test-Market Type:* Established Amelia Eternal markets.

*Test Markets to Be Used:* Austin, Texas; Denver, Colorado; San Diego, California.

*Test-Evaluation Criteria:* 1) Basic Amelia Eternal audit of consumer awareness, knowledge, and attitudes to be conducted in weeks ending 10/1/79; 4/1/80; and 10/1/80. Sample size: 1,000 per wave, allocated equally to each market. 2) Amelia Eternal monthly sales and sales-representative records aggregated across the test markets.

*Media Weight Level:* Local market weight projectable to $7,500,000 expenditure in defined Amelia Eternal established markets (58 percent of U.S.): Use Little America projection basis.

**Test 3**: Strategy to be tested:

*Strategy F:* Describe Amelia Eternal product lines in performance terms.

*Advertising Period:* October 6, 1979 - September 30, 1980.

*Test-Market Type:* Established Amelia Eternal markets.

*Test Markets to Be Used:* Cedar Rapids-Waterloo, Iowa; Portland, Oregon; Seattle-Tacoma, Washington.

*Test-Evaluation Criteria:* 1) Basic Amelia Eternal audit of consumer awareness, knowledge, and attitudes, augmented questionnaire, to be conducted in weeks ending 10/1/79; 4/1/80; and 10/1/80. Sample size: 1,000 per wave, allocated equally to each market. 2) Amelia Eternal monthly sales and sales-representative records aggregated across the test markets.

*Media Weight Level:* Local market weight projectable to $7,500,000 expenditure in defined Amelia Eternal established markets (58 percent of U.S.): Use Little America projection basis.

**Test 4**: Strategy to be tested:

*Strategy G:* Describe specific individual Amelia Eternal brand items in performance terms.

*Advertising Period:* October 6, 1979 - September 30, 1980.

*Test-Market Type:* Established Amelia Eternal markets.

*Test Markets to Be Used:* Dayton, Ohio; Sacramento-Stockton, California; and Salt Lake City, Utah.

*Test-Evaluation Criteria:* 1) Basic Amelia Eternal audit of consumer awareness, knowledge, and attitudes, augmented questionnaire, to be conducted in weeks ending 10/1/79; 4/1/80; and 10/1/80. Sample size: 1,000 per wave, allocated equally to each market. 2) Amelia Eternal monthly sales and sales-representative records aggregated across the test markets.

*Media Weight Level:* Local market weight projectable to $7,500,000 expenditure in defined Amelia Eternal established markets (58 percent of U.S.): Use Little America projection basis.

There was a hectic period, during the summer of 1979, when Aesop and Acton employees, working closely with Morgan Harris and Stanton Thornton of Amelia Eternal developed the five advertising campaigns to execute each of the five strategies to be tested, developed detailed media plans, and helped the Amelia Eternal organization develop plans for stepped up recruiting and sales activity.

Finally, the test advertising began to appear in the various test markets. As the test year progressed, measurements specified as the basis for test-market evaluation were made in each of the test markets. Key data for each of the tested campaigns are presented in Exhibits 14-1 through 14-32.

## *QUESTIONS FOR CASE 14*

1. Analyze the test-market data presented in Exhibits 14-1 through 14-32.
   a. Is the Strategy *I-A* program tested in Test 1 successful? What conclusions do you draw as a result of this test?
   b. Which strategy—B, F, or G—accomplishes most in established markets? What conclusions do you draw as a result of Tests 2, 3, and 4?
   c. Assume that there are 78 million homes in the United States. Assume that all costs, direct and indirect, account for 81.7 percent of each Amelia Eternal sales dollar and that the remaining 18.3 percent of each sales dollar is "available for profit, promotion, and/or advertising." Assume that sales for August and September 1979 are equal to one sixth of normal pretest-period sales in each group of test markets.
      (i) Does the test of advertising strategy *I-A* recapture its cost, or "payout" in the test year?
      (ii) Does the test of advertising strategy *B* recapture its cost, or "payout," in the test year?
      (iii) Does the test of advertising strategy *F* recapture its cost, or "payout" in the test year?
      (iv) Does the test of advertising strategy *G* recapture its cost, or "payout," in the test year?
      (v) Summarize the fiscal implications of the test-market results for the Amelia Eternal Company.

2. Two kinds of evaluative data—consumer survey, and sales—are presented in the exhibits. Discuss the value of each in evaluating the results of the test markets. If you were limited to one kind of information, which would be more valuable? Why? What is the value of the other, less-preferred, information? Explain.

3. The test-market results are presented as summary data aggregated across the three markets included in each test. Is this the ideal way in which to assess test-market results? Of what value might be test results for individual markets? How important is it to have test-result data on a market-by-market basis?

4. Test 3 and Test 4 specifications call for an "augmented questionnaire" in the "basic Amelia Eternal audit of consumer awareness, knowledge, and attitudes." What does this mean? Why is the use of an "augmented questionnaire" necessary in these tests?

5. Describe the timing of this test program. How are the consumer-research studies and the advertising test periods related to each other? Of what importance is this relationship to the success of the market tests?

6. The test plan specifies that established markets (58 percent of the U.S.) should receive a national media expenditure of $7,500,000 and that underdeveloped markets (42 percent of the United States) should receive a national media expenditure of $7,500,000. What is the meaning of this specification? Why must the pattern of national media expenditures be included in a test of advertising campaigns?

7. What is the "Little America" method of projection? Is it an appropriate projection method for this test? Explain why or why not.

**EXHIBIT 14-1**
**Specimen Data: Awareness of Amelia Eternal Company, 1979 and 1980; Test of Advertising Strategy I and A in Underdeveloped Markets**

| | | 10/1/79 | 4/1/80 | 10/1/80 |
|---|---|---|---|---|
| Women Fifteen Years and Older | Base | 992 | 972 | 1,006 |
| | | 100 | 100 | 100 |
| | | % | % | % |
| Unaided Awareness: | | | | |
| What door-to-door sales companies have you ever heard of? | | | | |
| Avon | | 60 | 58 | 62 |
| Encyclopedia Britannica | | 22 | 24 | 24 |
| Shaklee | | 21 | 19 | 23 |
| Electrolux | | 21 | 26 | 24 |
| Amway | | 13 | 15 | 9 |
| Amelia Eternal | | 2 | 12 | 42 |
| Other companies mentioned | | 42 | 41 | 40 |
| Don't know any direct or door-to-door sales companies | | 37 | 30 | 26 |
| (Average number of companies mentioned by those respondents who could identify a direct or door-to-door sales company) | | 2.9 | 2.8 | 3.0 |
| Aided Awareness: | | | | |
| Please tell me which of the companies on this list you are familiar with: | | | | |
| Avon | | 96 | 92 | 94 |
| Encyclopedia Britannica | | 90 | 91 | 83 |
| Amelia Eternal | | 6 | 35 | 72 |
| World Book Encyclopedia | | 54 | 52 | 48 |
| Amway | | 21 | 23 | 24 |
| Fuller Brush | | 78 | 76 | 74 |
| Electrolux | | 70 | 69 | 71 |
| Shaklee | | 24 | 25 | 23 |
| Direct Questioning about Amelia Eternal | | | | |
| Have you ever heard of the Amelia Eternal Company? | | | | |
| | Yes | 16 | 47 | 91 |
| | No | 84 | 53 | 9 |

*Source:* Audit of Consumer Awareness, Knowledge, and Attitudes: Underdeveloped Markets, Strategy I and A. Fall 1979; Spring 1980; Fall 1980.

**EXHIBIT 14-2**
**Specimen Data: Awareness of Amelia Eternal by Age, Income, and Education, 1979 and 1980; Test of Advertising Strategy I and A in Underdeveloped Markets**

| | | | | | | | | | | | | | |
|---|---|---|---|---|---|---|---|---|---|---|---|---|---|
| | October 1, 1979 | | | | | | | | | | | | |
| | | Age | | | | | Household Income | | | | Education | | |
| | Total | 15–24 | 25–34 | 35–49 | 50–64 | 65 & Older | Under $7,500 | $ 7,500 14,999 | $15,000 19,999 | $20,000 & over | Any College | Graduated High School | Did Not Graduate High School |
| Women 15 Years and Older | 992 | 208 | 188 | 218 | 238 | 140 | 298 | 297 | 149 | 248 | 248 | 417 | 327 |
| | 100 | 100 | 100 | 100 | 100 | 100 | 100 | 100 | 100 | 100 | 100 | 100 | 100 |
| | % | % | % | % | % | % | % | % | % | % | % | % | % |
| *Unaided Awareness* | | | | | | | | | | | | | |
| Ever heard of Amelia Eternal | 2 | – | 1 | 1 | 2 | 8 | 1 | 2 | 1 | 4 | – | 1 | 5 |
| *Aided Awareness* | | | | | | | | | | | | | |
| Familiar with Amelia Eternal | 6 | – | 2 | 4 | 7 | 23 | 4 | 6 | 7 | 8 | 3 | 7 | 7 |
| *Direct Questioning* | | | | | | | | | | | | | |
| Know of Amelia Eternal | 16 | 1 | 6 | 12 | 17 | 61 | 15 | 17 | 16 | 16 | 9 | 15 | 23 |
| | April 1, 1980 | | | | | | | | | | | | |
| Women 15 Years and Older | 972 | 204 | 185 | 214 | 233 | 136 | 292 | 293 | 146 | 241 | 243 | 408 | 321 |
| | 100 | 100 | 100 | 100 | 100 | 100 | 100 | 100 | 100 | 100 | 100 | 100 | 100 |
| | % | % | % | % | % | % | % | % | % | % | % | % | % |
| *Unaided Awareness* | | | | | | | | | | | | | |
| Ever heard of Amelia Eternal | 12 | 8 | 11 | 13 | 13 | 16 | 13 | 11 | 12 | 12 | 7 | 11 | 17 |
| *Aided Awareness* | | | | | | | | | | | | | |
| Familiar with Amelia Eternal | 35 | 30 | 32 | 34 | 37 | 45 | 30 | 36 | 34 | 40 | 26 | 33 | 44 |
| *Direct Questioning* | | | | | | | | | | | | | |
| Know of Amelia Eternal | 47 | 35 | 39 | 43 | 49 | 79 | 48 | 46 | 44 | 49 | 35 | 41 | 64 |

| | October 1, 1980 | | | | | | | | | | | | |
|---|---|---|---|---|---|---|---|---|---|---|---|---|---|
| | | Age | | | | | Household Income | | | | Education | | |
| | Total | 15–24 | 25–34 | 35–49 | 50–64 | 65 & Older | Under $7,500 | $ 7,500 14,999 | $15,000 19,999 | $20,000 & over | Any College | Graduated High School | Did Not Graduate High School |
| Women 15 Years and Older | 1006 | 211 | 191 | 221 | 241 | 142 | 301 | 302 | 151 | 252 | 252 | 423 | 331 |
| | 100 | 100 | 100 | 100 | 100 | 100 | 100 | 100 | 100 | 100 | 100 | 100 | 100 |
| | % | % | % | % | % | % | % | % | % | % | % | % | % |
| *Unaided Awareness* | | | | | | | | | | | | | |
| Ever heard of Amelia Eternal | 42 | 30 | 38 | 40 | 44 | 65 | 43 | 41 | 40 | 44 | 26 | 41 | 56 |
| *Aided Awareness* | | | | | | | | | | | | | |
| Familiar with Amelia Eternal | 72 | 68 | 70 | 70 | 72 | 83 | 69 | 73 | 71 | 75 | 59 | 70 | 85 |
| *Direct Questioning* | | | | | | | | | | | | | |
| Know of Amelia Eternal | 91 | 87 | 88 | 90 | 92 | 100 | 89 | 92 | 90 | 93 | 76 | 93 | 100 |

*Source:* Audit of Consumer Awareness, Knowledge, and Attitudes: Underdeveloped Markets, Strategy I and A. Fall, 1979; Spring 1980; Fall 1980.

**EXHIBIT 14-3**

**Specimen Data: Consumers' Ability to Name Amelia Eternal Products, 1979 and 1980; Test of Advertising Strategy I and A in Underdeveloped Markets**

| | | 10/1/79 | 4/1/80 | 10/1/80 |
|---|---|---|---|---|
| Women Fifteen Years and Older | Base | 992 | 972 | 1,006 |
| | | 100 | 100 | 100 |
| | | % | % | % |
| Have heard of Amelia Eternal Company | | 16 | 47 | 91 |
| Average number of household products named by each respondent | | 1.21 | 1.19 | .74 |
| Average number of makeup products named by each respondent | | 1.76 | 1.43 | .63 |

*Source:* Audit of Consumer Awareness, Knowledge, and Attitudes: Underdeveloped Markets, Strategy I and A. Fall 1979; Spring 1980; Fall 1980.

**EXHIBIT 14-4**

**Specimen Data: Consumers' Experience with Amelia Eternal Sales Representatives, 1979 and 1980; Test Advertising Strategy I and A in Underdeveloped Markets**

| | | 10/1/79 | 4/1/80 | 10/1/80 |
|---|---|---|---|---|
| Women Fifteen Years and Older | Base | 992 | 972 | 1,006 |
| | | 100 | 100 | 100 |
| | | % | % | % |
| Have heard of the Amelia Eternal Company | | 16 | 47 | 91 |
| Recall having been called upon by Amelia Eternal representatives | | 6 | 12 | 22 |
| Recall purchasing an Amelia Eternal household product | | 2 | 8 | 14 |
| Recall purchasing an Amelia Eternal makeup product | | 1 | 12 | 18 |
| Have been called upon by an Amelia Eternal sales representative in the past four weeks | | 2 | 6 | 14 |

*Source:* Audit of Consumer Awareness, Knowledge, and Attitudes: Underdeveloped Markets, Strategy I and A. Fall 1979; Spring 1980; Fall 1980.

**EXHIBIT 14-5**

**Specimen Data: Consumer Attitudes toward Amelia Eternal Sales Representatives, 1979 and 1980; Test of Advertising Strategy I and A in Underdeveloped Markets**

| | | 10/1/79 | 4/1/80 | 10/1/80 |
|---|---|---|---|---|
| Women Fifteen Years and Older | Base | 992 | 972 | 1,006 |
| | | 100 | 100 | 100 |
| | | % | % | % |
| Have heard of Amelia Eternal Company | | 16 | 47 | 91 |
| Have been called upon by an Amelia Eternal Sales representative in the past four weeks | | 2 | 6 | 14 |
| How would you rate the Amelia Eternal sales representative on friendliness? | | | | |
| Very friendly | | * | 69 | 64 |
| A little friendly | | * | 20 | 22 |
| Not too friendly | | * | 6 | 9 |
| Quite unpleasant | | * | 5 | 5 |
| How would you rate the Amelia Eternal sales representative on personal appearance? | | | | |
| Very well groomed | | * | 30 | 34 |
| Quite well groomed | | * | 32 | 34 |
| Not too well groomed | | * | 26 | 20 |
| Downright sloppy | | * | 12 | 12 |
| How would you rate the Amelia Eternal sales representative's enthusiasm for her products? | | | | |
| Very enthusiastic about products | | * | 85 | 82 |
| Somewhat enthusiastic about products | | * | 6 | 12 |
| Not too enthusiastic about products | | * | 5 | 4 |
| Unenthusiastic about products | | * | 4 | 2 |
| How would you rate the Amelia Eternal sales representative's knowledge about her products? | | | | |
| Very knowledgeable about products | | * | 25 | 20 |
| Somewhat knowledgeable about products | | * | 45 | 40 |
| Not too knowledgeable about products | | * | 20 | 25 |
| Doesn't know anything about products | | * | 10 | 15 |

*Base of respondents too small for percentaging.

*Source:* Audit of Consumer Awareness, Knowledge, and Attitudes: Underdeveloped Markets, Strategy I and A. Fall 1979; Spring 1980; Fall 1980.

**EXHIBIT 14-6**

**Specimen Data: Consumer Attitudes* toward the Amelia Eternal Company, 1979 and 1980; Test of Advertising Strategy I and A in Underdeveloped Markets**

| | | 10/1/79 | 4/1/80 | 10/1/80 |
|---|---|---|---|---|
| Women Fifteen Years and Older | Base | 992 | 972 | 1,006 |
| | | 100 | 100 | 100 |
| | | % | % | % |
| Have heard of the Amelia Eternal Company | | 16 | 47 | 91 |
| Attitude-Scale Ratings*: | | | | |
| 1. Amelia Eternal offers a broad line of household products | | 3.8 | 3.6 | 3.4 |
| 2. Amelia Eternal offers a broad line of makeup products | | 4.1 | 3.9 | 3.7 |
| 3. Amelia Eternal offers fashionable, up-to-date makeup products | | 3.0 | 2.8 | 1.6 |
| 4. Amelia Eternal representatives provide service that is pleasant and free from hard sell | | 7.4 | 7.6 | 7.9 |
| 5. Amelia Eternal representatives provide individual attention and continuing personal service | | 4.1 | 3.8 | 2.6 |
| 6. Amelia Eternal representatives offer a real alternative to shopping in stores | | 3.2 | 8.6 | 8.8 |
| 7. Amelia Eternal offers an opportunity to get to know and like a friendly representative | | 7.1 | 5.2 | 3.1 |
| 8. Amelia Eternal guarantees complete satisfaction from every product you buy | | 3.6 | 2.8 | 2.0 |
| 9. Amelia Eternal products are totally effective yet are completely harmless to their users | | 1.7 | 1.5 | 1.6 |

*Each respondent who had heard of the Amelia Eternal Company rated it on each attitude scale and gave the company a numeric rating varying from 1 (low) to 10 (high). The higher the consumer rating, the better Amelia Eternal scored.

*Source:* Audit of Consumer Awareness, Knowledge, and Attitudes: Underdeveloped Markets, Strategy I and A. Fall 1979; Spring 1980; Fall 1980.

**EXHIBIT 14-7**

**Specimen Data: Amelia Eternal Sales Representatives and Sales Representatives Per 10,000 Households,* 1979 and 1980; Test of Advertising Strategy I and A in Underdeveloped Markets**

| Last Day of: | | Sales Representatives | Sales Representatives Per 10,000 Household |
|---|---|---|---|
| July | 1979 | 350.3 | 2.14 |
| August | 1979 | 386.3 | 2.36 |
| September | 1979 | 445.3 | 2.72 |
| October | 1979 | 595.9 | 3.64 |
| November | 1979 | 620.4 | 3.79 |
| December | 1979 | 756.3 | 4.62 |
| January | 1980 | 852.9 | 5.21 |
| February | 1980 | 1,034.6 | 6.32 |
| March | 1980 | 1,214.7 | 7.42 |
| April | 1980 | 1,458.6 | 8.91 |
| May | 1980 | 1,471.1 | 8.99 |
| June | 1980 | 1,524.0 | 9.31 |
| July | 1980 | 1,553.5 | 9.49 |
| August | 1980 | 1,556.8 | 9.51 |
| September | 1980 | 1,547.0 | 9.45 |
| October | 1980 | 1,551.9 | 9.48 |

*The household population of strategy I and A test markets (Albany-Schenectady-Troy, New York; Birmingham, Alabama; Columbus, Ohio) television areas of dominant influence is approximately 1,637,000, as of January 1, 1980.

*Source:* Amelia Eternal Company Internal Records.

**EXHIBIT 14-8**

**Specimen Data: Monthly Dollar Sales Per Amelia Eternal Sales Representative, 1979 and 1980; Test of Advertising Strategy I and A in Underdeveloped Markets**

| Month of: | | Dollar Sales Per Representative |
|---|---|---|
| July | 1979 | $101.16 |
| August | 1979 | 99.25 |
| September | 1979 | 103.12 |
| October | 1979 | 116.50 |
| November | 1979 | 129.50 |
| December | 1979 | 151.63 |
| January | 1980 | 136.25 |
| February | 1980 | 138.75 |
| March | 1980 | 136.75 |
| April | 1980 | 150.13 |
| May | 1980 | 153.88 |
| June | 1980 | 125.75 |
| July | 1980 | 149.00 |
| August | 1980 | 150.13 |
| September | 1980 | 166.13 |
| October | 1980 | 153.00 |

*Source:* Amelia Eternal Company Internal Records.

**EXHIBIT 14-9**
**Specimen Data: Awareness of Amelia Eternal Company: 1979 and 1980; Test of Advertising Strategy B in Established Markets**

| | | 10/1/79 | 4/1/80 | 10/1/80 |
|---|---|---|---|---|
| Women Fifteen Years and Older | Base | 1,061 | 1,103 | 996 |
| | | 100 | 100 | 100 |
| | | % | % | % |
| Unaided Awareness: | | | | |
| What door to door sales companies have you ever heard of? | | | | |
| Avon | | 73 | 69 | 70 |
| Encyclopedia Britannica | | 35 | 34 | 33 |
| Shaklee | | 26 | 28 | 22 |
| Electrolux | | 20 | 21 | 18 |
| Amway | | 19 | 22 | 17 |
| Amelia Eternal | | 18 | 32 | 47 |
| Other companies mentioned | | 42 | 40 | 39 |
| Don't know any direct or door to door sales companies | | 36 | 30 | 24 |
| (Average number of companies mentioned by those respondents who could identify a direct or door-to-door sales company) | | 3.6 | 3.5 | 3.2 |
| Aided Awareness: | | | | |
| Please tell me which of the companies on this list you are familiar with: | | | | |
| Avon | | 97 | 94 | 98 |
| Encyclopedia Britannica | | 81 | 83 | 85 |
| Amelia Eternal | | 32 | 49 | 85 |
| World Book Encyclopedia | | 47 | 49 | 47 |
| Amway | | 26 | 25 | 27 |
| Fuller Brush | | 83 | 85 | 79 |
| Electrolux | | 69 | 70 | 69 |
| Shaklee | | 27 | 24 | 25 |
| Direct Questioning about Amelia Eternal: | | | | |
| Have you ever heard of the Amelia Eternal Company? | | | | |
| | Yes | 47 | 69 | 92 |
| | No | 53 | 31 | 8 |

*Source:* Audit of Consumer Awareness, Knowledge, and Attitudes: Established Markets, Strategy B. Fall 1979; Spring 1980; Fall 1980.

**EXHIBIT 14-10**

**Specimen Data: Awareness of Amelia Eternal by Age, Income, and Education, 1979 and 1980; Test of Advertising Strategy B in Established Markets**

| | | Age | | | | | Household Income | | | | Education | | |
|---|---|---|---|---|---|---|---|---|---|---|---|---|---|
| | Total | 15–24 | 25–34 | 35–49 | 50–64 | 65 & Older | Under $7,500 | $ 7,500 14,999 | $15,000 19,999 | $20,000 & over | Any College | Graduated High School | Did not Graduate High School |
| **October 1, 1979** | | | | | | | | | | | | | |
| Women 15 Years and Older | 1,061 | 223 | 202 | 233 | 255 | 148 | 318 | 318 | 159 | 266 | 265 | 446 | 350 |
| | 100 | 100 | 100 | 100 | 100 | 100 | 100 | 100 | 100 | 100 | 100 | 100 | 100 |
| | % | % | % | % | % | % | % | % | % | % | % | % | % |
| *Unaided Awareness* | | | | | | | | | | | | | |
| Ever heard of Amelia Eternal | 18 | 12 | 17 | 20 | 24 | 15 | 17 | 19 | 16 | 20 | 16 | 19 | 19 |
| *Aided Awareness* | | | | | | | | | | | | | |
| Familiar with Amelia Eternal | 32 | 22 | 33 | 34 | 36 | 36 | 34 | 31 | 33 | 31 | 33 | 30 | 34 |
| *Direct Questioning* | | | | | | | | | | | | | |
| Know of Amelia Eternal | 47 | 43 | 45 | 47 | 52 | 46 | 48 | 46 | 47 | 47 | 45 | 49 | 46 |
| **April 1, 1980** | | | | | | | | | | | | | |
| Women 15 Years and Older | 1,103 | 232 | 210 | 243 | 265 | 153 | 331 | 331 | 165 | 276 | 276 | 463 | 364 |
| | 100 | 100 | 100 | 100 | 100 | 100 | 100 | 100 | 100 | 100 | 100 | 100 | 100 |
| | % | % | % | % | % | % | % | % | % | % | % | % | % |
| *Unaided Awareness* | | | | | | | | | | | | | |
| Ever heard of Amelia Eternal | 32 | 27 | 29 | 31 | 34 | 42 | 34 | 32 | 31 | 30 | 29 | 31 | 35 |
| *Aided Awareness* | | | | | | | | | | | | | |
| Familiar with Amelia Eternal | 49 | 40 | 42 | 44 | 51 | 76 | 51 | 49 | 50 | 46 | 44 | 50 | 51 |
| *Direct Questioning* | | | | | | | | | | | | | |
| Know of Amelia Eternal | 69 | 54 | 59 | 67 | 73 | 100 | 70 | 70 | 68 | 67 | 65 | 68 | 73 |

**EXHIBIT 14-10 (Continued)**

| | October 1, 1980 | | | | | | | | | | | | |
|---|---|---|---|---|---|---|---|---|---|---|---|---|---|
| | | | | | | | | | | | Education | | |
| | | Age | | | | | Household Income | | | | | | |
| | Total | 15–24 | 25–34 | 35–49 | 50–64 | 65 & Older | Under $7,500 | $ 7,500 14,999 | $15,000 19,999 | $20,000 & over | Any College | Graduated High School | Did not Graduate High School |
| Women 15 Years and Older | 996 | 209 | 189 | 219 | 239 | 140 | 299 | 299 | 149 | 249 | 249 | 418 | 329 |
| | 100 | 100 | 100 | 100 | 100 | 100 | 100 | 100 | 100 | 100 | 100 | 100 | 100 |
| | % | % | % | % | % | % | % | % | % | % | % | % | % |
| *Unaided Awareness* | | | | | | | | | | | | | |
| Ever heard of Amelia Eternal | 47 | 44 | 43 | 48 | 46 | 58 | 48 | 46 | 47 | 47 | 46 | 44 | 51 |
| *Aided Awareness* | | | | | | | | | | | | | |
| Familiar with Amelia Eternal | 85 | 80 | 84 | 85 | 86 | 93 | 85 | 86 | 85 | 84 | 82 | 83 | 90 |
| *Direct Questioning* | | | | | | | | | | | | | |
| Know of Amelia Eternal | 92 | 91 | 92 | 93 | 90 | 96 | 93 | 90 | 91 | 94 | 90 | 93 | 92 |

*Source:* Audit of Consumer Awareness, Knowledge, and Attitudes: Established Markets, Strategy B. Fall 1979; Spring 1980; Fall 1980.

**EXHIBIT 14-11**
**Specimen Data: Consumer's Ability to Name Amelia Eternal Products, 1979 and 1980; Test of Advertising Strategy B in Established Markets**

| | | 10/1/79 | 4/1/80 | 10/1/80 |
|---|---|---|---|---|
| Women Fifteen Years and Older | Base | 1,061 | 1,103 | 996 |
| | | 100 | 100 | 100 |
| | | % | % | % |
| Have heard of Amelia Eternal Company | | 47 | 69 | 92 |
| Average Number of household products named by each respondent | | 1.59 | 1.32 | 1.21 |
| Average Number of makeup products named by each respondent | | 2.83 | 2.47 | 1.96 |

*Source:* Audit of Consumer Awareness, Knowledge, and Attitudes: Established Markets, Strategy B. Fall 1979; Spring 1980; Fall 1980.

**EXHIBIT 14-12**
**Specimen Data: Consumers' Experience with Amelia Eternal Sales Representatives, 1979 and 1980; Test of Advertising Strategy B in Established Markets**

| | | 10/1/79 | 4/1/80 | 10/1/80 |
|---|---|---|---|---|
| Women Fifteen Years and Older | Base | 1,061 | 1,103 | 996 |
| | | 100 | 100 | 100 |
| | | % | % | % |
| Have heard of the Amelia Eternal Company | | 47 | 69 | 92 |
| Recall having been called upon by Amelia Eternal representative | | 17 | 30 | 48 |
| Recall purchasing an Amelia Eternal household product | | 10 | 20 | 30 |
| Recall purchasing an Amelia Eternal makeup product | | 13 | 24 | 36 |
| Have been called upon by an Amelia Eternal sales representative in the past four weeks | | 9 | 18 | 30 |

*Source.* Audit of Consumer Awareness, Knowledge, and Attitudes: Established Markets, Strategy B. Fall 1979; Spring 1980; Fall 1980.

**EXHIBIT 14-13**
**Specimen Data: Consumer Attitudes toward Amelia Eternal Sales Representatives, 1979 and 1980; Test of Advertising Strategy B in Established Markets**

| | | 10/1/79 | 4/1/80 | 10/1/80 |
|---|---|---|---|---|
| Women Fifteen Years and Older | Base | 1,061 | 1,103 | 996 |
| | | 100 | 100 | 100 |
| | | % | % | % |
| Have heard of Amelia Eternal Company | | 47 | 69 | 92 |
| Have been called upon by an Amelia Eternal sales representative in the past four weeks | | 9 | 18 | 30 |
| How would you rate the Amelia Eternal sales representative on friendliness? | | | | |
| Very friendly | | 72 | 80 | 91 |
| A little friendly | | 18 | 15 | 7 |
| Not too friendly | | 6 | 3 | 2 |
| Quite unpleasant | | 4 | 2 | – |
| How would you rate the Amelia Eternal sales representative on personal appearance? | | | | |
| Very well groomed | | 42 | 56 | 65 |
| Quite well groomed | | 30 | 28 | 25 |
| Not too well groomed | | 18 | 10 | 9 |
| Downright sloppy | | 10 | 6 | 1 |
| How would you rate the Amelia Eternal sales representative's enthusiasm for her products? | | | | |
| Very enthusiastic about products | | 85 | 92 | 97 |
| Somewhat enthusiastic about products | | 12 | 7 | 3 |
| Not too enthusiastic about products | | 3 | 1 | – |
| Unenthusiastic about products | | – | – | – |
| How would you rate the Amelia Eternal sales representative's knowledge about her products? | | | | |
| Very knowledgeable about products | | 37 | 47 | 54 |
| Somewhat knowledgeable about products | | 44 | 35 | 40 |
| Not too knowledgeable about products | | 12 | 10 | 6 |
| Doesn't know anything about products | | 7 | 8 | – |

*Source:* Audit of Consumer Awareness, Knowledge, and Attitudes: Established Markets, Strategy B. Fall 1979; Spring 1980; Fall 1980.

**EXHIBIT 14-14**
**Specimen Data: Consumer Attitudes* toward the Amelia Eternal Company, 1979 and 1980; Test of Advertising Strategy B in Established Markets**

| | | 10/1/79 | 4/1/80 | 10/1/80 |
|---|---|---|---|---|
| Women Fifteen Years and Older | Base | 1,061 | 1,103 | 996 |
| | | 100 | 100 | 100 |
| | | % | % | % |
| Have heard of the Amelia Eternal Company | | 47 | 69 | 92 |
| Attitude-Scale Ratings* | | | | |
| 1. Amelia Eternal offers a broad line of household products | | 4.7 | 3.6 | 3.0 |
| 2. Amelia Eternal offers a broad line of makeup products | | 5.2 | 4.3 | 3.2 |
| 3. Amelia Eternal offers fashionable, up-to-date makeup products | | 4.7 | 4.0 | 3.6 |
| 4. Amelia Eternal representatives provide service that is pleasant and free from hard sell | | 8.1 | 8.9 | 9.4 |
| 5. Amelia Eternal representatives provide individual attention and continuing personal service | | 5.1 | 7.3 | 8.9 |
| 6. Amelia Eternal representatives offer a real alternative to shopping in stores | | 4.0 | 5.2 | 6.7 |
| 7. Amelia Eternal offers an opportunity to get to know and like a friendly representative | | 8.2 | 9.4 | 9.8 |
| 8. Amelia Eternal guarantees complete satisfaction from every product you buy | | 4.3 | 4.7 | 6.8 |
| 9. Amelia Eternal products are totally effective yet are completely harmless to their users | | 3.1 | 6.9 | 8.7 |

*Each respondent who had heard of the Amelia Eternal Company rated it on each attitude scale and gave the company a numeric rating varying from 1 (low) to 10 (high). The higher the consumer rating, the better the Amelia Eternal Company scored.

*Source:* Audit of Consumer Awareness, Knowledge, and Attitude: Established Markets, Strategy B. Fall 1979; Spring 1980; Fall 1980.

**EXHIBIT 14-15**

**Specimen Data: Amelia Eternal Sales Representatives and Sales Representatives Per 10,000 Households,* 1979 and 1980; Test of Advertising Strategy B in Established Markets**

| Last Day of: | | Sales Representatives | Sales Representatives Per 10,000 Households |
|---|---|---|---|
| July | 1979 | 2070.7 | 11.62 |
| August | 1979 | 2054.6 | 11.53 |
| September | 1979 | 2127.7 | 11.94 |
| October | 1979 | 2136.6 | 11.99 |
| November | 1979 | 2191.9 | 12.30 |
| December | 1979 | 2272.1 | 12.75 |
| January | 1980 | 2247.1 | 12.61 |
| February | 1980 | 2320.2 | 13.02 |
| March | 1980 | 2366.5 | 13.28 |
| April | 1980 | 2362.9 | 13.26 |
| May | 1980 | 2441.3 | 13.70 |
| June | 1980 | 2432.4 | 13.65 |
| July | 1980 | 2427.1 | 13.62 |
| August | 1980 | 2480.5 | 13.92 |
| September | 1980 | 2630.2 | 14.76 |
| October | 1980 | 2624.9 | 14.73 |

*The household population of Strategy B test markets (Austin, Texas; Denver, Colorado; San Diego, California) television areas of dominant influence is approximately 1,782,000, as of January 1, 1980.

**EXHIBIT 14-16**

**Specimen Data: Monthly Dollar Sales Per Amelia Eternal Sales Representatives, 1979 and 1980; Test of Advertising Strategy B in Established Markets**

| Month of: | | Dollar Sales Per Representative |
|---|---|---|
| July | 1979 | 184.12 |
| August | 1979 | 195.60 |
| September | 1979 | 201.59 |
| October | 1979 | 206.34 |
| November | 1979 | 204.29 |
| December | 1979 | 216.13 |
| January | 1980 | 211.67 |
| February | 1980 | 231.42 |
| March | 1980 | 226.81 |
| April | 1980 | 235.17 |
| May | 1980 | 246.92 |
| June | 1980 | 218.12 |
| July | 1980 | 231.63 |
| August | 1980 | 229.56 |
| September | 1980 | 241.13 |
| October | 1980 | 256.18 |

*Source:* Amelia Eternal Company Internal Records.

**EXHIBIT 14-17**
**Specimen Data: Awareness of Amelia Eternal Company and Selected Amelia Eternal Product Lines, 1979 and 1980; Test of Advertising Strategy F in Established Markets**

| | | 10/1/79 | 4/1/80 | 10/1/80 |
|---|---|---|---|---|
| Women Fifteen Years and Older | Base | 987 | 1,034 | 1,006 |
| | | 100 | 100 | 100 |
| | | % | % | % |
| Unaided Awareness: | | | | |
| What door-to-door sales companies have you ever heard of? | | | | |
| Avon | | 58 | 54 | 56 |
| Encyclopedia Britannica | | 42 | 43 | 38 |
| Shaklee | | 24 | 26 | 28 |
| Electrolux | | 19 | 24 | 17 |
| Amway | | 24 | 23 | 22 |
| Amelia Eternal | | 27 | 29 | 34 |
| Other companies mentioned | | 38 | 42 | 39 |
| Don't know any direct or door to door sales companies | | 42 | 40 | 39 |
| (Average number of companies mentioned by those respondents who could identify a direct or door to door sales company) | | 4.0 | 4.0 | 3.8 |
| Aided Awareness: | | | | |
| Please tell me which of the companies on this list you are familiar with: | | | | |
| Avon | | 89 | 87 | 91 |
| Encyclopedia Britannica | | 72 | 74 | 73 |
| Amelia Eternal | | 38 | 42 | 46 |
| World Book Encyclopedia | | 54 | 56 | 51 |
| Amway | | 31 | 38 | 34 |
| Fuller Brush | | 96 | 95 | 96 |
| Electrolux | | 58 | 60 | 54 |
| Shaklee | | 32 | 31 | 34 |
| Direct Questioning about Amelia Eternal: | | | | |
| Have you ever heard of the Amelia Eternal Company? | | | | |
| | Yes | 49 | 51 | 50 |
| | No | 51 | 49 | 50 |

*continued*

**EXHIBIT 14-17 (Continued)**

| | | 10/1/79 | 4/1/80 | 10/1/80 |
|---|---|---|---|---|
| Direct Questioning about Super Power Household Products: | | | | |
| Have you ever heard of Super Power Household Cleaning Products? | | | | |
| | Yes | 21 | 47 | 76 |
| | No | 79 | 53 | 24 |
| Direct Questioning about Eternal Cosmetic Products: | | | | |
| Have you ever heard of Amelia Eternal Cosmetic Products? | | | | |
| | Yes | 16 | 31 | 54 |
| | No | 84 | 69 | 46 |

*Source:* Audit of Consumer Awareness, Knowledge, and Attitudes: Established Markets, Strategy F. Fall, 1979; Spring 1980; Fall 1980.

**Specimen Data: Awareness of Amelia Eternal and Selected Amelia Eternal Product Lines, 1979 and 1980; Test of Advertising Strategy F in Established Markets**

| | October 1, 1979 | | | | | | | | | | | | |
|---|---|---|---|---|---|---|---|---|---|---|---|---|---|
| | | Age | | | | | Household Income | | | | Education | | |
| | Total | 15–24 | 25–34 | 35–49 | 50–64 | 65 & Older | Under $7,500 | $ 7,500 14,999 | $15,000 19,999 | $20,000 & over | Any College | Graduated High School | Did Not Graduate High School |
| Women 15 Years and Older | 987<br>100<br>% | 227<br>100<br>% | 197<br>100<br>% | 197<br>100<br>% | 217<br>100<br>% | 149<br>100<br>% | 276<br>100<br>% | 286<br>100<br>% | 168<br>100<br>% | 257<br>100<br>% | 276<br>100<br>% | 385<br>100<br>% | 326<br>100<br>% |
| *Unaided Awareness* | | | | | | | | | | | | | |
| Ever heard of Amelia Eternal | 27 | 22 | 24 | 26 | 29 | 41 | 26 | 28 | 23 | 29 | 20 | 26 | 34 |
| *Aided Awareness* | | | | | | | | | | | | | |
| Familiar with Amelia Eternal | 38 | 34 | 37 | 39 | 39 | 50 | 39 | 39 | 40 | 34 | 29 | 37 | 47 |
| *Direct Questioning* | | | | | | | | | | | | | |
| Know of Amelia Eternal | 49 | 42 | 44 | 47 | 50 | 74 | 47 | 51 | 50 | 48 | 40 | 50 | 56 |
| *Direct Questioning* | | | | | | | | | | | | | |
| Know of Super Power Products | 21 | 19 | 20 | 18 | 22 | 32 | 20 | 21 | 21 | 22 | 14 | 19 | 29 |
| *Direct Questioning* | | | | | | | | | | | | | |
| Know of Eternal Products | 16 | 14 | 14 | 16 | 17 | 22 | 17 | 17 | 14 | 15 | 12 | 16 | 19 |
| | April 1, 1980 | | | | | | | | | | | | |
| Women 15 Years and Older | 1,034<br>100<br>% | 238<br>100<br>% | 207<br>100<br>% | 207<br>100<br>% | 227<br>100<br>% | 155<br>100<br>% | 290<br>100<br>% | 300<br>100<br>% | 176<br>100<br>% | 269<br>100<br>% | 290<br>100<br>% | 403<br>100<br>% | 341<br>100<br>% |
| *Unaided Awareness* | | | | | | | | | | | | | |
| Ever heard of Amelia Eternal | 29 | 23 | 25 | 28 | 30 | 43 | 30 | 27 | 29 | 30 | 24 | 28 | 34 |
| *Aided Awareness* | | | | | | | | | | | | | |
| Familiar with Amelia Eternal | 42 | 35 | 38 | 38 | 42 | 63 | 44 | 38 | 40 | 45 | 35 | 41 | 49 |
| *Direct Questioning* | | | | | | | | | | | | | |
| Know of Amelia Eternal | 51 | 44 | 46 | 47 | 52 | 72 | 53 | 53 | 47 | 49 | 40 | 50 | 61 |
| *Direct Questioning* | | | | | | | | | | | | | |
| Know of Super Power Products | 47 | 37 | 45 | 48 | 51 | 58 | 46 | 45 | 49 | 49 | 36 | 49 | 54 |
| *Direct Questioning* | | | | | | | | | | | | | |
| Know of Eternal Products | 31 | 26 | 30 | 32 | 33 | 36 | 33 | 29 | 27 | 33 | 24 | 29 | 39 |

**EXHIBIT 14-18 (Continued)**

| | October 1, 1980 | | | | | | | | | | | | |
|---|---|---|---|---|---|---|---|---|---|---|---|---|---|
| | | Age | | | | | Household Income | | | | Education | | |
| | Total | 15–24 | 25–34 | 35–49 | 50–64 | 65 & Older | Under $7,500 | $ 7,500 14,999 | $15,000 19,999 | $20,000 & over | Any College | Graduated High School | Did Not Graduate High School |
| Women 15 Years and Older | 1,006 | 231 | 201 | 201 | 221 | 151 | 282 | 292 | 170 | 262 | 282 | 392 | 332 |
| | 100 | 100 | 100 | 100 | 100 | 100 | 100 | 100 | 100 | 100 | 100 | 100 | 100 |
| | % | % | % | % | % | % | % | % | % | % | % | % | % |
| *Unaided Awareness* | | | | | | | | | | | | | |
| Ever heard of Amelia Eternal | 34 | 26 | 29 | 32 | 35 | 54 | 35 | 32 | 36 | 34 | 28 | 33 | 40 |
| *Aided Awareness* | | | | | | | | | | | | | |
| Familiar with Amelia Eternal | 46 | 37 | 39 | 44 | 42 | 79 | 43 | 47 | 45 | 49 | 42 | 47 | 48 |
| *Direct Questioning* | | | | | | | | | | | | | |
| Know of Amelia Eternal | 50 | 46 | 47 | 47 | 51 | 64 | 51 | 50 | 49 | 49 | 42 | 48 | 59 |
| *Direct Questioning* | | | | | | | | | | | | | |
| Know of Super Power Products | 76 | 68 | 72 | 74 | 77 | 95 | 77 | 74 | 79 | 75 | 70 | 75 | 83 |
| *Direct Questioning* | | | | | | | | | | | | | |
| Know of Eternal Products | 54 | 47 | 49 | 53 | 56 | 70 | 49 | 56 | 53 | 57 | 44 | 51 | 66 |

*Source:* Audit of Consumer Awareness, Knowledge, and Attitudes: Established Markets, Strategy F. Fall 1979; Spring 1980; Fall 1980.

**EXHIBIT 14-19**

**Specimen Data: Consumers' Ability to Name Amelia Eternal Products, 1979 and 1980; Test of Advertising Strategy F in Established Markets**

| | | 10/1/79 | 4/1/80 | 10/1/80 |
|---|---|---|---|---|
| Women Fifteen Years and Older | Base | 987 | 1,034 | 1,006 |
| | | 100 | 100 | 100 |
| | | % | % | % |
| Have heard of the Amelia Eternal Company | | 49 | 51 | 50 |
| Average number of household products named by each respondent | | 1.49 | 1.94 | 2.76 |
| Average number of makeup products named by each respondent | | 2.43 | 3.72 | 4.96 |

*Source:* Audit of Consumer Awareness, Knowledge, and Attitudes: Established Markets, Strategy F. Fall 1979; Spring 1980; Fall 1980.

**EXHIBIT 14-20**

**Specimen Data: Consumers' Experience with Amelia Eternal Sales Representatives, 1979 and 1980; Test of Advertising Strategy F in Established Markets**

| | | 10/1/79 | 4/1/80 | 10/1/80 |
|---|---|---|---|---|
| Women Fifteen Years and Older | Base | 987 | 1,034 | 1,006 |
| | | 100 | 100 | 100 |
| | | % | % | % |
| Have heard of the Amelia Eternal Company | | 49 | 51 | 50 |
| Recall having been called upon by Amelia Eternal representative | | 21 | 28 | 34 |
| Recall purchasing an Amelia Eternal household product | | 9 | 14 | 16 |
| Recall purchasing an Amelia Eternal makeup product | | 12 | 13 | 20 |
| Have been called upon by an Amelia Eternal sales representative in the past four weeks | | 11 | 20 | 22 |

*Source:* Audit of Consumer Awareness, Knowledge, and Attitudes: Established Markets, Strategy F. Fall 1979; Spring 1980; Fall 1980.

**EXHIBIT 14-21**

**Specimen Data: Consumer Attitudes toward Amelia Eternal Sales Representatives, 1979 and 1980; Test of Advertising Strategy F in Established Markets**

| | | 10/1/79 | 4/1/80 | 10/1/80 |
|---|---|---|---|---|
| Women Fifteen Years and Older | Base | 987 | 1,034 | 1,006 |
| | | 100 | 100 | 100 |
| | | % | % | % |
| Have heard of the Amelia Eternal Company | | 49 | 51 | 50 |
| Have been called upon by an Amelia Eternal sales representative in the past four weeks | | 11 | 20 | 22 |
| How would you rate the Amelia Eternal sales representative on friendliness? | | | | |
| Very friendly | | 68 | 71 | 69 |
| A little friendly | | 20 | 22 | 24 |
| Not too friendly | | 7 | 4 | 3 |
| Quite unpleasant | | 5 | 3 | 4 |
| How would you rate the Amelia Eternal sales representative on personal appearance? | | | | |
| Very well groomed | | 38 | 42 | 44 |
| Quite well groomed | | 35 | 37 | 42 |
| Not too well groomed | | 13 | 12 | 10 |
| Downright sloppy | | 14 | 9 | 4 |
| How would you rate the Amelia Eternal sales representative's enthusiasm for her products? | | | | |
| Very enthusiastic about products | | 72 | 77 | 83 |
| Somewhat enthusiastic about products | | 14 | 12 | 10 |
| Not too enthusiastic about products | | 9 | 8 | 4 |
| Unenthusiastic about products | | 5 | 3 | 3 |
| How would you rate the Amelia Eternal sales representative's knowledge about her products? | | | | |
| Very knowledgeable about products | | 40 | 49 | 54 |
| Somewhat knowledgeable about products | | 40 | 32 | 38 |
| Not too knowledgeable about products | | 8 | 13 | 6 |
| Doesn't know anything about products | | 12 | 6 | 2 |

*Source:* Audit of Consumer Awareness, Knowledge, and Attitudes: Established Markets, Strategy F. Fall 1979; Spring 1980; Fall 1980.

**EXHIBIT 14-22**
**Specimen Data: Consumer Attitudes* toward the Amelia Eternal Company, 1979 and 1980; Test of Advertising Strategy F in Established Markets**

| | | 10/1/79 | 4/1/80 | 10/1/80 |
|---|---|---|---|---|
| Women Fifteen Years and Older | Base | 987 | 1,034 | 1,006 |
| | | 100 | 100 | 100 |
| | | % | % | % |
| Have heard of the Amelia Eternal Company | | 49 | 51 | 50 |
| Attitude-Scale Ratings* | | | | |
| 1. Amelia Eternal offers a broad line of household products | | 4.9 | 5.1 | 5.4 |
| 2. Amelia Eternal offers a broad line of makeup products | | 5.7 | 6.3 | 6.7 |
| 3. Amelia Eternal offers fashionable, up-to-date makeup products | | 3.9 | 5.1 | 7.0 |
| 4. Amelia Eternal representatives provide service that is pleasant and free from hard sell | | 6.5 | 6.3 | 6.4 |
| 5. Amelia Eternal representatives provide individual attention and continuing personal service | | 4.9 | 4.8 | 5.3 |
| 6. Amelia Eternal representatives offer a real alternative to shopping in stores | | 3.6 | 3.3 | 3.7 |
| 7. Amelia Eternal offers an opportunity to get to know and like a friendly representative | | 7.7 | 7.9 | 8.2 |
| 8. Amelia Eternal guarantees complete satisfaction from every product you buy | | 3.9 | 4.4 | 5.1 |
| 9. Amelia Eternal products are totally effective yet are completely harmless to their users | | 2.9 | 4.7 | 6.3 |

*Each respondent who had heard of the Amelia Eternal Company rated it on each attitude scale and gave the company a numeric rating ranging from 1 (low) to 10 (high). The higher the consumer rating, the better the Amelia Eternal Company scored.

*Source:* Audit of Consumer Awareness, Knowledge, and Attitudes: Established Markets, Strategy F. Fall 1979; Spring 1980; Fall 1980.

**EXHIBIT 14-23**

**Specimen Data: Amelia Eternal Sales Representatives and Sales Representatives Per 10,000 Households,* 1979 and 1980; Test of Advertising Strategy F in Established Markets**

| Last Day of: | | Sales Representatives | Sales Representatives Per 10,000 Households |
|---|---|---|---|
| July | 1979 | 2195.7 | 12.06 |
| August | 1979 | 2298.6 | 12.63 |
| September | 1979 | 2145.7 | 11.79 |
| October | 1979 | 2185.8 | 12.01 |
| November | 1979 | 2189.4 | 12.03 |
| December | 1979 | 2313.2 | 12.71 |
| January | 1980 | 2260.4 | 12.42 |
| February | 1980 | 2309.5 | 12.69 |
| March | 1980 | 2278.6 | 12.52 |
| April | 1980 | 2209.4 | 12.14 |
| May | 1980 | 2138.5 | 11.75 |
| June | 1980 | 2143.9 | 11.78 |
| July | 1980 | 2140.3 | 11.76 |
| August | 1980 | 2154.8 | 11.84 |
| September | 1980 | 2163.9 | 11.89 |
| October | 1980 | 2185.8 | 12.01 |

*The household population of strategy F test markets (Cedar Rapids-Waterloo, Iowa; Portland, Oregon; Seattle-Tacoma, Washington) television areas of dominant influence is approximately 1,820,000, as of January 1, 1980.

*Source:* Amelia Eternal Company Internal Records.

**EXHIBIT 14-24**

**Specimen Data: Monthly Dollar Sales Per Amelia Eternal Sales Representative, 1979 and 1980; Test of Advertising Strategy F in Established Markets**

| Month of: | | Dollar Sales Per Representative |
|---|---|---|
| July | 1979 | 170.42 |
| August | 1979 | 172.19 |
| September | 1979 | 174.83 |
| October | 1979 | 179.35 |
| November | 1979 | 176.42 |
| December | 1979 | 184.35 |
| January | 1980 | 192.13 |
| February | 1980 | 187.16 |
| March | 1980 | 174.32 |
| April | 1980 | 189.14 |
| May | 1980 | 178.36 |
| June | 1980 | 191.20 |
| July | 1980 | 185.32 |
| August | 1980 | 186.40 |
| September | 1980 | 188.13 |
| October | 1980 | 193.81 |

*Source:* Amelia Eternal Company Internal Records.

**EXHIBIT 14-25**
**Specimen Data: Awareness of Amelia Eternal Company and Selected Amelia Eternal Brands, 1979 and 1980; Test of Advertising Strategy G in Established Markets**

| | | 10/1/79 | 4/1/80 | 10/1/80 |
|---|---|---|---|---|
| Women Fifteen Years and Older | Base | 1,054 | 999 | 1,007 |
| | | 100 | 100 | 100 |
| | | % | % | % |
| Unaided Awareness: | | | | |
| What door-to-door sales companies have you ever heard of? | | | | |
| Avon | | 72 | 74 | 76 |
| Encyclopedia Britannica | | 31 | 32 | 29 |
| Shaklee | | 24 | 28 | 26 |
| Electrolux | | 28 | 24 | 22 |
| Amway | | 12 | 14 | 14 |
| Amelia Eternal | | 31 | 33 | 40 |
| Other companies mentioned | | 41 | 41 | 42 |
| Don't know any direct or door to door sales companies | | 24 | 26 | 25 |
| (Average number of companies mentioned by those respondents who could identify a direct or door to door sales company) | | 3.1 | 3.3 | 3.3 |
| Aided Awareness: | | | | |
| Please tell me which of the companies on this list you are familiar with: | | | | |
| Avon | | 85 | 84 | 81 |
| Encyclopedia Britannica | | 91 | 90 | 94 |
| Amelia Eternal | | 44 | 47 | 53 |
| World Book Encyclopedia | | 27 | 26 | 25 |
| Amway | | 29 | 30 | 32 |
| Fuller Brush | | 74 | 75 | 69 |
| Electrolux | | 64 | 66 | 61 |
| Shaklee | | 38 | 39 | 34 |
| Direct Questioning about Amelia Eternal: | | | | |
| Have you ever heard of the Amelia Eternal Company? | | | | |
| | Yes | 50 | 52 | 56 |
| | No | 50 | 48 | 44 |

*continued*

**EXHIBIT 14-25 (Continued)**

| | | 10/1/79 | 4/1/80 | 10/1/80 |
|---|---|---|---|---|
| Direct Questioning about Amelia Eternal Household Product Brands: | | | | |
| Have you ever heard of | | | | |
| Super Power Safe Laundry Detergent | | | | |
| | Yes | 14 | 20 | 32 |
| | No | 86 | 80 | 68 |
| Super Power Safe Dishwashing Detergent | | | | |
| | Yes | 10 | 18 | 40 |
| | No | 90 | 82 | 60 |
| Direct Questioning about Amelia Eternal Makeup Brands: | | | | |
| Have you ever heard of | | | | |
| Eternal Moisturizer | Yes | 6 | 12 | 27 |
| | No | 94 | 88 | 73 |
| Sheen Soft Shampoo | Yes | 4 | 10 | 20 |
| | No | 96 | 90 | 80 |
| Elegant Eve Cream | Yes | 4 | 12 | 27 |
| | No | 96 | 88 | 73 |

*Source:* Audit of Consumer Awareness, Knowledge, and Attitudes: Established Markets, Strategy G. Fall, 1979; Spring 1980; Fall 1980.

**EXHIBIT 14-26**
**Specimen Data: Awareness of Amelia Eternal Company and Selected Amelia Eternal Brands by Age, Income, and Education, 1979 and 1980; Test of Advertising Strategy G in Established Markets**

| | October 1, 1979 | | | | | | | | | | | | |
|---|---|---|---|---|---|---|---|---|---|---|---|---|---|
| | | Age | | | | | Household Income | | | | Education | | |
| | Total | 15–24 | 25–34 | 35–49 | 50–64 | 65 & Older | Under $7,500 | $ 7,500 14,999 | $15,000 19,999 | $20,000 & over | Any College | Graduated High School | Did Not Graduate High School |
| Women 15 Years and Older | 1,054 | 242 | 211 | 211 | 232 | 158 | 295 | 306 | 179 | 274 | 295 | 411 | 348 |
| | 100 | 100 | 100 | 100 | 100 | 100 | 100 | 100 | 100 | 100 | 100 | 100 | 100 |
| | % | % | % | % | % | % | % | % | % | % | % | % | % |
| *Unaided Awareness* | | | | | | | | | | | | | |
| Ever heard of Amelia Eternal | 31 | 26 | 29 | 30 | 32 | 42 | 32 | 29 | 30 | 33 | 24 | 30 | 38 |
| *Aided Awareness* | | | | | | | | | | | | | |
| Familiar with Amelia Eternal | 44 | 35 | 37 | 41 | 43 | 72 | 46 | 39 | 42 | 49 | 36 | 42 | 53 |
| *Direct Questioning* | | | | | | | | | | | | | |
| Know of Amelia Eternal | 50 | 44 | 47 | 49 | 51 | 64 | 52 | 49 | 50 | 49 | 41 | 48 | 60 |
| *Direct Questioning* | | | | | | | | | | | | | |
| Know of: | | | | | | | | | | | | | |
| Super Power Safe Laundry Detergent | 14 | 2 | 4 | 8 | 12 | 56 | 13 | 14 | 12 | 17 | 6 | 13 | 22 |
| Super Power Safe Dishwashing Detergent | 10 | – | 3 | 5 | 7 | 46 | 9 | 8 | 11 | 12 | 4 | 10 | 15 |
| *Direct Questioning* | | | | | | | | | | | | | |
| Know of: | | | | | | | | | | | | | |
| Eternal Moisturizer | 6 | – | – | 4 | 6 | 26 | 5 | 6 | 4 | 8 | 2 | 5 | 10 |
| Sheen Soft Shampoo | 4 | – | – | – | 3 | 22 | 3 | 4 | 3 | 6 | 1 | 3 | 8 |
| Elegant Eve Cream | 4 | – | – | – | 2 | 23 | 2 | 5 | 4 | 6 | – | 2 | 10 |

**EXHIBIT 14-26 (Continued)**

| | April 1, 1980 | | | | | | | | | | | | |
|---|---|---|---|---|---|---|---|---|---|---|---|---|---|
| | | Age | | | | | Household Income | | | | Education | | |
| | Total | 15–24 | 25–34 | 35–49 | 50–64 | 65 & Older | Under $7,500 | $ 7,500 14,999 | $15,000 19,999 | $20,000 & over | Any College | Gradu-ated High School | Did Not Graduate High School |
| Women 15 Years and Older | 999 | 220 | 210 | 210 | 219 | 140 | 280 | 289 | 170 | 260 | 290 | 389 | 320 |
| | 100 | 100 | 100 | 100 | 100 | 100 | 100 | 100 | 100 | 100 | 100 | 100 | 100 |
| | % | % | % | % | % | % | % | % | % | % | % | % | % |
| *Unaided Awareness* | | | | | | | | | | | | | |
| Ever heard of Amelia Eternal | 33 | 24 | 26 | 29 | 32 | 65 | 32 | 31 | 33 | 36 | 27 | 31 | 41 |
| *Aided Awareness* | | | | | | | | | | | | | |
| Familiar with Amelia Eternal | 47 | 42 | 44 | 46 | 47 | 61 | 49 | 48 | 47 | 44 | 42 | 45 | 54 |
| *Direct Questioning* | | | | | | | | | | | | | |
| Know of Amelia Eternal | 52 | 45 | 48 | 48 | 53 | 73 | 53 | 50 | 49 | 55 | 46 | 52 | 57 |
| *Direct Questioning* | | | | | | | | | | | | | |
| Know of: | | | | | | | | | | | | | |
| Super Power Safe Laundry Detergent | 20 | 7 | 14 | 19 | 21 | 50 | 21 | 17 | 19 | 23 | 12 | 18 | 30 |
| Super Power Safe Dish-washing Detergent | 18 | 3 | 7 | 12 | 19 | 65 | 16 | 20 | 19 | 17 | 13 | 15 | 26 |
| *Direct Questioning* | | | | | | | | | | | | | |
| Know of: | | | | | | | | | | | | | |
| Eternal Moisturizer | 12 | 2 | 8 | 10 | 11 | 39 | 9 | 10 | 11 | 18 | 6 | 11 | 19 |
| Sheen Soft Shampoo | 10 | 2 | 7 | 8 | 8 | 33 | 9 | 8 | 7 | 15 | 4 | 7 | 19 |
| Elegant Eve Cream | 12 | 3 | 5 | 9 | 11 | 42 | 9 | 11 | 12 | 17 | 7 | 10 | 19 |

| | October 1, 1980 | | | | | | | | | | | | |
|---|---|---|---|---|---|---|---|---|---|---|---|---|---|
| | | Age | | | | | Household Income | | | | Education | | |
| | Total | 15–24 | 25–34 | 35–49 | 50–64 | 65 & Older | Under $7,500 | $ 7,500 14,999 | $15,000 19,999 | $20,000 & over | Any College | Graduated High School | Did Not Graduate High School |
| Women 15 Years and Older | 1,007 | 232 | 201 | 201 | 222 | 151 | 282 | 292 | 171 | 262 | 282 | 393 | 332 |
| | 100 | 100 | 100 | 100 | 100 | 100 | 100 | 100 | 100 | 100 | 100 | 100 | 100 |
| | % | % | % | % | % | % | % | % | % | % | % | % | % |
| *Unaided Awareness* | | | | | | | | | | | | | |
| Ever heard of Amelia Eternal | 40 | 35 | 37 | 39 | 41 | 52 | 39 | 41 | 42 | 39 | 32 | 38 | 49 |
| *Aided Awareness* | | | | | | | | | | | | | |
| Familiar with Amelia Eternal | 53 | 46 | 48 | 50 | 51 | 77 | 54 | 50 | 52 | 56 | 45 | 52 | 61 |
| *Direct Questioning* | | | | | | | | | | | | | |
| Know of Amelia Eternal | 56 | 49 | 51 | 53 | 54 | 79 | 55 | 57 | 57 | 56 | 49 | 54 | 64 |
| *Direct Questioning* | | | | | | | | | | | | | |
| Know of: | | | | | | | | | | | | | |
| Super Power Safe Laundry Detergent | 32 | 20 | 25 | 27 | 29 | 72 | 30 | 34 | 32 | 32 | 28 | 30 | 38 |
| Super Power Safe Dishwashing Detergent | 40 | 32 | 33 | 36 | 38 | 71 | 41 | 41 | 38 | 39 | 35 | 37 | 48 |
| *Direct Questioning* | | | | | | | | | | | | | |
| Know of: | | | | | | | | | | | | | |
| Eternal Moisturizer | 27 | 12 | 20 | 22 | 23 | 72 | 26 | 29 | 26 | 27 | 20 | 26 | 34 |
| Sheen Soft Shampoo | 20 | 15 | 17 | 17 | 19 | 37 | 18 | 19 | 21 | 23 | 14 | 16 | 30 |
| Elegant Eve Cream | 27 | 14 | 20 | 22 | 23 | 70 | 29 | 25 | 26 | 28 | 23 | 24 | 34 |

*Source:* Audit of Consumer Awareness, Knowledge, and Attitudes: Established Markets, Strategy G. Fall 1979; Spring 1980; Fall 1980

**EXHIBIT 14-27**
**Specimen Data: Consumers' Ability to Name Amelia Eternal Products, 1979 and 1980; Test of Advertising Strategy G in Established Markets**

| | | 10/1/79 | 4/1/80 | 10/1/80 |
|---|---|---|---|---|
| Women Fifteen Years and Older | Base | 1,054 | 999 | 1,007 |
| | | 100 | 100 | 100 |
| | | % | % | % |
| Have heard of the Amelia Eternal Company | | 50 | 52 | 56 |
| Average number of household products named by each respondent | | 1.72 | 1.99 | 2.87 |
| Average number of makeup products named by each respondent | | 2.79 | 4.01 | 5.02 |

*Source:* Audit of Consumer Awareness, Knowledge, and Attitudes: Established Markets, Strategy G. Fall 1979; Spring 1980; Fall 1980.

**EXHIBIT 14-28**
**Specimen Data: Consumers' Experience with Amelia Eternal Sales Representatives, 1979 and 1980; Test of Advertising Strategy G in Established Markets**

| | | 10/1/79 | 4/1/80 | 10/1/80 |
|---|---|---|---|---|
| Women Fifteen Years and Older | Base | 1,054 | 999 | 1,007 |
| | | 100 | 100 | 100 |
| | | % | % | % |
| Have heard of the Amelia Eternal Company | | 50 | 52 | 56 |
| Recall having been called upon by Amelia Eternal representative | | 23 | 25 | 30 |
| Recall purchasing an Amelia Eternal household product | | 10 | 12 | 13 |
| Recall purchasing an Amelia Eternal makeup product | | 15 | 17 | 16 |
| Have been called upon by an Amelia Eternal sales representative in the past four weeks | | 13 | 19 | 23 |

*Source:* Audit of Consumer Awareness, Knowledge, and Attitudes: Established Markets, Strategy G. Fall 1979; Spring 1980; Fall 1980.

**EXHIBIT 14-29**

**Specimen Data: Consumer Attitudes toward Amelia Eternal Sales Representatives, 1979 and 1980; Test of Advertising Strategy G in Established Markets**

| | | 10/1/79 | 4/1/80 | 10/1/80 |
|---|---|---|---|---|
| Women Fifteen Years and Older | Base | 1,054 | 999 | 1,007 |
| | | 100 | 100 | 100 |
| | | % | % | % |
| Have heard of the Amelia Eternal Company | | 50 | 52 | 56 |
| Have been called upon by an Amelia Eternal sales representative in the past four weeks | | 13 | 19 | 23 |
| How would you rate the Amelia Eternal sales representative on friendliness? | | | | |
| Very friendly | | 74 | 77 | 76 |
| A little friendly | | 19 | 18 | 19 |
| Not too friendly | | 5 | 3 | 2 |
| Quite unpleasant | | 2 | 2 | 3 |
| How would you rate the Amelia Eternal sales representative on personal appearance? | | | | |
| Very well groomed | | 40 | 42 | 44 |
| Quite well groomed | | 27 | 30 | 35 |
| Not too well groomed | | 20 | 22 | 20 |
| Downright sloppy | | 13 | 6 | 1 |
| How would you rate the Amelia Eternal sales representative's enthusiasm for her products? | | | | |
| Very enthusiastic about products | | 78 | 80 | 81 |
| Somewhat enthusiastic about products | | 12 | 14 | 16 |
| Not too enthusiastic about products | | 7 | 5 | 2 |
| Unenthusiastic about products | | 3 | 1 | 1 |
| How would you rate the Amelia Eternal sales representative's knowledge about her products? | | | | |
| Very knowledgeable about products | | 42 | 51 | 62 |
| Somewhat knowledgeable about products | | 37 | 41 | 37 |
| Not too knowledgeable about products | | 14 | 5 | 1 |
| Doesn't know anything about products | | 7 | 3 | - |

*Source:* Audit of Consumer Awareness, Knowledge, and Attitudes: Established Markets, Strategy G. Fall 1979; Spring 1980; Fall 1980.

**EXHIBIT 14-30**
**Specimen Data: Consumer Attitudes* toward the Amelia Eternal Company, 1979 and 1980; Test of Advertising Strategy G in Established Markets**

| | | 10/1/79 | 4/1/80 | 10/1/80 |
|---|---|---|---|---|
| Women Fifteen Years and Older | Base | 1,054 | 999 | 1,007 |
| | | 100 | 100 | 100 |
| | | % | % | % |
| Have heard of the Amelia Eternal Company | | 50 | 52 | 56 |
| Attitude-Scale Ratings* | | | | |
| 1. Amelia Eternal offers a broad line of household products | | 4.7 | 4.6 | 4.3 |
| 2. Amelia Eternal offers a broad line of makeup products | | 4.4 | 5.4 | 5.0 |
| 3. Amelia Eternal offers fashionable, up-to-date products | | 3.7 | 5.6 | 7.9 |
| 4. Amelia Eternal representatives provide service that is pleasant and free from hard sell | | 6.2 | 6.1 | 6.0 |
| 5. Amelia Eternal representatives provide individual attention and continuing personal service | | 5.0 | 4.8 | 4.7 |
| 6. Amelia Eternal representatives offer a real alternative to shopping in stores. | | 3.3 | 3.7 | 3.9 |
| 7. Amelia Eternal offers an opportunity to get to know and like a friendly representative | | 6.8 | 6.9 | 6.4 |
| 8. Amelia Eternal guarantees complete satisfaction from every product you buy | | 4.6 | 5.4 | 7.2 |
| 9. Amelia Eternal products are totally effective yet are completely harmless to their users | | 3.3 | 3.7 | 4.1 |

*Each respondent who had heard of the Amelia Eternal Company rated it on each attitude scale and gave the company a numeric rating varying from 1 (low) to 10 (high). The higher the consumer rating, the better the Amelia Eternal Company scored.

*Source:* Audit of Consumer Awareness, Knowledge, and Attitudes: Established Markets, Strategy G. Fall 1979; Spring 1980; Fall 1980.

**EXHIBIT 14-31**
**Specimen Data: Amelia Eternal Sales Representatives and Sales Representatives Per 10,000 Households,* 1979 and 1980; Test of Advertising Strategy G in Established Markets**

| Last Day of: | | Sales Representatives | Sales Representatives Per 10,000 Household |
|---|---|---|---|
| July | 1979 | 2148.7 | 11.98 |
| August | 1979 | 2137.2 | 11.92 |
| September | 1979 | 2165.9 | 12.08 |
| October | 1979 | 2280.7 | 12.72 |
| November | 1979 | 2149.8 | 11.99 |
| December | 1979 | 2162.3 | 12.06 |
| January | 1980 | 2208.9 | 12.32 |
| February | 1980 | 2226.9 | 12.42 |
| March | 1980 | 2332.6 | 13.01 |
| April | 1980 | 2323.7 | 12.96 |
| May | 1980 | 2280.7 | 12.72 |
| June | 1980 | 2368.5 | 13.21 |
| July | 1980 | 2269.9 | 12.66 |
| August | 1980 | 2235.8 | 12.47 |
| September | 1980 | 2293.2 | 12.79 |
| October | 1980 | 2332.6 | 13.01 |

*The household population of strategy G test markets (Dayton, Ohio; Sacramento-Stockton, California; Salt Lake City, Utah) television areas of dominant influence is approximately 1,793,000, as of January 1, 1980.

*Source:* Amelia Eternal Company Internal Records.

**EXHIBIT 14-32**

**Specimen Data: Monthly Dollar Sales Per Amelia Eternal Sales Representative, 1979 and 1980; Test of Advertising Strategy G in Established Markets**

| Month | | Dollar Sales Per Representative |
|---|---|---|
| July | 1979 | 181.48 |
| August | 1979 | 184.26 |
| September | 1979 | 179.42 |
| October | 1979 | 176.35 |
| November | 1979 | 168.49 |
| December | 1979 | 170.35 |
| January | 1980 | 176.49 |
| February | 1980 | 174.72 |
| March | 1980 | 178.86 |
| April | 1980 | 179.53 |
| May | 1980 | 180.42 |
| June | 1980 | 181.77 |
| July | 1980 | 179.72 |
| August | 1980 | 160.14 |
| September | 1980 | 175.37 |
| October | 1980 | 172.14 |

*Source:* Amelia Eternal Company Internal Records.

# Index

## A

# B



# C

# L



# M



# N

# T

# U



# V



# W